SIR ERNEST MAC
THE IMPORTANCE OF BE...

As a conductor, organist, pianist, composer, educator, writer, administrator, and musical statesman, Sir Ernest MacMillan stands as a towering figure in Canada's musical history. His role in the development of music in Canada from the beginning of this century to 1970 was pivotal. He conducted the Toronto Symphony Orchestra for twenty-five years, and the Toronto Mendelssohn Choir for fifteen. He was principal of the Toronto (now Royal) Conservatory of Music and dean of the University of Toronto's Faculty of Music. He founded the Canadian Music Council and the Canadian Music Centre, and was a founding member of the Canada Council. He was also the first president of the Composers, Authors, and Publishers Association of Canada.

Ezra Schabas provides not only the first detailed biography of MacMillan, but also a frank, richly detailed, and handsomely illustrated account of the Canadian music scene. He tells of MacMillan's rise in Canada, from his early years as a church organist to his international successes as a guest conductor; from his internment in a German prison camp to the knighthood conferred on him by King George V. As Robertson Davies said of MacMillan, 'It is on the achievements of such men that the culture of a country rests. Their work is not education, but revelation, and there is always about it something of prophetic splendour.'

EZRA SCHABAS has been active as a performer, teacher, and musical administrator in Canada for over forty years. He is Professor Emeritus in the Faculty of Music, University of Toronto, and former principal of the Royal Conservatory of Music. He is author of *Theodore Thomas: America's Conductor and Builder of Orchestras, 1835–1905*.

Sir Ernest MacMillan

THE IMPORTANCE

OF BEING

CANADIAN

EZRA SCHABAS

University of Toronto Press
Toronto Buffalo London

© University of Toronto Press Incorporated 1994
Toronto Buffalo London
Printed in Canada

Reprinted in paperback 1996

ISBN 0-8020-2849-7
ISBN 0-8020-7871-0

Printed on acid-free paper

Canadian Cataloguing in Publication Data

Schabas, Ezra, 1924–
Sir Ernest MacMillan

Includes bibliographical references.
ISBN 0-8020-2849-7 (bound) ISBN 0-8020-7871-0 (pbk.)

1. MacMillan, Ernest, Sir, 1893–1973.
2. Music – Canada – 20th century – History and criticism.
3. conductors (Music) – Canada – Biography.
4. Musicians – Canada – Biography.
5. Composers – Canada – Biography. I. Title.

ML422.M35S35 1994   780'.92   C94-931158-8

The author and publisher gratefully acknowledge the financial assistance
of The SOCAN Foundation.

This book has been published with the help of a grant from the
Canadian Federation for the Humanities, using funds provided by the
Social Sciences and Humanities Research Council of Canada.

Unless otherwise noted, the illustrations are from the following sources:
Clare (Mazzoleni) Piller Family Collection (CPFC),
Sir Ernest MacMillan Fonds (ECMF),
Keith MacMillan Family Collection (KMFC),
and Toronto Symphony Orchestra Archives (TSOA).

For Ann

Contents

Illustrations following pages 30 and 190

Preface

When I first travelled in Canada for the Royal Conservatory of Music in the early 1950s, performing musicians, composers, music teachers, and assorted music lovers almost always asked me, 'And how is Sir Ernest?' I knew that he was the conductor of Toronto's two leading musical organizations, the Toronto Symphony Orchestra (the TSO, as it was called) and the Toronto Mendelssohn Choir, but I had no idea that he was so well known, had so many friends throughout the country, and was so central to Canada's musical life. I usually responded that I knew him only slightly and that to my knowledge he was doing well, thank you very much.

Not long after, I was fortunate to play the clarinet under his direction and, in the 1960s, to work with him on Canadian Music Council business. It was a pleasure to hear him speak with insight and substance on musical matters. I saw him for the last time at his home in late 1968. We talked about my plans for a sabbatical leave from the University of Toronto, and he was encouraging and supportive.

In the late 1980s I began to sense that interest in serious – or 'classical' – music in Canada was levelling off, perhaps even declining. There were no new orchestras being formed and some of the existing ones were in dire financial straits because of shrinking audiences and poor public and private support. Music was getting short shrift in the elementary and secondary schools, music schools were struggling to survive, and the CBC's budget for live music was decreasing. Only opera and early music were holding their own or growing in public popularity.

Concerned about what the future might hold, I decided to look to the lessons of the past, to the postwar period, to the 1950s and 1960s, to the people who made things happen in those years of musical growth. This led me inevitably to Sir Ernest (that was how we *always* spoke of him) and to his achievements. For over four decades, he had patiently and unrelentingly led Canadians out of their musical wilderness.

Sir Ernest MacMillan *is* twentieth-century Canada's major musical figure. He was a conductor, composer, organist, teacher, examiner, festival adjudicator, arts planner, educational administrator, ethnomusicologist, speaker, and writer. He conducted the TSO (1931–56) and the Toronto Mendelssohn Choir (1942–57). He founded and was first president of the Canadian Music Council (1949–66) and was president of the Canadian Music Centre (1959–70). He was also first president of the Composers, Authors and Publishers Association of Canada (CAPAC) (1947–69), president of Jeunesses Musicales du Canada (1962–4), and a founding member of the Canada Council (1957–63). And he was principal of the Toronto (now Royal) Conservatory of Music (1926–42) and dean of the Faculty of Music of the University of Toronto (1927–52). Over sixty Sir Ernest MacMillan Fine Arts Clubs flourished in Canadian high schools from 1936 until the late 1960s.

MacMillan conducted every important Canadian orchestra as well as major orchestras in the United States, Britain, Australia, and Brazil. As an organist in the 1920s and 1930s, he played widely in Canada and abroad and many thought he had no equal. He composed religious music, music for the stage, and music for orchestra, orchestra and chorus, a cappella choir, voice, keyboard, and chamber groups, and transcribed and arranged a wealth of French and English folk tunes and Native music. Throughout his life he promoted Canadian artists, and, for its first six years (1959–65), conducted the CBC Talent Festival.

Raised as a Presbyterian – his father was a minister and noted hymnologist – MacMillan, while still in his teens, committed himself to serving Canada. This narrative in great part addresses this commitment. It also tries to come to grips with his underlying ambivalences – how this same sense of service and responsibility to his country and its people conflicted with his desire to develop his own extraordinarily promising artistic career to its fullest. The end result was a rich and complex life, with Canada the principal beneficiary.

Coming as it does twenty years after his death, this is, surprisingly, the first full-length biography of Sir Ernest MacMillan. Its publication follows immediately upon the centenary of his birth. In recalling our brief encounters, I regret that I did not know him better, but then I remind myself that being at some distance may have helped me to view his strengths and weaknesses more clearly. It is easy indeed to be overwhelmed by Sir Ernest's accomplishments, to write only paeans of praise – much as he may deserve them – and little else. I hope that I have succeeded in writing a balanced appraisal, even though I confess to admiring him even more now than when I first began working on this account of his life.

Acknowledgments

I wish to thank first the late Keith MacMillan, Sir Ernest MacMillan's older son, for encouraging me to embark on this biography shortly before he died. He left me the fruits of his extensive research and organization of material, including correspondence, many interviews, detailed analyses of Toronto Symphony concerts during Sir Ernest's tenure as conductor, a daily chronology of his father's life, excerpts from letters and press clippings, lists of letters, press notices, and Sir Ernest's writings, and some five chapters of a draft biography of his father, all of which have proved invaluable. I have thought of Keith constantly as I worked away at this challenging task over the past thirty months.

I thank next Ross MacMillan, Sir Ernest's younger son, and Patricia MacMillan, Keith's wife, for giving me complete access to the Sir Ernest MacMillan fonds at the National Library and to Keith MacMillan's papers. Their help in many other ways has been exemplary. I also thank other members of the MacMillan family – Keith and Patricia's second son Donald, Andrea Mazzoleni, Clare (Mazzoleni) Piller, Jocelyn Podhalicz, and Marion LeBel – for sharing their memories, letters, and papers.

I give special thanks to the archivists and librarians who assisted me, in some cases well beyond the call of duty. In particular, I thank Maureen Nevins, contract archivist-researcher at the National Library, who processed the MacMillan fonds, and, most recently, the Keith MacMillan fonds, and unselfishly shared her knowledge of its holdings with me whenever required. I also thank Timothy Maloney, director of the Music Division of the National Library, and Stephen Willis, head of the Manuscript Collection, for expediting my research. Richard Warren, Toronto Symphony archivist, was a constant and informed supporter. He was always cheerful, no matter how many times I asked him for more – and still more – information. Thanks go to Gail Donald, coordinator, and Deborah Lindsey, researcher, of the CBC Radio Archives (Toronto), and Leone Earls, head librarian of the CBC Reference Library (Toronto); Mark Hand, librarian, Canadian Music Centre (Toronto); Garan Wells, university archivist and Harold Averill, assistant university archivist, University of Toronto archives; Kathleen McMorrow, head, and Suzanne Meyers Sawa, librarian, the University of Toronto Faculty of Music Library; Raymond Peringer, archivist, Toronto Arts and Letters Club; Nicholas Barakett and Annette Wengel, librarians, Metropolitan Toronto Reference Library; Judith McErvel, archivist, Massey Hall and Roy Thomson Hall; Net Watson, archivist, Toronto Mendelssohn Choir; Vera Gardiner, archivist, Timothy Eaton Memorial Church; Joan Baillie, archivist, Canadian Opera Company; Joan Links and other staff, microtext room at the Robarts Library; and Jeff Walden of the BBC Written Archives Centre.

Many people have generously loaned or given me papers, photographs, and audiotapes. I thank Robert Creech for his extensive archival material on the Canadian Music Council and the Canadian Music Centre, Robert Rosevear for his taped recollections and archival material about the University of Toronto's Faculty of Music, Irene Rowe for a copy of her dissertation and other material on TSO children's concerts, and Gaynor Jones for her Toronto Conservatory material. I am also indebted to Gilles Lefebvre of Jeunesses Musicales du Canada, John Beckwith of the University of Toronto, Patricia Wardrop of the *Encyclopedia of Music in Canada*, Maud McLean of the Toronto Mendelssohn Choir, former CBC producer Carl Little, and retired Royal Conservatory teacher Wilfred Powell, for letters, documents, press clippings, and other items.

Louis Applebaum, Victor Feldbrill, and Geoffrey Payzant helped me enormously in sharing their recollections and views of Sir Ernest with me, as did John Beckwith, who also assisted me in reviewing Sir Ernest's compositions. I thank the following for their interviews with me: Louis Applebaum, John Beckwith, Helen Bickell, Edith Binnie, John Cozens, Victor Feldbrill, Frances Gage, Gordon Hallett, Maria Baumeister Kiors, John Lawson, Marion LeBel, Roy Loken, Donald MacMillan, Patricia MacMillan, Ross MacMillan, Lois Marshall, Mary Mason, Andrea Mazzoleni, Oskar Morawetz, Geoffrey Payzant, Harvey Perrin, Clare (Mazzoleni) Piller, Jocelyn Podhalicz, Laure Rièse, Paul Scherman, Muriel Gidley Stafford, Jean Tory, Nora van Nostrand Wedd, John Weinzweig, and Ethelwyn Wickson. Among the many people who talked with me about Sir Ernest and/or provided me with information and other services are Bernadette Antonacci, Mary Barrow, Eddy Bayens, Boris Berlin, Claude Bissell, M. Suzanne Bradshaw, Ruth Budd, Joe Cartan, Robin Elliott, Frank Fusco, Avrahm Galper, Clyde Gilmour, Francess Halpenny, Morry Kernerman, William Kilbourn, Marie Korey, William Littler, Jan Matejcek, John Mills, Carl Morey, Paul Pedersen, Eugene Rittich, William Rogers, Gwenlyn Setterfield, Peter Simon, Len Starmer, Sandy Stewart, Berul Sugarman, Vincent Tovell, Hazel Walker, Kenneth Winters, and the management of the Toronto Symphony. I thank Ron Schoeffel, editor-in-chief of the University of Toronto Press, for his unwavering support since I embarked on this biography, Robin Elliott, for editing the manuscript so imaginatively and thoroughly, Anne Forte, for her astute and cheerful management of its publication, and Antje Lingner, for the book's elegant design.

I wish to acknowledge the support of the following institutions for grants for travel, research assistance, and other expenses: The SOCAN Foundation, the University of Toronto Research Services, the Founders Fund of The Corporation of Massey Hall and Roy Thomson Hall, the Toronto Symphony Orchestra, and the Royal Conservatory of Music.

Finally, I would like to thank my wife, Ann, with all my heart. She has worked with me from the outset as a researcher and then, once the writing got under way, as an uncompromising editor. If this book has merit it is as much her doing as mine.

Abbreviations

ABC	Australian Broadcasting Corporation
AFM	American Federation of Musicians
BBC	British Broadcasting Corporation
CAC	Canadian Arts Council
CAPAC	Composers, Authors and Publishers Association of Canada Ltd
CBC	Canadian Broadcasting Corporation
CC	Canada Council
CISAC	Confédération Internationale des Sociétés d'Auteurs et Compositeurs
CMC	Canadian Music Centre
CMCl	Canadian Music Council
CMH	Canadian Musical Heritage series
CMJ	*The Canadian Music Journal*
CPR	Canadian Pacific Railway
ECM	Ernest Campbell MacMillan
EMC2	*Encyclopedia of Music in Canada*, second edition (Toronto 1992)
JMC	Jeunesses Musicales du Canada
KMF	Keith MacMillan fonds
NLC	National Library of Canada, Music Division
RCM	Royal Conservatory of Music of Toronto
TCM	Toronto Conservatory of Music
TMA	Toronto Musicians' Association
TMC	Toronto Mendelssohn Choir
TSO	Toronto Symphony Orchestra
UTA	University of Toronto Archives
VSO	Vancouver Symphony Orchestra

Sir Ernest MacMillan

Sans la musique, un État ne peut subsister.

Molière

Music, the most social of the arts, possesses supremely that unifying power which, given due support, will play a unique part in fostering and preserving the spirit of devotion that welds together a great nation.

Ernest MacMillan

1. A Gifted Child

Ernest MacMillan was on his way home after almost five years in Europe. It was January 1919 and he was twenty-five years old. He had been trapped for four years in German prisons as a civilian internee. Yet, bad as that had been, he knew that he was lucky not to have been killed or maimed in the trenches of Vimy Ridge or Passchendaele like so many other young Canadians. He wondered what Canada would be like, what musical opportunities would be awaiting him. Would Elsie, his betrothed, still love him? And, as he stood on the deck of the *Minnedosa* crossing the wintry North Atlantic, he thought – inevitably – of his father, Alexander MacMillan, and the Atlantic crossing *he* had made thirty-three years earlier. For his father, the crossing had indeed been a trip into the unknown.

In 1886, Alexander was a determined twenty-one-year-old theology student with a deep love of music. Slight of build and of medium height, he had set out from Scotland in March 1886 for a summer of missionary work in 'Manitoba and the North West.'[1] Scotland's Presbyterians saw English Canada as a potential bastion of their church and were busily – and successfully – making good Presbyterians out of the settlers and the Natives. The tiny *State of Georgia* tossed up and down like a cork on the North Atlantic's high seas, but Alexander had strong sea legs, fortunate in view of ensuing events – he would cross the Atlantic fifty-five times in all during his lifetime. After thirteen days at sea his ship docked in New York, but Alexander, feeling quite out of place in that noisy, bustling American city with its many nationalities speaking as

many different tongues, headed directly for Canada, where his
rich Scottish accent could be understood more readily by fellow
Scots who had settled there. Travelling by way of Niagara Falls, he
was overwhelmed by the sight and, more significantly, the sound
of the mighty cataract. 'It seemed that every note the human ear
can receive was being sounded, and yet without any sense of
discord. I felt, too, that if my power of hearing had been greater
I might have heard deeper and higher tones.'[2]

Toronto was the next stop, and then it was on to Winnipeg, a
thousand miles to the west and not easily accessible – he travelled
by boat a good part of the way. It was just one year after the Riel
Rebellion had been crushed, and the West was developing rapidly, with Winnipeg, geographically the most central city in the
Dominion, on its way to becoming a major rail hub. Church
authorities assigned Alexander to the Fort Frances mission in
northwestern Ontario, close to the U.S. border, where he
preached to settlers for the entire summer. Down river, too, was
a Native reserve, where he often mingled with the inhabitants,
learning their customs and gaining their confidence.

Our young minister-to-be's introduction to Canada concluded
with the coming of autumn. He made the long journey back to
Scotland by way of North Dakota, Minnesota, Wisconsin, Illinois,
and eventually Toronto, the Thousand Islands, the St Lawrence
River, Montreal, and Quebec City, where he boarded the
Sardinian bound for Glasgow. Alexander's trip to the New World
had been prompted by an 'impulse' to live in Canada, and the
summer's experiences had turned his impulse to resolve. Determined to serve man and God and raise a family in this great new
country, he finished his studies the next year and returned to
Canada to seek an assignment.

An offer to head a congregation was not long in coming. Auburn and Smith's Hill, two small neighbouring Ontario towns on
Lake Huron near Goderich, were seeking a minister and had
already heard twenty-seven aspirants for their post. Alexander was
invited to preach for two Sundays, and, soon after, the elders of
both churches chose him for the position. He accepted readily
and was duly ordained in September 1887. 'It was to me a solemn
hour,' Alexander would later write, 'as it meant not only taking

upon me the cure of souls, but being consecrated to the office of the Holy Ministry.'[3]

The Presbyterian church was on the way to becoming the largest Protestant denomination in Canada when Alexander became one of its ministers. Most of its followers were Scots of humble origin, whose sturdiness and industry had enabled them, half a century earlier, to clear and develop the country's virgin land. Now they were not only prosperous farmers but also ministers, statesmen, doctors, lawyers, merchants, and manufacturers. To work to one's limit was ingrained in these hardy people, who passed this ethic down from generation to generation.

Alexander met the expectations of his congregation and used Auburn as his musical proving ground. Some Presbyterian churches of the day still forbade both organs and hymn singing, believing that music for worship should consist solely of the singing of psalms from the Scriptures, but Alexander found this too limiting. Believing that 'the psalms alone were not adequate to Christian worship, as all of them had been composed prior to the Christian era and not a few reflected a stage of belief which had been transcended by the teaching of Christ,' he introduced hymns into the service.[4] Fortunately, his congregation responded happily, and this success helped him to chart his professional future.

He also found out how lonely a bachelor's life in rural Ontario could be. Luckily, in 1889, he met Wilhelmina Catherine (Winnie) Ross; they fell in love and were married the next year.

Winnie, the daughter of Presbyterian minister Alexander Ross and his wife, Isabella, was a tall and beautiful young woman who loved music and, like her husband, played the piano well. Her parents, although on a limited minister's stipend, had made certain that their daughters attended good private schools for young ladies where they were taught music and the other arts, but not the fundamentals of housekeeping.[5] After Winnie had a family, she had difficulty managing her children and the manse and had frequent depressions. Alexander's trips to Scotland on church business did not help, although on at least one occasion she accompanied him, leaving her children with her sister Christina. All in all it was a happy marriage.[6]

Winnie's father was the dour and forbidding minister of a Gaelic-speaking Presbyterian congregation in Woodville, Ontario. He was a stern and unyielding fundamentalist with narrow interests who had migrated from Scotland to Nova Scotia in 1860 to become minister of Pictou's Knox Church. It was there that he had met and married the attractive Isabella Sutherland, the widow of Ross's predecessor and already the mother of three children. Five more children, all girls, resulted from the union, although only three reached adulthood. Winnie, the youngest, was born in 1870, and, some years later, the family moved to Ontario. Ross ruled his family with an iron hand and showed little tolerance for anything other than controlled Christian behaviour.

Indeed, Winnie's father made such a strong impression on his grandson, Ernest MacMillan, that he once referred to him – with apologies to the *Reader's Digest* – as the 'Most Unforgettable Character I Have Known.'[7] He remembered grandfather Ross as 'formidable, of impressive dignity, [and] fully convinced of the rightness of his views and of the errors of everyone who differed from him. He personified the Calvinistic tradition with all its logic (if one accepted its premises) and all its rigidity. His journals ... reveal the man himself – austere, humble before the Almighty but holding his head high before all human beings, with whom – even in his household – he avoided too close contacts.'[8] Evidently Ross took little interest in the female sex, only men being of consequence to him. Nor did he see a need for affection from family and friends, perceiving such feelings as weakness. At his funeral, Winnie 'laid her hand on his and, with tears in her eyes, murmured: "Oh papa, why did you never let me love you?"'[9]

The Ross household was not a relaxed or happy one, and Winnie welcomed the chance to leave it behind to marry a man who differed so much from her father. Alexander MacMillan, by way of contrast, was tolerant and compassionate, with an attractive sense of humour, a prodigious memory, and a love of poetry. He viewed the ministry as a calling of duty and joy. As his children were growing up, they heard 'more of love and less of the fear of God' than did many of their friends. Ernest, in his later years, paid tribute to his father, saying that he was saintly and that it was 'an inestimable privilege and inspiration to know him.'[10]

After their marriage, Alexander and Winnie stayed in Auburn for a year and a half and then spent a few months in Scotland, Alexander to study and preach, and Winnie – as proudly Scottish as her husband – to visit the towns and churches of her ancestors. On their return to Canada, Alexander was called to a parish in Mimico, a western suburb of Toronto on Lake Ontario. He was delighted with its progressive congregation and the new electric street railway which made Toronto readily accessible. Much as he and Winnie had liked Auburn, they looked forward to the cultural advantages of the city.

In that last decade of the nineteenth century, 'Toronto the Good' was a thriving if slow-paced commercial centre of some 160,000 inhabitants. Its people, mainly of English and Scottish origin, were both thrifty and God-fearing, and their banks and churches were everywhere. Churchgoers were provided 'with a moral pathway through the hazards of a materialistic world,' so that 'material success was combined with moral fulfilment.'[11] Values of religion thus came to terms with those of business. Protestantism ruled supreme, controlling not only the city's work life but also its leisure life. Temperance was the watchword and everything and everybody came to a halt on Sundays and other Christian holidays.

Protestantism was also ingrained in Ontario's schools, where a 'secularized version of the basic story of Christian redemption' reinforced the teachings of the church.[12] The schools had vastly different expectations for boys and girls: boys were groomed to become powerful, practical, active, ambitious, and competitive; girls to become moral, spiritual, reflective, and emotional. Subjects and professions were chosen accordingly. Men took on the world while women attended to the home. But Alexander did not subscribe to these gender stereotypes, and, although his wife filled a traditional role, his daughters would not.

Torontonians made music mainly in their churches and homes – families would group around the parlour piano playing and singing together. There were also some important community choirs, the most prominent being F.H. Torrington's Toronto Philharmonic Society, which, for almost twenty years, had been performing such ambitious works as Handel's *Messiah*, Mendels-

sohn's *Elijah*, and Haydn's *Creation*. The high quality of Toronto's
choral singing owed much to British church traditions. By contrast, the city's orchestral playing was sadly underdeveloped.
There were several attempts to form an orchestra, and the most
successful was Torrington's Amateur Orchestra. It accompanied
the choir, of course, and also played movements of symphonies
of the classical and early romantic period, but little else. Torontonians heard orchestral music played well only by visiting groups
from the United States.[13] Local opera was almost non-existent,
Protestant Toronto's exposure to this worldly art being limited
mainly to occasional visits from touring companies from Montreal
and the United States.

Once established in Mimico, Alexander became involved in
Presbyterian musical affairs. His knowledge of music, church
history, and worship soon led to his appointment to a committee
of the church's General Assembly charged with revising the 1880
Protestant Hymnal, a project for which he was admirably suited. In
due course, he took full charge, and his reputation as a
hymnologist spread rapidly in the Presbyterian church.[14]

And then on 18 August 1893 the young couple's first child and
only son was born. It was, reportedly, a very stormy night and
Winnie had a difficult delivery, as she would have with the births
of her three other children, Dorothy, Jean, and Winifred. The
boy was baptized in the Mimico church by grandfather Alexander
Ross and named Ernest Alexander Campbell. His first given
name, Ernest, had no family association; his second, Alexander,
was after his father and his maternal grandfather; and his third,
Campbell, was after his maternal forebears, a ministerial family of
Kildonan, Sutherlandshire, who traced their roots back to Alexander Knox.[15] Ernest was truly a Scottish Canadian!

From a very early age he showed extraordinary musical talent.
His father wrote that 'when scarcely a year old he had prefer-
ences when certain tunes were sung to him. At one he would
turn down the corners of his mouth preparatory to vocal protest,
while at another he would laugh and crow.'[16] In 1896 Alexander
was transferred to St Enoch's Church in the flourishing Toronto
neighbourhood later known as Cabbagetown.[17] The family's new

home was roomy enough to house both a piano and a small Estey
organ, and the two instruments were kept tuned together. Winnie
would play the piano and Alexander the organ, and soon the boy
was playing the tunes he heard – sometimes on the piano, sometimes on the organ, first with one finger, and then, seemingly
without effort, with both hands. His mother, often alone because
of Alexander's extended trips to Scotland on hymnology matters,
played the piano frequently, and this helped to heighten Ernest's
musical awareness. Thus, as sometimes happens with musically
gifted children, he learned to read music before learning to read
words.

In later life Ernest would deny that he had been a child prodigy, preferring to describe himself as precocious. He did not begin
formal music lessons until he was eight, his parents having taught
him more or less informally until then. He was never forced to
practise: he played when he wished and, one surmises, how he
wished. In time his mother refused to play when he was within
earshot, because he played so much better than she did. According to his father he played better than either of them.[18] One
story, on good authority, tells how fun-loving Ernest even served
as surrogate pianist for a young friend. He would practise on her
piano so that she could play outdoors without her mother knowing – and her mother never found out![19] Having had such a
happy introduction to music, Ernest felt nothing but sadness all
his life for those musically gifted children who are pushed, ca-
joled, and exploited by ambitious parents.

His talent aside, Ernest was a typical boy with interests in many
things other than music. First came survival. He attended Rosedale Public School, where the renowned pedagogue Amelia
Simms was principal. Ernest avoided the strap, widely used in
Toronto schools at that time, by 'good behaviour mingled with
a certain degree of caution and cunning.'[20] Alexander proudly
recalled how his son 'took real interest and pleasure in the
school work and was usually first or almost first in each class.'[21]
Ernest remembered it differently: 'While I did not dislike my
lessons, I decidedly preferred *to be outside having a good time,* especially in winter when a snow-fight could enliven the recreation
hour.'[22]

In true boyish fashion, Ernest had his mishaps too. One winter day while on a sleigh-ride outing, he fell from the sled and a horse immediately behind stepped on his face.[23] Fortunately the injury was not serious. And there was another frightening experience. While out playing one day, an older lad – so the story goes – suddenly lifted him by his arms and dangled him over the guard-rail of the Sherbourne Street viaduct above the Rosedale ravine. Ernest and the other children present screamed in terror until the bully finally set him back safely on his feet.[24] Did the experience leave lasting traumas? We shall never know. Ernest could also be mischievous. When he was nine, he wrote to his mother – she was in Scotland at the time – about being chased by a 'cop' for illegally riding his bicycle down Winchester hill.[25]

One more word about his early schooling. Ernest was strong in the three Rs but, despite his dexterity at the keyboard, very clumsy when it came to manual skills – he claimed to be unable to drive a nail in straight. In art classes, too, his drawing ability was virtually non-existent, although he acknowledged that these classes did teach him to use his eyes.

Ernest's musical development had a real boost when he was seven. St Enoch's acquired a pipe organ and he fell in love with the instrument:

I lost no time in climbing on the organ bench and from then on for many years the organ was the object of my chief devotion. The instrument at St. Enoch's was of the old 'tracker action' type and the touch was the heaviest I have ever known – not merely a childish impression, for I confirmed it many years later. The motor was controlled by an open switch which I was forbidden to touch; it was inconvenient and humiliating to have to ask a grown-up to move it for me. I could reach the pedals only by sitting on the very edge of the seat, but I managed to find my way about and become familiar with the various stops as well as the functions of the swell and combination pedals.[26]

Alexander recalled his son's excitement as he skipped home from school, 'asking me to turn on the electric motor ... He played quite elaborate music, delighting especially in the works of Handel and Bach.'[27] Young Ernest made such progress that he soon became unofficial organist at St Enoch's, playing for Sunday school sessions and occasional services. And, although this tale could be apocryphal, he was sometimes so impatient to play that he would unceremoniously push the church organist, Maitland Johnson, off his bench and take over.

At eight, he began organ lessons with Arthur Blakeley, organist at the Sherbourne Street Methodist Church, which boasted an electrically powered four-manual organ. Ernest amusingly described Blakeley as 'a curious, eccentric character – fundamentally musical but with a touch of the charlatan. I remember how he used to delight his audiences with a "Storm Fantasia," for which the church lights were extinguished and lighting effects supplied by someone working a switch behind the organ.'[28] The ingenious Blakeley often had his mind on things other than teaching. He owned a motor boat which he used for duck-shooting on Lake Ontario, an activity which frequently had a higher priority than giving organ lessons, even to his best student. On one occasion, Ernest was practising on Blakeley's organ when he heard shooting coming from the basement. It was Blakeley killing rats, not ducks![29]

As an organ teacher, Blakeley was casual in matters of fingering and technique, but he did teach Ernest how to treat the organ 'as a genuinely musical instrument.'[30] There were other benefits, too, in studying with Blakeley. Ernest was the keyboard soloist and accompanist for the Blakeley boys' vocal trio, which, under Blakeley's direction, performed light music – an arrangement of 'Abide with Me' was a favourite – in Toronto and southern Ontario churches.[31] It was good experience for Ernest, who, because he did double duty as soloist and accompanist, gained experience in playing on many different organs.

Alexander MacMillan, thinking of his son's future, encouraged his participation in the group because 'he not only advanced rapidly in musical understanding but became accustomed, quite naturally and without consciousness of nervous strain, to perform in public.'[32] It was the beginning of the lighter side of Ernest's music-making, a facet of his career in which he revelled throughout his life. He loved to act, particularly in a musical context, and Blakeley helped this brilliant son of a sober and thoughtful

Presbyterian minister to lose whatever inhibitions he may have had.

Ernest was also 'creative' when it came to religious services: 'Little egotist that I was, I rather liked to invent my own games and run my own show. As a son of the manse I played at conducting church services – but not on the family Presbyterian model. The colour and aesthetic qualities of the Anglican ritual, especially of the "High Church" type, appealed to me strongly ... My own services were "High" and, when my liturgical knowledge failed, I invented a ritual of my own.'[33] To help out in his ritual Ernest would press his three sisters into service. '[I] had them robed in dressing gowns (cassocks) and bed-sheets (surplices), while I, in similar attire with the addition of improvised stole and hood, conducted the service.' Occasionally visitors played the part of the congregation and dropped the odd coin in the collection box, but Ernest, always truthful, admitted that neither money nor religious fervour were behind the make-believe services. He was motivated by 'the opportunity for histrionic display ... I have,' he admitted, 'always enjoyed some dressing up and acting a part.'[34]

At ten he asked his father to give him the dollar required to take the entrance examination for Jarvis Collegiate, a high school in central Toronto. Alexander felt he was far too young and unprepared academically, but Ernest said, 'Well, if you'll risk the dollar, I'll risk the exam.'[35] He got the dollar, passed the exam, and spent the next year – an extremely happy one – enjoying the different teachers and subjects at Jarvis. Too young to join the school's cadet corps and looking for fun, he organized his own army, 'selecting as General the tallest boy in our class – a good-natured and quite unmilitary youth – while I acted as Chief of Staff. I then found it necessary to organize an opposing army and had some success in doing so, but fortunately the projected battle never came off, for, after assiduously digging trenches at the crest of the Don Flats, we were discovered by the police and compelled to fill them in. Thus ended my military career.'[36]

Composing came naturally to Ernest. His first effort, at age nine, was an oratorio which 'dealt with a subject no less formidable than the Resurrection. I have taken care,' he said many years later, 'that it shall not be resurrected.'[37] The piece was never completed, although he evidently did more work on it when he was fourteen. In his early teens, he wrote other less ambitious compositions, none of which were more than good student efforts, although family and friends made much of them, to his great annoyance and embarrassment. *He* knew that they were minor efforts at best.

He also showed an early love for literature. There were many books in the cultivated MacMillan household, and Ernest read voraciously – Walter Scott, Shakespeare, the Bible. Scott even competed for a time with Bach. One day Alexander MacMillan, hearing Ernest playing the piano, leaned over to identify the piece and found that Ernest was reading *Guy Mannering* while playing a Bach fugue – such were his powers of concentration![38]

April 1904 was an eventful month. During the first week, he played the Massey Hall organ for the first time, for the Methodist Social Union's 'Festival of the Lilies.'[39] Despite the notoriously poor instrument, the press was full of praise. 'It seemed almost eerie to see the youngster commanding so much music, this lad in a white sailor suit, whose feet could barely reach the pedals.'[40] Then two weeks later he attended a joint recital by two English musicians, organist Edwin Lemare and baritone Watkin Mills, at Metropolitan Church in downtown Toronto. Lemare ended the concert with his version of the *Entry of the Gods to Valhalla* from *Das Rheingold* (playing transcriptions from Wagner's music dramas was a fashionable practice among virtuoso organists of the day). This set an appropriate mood for what followed, for, as Ernest later recalled, when he and his father emerged from the church, they 'were startled by a vivid red glow in the sky. I was forcibly prevented from rushing into the threatened area, although we came as near it as he thought safe.'[41] It was, of course, the great fire of 1904 which devastated many acres of the city's warehouse district, a spectacle to remember for a lifetime.

While in Toronto, Lemare visited Blakeley's church, and Blakeley proudly showed off Ernest, who was playing a piece which Lemare had not heard before. After inquiring about its name and composer, he was 'astonished' to learn that the boy was, in fact, improvising.[42] Blakeley loved to tell stories about Ernest. Another of his favourites was of how, when Ernest first

started to take lessons, he had to walk on the organ pedals because there was no other way he could reach them.

Following his Massey Hall debut, Alexander began taking his
young son with him on Sunday visits to out-of-town churches,
where Alexander would give a guest sermon and Ernest would
play a few pieces on the organ to entertain the congregation. And
his success at the 1904 Lilies Festival led to a return engagement
the following April, only this time he shared the program with
none other than 'Mr Blakeley's Boys.' He was getting more attention from indulgent listeners than was good for him when the
family left Toronto for an extended stay in Scotland.

In that spring of 1905 Alexander MacMillan was suffering from
overwork brought on by doing too many jobs – his St Enoch's
duties, his hymn writing and editing, his lecturing at the University of Toronto, and his occasional teaching at several ladies colleges. With four children to support – Ernest now had three
younger sisters – he needed the income, but the strain was taking
its toll. Alexander therefore leaped at the church's offer of a year
in Edinburgh to regain his strength and to work at hymnology.
Ernest had already been to Scotland with his parents for a two-
month stay in the summer of 1901, and looked forward to returning for what was to be one year, but which became three.

  After a summer in Scotland's south country, the family settled
in Edinburgh, and Ernest went through the transition from prodigy to serious music student. Indeed, the move to Edinburgh
could not have been more opportune for young Ernest, because
the city's cultural life was so much richer than Toronto's. He
excitedly attended the Scottish Orchestra's concerts each week,
score in hand, storing away what he heard in his extraordinary
musical memory; it was the beginning of his lifelong infatuation
with the orchestra. There were also other concerts featuring
outstanding artists in unusual programs. The renowned harpsi-
chordist Wanda Landowska introduced him to Bach, and this
inspired him to study his *Well-tempered Clavier*, the so-called 'Forty-
eight,' inside out. Landowska's playing helped him to gain
insights into Bach's music which would, as he matured musically,
place him in the forefront of Bach interpreters. The 'Forty-eight'

became his musical bible. His mother gave him the complete volume for Christmas in 1906, and, in later years, he would vividly illuminate its contents for students and finished musicians alike.

His parents, having decided that it was time for him to study the organ seriously, sent him to the distinguished forty-year-old blind organist Alfred Hollins, who was more than pleased to teach this brilliant Canadian boy who gave every indication of emulating his own career as a virtuoso organist. Unlike Ernest, who had no formal piano lessons in his childhood, Hollins had studied piano first and thus had built up fundamental keyboard skills before turning to the larger instrument. Indeed, he had been a piano prodigy and had played Beethoven's Concerto No. 5 at London's Crystal Palace while still in his early teens. Later, he had studied organ in Germany, had been soloist with orchestras in New York and Boston, and had held several important organ posts in England before returning to his native Edinburgh in 1897 to become organist of the Free St George's Church.

All too soon, as is often the case with extremely gifted students, Hollins was treating Ernest more as a colleague than a pupil, and thus was not as strict a pedagogue as the youth needed, or as Ernest, at least later, thought he had needed. Nonetheless, Ernest was emphatic in his praise of Hollins:

He set me an excellent example in rhythmical playing (a thing some organists never learn) and, having a very keen ear, was usually able to detect faults in my fingering and pedalling with uncanny precision. When in doubt he would put his hand over my fingers or even dive down to feel what my feet were doing. I often had the privilege of guiding him to a new organ; it was remarkable to see how he found his way about the stops and other accessories by touch alone. I must have been unconsciously inspired to gain some of the same facility – invaluable in reading new music, when a moment's distraction from the printed page might result in losing one's place.[43]

As time went on, Ernest would deputize for Hollins at St George's and elsewhere, rehearsing the choir and taking services. Alexander MacMillan described one of Ernest's Sunday appearances:

It was a great surprise to the congregation to see a lad of thirteen years, dressed in Norfolk suit and Eton Collar, discoursing music on the organ in the grand manner and controlling the choir and the singing of the people ... On that occasion the last of the hymns to be sung was ... 'O God Our Help in Ages Past.' Immediately after ... the Benediction Ernest began to improvise on the tune and continued to do so many minutes in a manner that was astonishing to the large proportion of the congregation who remained to listen.[44]

Eager to perform, the young organist also gave recitals in Edinburgh and other parts of Scotland, and even in England. Ernest, abounding in Scottish national pride, was particularly pleased when, after a recital in Kirriemuir, an inspired admirer wrote a poem in typical Burns metre which Ernest treasured all his life.[45] The poem, after describing the organ as 'A kist o' whistles near as auld as Jubal's day,' went on:

> But, deil may care, he set it goin'
> The man wha had tae dae the blawin'
> Could scarce get time his breith tae draw in
> He worked sae sair
> Keepin' the bellowses and pipes
> Weel filled wi' air.
>
> The folk wha heard him a' admired
> His style, and as they oot retired
> A siller offerin' was desired
> Which was maist fit
> A few gied less, but less gied mair
> Than thrup'ny bit.

Ernest's general education was neglected. He did not attend school at all during his first year in Edinburgh and only half-days, at Viewpark School, during the second.[46] This spell at Viewpark gave him some sorely missed time with others his own age, which his other Edinburgh activities did not. Of more significance, as time would tell, were the classes in music theory and history at Edinburgh University's Faculty of Music which he was allowed to attend. One professor in particular, Reid Professor Frederick Niecks, gave Ernest the first academic thrust to his musical studies. Niecks was an accomplished scholar and writer. He had studied philosophy and history at Leipzig University, was the author of treatises on music theory and history and of much-praised biographies of Chopin and Schumann, and served as music critic for the *Monthly Musical Record* and the *Musical Times*. He was also an accomplished performer. Before leaving Germany he had been a violin soloist and concert-master, and later in Scotland was violist with the Edinburgh String Quartet and organist at a church in Dumfries. Ernest was one of Niecks's star pupils in harmony and counterpoint classes that year and even earned a medal in advanced harmony. He credits Niecks with giving him 'an insight into musical history such as no one before or since has done.'[47]

By the time Ernest took classes at Edinburgh University, he was a mature thirteen-year-old, and his well-developed social skills endeared him to his fellow students, all of whom were, naturally, several years his senior. One student, Julius (Jimmy) Morison, treated Ernest on absolutely equal terms, addressing him in correspondence as 'my dear old chap' and sharing with him intimacies typical of young men.[48]

But Ernest was taken down a peg when, halfway through the year, he went to London to take the qualifying examinations for the Licentiateship of the Royal Academy and was 'well ploughed' for his efforts. The cocky young musician deserved the setback, for he had been under-prepared in sight-playing, sight-reading, and transposition.[49] The failure was, however, instructive, and when Ernest returned to Edinburgh he promptly began theory and composition studies with Dr W.B. Ross, a strict and thorough teacher and a demon for accuracy who insisted on the very best from his students. Ross taught composition along conservative lines, and his pupils learned well how to satisfy the 'exercise' requirements for degrees from important British musical institutions. Within six months Ernest earned the Associateship of the Royal College of Organists (ARCO), an examination which, according to his proud father, 80 per cent of adult applicants failed.[50] (He never retried the Royal Academy's Licentiate.) One assignment he did, on George Grove's *Beethoven's Nine Symphonies*, left him with a comprehensive understanding of these great works, so useful for any conductor. Given his prodigious memory, which had already aroused admiration in Edinburgh's musical circles, he may well have learned them all by heart at that time.

Gifts and pleasures came with his accomplishments. Because of his parents' delight and pride over his medal in harmony, they gave him a much-coveted set of *Grove's Dictionary of Music and Musicians* and then allowed their exuberant prodigy to go by himself on a bicycle trip through Scotland to get to know the West Highlands, the island of Arran, Burns country, and Perthshire. He was also treated to a week in London with his mother, and the two of them, on a tight budget, walked through much of the great city. In a letter to his father addressed 'Dear Male Parent,' he mentioned seeing original Wagner and Mendelssohn manuscripts and, although impressed, he added flippantly: 'no one but the composer could make [them] out.' He also described St Paul's Cathedral irreverently as 'a very ornamental place – very cleverly gotten up.'[51] He signed the letter 'Dacey,' the affectionate nickname by which he was known to his family.

The MacMillans made a number of lasting friends in Edinburgh, including, most notably, Margaret Maclean and Mary Lothian, two women who ran a toy shop called the Albert Bazaar and whom Ernest would later come to address 'with transatlantic impudence' as Peggy and Polly.[52] In the summer of 1907, Alexander had to return to Canada to resume his duties at St Enoch's, and taking his two older girls, Dorothy and Jean, with him, he left Winnie, Ernest, and Winifred in Scotland so that Ernest could prepare for entrance to Oxford. It was another year of serious study for Ernest, with his mother and a wider surrogate family of Edinburgh friends encouraging him. Winnie described to her sister how her son played Santa Claus for the 1907 Christmas (his passion for dressing up was always ready to surface): '[He] was puffing and blowing, with two big white bags on his back. The firelight just gave the required light and Santa's red nose, purchased by Ernest for a penny (wax, it was) was just beautiful. He had a red toque, edged with ermine (no, I mean cotton wool), coat of Alex's, edged likewise ... Ernest then presented the gifts, all carefully packed by himself.'[53]

Then in the spring of 1908, his third and final year in Edinburgh, Ernest matriculated for the Oxford BMus. Preparing for both the ARCO and the Oxford admission had pushed him to his utmost. At fourteen his musical credentials were already impressive, his general education had been sporadic but effective thanks to his enquiring mind, and he had heard some of Great Britain's leading orchestras, choirs, and soloists. The time had come to go home.

2. *Choosing a Career*

Before returning to Canada from Scotland, Ernest had accepted the position of organist-choirmaster at the Knox Presbyterian Church in Toronto – his first real job. He began his duties in September 1908, and things went badly from the start. The church had recently moved to a new building at the corner of Spadina and Harbord, a residential area near the University of Toronto campus. It had not yet installed an organ, and Ernest had to make do on a small harmonium for several months. Once the organ was in place, he launched a variety of musical activities, but the church elders, instead of being pleased, viewed his initiatives as unwelcome intrusions in the life of their church!

Clearly upset, Ernest soon realized that he should never have taken the job. His father, a leader in Presbyterian reform who believed in more widespread and creative use of music in the service and who knew Knox's fundamentalist position, should have warned him. Now Ernest had nothing to look forward to but musical frustration and unpleasantly long and grim sermons. 'Every Sunday evening for the greater part of one year we listened to an exposition of the Book of Ecclesiastes and went home with the words "Vanity of vanities, behold all is vanity" ringing in our ears.'[1] He persevered, yet confrontation was inevitable.

It finally came late in 1909, his second year at the church, when the chairman of Knox's music committee arrogantly took the brilliant young organist to task and laid down strict rules: the choir *and* the organ must be used for the opening hymn (Ernest preferred that the choir sing a cappella); the hymns must be sung more rapidly; Ernest must not use his hands and arms so much when leading the choir in anthems; he must finish anthems promptly upon the completion of the collection so that the minister not be delayed; monthly organ recitals and a quarterly Service of Praise must be 'sanctioned and controlled' by the music committee.[2]

Ernest gritted his teeth and still hung on. There was even a brief reprieve in May 1910, when he pleased the most severe fundamentalists at Knox with his dirge of 'particular solemnity' and 'special beauty' for the late King Edward VII's memorial service.[3] But three months later his plans for the next season came under fire at a meeting of the Session, the group responsible for the congregation's spiritual well-being. This was more than he could take, and, with his father's support, he resigned. His choir, more aware than the elders of the loss, gave the young director a handsome gold watch, which he treasured for the rest of his life. The Knox appointment had shown him the many problems faced by a church organist-choirmaster and raised serious doubts in his mind about whether a career in church music was really for him.

The difficulties notwithstanding, Ernest had used his time at Knox to good personal advantage. He had practised organ diligently, had studied many scores ranging from symphonic works to Bach's church cantatas, and had begun to develop a reputation as a soloist. Following his October 1909 recital to inaugurate the new organ at Toronto's St John's Presbyterian Church, *Saturday Night*, a popular Toronto weekly which gave attention to the arts, wrote: 'Mr. MacMillan, who until a few years ago was known as a clever child prodigy in local musical circles, performed an exacting programme (the principal work was Bach's *Prelude and Fugue in B Minor*) in very capable fashion ... With continued ripening and development of his powers he will eventually take his place amongst our foremost Canadian organists.'[4]

With Knox behind him, Ernest looked around for more challenges and credentials and set his sights on earning the Fellowship of the Royal College of Organists (FRCO) and the BMus at Oxford, both degrees to be earned solely by examinations. He also made plans to attend the University of Toronto to study history and political science, subjects which, he believed, would broaden his horizons. To this end he engaged tutors in mathematics and German, two subjects in which he needed more grounding to gain university admission. Here fate played into his hands – his German tutor was a young woman with whom he established immediate rapport, and who would eventually become his wife and lifelong companion. She was (Laura) Elsie Keith, who was a year and a half older than Ernest and one of four children of a well-known and prosperous Toronto family. Her father, Alexander Keith, was an engineer and inventor of household appliances. Her mother, Jessie Elizabeth, was the daughter of Duncan Forbes, the 'king of curlers,' and her uncle, J.C. Forbes, was a prominent artist. Elsie was in her second year at the university, majoring in modern languages. She was bright and perceptive, good at sports, charming, and diminutive – she was just under five feet tall.

Actually, Ernest had met her casually in 1908, soon after his return from Scotland, and remembered her as 'very lively and much more at home with the male sex than the Scottish girls I had known. She captured my fancy at once. I think my fate must have been settled from that moment, although it was not until five years later that I told her so.'[5] At the time, the tutoring sessions led to friendship, and, of course, helped Ernest pass his entrance examinations to the university.

He returned to Scotland in the late fall of 1910 to study with his Edinburgh teachers, and in January took the FRCO examination, astounding everyone by standing first among the nineteen finalists (from a field of 113 applicants) to win the coveted Carte-LaFontaine prize.[6] Encouraged, he stayed on in Britain to sit for his Oxford BMus examinations. That degree was attained in May 1911, also with impressive standing. Ernest was so jubilant about his marks that Dr Ross, his principal Edinburgh teacher, had all he could do to dissuade him from working immediately towards his doctorate; he thought that the young scholar had much to learn about other things before pursuing more degrees in music.[7]

During this Edinburgh visit, and with Elsie 4,000 miles away, the romantic Ernest fell in love with a Scottish girl, Lilian Hardie. Polly Lothian wrote to Ernest's father: 'You will have heard all about the "daughter-in-law elect," but remember the son is *very* much in love with her, so please make allowances for that when he is describing her beauty.'[8] There was, however, no formal engagement, and no more was heard of the romance.[9]

At seventeen, the gifted Ernest wasn't sure what kind of a musical career he wanted. He wrote to his father about studying in Germany, as most serious North American music students did, and mentioned Berlin or Leipzig for piano and composition. He also wrote about how much he wanted to visit the Wagner Festival at Bayreuth. At the same time, he was drawn to attending university and socializing and enjoying 'genial companions and the camaraderie of university life.'[10] This was understandable for one who had practised when others played, had had no formal schooling in his early teens, and had missed making friends with youths his own age. Ernest was also concerned that he wouldn't like living in Germany alone, dealing with a language he barely spoke, adapting to new and strange customs and people. Sober, provincial Canada, which meant home, security, and family to him, was a known quantity. He already had enough credentials to get a teaching post at a conservatory or, with more study, at a university, tempting prospects and practical solutions to earning a living.

Yet, he wondered, were these goals lofty enough for a musician of his ability? After Oxford he could have – perhaps should have – changed course and sought a career as an orchestral and operatic conductor. He loved the orchestra and had a fine sense for the dramatic, a strong theoretical background, and an amazing memory. He played the piano well, was a natural accompanist, and improvised brilliantly. Moreover, he could project his feelings and emotions to others – already borne out by his conducting the Knox Choir – and had an outgoing personality and rare leadership qualities. In sum, he had all the attributes to become a conductor of the first rank.

But there was Alexander MacMillan, who wanted his son to be a professor, a head of a music school, or a leading church musician, all responsible and honourable positions that, by their very nature, served others. He failed to comprehend the breadth and depth of his son's talent and the international career it could lead to, and Ernest was very much influenced by his father. In fact both of their visions were limited because they had lived only in Toronto and Edinburgh, cities which lacked the quality and diversity of musical life of Berlin, Leipzig, London, Paris, and New York. Ernest had had a taste of what a great city could offer him from his few brief visits to London, but failed to attach enough importance to it. Even if he had, his father still might not have understood.

And yet, intuitively, Ernest resisted the pull back to Toronto. He wrote his father again, this time to express his fear that he would 'deteriorate into a mere church musician ... Being a church organist is no fun. That is why I intend giving up the organ as soon as I can ... I am afraid of settling down to be a local musician.'[11] Patiently, Alexander avoided a confrontation with his son and found him an attractive organist post at St Paul's Church in Hamilton, a city some forty miles west of Toronto. The post would dovetail nicely with his studies at the University of Toronto. Ernest finally surrendered.

His return home in 1911 meant that he would be part of the world of the church, the university, and the Canadian middle class. The values his father had instilled in him, and his father's manipulation of events, discouraged Ernest from biting the bullet and going off into the unknown. Going home was probably the right decision for him personally, but not, perhaps, for the full realization of his enormous musical talent. In any event, he passed up the chance, at the right time in his life, to prepare properly for a conducting career, a career which he later wanted to pursue more than anything else.

There were, undoubtedly, compensations to being home again. His city and country seemed to be changing for the better. Thanks to a flourishing economy, Toronto's population was growing, and the city was even building skyscrapers. Canada's Liberal government, led by Sir Wilfrid Laurier, had just been deposed after fifteen years in power, but during its term it had helped Canadians to develop a modicum of national confidence and pride, and to feel some independence from Britain and the United States. Laurier had encouraged immigration and the settling of the West, supported increased international trade, and paved the way for more railways.

There was improvement, too, on the musical front. The Toronto Symphony Orchestra had been founded in 1906 by Frank Welsman, a Toronto Conservatory teacher, and gave its first concert on 11 April 1907. It was now performing regularly at Massey Hall with passable proficiency, playing major works by the great eighteenth- and nineteenth-century symphonic composers. In addition there were several outstanding secular and church choirs in the city, which established Toronto as the choral capital of North America. The finest was the Mendelssohn Choir, which had been founded in 1894 by A.S. Vogt, by all accounts an excellent choral conductor. Ernest considered Vogt's reading of Pierné's *Children's Crusade* particularly good, and, years later, following his own reading of the work with the Conservatory Choir, modestly doubted that he had 'ever achieved the effect produced by Vogt.'[12]

Ernest enjoyed his three years at 'Varsity,' as the university was affectionately called. He had some excellent professors, most notably George Wrong and James Mavor, and his social life, as he had hoped, flourished. The *Phi Kappa Pi* fraternity, wanting 'to look him over' before proposing him for membership, invited what they thought was a stuffy classical musician to dinner. After the meal, to their surprise and delight, he sat down at the piano and played popular songs of the day, Gilbert and Sullivan tunes and, it was rumoured, some off-colour poems he had set to music. Doubts gone and hearts won over, the fraternity members promptly asked him to join.[13]

During his first year, Ernest helped his father prepare a new university hymn book and was rewarded with a trip to England to check the proofs at the Oxford University Press. Four of his own tunes were included in what turned out to be a fine volume.[14] One of them, 'Benedicte, Omnia Opera,' to a text by John Milton, shows that Ernest's approach to hymn writing was anything but bloodless. Its first six notes, which encompass a range of an octave and a half, exclaim, 'Ring out, ye crystal spheres.'[15] Alas, Ernest had been in England only a few days when word came that his father had been struck by lightning in his Toronto home and had suffered burns and shock. In London at the time with his twenty-three-year-old cousin Isabel Gunn (Christina's daughter) and Edinburgh friend Polly Lothian, he made plans to return home to lead the family but, on hearing that his father's injuries were slight, stayed on to finish his proofing assignment.[16]

Elsie Keith was also visiting in London that summer, and their friendship blossomed. Together they took in the sights, from a service at Westminster to the soapbox orators at Hyde Park. Isabel wrote to her mother that Ernest was very much in love with Elsie. 'He talks about her incessantly and wonders if she would think he was too young for her and is much hurt when Miss Lothian and I laugh.'[17] At the same time, Isabel expressed concern about her young cousin: '[He] is a wearing person to be with. He isn't well, looks anemic, and gets so depressed ... I think he is worried about what he will do next winter. He seems to feel that the family can't get along on the salary the University would pay him – the news that Uncle Allie might have to rest for some time makes him more inclined to this. He doesn't seem to like the idea of going to Chicago but talks of keeping on at Hamilton – however, he is so changeable one can't tell what he'll do.' Isabel was referring to two new job offers Ernest was mulling over – assistant organist at the university, a post that would allow him to continue his studies, and an attractive post at Chicago's Fourth Presbyterian Church, which would not.

In this same letter, Isabel provided a few more candid observations about Ernest. She accused him of putting on airs and mentioned that he 'evidently likes to impress the people here with his blasé knowledge of London.' And then she praised him:

Not a word does he ever say to give a hint of his attainments. I think it is fine the way he has kept his head about the wonders he has done. Poor child, he is such a child in a way, it must be hard to have the capacity to do anything and to have to choose one thing – he wants to study in Oxford – he wants to have the university organ and organize a choir – he wants to go to Germany and lead a Bohemian life – he wants to take piano lessons and learn a string instrument.

After considerable thought, Ernest turned down the Chicago job and opted to stay on at the University of Toronto for his second year of study. It was a wise decision. He formed the University Musical Society, which sponsored concerts and lectures, and, to his surprise and pleasure, he was elected president of his class. It also pleased him that, as assistant organist, the university paid him well for Sunday services and the occasional official event. Convocation Hall, where most of the services and events took place, had an excellent organ.

And then there was Elsie. They saw much of one another, and, more and more, Ernest grew to love 'this fiercely individualistic and strong feminist ... with a mind of her own and, when she needed it, a will of steel ... She was a warm, impulsive, intensely feeling person – on the one hand with a broad streak of common sense and on the other with a strong artistic sensibility in literature, music, and painting.'[18] Now the two young people needed something to bring their feelings to a head.

The catalyst was Ernest's departure, on 25 June 1913, for Murray Bay, a summer resort on the St Lawrence River in Quebec where he had a two-month job as church organist in exchange for his expenses. His father was to be visiting minister at the same church.[19] When Ernest stopped off to say goodbye to Elsie he found himself in the hallway of her home, resplendent with straw hat, cane, and cigar, 'blurting out his long pent-up feelings.' On this their 'day of revelation,' as they would henceforth call it, Ernest and Elsie declared their love for each other. After deciding to announce their engagement in September, they parted.[20]

Letters followed thick and fast. For the first few weeks they each wrote at least once and often two or three times daily. Ernest shared his innermost thoughts and feelings with Elsie, as he would for the rest of his life. She was his confidante, his sounding-board, and his constant support, and she would grow to understand him like no other. Ernest's letters were ardent. Elsie's were too, but with more reserve, as one would expect of a well-brought-up Toronto woman in the year 1913. En route to Murray Bay, Ernest charmingly begged her indulgence: 'This is my first attempt at a love-letter, so if you find any faults in it, they may be set down to inexperience and – may I hope it? – be pardoned?'[21] He feigned modesty by saying that he feared he was not good enough for her, while comparing himself to Beethoven, who had looked for a woman to love him and strengthen him in virtue.

'You will encourage my virtues, such as they are, and rid myself of my vices ... moral cowardice ... a dread of facing facts squarely ... and a habit of beating around the bush.'[22]

Ernest wrote much about morality and ethics, and, especially, about his future.[23] 'The highest life is gained through sacrifice and service,' he said. Clearly no soothsayer, in view of how events would unfold, he spelled out his plans. First, he would do the D Mus work for Oxford. If he passed the preliminary examinations, he would be ready to take the qualifying examinations in November 1915. Then, if his composition was accepted by the jury, he would have the doctorate by the following June. He would spend the winter of 1915–16 in Oxford, where, incidentally, he would also write his Toronto MA thesis, 'which would be a comparatively easy matter.' Another *Presbyterian Book of Praise* was also in the offing, and he expected to be called upon to edit it and see it through publication in England.

But, he stressed, these plans were for Elsie's eyes only, for he would not like others to know about them in case they fell through. Once these things had been completed he hoped to become a professor of music at Toronto, 'the best centre around in which to work for the "cause" of music in Canada.' Although only nineteen, the son of Alexander MacMillan was already preparing to commit himself to his country's musical life, much as his father had committed himself to its religious life. Yet the enormity of all this was plaguing him with doubts. Two days later, after more reflection, the young Canadian idealist wrote with startling insight about the state of the arts in Canada:

I often wonder whether I ought to stick to music as a profession. Somehow the feeling grows upon me more and more that Canada is not yet ripe for the development of a national art, and that any attempt to foist upon her a purely artificial product must result in failure. After all, real art must spring from the heart of the people, and one might almost believe that the whole social scheme would need to be reorganized before there will be any opportunity for artistic development. No amount of patronage from the 'upper classes' will ever suffice to produce great music, and the commercial money-grubbing spirit of all America – and England too – today will eventually choke whatever possibilities lie before us. The musical profession needs the nation at its back, and the fact that it is not so would seem a very excellent reason for the poor ideals of art the average Canadian has ...

Time after time I have wished to enter the ministry, but I cannot accept the dogmas the church forces upon its servants, and I am not ready to put myself in a false position. But I firmly believe that the preacher must precede the artist, and that social reformation must accompany the flowering forth of a nation's artistic production. The hopelessness of trying to inspire the public ... with great ideals is more and more growing upon me, yet I fear I have not the heroic spirit which goes in the face of all opposition and will admit no compromise. The musical profession is becoming as commercial as everything else – even the church has caught the money-getting spirit. If we could find a band of uncompromising idealists who understood their work and were prepared to sacrifice everything for it, there might be some hope, but where are they? I shall never forget what Dr. Herridge of Ottawa (one of my heroes) said ... He hoped that I would live to combat 'musical philistinism' in Canada – and it certainly needs combatting.[24]

Extremely conscious of being in French Canada, he questioned why the French-speaking Canadians he met did not want to learn English. He firmly believed that this was inhibiting Quebec's development, as was the Catholic church's extraordinary influence and backwardness. 'Quebecers will wake up some day,' he prophesied, 'and then we will have to make up for lost time.'[25] (A decade later he would realize how important French was for francophones and why anglophones needed to study French to understand French Canada better. And he practised what he preached by learning French – although never to his complete satisfaction.)

His letters grew more moderate in tone and dropped off in number towards the end of July because of his increasingly busy social life. He naïvely told Elsie about the pretty girls he was meeting and the dances he was attending, and wrote in detail about a Mrs Antoinette Burgess and her 'bratty' fourteen-year-old daughter, Barbara. Mrs Burgess, a wealthy and cultivated Bostonian, was quite taken with Ernest's ability and personality and took him all over the Murray Bay area by boat and private carriage in fine style. She knew much about the musical life of Boston, New York, London, and the cities of continental Europe, and filled Ernest's envious ears with fascinating stories about the famous musicians she numbered among her friends. Such tales convinced him all the more that Toronto was a musical backwater and that the organ loft and the cloistered university were holding back his development and keeping him away from the real world of music. On another tack, he complained to Elsie about the deplorable state of musical criticism in Toronto. And then, in one of his typically self-deprecatory moods, he said, 'I have no better critic than myself, and I am both biased and incompetent.'[26]

By mid-August the not-so-serious young church organist was heavily involved in rehearsing Murray Bay vacationers in a variety show, and he assured Elsie that most of the participants were middle-aged, although it was probably a half-truth for her sake. He also told Elsie that his skills as an all-round pianist had been confirmed by a teenager who, after hearing him play at a party, had called him the best ragtime player she had ever heard – next to the one at the Strand in Montreal![27] It was indeed true that his remarkable ear and improvisatory skills enabled him to play music of any style, whenever the spirit moved him. His letters by then had become frank accounts of the good times he was having and of how much he was enjoying the attention which was being showered upon him. These letters contrast sharply with his earlier ones, in which he had told Elsie that their love would be 'firmer with separation.' Firmer or not, their love did survive the separation and, when he returned to Toronto at the summer's end, their engagement was announced and a betrothal reception followed. The sweethearts planned a long engagement, but little did they realize *how* long it would be.

In September 1913, Ernest began his third year at Varsity, and to convince himself that he was a solo artist, he gave a formal organ recital at the university. Meanwhile, Antoinette Burgess, wanting to show him off to her Boston friends and sensing that he wanted to see more of the musical world she had tantalized him with during the summer, invited him to Boston for Christmas. As she

Winnie Ross when she first met Alexander MacMillan. (CPFC)

Alexander MacMillan when Ernest was six. (KMFC)

The MacMillan family in Scotland in 1883. Alexander is standing left.
(KMFC)

OPPOSITE:

Ernest at seven months and as a precocious three-year-old. (KMFC)

The Reverend Alexander Ross, Ernest MacMillan's maternal grandfather, c. 1875. (KMFC)

Seven-year-old Ernest with sisters Dorothy and Jean. (KMFC)

Ernest when he first played the organ at Massey Hall
at age ten. (KMFC)

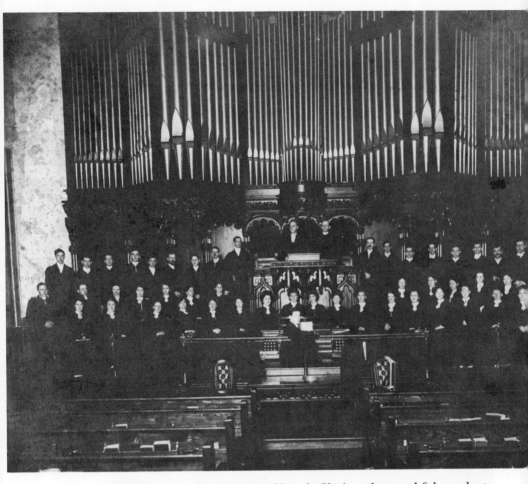

The 1910 Knox Presbyterian Church Choir – the youthful conductor is at the console – in its new building on Spadina Avenue. (KMFC)

OPPOSITE:

A dapper Varsity undergraduate. (KMFC)

bottom: Ernest happily wearing his Oxford hood in 1911. (KMFC)

Ernest prior to an organ recital
in Newcastle, Ontario.
(KMFC)

Five Ruhleben internees. Ernest, dressed informally, is standing on the right. Benjamin Dale is seated centre. (ECMF)

The all-male cast, orchestra, and production staff of Ruhleben's *Mikado*. Conductor Ernest MacMillan is front centre. (ECMF)

Timothy Eaton Memorial Church on Toronto's St Clair Avenue
c. 1920. MacMillan conducted Bach's *St Matthew Passion* there for
the first time in 1923. (Eaton Memorial Church Archives)

Elsie MacMillan in the mid-1920s. (KMFC)

Amice Calverley's drawing of bespectacled, pipe-smoking Ernest in his early thirties. (KMFC)

Newly appointed Toronto Conservatory principal Ernest MacMillan in his office, October 1926. (KMFC)

Composer of 'Stop All This Idle Chatter' Frank Bolton (Native name
Geetiks) donning his regalia. Ernest MacMillan assists.
(Canadian Museum of Civilization)

Hugh the drover (Allan Jones) and John the butcher (Randolph
Crowe) facing off in Vaughan Williams's opera *Hugh the Drover*.
(Canadian Opera Company Archives)

A youthful representative of the Sir Ernest MacMillan Fine Arts Clubs presenting a gift to its patron. (ECMF)

Ernest relaxing with his sister Winifred (left) and her piano-team partner, Kay Irwin. (CPFC)

The Lausanne Anglo-American Conference of 1931. Left to right:
Allan Sly, Boris Berlin, Ernest MacMillan, and Géza de Kresz.
(ECMF)

Reginald Stewart, Philadelphia Orchestra conductor Eugene
Ormandy, and Sir Ernest having a good laugh during Ormandy's visit
to Toronto in 1938. (ECMF)

Igor Stravinsky and Ernest MacMillan jauntily posing for the camera.
Stravinsky conducted the TSO in 1937. (ECMF)

Sir Ernest conferring with Georges Enesco and Czech conductor
Henry Svoboda in February 1939. Note photo of Stokowski on
the wall. (ECMF)

The renovated 1948 Massey Hall as seen from the stage. (KMFC)

had anticipated, he jumped at the opportunity and was much impressed by the city's cultural riches, particularly the Boston Symphony Orchestra, which was probably the finest on the continent. By comparison, Toronto, not that much smaller than Boston, was still struggling to get its fledgling orchestra off the ground. The generous Mrs Burgess took Ernest to several symphony concerts, and introduced him to conductor Karl Muck. He wrote Elsie: 'The great man might have been interested in me, since he shook hands with me four times and gave me good advice for studying.' However, Ernest didn't say what the advice was.[28]

The Boston Opera was doing *La Bohème*, with the celebrated Maggie Teyte as Mimi, and *Madama Butterfly*, and he enjoyed both performances immensely.[29] He also heard pianist Harold Bauer and violinist Jacques Thibaud, two of the finest musicians of the day, give a joint recital at which they played the Franck Sonata and the Beethoven *Kreutzer* Sonata. 'It was one of the most magnificent performances I have ever listened to ... There is no display for display's sake about Bauer, and his playing is so satisfying,' wrote the ecstatic Ernest. He vowed that, when the time came for him to study piano seriously, he wanted Bauer as his teacher.[30] Before returning to Toronto, he gave two organ recitals, the first at a local church and the second at the Harvard Club, where the printed program identified him as Ernest Campbell Machillon![31]

Inspired, Ernest, with the help of his University Musical Society, adventurously planned to feature himself in a novel concert on 16 March 1914 of organ concertos by Handel, Rheinberger, and Bossi, and engaged an orchestra of mainly Toronto Symphony players with Luigi von Kunits as conductor. Von Kunits, a gifted Viennese violinist, had been a concert-master and soloist with a number of leading European and North American symphony orchestras, and had recently turned down the conductorship of the Philadelphia Orchestra because of a weak heart. (The Philadelphia post was given to Leopold Stokowski, the second choice!) Instead, he preferred to settle in Toronto and teach at the Canadian Academy of Music.

Attendance at the concert was poor. In fact, Ernest said that it was the smallest audience he had ever seen in Convocation Hall.[32] The admission charge to help pay the fees for the orchestra and conductor probably kept people away. To make matters worse, as Ernest later pointed out, 'the press was not too cordial, agreeing on the whole with Hector Berlioz that "the organ was Pope and the orchestra King" – a not over-congenial pair.' [33] Luckily, the prudent Ernest had three wealthy guarantors, Sir Edmund Walker, Sir Edmund Osler, and Mr – later Sir – Joseph Flavelle, who covered the $300 loss.[34] Toronto knew that it had an outstanding organist in its midst but was not yet ready to pay to hear him.

Elsie, meanwhile, was in Bermuda with her mother, for health and other undisclosed reasons. Letters flowed between them as they had the previous summer and Christmas. Since she had missed his March concert, he described it for her and told her how excited he was about von Kunits's conducting. 'He doesn't hold his men in as Welsman does ... The Toronto Symphony men seem to have under von Kunits a life and spice of their own playing which I had not observed in them before.'[35]

His disappointment with the concert convinced Ernest all the more that, if he was to advance musically, he must leave Toronto and work abroad, and he began to think seriously about deferring his final university year to study piano and composition in Paris. His unofficial patron, Mrs Burgess, urged him on, while his love for Canada, for his family, and for Elsie held him back. He asked Elsie, 'How long shall we be able to stand Toronto?' and then, with almost premonitory concern, 'Are we or are we not going to have a chance to be *young* together? ... I am growing more depressed at the thought of going to Paris.'[36]

But he put his doubts aside and, fixing his travel plans for late May (he would travel with the Burgesses), plunged into a month of activity – writing his end-of-year examinations, helping his parents move house, welcoming Elsie back from Bermuda, and preparing for Europe. Alexander and Winnie were, all the while, quietly resentful of Mrs Burgess's intrusion into their beloved son's life and looked with considerable suspicion on the attention she was showering on him. Yet either they said nothing or what they said fell on deaf ears, because once Ernest had made up his mind to go he wavered no more.

And so, with Antoinette and Barbara Burgess, Ernest MacMillan set out for Europe without any inkling that he was beginning a four-and-a-half-year adventure.[37] They first stopped in New York, where he inspected several impressive church organs and gaped at the new Woolworth Building (although he thought the smaller Metropolitan Life Building more 'artistic') and then boarded the *Kronprinz Wilhelm.*

In that summer of 1914, 'la belle époque' was drawing to a close in beautiful Paris. Ernest was enthralled by its museums, galleries (he was being 'converted' to impressionism), theatres (he thought them better than London's), and opera – he saw Wagner's *Parsifal*, Debussy's *Pelléas et Mélisande*, and Gustave Charpentier's quintessentially Parisian opera *Louise*. Versailles and Chartres were on his itinerary as was a visit to the Trocadero to see pupils of Isadora Duncan in action. But after two weeks of sightseeing and fun, the work ethic which ruled his life intervened – he told Elsie that, although he couldn't refuse to accompany Mrs Burgess to 'places of interest,' he would rather be composing and practising piano.[38]

Since he could not enrol in the famed Paris Conservatoire until October, he sought out Harold Bauer, who was living in Paris, but to Ernest's great disappointment Bauer was not available for private lessons. However, he found a suitable alternative, Thérèse Chaigneau, a star pupil of Bauer's and, incidentally, the wife of composer Walter Rummel. 'In a way,' he wrote Elsie, 'I might have preferred a man, who could really swear at me and make me tremble when I make a mess.'[39]

At the long-awaited first lesson on 3 July, Chaigneau assigned her twenty-one-year-old student scales and other technical work, and the C-sharp Minor Prelude and Fugue from Bach's *Well-tempered Clavier*. This was just what Ernest wanted. He worked nine hours a day and pleased his teacher mightily. His next assignment – impressive for a self-taught 'beginner' – included two Beethoven sonatas. Then, after putting out feelers for a composition teacher, he set out for Bayreuth with the Burgesses to attend the Wagner Festival, expecting to settle the matter when he returned. Alas, it would be a long time before he would see Paris again.

Going to Bayreuth was then, as now, almost a religious pilgrimage. Ernest, like other visitors to this sleepy Bavarian town, fell under the spell of Richard Wagner, his festival theatre, and his music dramas. First came *Das Rheingold* on 26 July. 'How to describe the performance?' he asked Elsie. 'It is really quite beyond me. I don't mean to say that it was perfect – I suppose the more modern opera houses have more remarkable staging, though this was very wonderful.' He noted that some of the singers were good and some not so good, but there was no question about the orchestra: 'Nothing could be finer ... [It] is recruited from all the towns in Germany, and even from Boston.'[40] Ernest also marvelled at the theatre's unsurpassed acoustics and its totally hidden orchestra pit.

It was Europe's fateful summer. While Ernest was enjoying Bayreuth, elsewhere in Europe calamitous events were unfolding. On 28 June, the Austrian Archduke Franz Ferdinand had been assassinated at Sarajevo. Exactly one month later Austria-Hungary declared war on Serbia. Russia mobilized two days later. On 1 August, at an intermission during *Parsifal*, Ernest overheard Karl Muck, who was conducting the performance, tell Mrs Burgess that Germany had declared war on Russia.[41] In quick succession, Germany invaded France and Belgium. Left with little choice, England and, by extension, Canada declared war on Germany on 4 August.

Although the 'Guns of August'[42] were being put in place all over Europe, Ernest was too immersed in Wagner to note what was happening and, when he did, it was too late. Yet it was not all his fault – many foreign visitors in Germany stayed on complacently after 1 August. On 3 August Ernest did seek the advice of Charles S. Winans, the American consul in nearby Nuremberg (the British consul had already left the country), but Winans, who had just arrived from Spain, knew little about Germany and couldn't speak German. Unwisely, he advised Ernest to return to Bayreuth to await further developments, and added reassuringly that, if England entered the war, Ernest would probably be sent to a neutral country such as Holland.

'Innocent and trusting,' Ernest stayed on in Bayreuth until the end of August, when the Burgesses left for the United States. Then, because he couldn't leave Germany to return to Paris, he went to Nuremberg, where life was continuing much as in peacetime.[43] He took a room in a small pension, improved his German, enjoyed Nuremberg's historic old town and medieval architecture (this was where Albrecht Dürer had been born and Hans Sachs and his mastersingers had worked), and wondered what would happen to him.[44] Ernest also worked diligently on the first two movements of a string quartet – he had sketched the third movement in August while at Bayreuth – and took viola lessons. He spent his leisure time playing piano duos and chess with Benjamin Dale, a talented British composer who, along with several other Englishmen, was living in the same pension.[45]

His concern about the war did not prevent him from enjoying the city's musical life, which was far superior to Toronto's. Nuremberg had its own opera house and orchestra, although the latter was no longer up to full strength because many of its players had been called up to fight. It wasn't until November, when British male civilians in Germany (including those at Ernest's pension) were rounded up and interned, that Ernest had real cause for worry. Inexplicably, he was left alone. Perhaps there had been a mix-up about his status. As early as September, the German police had posted notices requiring all enemy aliens to register, but Ernest had failed to read the small print with sufficient care. He thought he *had* registered when he had reported himself as a visitor-tourist, but that wasn't what the notice meant. (He speculated later that the official to whom he had reported may have mistaken Canada's Toronto for Italy's Taranto and, accordingly, not realized that he *was* an enemy alien.) Disaster struck in early January 1915. He was arrested for violating the Defence of the Realm Act, fingerprinted, and, after a brief trial, fined 3,000 marks and sentenced to two months' solitary confinement.

Ernest wired Peggy Maclean for funds to pay the fine, and she, in turn, wired Alexander MacMillan, but, in the end, Consul Winans came to the rescue and provided the money. All things considered, Ernest was not treated badly during those two months in prison, perhaps thanks to Mrs Burgess. Through her family connections, she had been able to bring his plight to the attention of President Woodrow Wilson, who then advised the Secre-

tary of State to see that everything possible be done for Ernest.[46]
Nevertheless, he was only allowed to write one letter each month.
He could receive more. In his first letter he wrote, 'I am *not*
grumbling at my fate, nor at the German government! I certainly
shouldn't have been such a fool as I was, and I must say, nothing
could have been fairer than the trial they gave me.'[47]

To help pass the time, Winans brought him several books,
including Goethe's *Wilhelm Meister*, which improved his German,
and a complete Shakespeare. But imprisonment also meant poor
food, an uncomfortable bed, and dreary Sunday services with a
German chaplain inveighing 'against the sins of England.'[48] Yet
even these services had their bright side, for Ernest heard and
sang many German chorales, some of which were actually new to
him. Most important, he kept calm and did not irritate the prison
authorities, who treated him well and generously excused him
from manual labour because he was an accomplished organist.
He was allowed to exercise in the prison yard with other inmates,
although he was forbidden to speak to them. Years later, Ernest
spoke rather lightly about his time in the Nuremberg jail, but he
must have been quite frightened at the time. In all, it was an
extraordinary experience for a young man who had, until then,
led a more or less sheltered and predictable life. On 19 March,
having served his sentence, he was taken under armed guard to
Ruhleben, several hundred miles to the north. A new and important chapter in his life was beginning.

3. Life behind Barbed Wire

Ruhleben – peaceful life! – was an internment camp close to the industrial town of Spandau on the outskirts of Berlin. Formerly a popular racetrack, it consisted of three grandstands, eleven brick stables (used as barracks for the internees), and an administration building. The Germans had created the camp in reprisal for Britain's internment of German nationals. In all, over 4,000 men of all ages, mainly British but also a few Canadians and other British subjects from the far-flung Empire, were imprisoned there. About a third of the internees were merchant seamen and fishermen whose boats had been stranded in German harbours, a quarter were businessmen, a fifth were academics, students, artists, and musicians, and a sixth were skilled and unskilled workers.[1]

By the time Ernest arrived, in March 1915, Ruhleben had been in operation for over four months, and its inmates had suffered through a cold and miserable winter. Yet, what had started as a disorganized assembly of distraught civilians caught unexpectedly in a warring country had already transformed itself into an active and purposeful community determined to make the best of what it firmly believed would be a short period of imprisonment. Living conditions were primitive. Men slept on straw mattresses in horse stalls and lofts, with one blanket their only protection against the cold. There were few wash-basins, only cold showers, and, in the early days, humiliating toilet conditions. As for the food, it was barely adequate and its quantity and quality deteriorated the longer the war lasted. Black prisoners from Africa were

quartered in a separate barrack as were many Jews, the latter by
their own choosing, since a Berlin caterer had offered to prepare
kosher food for those requesting it. (The Jewish barrack was
disbanded in 1916.) In any case, there is little evidence of prejudice towards Jews or blacks.[2] The several hundred pro-German
prisoners were separated from the others to prevent confronta-
tions and were given the opportunity to serve with the German
army. Few did.

Ruhleben was, however, by no means a Second World War kind
of concentration camp. German prison guards, except for the
odd sadist, treated the prisoners fairly and reasonably, and
towards the end of the war the prisoners ate even better than
their captors, thanks to food parcels from families and friends.
Generally, the more affluent the prisoner the better he fared,
although the British government eventually allocated funds to
help the less-fortunate ones. Luckily, Ernest received a steady flow
of parcels from family and friends.

After some months, Ruhleben authorities granted the prisoners
self-government. Joseph Powell, a German-speaking English film
distributor, was appointed 'Captain of the Camp,' and he was
assisted by German-speaking sub-captains, who, of course, varied
in their leadership skills. There are bound to be difficulties when
men are forced to live together in close quarters. That there were
so few at Ruhleben is a tribute to its keepers, its self-government,
and, one must surmise, British attributes of fair play and good
behaviour.

Once the Ruhleben community had taken shape, the prisoners
threw themselves into a variety of absorbing activities. They published a camp newspaper and several journals; they formed associations, clubs, and societies; and they produced plays, musical
comedies, concerts, and entertainments of all kinds, involving
hundreds of prisoners on- and off-stage. Classes and lectures were
started, and these led to a camp school with course offerings in
languages, the arts and sciences, and nautical subjects for seamen.
The school at its peak had close to 250 teachers in seventeen
departments with a student enrolment of over 1,000. A wide
range of sports activities also sprang up, despite the constraints of
a shortage of space. Ruhlebenites became famous for coming to

grips positively with their unfortunate plight, and their activities were well publicized in Britain during the war.

For Ernest, being at Ruhleben after two months in the Nuremberg jail was a great morale booster. Now he was with English-speaking and law-abiding men, and opportunities for rewarding activity abounded. Ernest soon became associated with a group of intelligentsia – musicians, actors, directors, artists, and academics. Welcomed into their midst, he worked and socialized with them easily, and was given the nickname 'Mac.' His innate qualities served him well. He was a well-mannered extrovert in a sea of reserved Englishmen, and, thanks to his egalitarian Canadian background and his positive and constructive attitude towards others, he was popular with men of all classes and all levels of education. Even his Presbyterian upbringing was an advantage. He had been taught not to complain when denied material things, and this helped him to adapt to Ruhleben's austerity more easily than many of his fellow middle-class inmates.

As expected, there were groups, and groups within groups. 'The Englishman must have his club,' Ernest wrote, and he was asked to join the one whose members were chiefly artists and musicians. Called the Corner House, it was quartered in a lean-to at the side of a barrack. 'Effective murals decorated the walls: a large painting by the versatile Charles Winzer, depicting the Café de la Paix in Paris, adorned one end and served as a reminder of happier days.'[3] When Ernest was depressed, which was often, he especially appreciated the club's ambience and camaraderie, for it was a refuge where homesick men could bond and share common interests. The Corner House had a piano which Ernest would play – even ragtime pieces – to the delight of his fellow prisoners.[4] And it was there that he resumed his friendship with Benjamin Dale and shared many a musical idea with him. Dale, eight years older than Ernest, had already had some of his compositions performed and published in Britain.

Within a month Ernest was writing music for a comedy revue titled *Don't Laugh*. The producer was John Roker, a former ballet-master of the Metropol Theatre in Berlin. Roker had much experience in directing revues and ran the show professionally. Ernest conducted the performances and chalked it all up to experience.

'A conductor who can follow the unrhythmical eccentricities of
a music-hall comedian can follow anybody, and some distinguished artists can be eccentric enough.'[5] According to fellow-
inmate Israel Cohen, *Don't Laugh* was 'a tribute to the wondrous
power of costume, paint, and powder in transforming a number
of athletic youths into a bevy of alluring beauties,' and Roker
thought that the show's cheerfully wistful 'Ruhleben Beauty
Chorus' had the 'real revue touch.'[6] The chorus, needless to say,
was entirely male, and sang in a high falsetto. Several of the
songs, as expected, dealt with life at Ruhleben. One goes like this:

> Line up, boys, and sing the chorus,
> Shout this chorus all you can,
> We want the people there,
> To hear in Leicester Square,
> That we're the boys that (*slap*) never get downhearted.
> Back, back, back again in England,
> There we'll fill a flowing cup,
> And tell them clear and loud of the Ruhleben crowd,
> That always kept their pecker up.

This chorus did not die after the show closed – for the next three
years it was 'repeated with gusto' at the camp and, for many years
after sung at camp reunions.

Ernest, ambivalent or perhaps embarrassed about his accomplishments in this alien field (it was a much bigger and more
risqué venture than the Murray Bay variety show), told Elsie, a bit
stuffily, that 'some of the songs are quite clever and amusing but
I want to be finished and done with the music, which is of the
"popular" variety.'[7] Within two months he moved on to symphonic music. Shortly after the camp had opened, an orchestra
had been started by F. Charles Adler, an English conductor a few
years older than Ernest, and it was not long before several camp
conductors, including Ernest, were sharing it. Although makeshift, the orchestra was reasonably good – there were some very
fine string players, with the winds and brass less accomplished.
Fortunately, Quentin Maclean, an organist who had been studying
in Leipzig with Max Reger and Karl Straube, skilfully used the

harmonium to substitute for missing instruments, which no doubt
helped prepare him for his career as a theatre organist in Britain
and, later, in Canada.

Early on, in June 1915, the camp orchestra offered Ernest his
first serious conducting assignment – Bizet's *L'Arlésienne Suite*. The
players must have been pleased, for, in November, he led them
in a full concert, with Canadian pianist Harry Field playing Liszt's
E-flat Concerto – poor Field had to cope with a stubborn damper
pedal. The following month, Ernest, along with several others,
was kept busy composing music for a Christmas pantomime,
Cinderella. Again, he was chosen to conduct the performances.

Towards the end of 1916, he became involved in that all-time
Gilbert and Sullivan favourite, *The Mikado*. Unquestionably, it was
the high point of his musical comedy career, and the circumstances surrounding the preparation of the work made its success
all the more noteworthy. There was a copy of the libretto in the
camp, but, unfortunately, no score. Undaunted, five musicians –
Dale, Charles Weber, A.G. Claypole, Waldemar Pauer, and Ernest
– resolved to create one by literally reconstructing the music from
memory. The score they came up with was quite remarkable both
for its accuracy and for the way it was custom-designed to fit the
camp's unusual human and physical resources. Ernest, who had
contributed the lion's share, went on to conduct the thirteen
performances to enthusiastic audiences of prisoners *and* captors.
There was even a special performance for James Gerard, the
American Ambassador to Germany who had indirectly looked out
for Ernest when he was in the Nuremberg prison, and who did
much, in the early years of the war, to persuade the Germans to
improve Ruhleben's living conditions. To the delight of the
MacMillans and their friends, that performance was cheerfully
noted in the *London Illustrated News*. Ernest wrote to his family
when *The Mikado* was in rehearsal and, significantly, told them
how much he was enjoying conducting:

It keeps me from the blues, and I think it will not be all bad. It was ...
heavy work scoring it (the score is at least two inches thick) but there
is a lot of fun in it, too ... There is a great pleasure to be gained, for
me, conducting even an amateur orchestra. I haven't touched an organ

for two years and a half, but I fear I shall find its colours pale mournful-
ly before the richness of the strings. Why didn't I learn the fiddle when
I was ten? And yet there is very little in my life I would care to unlive,
and I wouldn't *be* any one else for the world! Not even if I were out of
Ruhleben.[8]

Ernest's artistic triumphs at Ruhleben were not confined to
music. He created quite a stir as a female impersonator or, more
accurately, as a player of female roles, for a number of delightful
performances of the Ruhleben Dramatic Society. Presbyterianism
being what it was, the MacMillan children had not been taken to
the theatre by their parents, but Ernest had always enjoyed acting
– recall the Arthur Blakeley trio, his Anglican rituals with his
sisters, his 'army' at Jarvis, and his impersonation of Santa Claus
in Edinburgh. At age ten, he had even tried to write a play based
on Christopher Columbus.[9] Now Ruhleben's active theatrical life
was providing him with a stage on which to show off his innate
acting talent.

His first role was the maid opposite Timothy Eden (Anthony
Eden's older brother) in R.C. Carton's comedy *Mr. Preedy and the
Countess*. His performance made such a hit that he was next assigned Lady Bracknell in Oscar Wilde's *The Importance of Being
Ernest*. With his lorgnette and deep contralto voice, he had audiences convulsed with laughter – he may, indeed, have been the
one to make male Bracknells fashionable! After that it was nothing but female roles for him. His next was 'the seductive part of
Phrynette the laundress' in André Wormser's pantomime, *L'En-
fant prodigue*, for which he also re-scored the music. Israel Cohen
thought that this production was Ruhleben's 'most notable triumph ... from an artistic point of view.'[10]

In fact, nothing was beyond the Ruhleben Dramatic Society –
Greek plays, farces, works in French and German, even Shake-
speare and Shaw. In 1916 it marked the 300th anniversary of
Shakespeare's death with productions of *Twelfth Night* (Ernest as
Maria) and *Othello* (Ernest as Bianca). Late in 1916 Ernest
broadened his range to produce, as well as act in, Shaw's *Fanny's
First Play* (he took the role of Darling Dora). In his usual under-
stated way he wrote, 'I do not fancy myself as producer, but

Shaw's lines, reasonably well enunciated, carried the thing off and the audience appeared to enjoy it.'¹¹ It was his last appearance on the Ruhleben stage. For the remaining time at the camp he limited himself to music; his dramatic flair was not to burst forth again until many years later and in markedly different circumstances.

There is no question that Ernest's conducting, composing, and arranging for the stage at Ruhleben made him more versatile and his musical taste more catholic. He learned to value functional music as long as it was 'good' and lifted men's spirits, which it certainly did at Ruhleben. And, as if these musical and theatrical activities were not enough, he also lectured to the Ruhleben Historical Circle on such diverse subjects as 'The Viennese Classicists,' 'Debussy,' and 'English Composers – Handel to Delius.' Together with Benjamin Dale, he gave ten talks on the Beethoven symphonies. Also, drawing on his knowledge of political science, he lectured soberly on 'Milestones in Canadian Constitutional Development.'

But it was his experiences as a fledgling symphonic conductor which had the most significance for his future. Such experiences might have come about in the normal course of events, by training at the Paris Conservatoire or by being a repetiteur in a German opera house. Since neither was to be, Ruhleben was his conducting launching pad: it gave him an orchestra with all the time in the world to play music just for pleasure – a windfall for any young conductor. Ernest also learned a great deal by observing other, more mature Ruhleben conductors at work. Unfortunately, only Charles Weber, who would become the conductor of the Carl Rosa Opera Company of England after the war, gave him any formal instruction and this was limited; in retrospect, more lessons would have been useful. In any event, he was one of the most popular conductors at the camp, if not *the* most popular. Not only did the orchestra choose him to conduct more often than anyone else, but he was also a favourite choice of directors looking for someone to conduct theatrical events. In Ruhleben's final year he was made head of all musical activities.

Two years into his Ruhleben incarceration, Ernest shared with Elsie his thoughts about a conducting career. 'Since coming here,

I have found that I have a natural talent for conducting which I should greatly like to develop; how, where, and when remains to be seen.'[12] And four months later, with an eye to the future and a fine sense for the practical, he continued:

You know, I've a good mind to begin agitating for a Toronto opera company when I return – beginning in a modest way, but entirely a local venture. If we could find some Maecenas willing to finance the scheme as Beecham is doing in Manchester, it might turn out to be a huge success in the end. There is no end of good voices in Toronto, but of course you need experienced teachers and, above all, money. Popular prices and all operas (and comic operas) in English should be the program, and it could easily be worked hand in hand with any purely dramatic scheme.[13]

In the same letter, he accurately predicted that the war would alter Canada's colonial mentality for the better. 'There would be more public spirit at home now than before the war, and it ought to be directed into the proper channels when the war comes to an end. However, there's time enough for that.'

In 1916 several hundred internees – those over forty-five and the infirm – were released from Ruhleben, and a number of them met in London early in 1917 to discuss ways of getting their fellow prisoners home. Alexander MacMillan was in London at the time and attended the meeting, where he was reassured by many present that Ernest was in good form and busy with music and drama. Alexander had recently arrived in England to deliver his revised *Book of Praise* (which Ernest was to have helped him prepare but obviously couldn't) to Oxford for publication. Fearful of disaster on the trip over, Alexander had the manuscript sewn into his overcoat, which he wore at all times. His fears were not unfounded, for the ocean crossing had been perilous, with his ship dodging U-boats on several occasions. One submarine even surfaced on the last night of the journey – a full moon was out in all of its glory – but was finally outmanoeuvred by the unarmed merchant ship.[14] In Edinburgh a few weeks after the London meeting, Alexander heard Israel Cohen give a speech about Ruhleben. When Cohen mentioned Ernest's contributions to camp life, there was a spontaneous round of applause. Edinburgh had not forgotten its young organ virtuoso.[15]

Ernest put his academic work on hold for the first two years at Ruhleben. In May 1915 he had heard that he had been awarded his University of Toronto BA *in absentia* in recognition of his plight and the high grades he had earned during his first three years, but it wasn't until 1917 that he decided to tackle the Oxford DMus. He would first have to pass several written examinations in harmony, counterpoint, and allied subjects, and then compose an 'exercise' – a major work for chorus and full orchestra with an orchestral overture in sonata form and at least one choral section in eight parts to demonstrate his skill in polyphonic writing. With the help of a Dr Logie, a fellow-prisoner, he arranged to sit for the written examinations at Ruhleben. After obtaining the required theory books, he spent endless hours from April to November, studying their contents from cover to cover. Then, happily, he heard that 'the Oxford authorities proved themselves exceptionally generous (the war seems to have revolutionized even Oxford!) and excused me from the examinations.'[16]

He immediately plunged into the preparation of the exercise, choosing to write a secular oratorio based on the Swinburne poem *Ode to England*. Luckily he found a small cubbyhole in which to work (a lack of privacy was a major problem at Ruhleben) and rented a piano for an hour a day. There was, however, one thing he had not thought of when he chose *England* – that such a clearly patriotic, flag-waving text might offend his German captors, who, in the worst scenario, might refuse to post it. As his work progressed, his concern grew.

Fortunately, all went well. He finished writing *England: An Ode* (as he named it) on 15 April 1918, and dispatched it, without mishap, to Oxford. On 13 June, he received word that the work had been accepted by his three illustrious examiners, Sir Hugh Allen, Sir Walter Parratt, and Dr Ernest Walker. Unassumingly and nonchalantly, he wrote to Elsie, 'It might have been a waste of time outside to put in a lot of time at such work, but here it was an occupation which kept me going all last winter without involving too great a strain.'[17] As usual, he was playing down his achievement, but his ability was such that he probably *did* do it without any great effort, as he said, 'between meals.' Ernest also confessed to Elsie that, although *England*'s text was timely, his feelings towards Swinburne were cool. (The poem is of dubious merit.) Characteristically, he wrote, 'I didn't set the whole poem, and the result is somewhat unbalanced and occasionally scrappy ... but I think a good deal of it would sound well.' Modesty aside, he was genuinely pleased with the work, and, make no mistake, he was well aware of the degree's importance in the academic world.

England consists of a long overture followed by three choral sections, and is scored for soprano, baritone, chorus, and orchestra. The overture opens with a militant theme that resembles in feeling parts of Strauss's *Don Juan* and *Ein Heldenleben*. In Ernest's own words, it 'may be said to typify England in action – England as a force in the world at large.'[18] Richly scored and with everchanging harmonies, it moves on to a contrasting lyrical second theme, heard first in the clarinet and reminiscent of Elgar. This soon leads to a romantic climax followed by a codetta theme – something of a cross between the first two themes with Celtic echoes and whole-tone scales. There is a development section, which, as expected, dwells on the exposition themes. It is inventive, busy, restless, and dense in texture, as is the recapitulation. The overture concludes with a grand climax in the manner of Richard Strauss.

The first choral section (Part One) begins with the second main theme of the work, which Ernest intended to portray 'the stability of England.' Forthright and demanding attention, it is followed by an emphatic chorus, 'Sea and strand, and a lordlier land.' After two stanzas, which vary in tempi and dynamics, comes an Allegro marziale section, begun by male voices alone singing a stanza which epitomizes the best or, depending on one's point of view, the worst of the British Empire:

Fame, wherever her flag flew, never forbore to fly with an equal wing;
France and Spain with their warrior train bowed down before her as
  thrall to king;
India knelt at her feet, and felt her sway more fruitful of life than
  spring.

This chorus evolves from a two-part to an eight-part *pianissimo* section, followed by an attractive two-stanza baritone solo, 'All the terror of time, where error and fear were lords of a world of slaves.' The orchestra reiterates previously heard themes in different guises, at times almost overwhelming the solo voice. The final stanza of Part One, for six-part chorus, shows some adroit counterpoint in view of the wide leaps in the theme, and ends softly with a widely spaced chord in ten parts.

Part Two's mood is at first quieter and more pastoral; it opens with a soprano solo, 'Music made of change and conquest.' Here, as throughout the work, Ernest shows how well he understood prosody and voices, in large part an outcome of his experiences with choirs in Edinburgh and Toronto. There follows a beautiful four-part women's chorus, 'Where the footfall sounds.' Part Two ends with an Elgarian flourish both in text and music – 'England yet shall stand!'

Almost as an anticlimax, a quiet orchestral interlude leads the listener into Part Three, which begins with 'From the springs of the dawn,' a complex and sometimes frenetic eight-part fugal chorus in 9/8 time, both dazzling and unsettling by its very industry. The voices are brought together, the metre changes, there is a *stringendo*, then a unison passage in all parts which leads to a grand conclusion. Ernest did not try to break new ground with *England*, but wisely gave the examiners what they wanted. In the process he reached some heights, but perhaps not as many as he might have if he had not been bound by Oxford's strictures. In itself, composing such a large-scale forty-minute work was no small feat, especially for a prison camp inmate.

England was first reviewed by 'G.G.' (probably George Gardner) in *The Musical Times*, the review ended by stating of the work 'It is tolerably certain that all who make its acquaintance will await with keen interest further work from the same accomplished pen.'[19] The first two performances both occurred the next year, in the spring of 1921. One was by the Sheffield Musical Union, a leading English choir, with Henry Coward conducting, and the other was by Toronto's Mendelssohn Choir at Massey Hall, with Herbert Fricker conducting. A Sheffield critic began his review with a whimsical reference to Oxford's requirements. 'The work contains a few sacrifices to the academic gods whose minds are broader now than they were twenty years ago ... but they are made to fall naturally into place; in fact, (except in the rather prolix Overture), Dr. MacMillan has succeeded in making virtues of necessities.'[20] The same critic praised Ernest's composing technique, several of his choruses (especially the difficult eight-part one), and his 'rhythmic variety and rhythmic justice in the setting of Swinburne's words. Taken as a whole, *England* achieves much and promises more.'

Toronto critics said little of substance about *England.* The erratic Augustus Bridle reported that it was 'intellectual rather than emotional; not big in imagination; very seldom highly melodic.'[21] He liked the scoring for orchestra and the choral fugue, and predicted that 'ten years from now MacMillan should turn out some big colourful Canadian work, not written for a degree but torn out of national experience.' The *Mail and Empire* critic liked Ernest's handling of Swinburne's rhythms and the 'exalted confidence' and 'virility' of the work as a whole.[22]

Ernest's other serious, although smaller, composing effort at Ruhleben was *Three Songs for High Baritone,* to be sung by Aleel in William Butler Yeats's play *The Countess Cathleen.* The first and most noteworthy song, 'Were I but Crazy for Love's Sake,' has a youthful spontaneity which reinforces Aleel's rather strange dramatic exclamations.[23] The piano is an extremely imaginative partner, playing glissandos, tremolos, and *una corda* arpeggios, which give an almost impressionistic feel to the accompaniment, and soft syncopated chords, which dramatize the *sotto voce* words of the singer. Even a few spoken words are used. The song is another example of how well Ernest understood prosody and, for that matter, drama in music.

MacMillan's recollections in his 'Memoirs' make his time at Ruhleben sound like an active and interesting interlude, during which he learned much, made many friends, and received two university degrees. True as all this was, there were times when he despaired that the war would ever end and that he would ever leave the camp. Fortunately, there were many letters from Elsie and from his parents and sisters, especially Dorothy, who was a leading Varsity personality during the war years. A major in modern languages, she was president of the university's Modern Language Society and a leading member of the University College Dramatic Society. Since there were few men about, she, like her brother, played opposite-sex roles, most notably Benedick in *Much Ado about Nothing*. Ernest heard that she looked handsome in satin brocade breeches and lace ruffles, but it was Dorothy's racy novel, serialized in the university newspaper, *Varsity*, that brought her the most fame and notoriety.

To be sure, Ernest took great care to put up a good front in his letters to his family, always depicting conditions brighter than they actually were, but his letters to Elsie were much franker. As early as mid-July 1915 he told her how depressed he was, despite the success of *Don't Laugh*.[24] Before he had gone away, she had become accustomed to his changing moods and states of depression, but now, because of the distance and the trying circumstances, they affected her more. Since all letters in and out were censored, it was hard for them to write on a deeply personal level, and this contributed to a gradual estrangement. After all, they had not seen each other since May 1914. People change and, although Elsie kept in close touch with the MacMillan family, it was, understandably, a strain for her to be with them without Ernest. The MacMillans were hospitable and cordial towards her, but their reserved affection was not what she was used to – she was more spontaneous and outgoing and not ashamed to be seen caring.

Towards the end of 1916, the separation was taking its toll. Elsie wrote sadly, 'The realness between us seems to have gone' and 'There's nothing real that I may write about.'[25] Ernest, deeply into *The Mikado*, replied, 'While I am rotting away I sometimes have the feeling that the girl I love is slipping away from me. Perhaps we shall never be so close together again. It will never be the same as in the old days. We are both too changed for that. But may we hope for something better and stronger? I have the feeling that I shall have to win you over again.'[26]

Almost a year later, Elsie innocently mentioned to Ernest that she had been seeing another young man, and this upset him enough to write that if she wished 'to part company' with the

ring he had given her he would understand. Totally despondent
– he had just begun *England* – he wrote about the end of the war
not being in sight and about feeling 'so powerless in everything
I attempt. I have tried hard to write music but no ideas come that
are not banal. I take refuge in beautiful and fatuous complexi-
ties.'[27]

Their rift healed and Elsie wrote lovingly when she heard the
news of his doctorate:

My own very dearest Doctor – The altogether overwhelming news has
just been really confirmed. My darling – if only I could speak my happiness to you alone! I am too filled with admiration, and wonder, and love
to express myself at all. Dear, you will never have to exact the 'wifely
honour' that is your masculine due – I would Katherine you till you are
bored to tears! Indeed, I don't know whether the honour I bear you, or
the love, is the greater ... And now, Dr. MacMillan, F.R.C.O., B.A., etc.
etc. etc. – tell me, out of your wealth and depth and variety of knowledge, whether, on state occasions, I shall be Mrs. Dr. – ? And let me tell
you that in this day of Female Emancipation I have no intention of
being outdone by a mere man.[28]

Elsie's delight with Ernest's new title was in interesting contrast
to what she had to say about the use of another kind of title. The
year before, she had written about meeting Sir John Eaton at a
garden party: 'Did you know that he was a Sir? We have a whole
retenue [Elsie was always a bad speller, which sometimes drove
Ernest frantic] of Courtly Knights now-a-days ... Isn't it ridiculous
and disgusting too? ... It is a fine custom for a country to acknowledge public service (*when rendered*) by some sort of honorary
degree – but a Sir and his Lady – particularly the Lady is too
much for my gravity.'[29] To which Ernest made no comment.

News of the horrendous Halifax explosion of 6 December 1917,
which killed 1,600, injured 9,000 others, and levelled most of the
city's north end, reached Ernest through another Canadian prisoner, Winthrop Bell, who would be a good friend in later years.
The disaster had a profoundly disturbing effect on him, and he
wrote grimly to Elsie that it was caused 'by a substance deliberately manufactured by man. One wonders how far the destruction of

mankind can be carried ... Perhaps some day we shall find a means for blowing Mother Earth to atoms.'[30] (The Halifax calamity was, in fact, the greatest man-made explosion before Hiroshima.) Halifax, the anguish of the war, and his distance from his father and from Presbyterianism all contributed to Ernest's diminishing interest in religion, and, although he never wrote about it, he was no longer an active Presbyterian. He could live with Presbyterianism, respect it, and take part in its rituals, but he could no longer love it. God, Jesus, and the Scriptures remained with him but more passively so in the years that followed.

By early 1918, Germany had lost the war in the Middle East and in East Africa. In March it launched its final assault on the western front, but by mid-August the German military knew the end was near. Sadly, it took until 11 November for hostilities to cease, with thousands more killed in the interim. The loss of nearly eight million lives in the Great War was horrible beyond belief.

In the war's final year, Canada suffered from runaway inflation, newspapers in 'enemy' languages were frowned upon or forbidden, and there were food and fuel shortages. Prohibition was enforced by all the provinces except Quebec. England's handling of the western front and its all-too-frequent cavalier use of Canadian troops as cannon fodder so disenchanted English Canadians that their ties to the mother country were forever loosened. At the same time, the conscription crisis – the government had failed to enlist Quebec's support in fighting the war – was creating a rift between English and French Canadians which would be hard to heal. One brighter note was that women were now franchised in six of the nine provinces. This was the Canada Ernest would return to after leaving Ruhleben on 24 November 1918.

4. No Finer Organist

A quick and successful revolution in the fall of 1918 brought down Germany's military regime. At Ruhleben, the guards dismissed their leaders and freed their prisoners, then asked the latter to be tolerant of the German people, who had deposed their autocratic leaders and were looking forward to establishing a democracy. Three weeks after the armistice, Ernest wrote to his father: 'There seems to be ... doubt here as to the genuineness of the revolution, but to the mind of anybody who was in Berlin during the last few weeks there can be no doubt whatever ... One German soldier told me he believed it was the first time in history that a nation was glad to have been beaten.'[1] Berlin, Ernest went on, had a severe food shortage and was hoping for relief from abroad. Unfortunately, little was forthcoming. The Weimar Republic, the outcome of a spontaneous and well-intentioned political and social revolution, was weakened by the vengeful Allies and their humiliating peace terms.

Before his departure from Ruhleben, Ernest had visited Berlin to attend performances of Brahms's *German Requiem* and Beethoven's *Fidelio*. Years later he wrote about the *Fidelio*:

I confess that tears filled my eyes when, in the fifth bar of the overture, the two horns sounded their notes with perfect clarity and security. I had almost forgotten that horns could sound like that! Sitting beside me was a girl eating a baked potato which her escort had brought with him as a special treat. Food was at a premium and the value of the mark was dropping like a stone down a well. Yet the Berliners had to have their music. On Busstag (Repentance Day) I attended a performance of Brahms's *Ein deutsches Requiem*, and, though I doubt if the German people felt much repentance for their national sins, they too had suffered grievously, and hearing Brahms's noble music under such conditions was impressive beyond words.[2]

Free at last, Ernest and his fellow prisoners had slowly made their way by train across Germany and then by Danish boat across the North Sea to Leith, Edinburgh's port city, where they were welcomed by 'cheers on all sides, shooting of sirens from destroyers, waving of flags, and all kinds of demonstrations ... I shan't attempt to describe my feelings.'[3] He was embarrassed by the goodness of everyone. Polly Lothian was at the pier to meet him – she and Peggy Maclean had regularly sent him parcels and exchanged innumerable letters with the MacMillans about the welfare of their 'Dacey boy.'

Thinner but otherwise none the worse for wear, Ernest had his first hot bath in four years, followed by a succulent steak dinner, which he later described as his 'most memorable meal.'[4] He savoured to the hilt his new freedom, and wandered about Edinburgh 'as though in a dream ... I would often look over my shoulder to make sure that my speaking English was not attracting unfavourable attention ... I remember stopping a young officer to ask some question or other and being struck by the courtesy with which I was answered; we had become used to being barked at when we spoke to men in uniform.'[5] But it was not long before he began to feel uncomfortable at being fêted as a kind of hero. While there is little doubt that he would have enlisted had he not been interned, he was quick to remind others that 'probably no one ... did less for the war effort.'[6]

During his stay in Edinburgh, his old teacher Alfred Hollins invited him to play for a Sunday evening service and described Ernest's performance in glowing terms:

Although he had not touched an organ for over four years and it was much longer than that since he had last played St. George's organ, one would have thought he had been using it uninterruptedly all his life. For the opening voluntary he played from memory the slow movement of Mendelssohn's *Second Sonata*. It must have been eleven or twelve years since he had studied it with me, and I was delighted to find that he had not forgotten a single thing I had taught him about registration. For instance, I had told him to put on the tremulant at a certain point, and sure enough on it came ... His concluding voluntary was the *St. Anne's Fugue*.[7]

Ernest went from Edinburgh to London to see the Novello company about publishing his *England*, stopping en route in Sheffield to visit his father's brother John and to meet Henry Coward, who would lead the first performance of *England* two years later. Then it was back to Edinburgh to surprise Polly and Peggy on New Year's morning. 'He thought it would be nice to be with us over the New Year,' wrote Peggy to Alexander MacMillan. 'His bright refreshing ways and so much of the boy spirit is still left in him.' And then she hesitatingly and yet so affectionately went on: 'There is a little confession I feel I must make. When Ernest first came we thought he looked rather bloodless and, having some good port wine in the house ... we gave Ernest a little at dinner each day ... As you know we are abstainers in the ordinary way ... This was simply given as medicine, so I hope you will not mind.'[8]

Peggy and Polly fussed over him like mother hens and even meddled in his professional affairs. Unbeknown to Ernest but with the best of intentions, Peggy had written to the secretary of King George V, asking that *England* be brought to His Majesty's notice, believing that this would help promote the work and bring Ernest distinction. When Ernest found out about her letter, she suggested he seek permission to dedicate the piece to the King. Ernest, who was feeling very Canadian, became annoyed with her on both counts, and she had to write again to the King's secretary – it must have been extremely difficult for her – to put the whole matter to rest.[9]

Homeward bound at last, Ernest arrived in Saint John, New Brunswick, on 27 January 1919. As luck would have it, his father was in Halifax, and Ernest surprised him, first with a phone call from Saint John, and then with a reunion in Halifax.[10] Alexander must have had friends in high places, for he quickly arranged for

Ernest, as a returning 'prisoner of war,' to travel on to Toronto at no cost and in first class, as well. And so Ernest arrived home on 4 February to the welcoming arms of the rest of his family – and Elsie. As soon as they met, they knew that their feelings towards each other had not changed. Jokingly, she accused him of having picked up an English accent, which was probably true, since he had lived with Englishmen for nearly four years. In fact, for the rest of his days, he had a slight but completely natural English-Scottish lilt to his speech, the English part from Ruhleben and the Scottish part from his years in Edinburgh. However, Robertson Davies called it '*real* Canadian, not the English-accented speech affected by some Canadians.'[11] Ernest's speech was clear and precise, and served him admirably.

As expected, Toronto's musical life had changed considerably since Ernest's departure in 1914. The Toronto Symphony had disbanded in 1918 after barely weathering the war years, and the city was without an orchestra. A.S. Vogt had left the Mendelssohn Choir because of his demanding duties as principal of the Toronto Conservatory of Music (it was growing rapidly under his leadership) and as dean of the newly established Faculty of Music at the University of Toronto. Herbert Fricker, an organist and former conductor of the Leeds Philharmonic, had succeeded Vogt as Mendelssohn Choir director.

For Ernest, as for others who had spent the war years overseas for whatever reason, readjusting to Canadian life had its problems. In the company of his family, he was, for a while, uncharacteristically contentious, hostile to organized religion, and disillusioned with established institutions of all kinds.[12] But he soon settled down, and within weeks his father was proposing that he do an organ recital tour of western Canada in April and May. Ernest agreed and, to make the engagements more marketable, he also gave a short talk at each concert about his Ruhleben experiences. He was not overly enthusiastic about the venture – he had no wish to leave Elsie after such a long absence and, furthermore, lacked confidence as a public speaker – but after Elsie's urging, he went ahead with it.

Once more there was a steady flow of letters between them. Thinking of Ernest's academic future, Elsie wrote about a

'Torrington Memorial Chair in Music' proposed for the University of Toronto's Faculty of Music, and enclosed an anonymous letter to the press which urged: 'If a chair of music is established it is to be hoped that only a pure Britisher – born of Empire stock – should be given that important position.'[13] (Toronto's mind-set at the time was such that comments of this kind went unchallenged.) It was a clear, if indirect, attack on Vogt, whose name sounded 'foreign' to English Toronto, but who had in fact been born in Canada of Swiss-German parentage. Even the usually unprejudiced Elsie seemed inclined to side with the letter-writer – perhaps her loyalty to Ernest was getting in the way of her judgment.

In his reply, Ernest said that, while he didn't think of Vogt as a foreigner, he disliked him and thought him the wrong man for the job. 'Willan, or even Ham, would be better.' (British organist and composer Healey Willan had come to Canada in 1913 to head the Conservatory's theory department and to take on the position of organist at St Paul's Anglican Church. Albert Ham, also a British organist, was head of music at St James' Cathedral and taught at the Conservatory.) 'Von Kunits, who is an out-and-out Hun, would fit such a position well.' (He was using 'Hun' to mean 'typically German,' not pejoratively.) Then he said what was really on his mind: 'Shouldn't mind the position myself, for that matter.'[14] As it turned out, the Torrington Chair never came to pass.

The tour was an all-round success and provided Ernest with an indirect bonus – his first trip to central and western Canada. He saw the Canadian Shield, the Prairies, the Rockies, the Pacific Coast, and the country's burgeoning western cities. He praised Winnipeg's wide business streets, saying that they gave the city 'the appearance of a big metropolis (which it is certainly going to be before long) – an appearance which Toronto certainly lacks,' and marvelled at the Rockies: 'All that I have read fails entirely to do the mountains justice ... They are stand-offish and decidedly Pagan. One believes in Odin and Thor here. The valley of the Columbia River, however, is altogether lovely, while the mountains threaten it.'[15]

Organist Charles Peaker, who later would study with Ernest, heard him play in Saskatoon and described him, over half a century later, as 'tall [he was five feet ten], dark, and debonair, rather too pale from his incarceration ... He came in looking like a royal duke ... and thundered into the *F Minor Overture* of Alfred Hollins.'[16] About halfway through the recital, 'he went to the pulpit to tell us about his four years in Ruhleben, and I must say it was very stilted. He didn't like talking about himself. Very thankfully, he came back to the organ bench and played the great *G Minor* so sumptuously that those Presbyterians cheered.' (Peaker was, at the time, a Congregationalist.)

As was to be expected on such a tour, Ernest played on a wide range of organs. The one in Regina 'was a joke bordering on the tragic,' and the one in Calgary was 'the best yet.' Performing artists, he soon learned, were pioneers who had to be ready for any eventuality. There were bonuses too. Ernest commented on the elegant and very English Empress Hotel in Victoria, where the ritual of afternoon tea to the accompaniment of discreet background music was observed, and noted that 'it is probably the only hotel in Canada that isn't peppered up with spittoons.' And he was surprised to find that farmers on the prairies and miners in Nanaimo had 'motors.' As the tour went on his mood improved. 'It brings in the shekels, and I am getting very mercenary these days ... Incidentally, I find it a very easy way of making money – and not too distasteful a way either.'[17]

Returning to Toronto, Ernest began looking for work, and it was not long in coming. In July he was appointed to the faculty of the Canadian Academy of Music, one of three music schools in the city, the other two being the Toronto Conservatory and the Hambourg Conservatory. (As a boy, he had heard members of the Hambourg family perform in Edinburgh.) The Academy had been founded by the wealthy Albert Gooderham in 1911, and had absorbed the Toronto College of Music in 1918. Gooderham wanted gifted students to study in Canada instead of abroad and, to this end, brought prominent musicians from Europe and the United States to teach. This lent honour to Ernest's appointment. The terms were good: he would teach a prescribed number of lessons and classes for a substantial guaranteed salary, and he could, of course, earn more by giving lessons and classes beyond the prescribed number.

In September, Ernest participated in a Canadian Guild of Organists recital, collaborating with, among others, Healey Willan and Richard Tattersall (another organist who had emigrated from Britain); Willan and Tattersall would become two of his closest friends. Organ recitals at the Academy and nearby centres soon followed. He also played piano on occasion with the Academy String Quartet, led by von Kunits, who liked Ernest's musicianship in spite of his limited technical skill.

Toronto's artistic and literary circles also beckoned. He was invited to join the Arts and Letters Club, an active meeting place for artists and academics committed to developing Canadian culture, albeit in the English mould. Ernest soon became a prominent member, serving on discussion panels and arranging musical events. Other members in his day included Willan, pianist and conductor Reginald Stewart, critic Augustus Bridle (one of the club's founders), and the landscape painters known collectively as the Group of Seven.

All the while Ernest was seeking a suitable church organist-choirmaster position; his need for a steady income (in order to marry) suppressed his distaste for such work. At last, in the fall of 1919, Timothy Eaton Memorial Church, one of the most prestigious and richest congregations in Canada, made him an offer which he accepted with alacrity. The post was a real plum: excellent pay, a splendid four-manual organ, and a good budget for soloists and special concerts. The time had come for vows.

Ernest and Elsie were married on the afternoon of 31 December at St Andrew's Presbyterian Church in downtown Toronto – the same church in which Elsie's mother and father had been married. Alexander officiated.

We had intended it to be as informal as possible; no invitations had been sent out and no reception was to be held after the ceremony. Nevertheless word had got around and hundreds of friends were present. We had hoped to make our getaway unobtrusively but had reckoned without the weather. As we arrived at the door, the sexton met me with overcoat, hat, and galoshes. I was unable to put on the last before friends came swarming around, all eager to shake hands and wish us well; it was absurd and most undignified to hold out one hand while standing on one foot and struggling into my galoshes with the aid of the other. Elsie meanwhile stood by, graciously receiving our friends; she had (perhaps intentionally) neglected to provide herself with foot protection other than a pair of very light slippers ... but, as on many subsequent occasions, she preserved her dignity much more successfully than I. Finally we made our escape and were duly launched into married life.[18]

On 19 January, after a ten-day honeymoon, a full-scale wedding reception was held at the Keith home in Toronto's Casa Loma district. It followed a Women's Musical Club of Toronto afternoon concert at which Ernest played the Franck *Quintet* with the Academy String Quartet. It was not his first appearance for the club – he had played the Toronto Conservatory organ at a club concert when he was fifteen. Combining business with pleasure, he invited the audience *en masse* to the reception, to be joined, in the early evening, by relatives and friends. Elsie, resplendent in a trained robe of white satin with georgette and pearls, was beginning her lifelong role as hostess *par excellence*. It was a gala party.

They were not long in starting a family. Their first son, Keith, was born on 23 September 1920, and their second son, Ross, arrived on 17 November 1923. Both boys thrived, but two other baby boys died at birth – one in 1922 and the other in 1925. Elsie's tiny frame may well have been the problem. She bore the tragedies well but, like any mother, talked wistfully throughout her life about the two lost babies. In May 1922, shortly after the first stillbirth, she wrote a heart-rending letter to Ernest, who was examining Toronto Conservatory candidates in Montreal.

The boy and the closeness to you are the only things that really help. He is asleep – holding his penguin and looking too lovely to be true ... The wee one was like him – if only we did not have to wait so long! I don't think the craving will ever be satisfied until there is another. The milk comes again and again with thinking of him. I want you so awfully dear. It is strange because it has always been my way to shrink from the people I cared most about when I was hurt. But this is ours, and just as keenly yours as mine.[19]

To help Elsie in this trying period, Ernest's sister Dorothy and her close friend Evangeline Olmsted often walked baby Keith in his perambulator. For fun-loving Dorothy, nothing was sacred, even her father's work. On one occasion she jokingly told Evangeline that, in the MacMillan house, 'The Book' was no longer the Holy Bible but the hymn book Alexander was revising.[20] She was also a rebel. One of Evangeline's stories, in particular, bears this out and sheds some light on Ernest's role as older brother:

One afternoon Dorothy arrived in a very exalted mood with the news that she was about to elope with Campbell McInnes, a tenor [McInnes was a baritone] concert singer who had made a considerable stir in musical circles in Toronto. I had heard him sing in Dorothy's company but I had no idea that they knew each other well. Dorothy said that Mr. McInnes had taken passage for them both on a ship out of Montreal and that she proposed to join him there just before sailing time. She was taking the overnight train to Montreal. We bade each other a fond farewell and I sat down to consider whether I ought to warn the family. I was still absolutely undecided when the telephone rang. It appeared that Dorothy had left a note for her mother in her room. I admitted that I thought Dorothy was on her way to Montreal. The next news I had was from Dorothy herself, who said that Ernest had driven to Montreal, come on board before the boat sailed, told Mr. McInnes exactly what he thought of him, and persuaded Dorothy to return to Toronto. I did not then know that Mr. McInnes had two sons and a wife who had divorced him a few years before, and I am not sure that Dorothy did either.[21]

Ernest MacMillan's conducting first caught the attention of Toronto's musical public on 23 March 1921, when he led his Eaton Memorial choir, augmented with singers from two other churches, and a professional orchestra of forty-six players, in a performance of the Brahms *German Requiem*. It is a deeply personal work sung to texts from the German Bible, and its humanistic approach to God and religion had profoundly moved Ernest when he first heard it in Berlin after his release from Ruhleben. The press unanimously acclaimed the performance and its young conductor. Hector Charlesworth of *Saturday Night*, who served as both music critic and editor of the magazine through the years, wrote astutely:

The mere fact that such a stupendous work was chosen indicated the soaring ambition of Dr. MacMillan, and he more than justified it by the results achieved ... If Dr. MacMillan had provided even what critics call, for convenience sake, a 'creditable' performance, it would have been a notable achievement; but it was more than that – it was, in the opinion of every professional musician who heard it, astonishingly fine, and to them it demonstrated ... that Dr. MacMillan is a force to be reckoned with in Canadian music.[22]

The *Mail and Empire* critic agreed, saying that Ernest's contribution was the 'outstanding feature' of the performance and that 'his future work will be watched with interest, for he gave the impression of having great reserves.' Interestingly, the review also pointed out that 'German' or 'Deutsches' had been discreetly omitted from the title of the work on program announcements, 'the reason ... being of course obvious.' There was still much anti-German feeling thirty months after the armistice.[23]

An incident during the preparation of the performance caused MacMillan considerable distress, but was typical of narrow-minded Toronto at the time. He had called his one orchestra rehearsal for a Sunday afternoon, because Toronto's orchestral players were too busy working in theatres during the week. When news of the rehearsal leaked, the local police threatened to charge conductor and players for breach of the Lord's Day Act, which forbade 'unlawful activities,' such as music-making for money on the Sabbath.[24] That the rehearsal was being held in a church and the work was religious meant nothing to the Lord's Day arbiters. The indignant Eaton Memorial Church dug in its heels and vowed to fight for the musicians if the police carried out their threat. The situation looked grim, but luckily the local constabulary's bark was worse than its bite. In the absence of Reverend W.F. Rochester, the secretary of the Lord's Day Alliance, the 'moral watchdogs' of the Act, there was no one to advise the police about the appropriateness of the charges, and so the rehearsal proceeded as planned and the police did nothing.

It was in the 1920s that MacMillan did most of his major work as an organist. Within two years of his return to Canada he was

considered by other Canadian organists as one of the best if not
the best in the country, and soon his reputation spread to the
United States. On 2 August 1922, he gave a recital at the annual
convention of the National Association of Organists in Chicago
that stunned the discriminating audience. Modestly, MacMillan
was sure that his playing at the convention was surpassed by
Lynnwood Farnam's. (Farnam was an expatriate Canadian organist who had settled in New York.) He admired both Farnam's
consummate musicianship and his 'complete composure and ease
at the console.' From Farnam he learned that 'the first principle
of good organ technique is ... balancing one's weight on the
organ bench,' something which, however obvious, many organists
fail to do.[25] *Diapason*, a leading American organ journal, dodged
comparisons: 'When one looked at Dr. MacMillan and Mr.
Farnam one realized what giants had just grown up in the organ
world on this continent and what encouragement for the future
of organ playing was held out by their presence ... MacMillan, like
Farnam, played his entire program from memory.'[26]

As MacMillan's organ skills grew, so did his preference for
playing the music of Johann Sebastian Bach, the composer who
knew and wrote for the instrument like no other. He could practise without interruption, day and night, summer and winter
(unlike many other churches Eaton Memorial was kept warm at
all times), which allowed him to learn most of Bach's organ works
from memory. This led to his first series of all-Bach recitals on
four successive Saturdays, beginning 19 March 1922. He gave a
similar series the next year and increased the number of recitals
to five in 1924 and 1925. In the eighteen recitals over the four-
year span, the young organist played nearly all of Bach's preludes
and fugues, chorale preludes, trio sonatas, toccatas, passacaglias,
and other short pieces, and repeated only a handful. It was an
impressive achievement.

The 1925 Bach series captured the most press. Lawrence Mason, the enthusiastic critic of the *Globe* and a Yale PhD, had been
disappointed with MacMillan's 1924 recitals but found his 7
March 1925 concert 'truly amazing,' particularly the five chorale
preludes which disclosed 'a totally new and undreamed of Bach
... Here is devotional music of the sincerest type, but radiant and

simple, not austere and difficult – at least as played by this masterly executant and interpreter.'[27] Mason went on in his usual mix of richly descriptive and syrupy language:

The pure liquid sprays of perfectly rounded notes of the Prelude and Fugue in A Major called forth some deliciously different registrations, while the fugue was again an absolute revelation ... He invests each entrance with a deft and tiptoe archness and each voice with an individuality of its own, so that the progressive evolution and treatment have a zest and relish that are a continual delight to the mind, while the aesthetic sense is ravished by the colour, warmth, delicacy, grace and beauty of the music, as music.

Ernest did not play Bach 'orchestrally,' tempted as he was by the large eighty-nine-stop romantic organ at Eaton Memorial and the Toronto Conservatory's equally romantic smaller instrument he used occasionally. As Mason suggested, MacMillan highlighted the master's harmonic and polyphonic structures and melodic lines, knowing that the composer's values lay in them. Years later, MacMillan explained that Bach's texture was 'so intricate as to escape even the most sophisticated ear: only after extensive analysis do all the details reveal themselves in relation to the whole.'[28] Analyse them he did, yet, fearing that too much of it could work against the holistic approach he sought when performing Bach, he warned organists not to get buried in detail and not to forget to address 'Bach's theological bent, the intellectual side of his religious life, which expresses itself through his music.' To reinforce this view, which was much in accord with the great Albert Schweitzer's, he reminded his listeners that Bach appended to many of his works *Soli Deo Gloria* (To God Alone the Glory).

Having failed to find meaning in religion in the aftermath of the war and its terrible carnage, MacMillan was now finding it in the music of the great master. A generation later, in prose clear to layman and professional alike, he emphasized that

all musicians sit at the feet of Bach. The performer's training ... is based on an intensive study of his works. Both technical study and power of expression can be immensely expanded through such a study. To the composer he represents supreme mastery over melodic, harmonic, and contrapuntal resources and few of his successors have even approached that sense of structural balance that deals equally successfully with a miniature and with an immense design such as that of the *Goldberg Variations.* To the historian he is a focal point – perhaps *the* focal point – in all musical history, drawing as he does deep inspiration from the riches of the past and experimenting with such boldness that the most 'advanced' composers of today base many of their own experiments in essence on his procedure.[29]

Yet by no means did he confine all of his organ playing to Bach. In the fall of 1922 he gave two Eaton Memorial recitals that included nineteenth- and twentieth-century works. The first featured Healey Willan's *Introduction, Passacaglia, and Fugue* – MacMillan played Canadian music whenever possible – and the second was an all-Franck evening commemorating the composer's hundredth birthday. His success in Chicago led to other recitals in the United States over the next few years, all of which earned glowing reviews, not only for his magnificent playing but also for his repertoire. In New York in 1923, he was applauded for 'covering a large field' (he played the music of thirteen different composers) and in Washington in 1924, for including the works of 'four living composers.'[30] That year MacMillan teamed up with British pianist Claude Biggs for two unusual recitals (organ and piano are rarely played together), and the Toronto and New York press praised their programs as much for their originality as their artistry. For the New York program, MacMillan and Biggs together played their own versions of Brahms's *Variations on a Theme of Handel*, Debussy's *La Cathédrale engloutie*, and Chopin's *Étude in C Minor*. They each played several solo works as well.

Both in the United States and in Canada, listeners admired MacMillan's playing for its accuracy, colour, and interest, and even more so for its motion and rhythmic drive. It has been said with some justification that the organ can be the most impersonal of instruments, but, when MacMillan played, his personality shone through the sounds of the mighty instrument like a beacon. According to Henry T. Finck, a senior New York critic, MacMillan was 'a real Berlioz in the art of orchestrating' and 'his technique was faultless.'[31] Hugh Ross, an English organist and conductor who would later head New York's Schola Cantorum and the choral department at Tanglewood, heard MacMillan in Winnipeg and wrote:

[He] has not only the sure touch and attractive brilliance which are expected nowadays from virtuosos, but his playing and program express the attitude which give his work an individuality of its own. It would be possible to dilate at some length upon special virtues ... the phrasing which ornamented the older music, the special attention paid to the phrasing in the pedals, the sure memory which gave the player complete concentration on his work, the understanding of *rubato* ... and the perfect appreciation which made the last phrase of the Bach *Adagio* the most beautiful moment in the whole recital.[32]

At best, organ recitals have limited audience appeal, and MacMillan's were no exception. Nevertheless, he had a substantial coterie of loyal followers, and when he played in the United States, he was hailed as the 'Marcel Dupré of the North.' (Dupré was a French organ virtuoso and composer who toured North America frequently.) In January 1925, Dupré played in Toronto on the Eaton Memorial organ, and the press reviewed him, as usual, with great favour. Yet, only three days later, MacMillan gave a Bach concert at the Toronto Conservatory that brought on a near panegyric by Hector Charlesworth:

This young Canadian is, in virtuosity, enthusiasm, and authority of style, one of the outstanding organists not merely of Canada but of North America ... After the recital of Marcel Dupré, comparisons were inevitable, but Dr. MacMillan had no reason to fear them. His final number, the great *Fantasia and Fugue in G Minor*, was a dazzling triumph of virtuosity. In the *Trio Sonata in D Minor*, the *Vivace* was particularly superb. The insouciance and charm of ... the *Pastorale in F* was wonderfully fascinating ... His performance of ten Christmas preludes from the *Little Organ Book* was notably fine in lyrical ease and sincerity.[33]

It seemed almost predestined that, given his absorption with Bach, MacMillan would move on from his organ music to his liturgical works. If, as has been said, all musical roads lead to Bach, then, to get to the very essence of Bach, all Bach roads lead to the *St Matthew Passion,* and MacMillan set his sights on it. Surprisingly, Bach's choral music had not been done often in Toronto churches prior to the 1920s. The city's English-trained organists and choirmasters leaned more to Handel, Haydn, and nineteenth- and early-twentieth-century romantic composers. Elsie MacMillan, who understood Toronto's musical attitudes and tastes better than most, noted with some irony that 'Bach was regarded by the average congregation as a sort of spring tonic – beneficial, but a little hard to take. I well remember one of the most faithful attendants of my husband's Bach organ recitals at the Eaton Memorial telling me how she persuaded several of her friends to come too "because," she said, "you may not enjoy it but it is good for you."'[34]

To return to the *St Matthew Passion,* like other passion music it is a musical setting of the Gospel story as told by one of the evangelists. Bach's setting calls for two choirs and two orchestras. Dramatic and yet devotional, it uses biblical text for the basic narrative sung by the Evangelist, Jesus, and the *turba* (chorus). Picander, a Leipzig writer and contemporary of Bach, did the poetic texts for the arias and large choruses, while the chorales, which conclude each section, are based on Lutheran hymns. The lyrical Part One deals with the conspiracy, the taking of Jesus, and the flight of the disciples. The dramatic Part Two relates Peter's denial, Pilate's judgment, the death of Judas, Golgotha, the Crucifixion, and the death and burial of Jesus. It is a work of remarkable unity owing, principally, to the empathic collaboration of Bach and Picander.

Toronto organist G.D. Atkinson had done excerpts from the *St Matthew Passion* with his Sherbourne Street Methodist Church Choir in 1921 and 1922, and Bridle, who was at Atkinson's first performance, recalled that 'a young man stood next to me at the back wall of the gallery and sang all the chorales in the bass by heart. He had no score. He seemed to have heard the work somewhere.'[35] The 'young man' was, of course, Ernest MacMillan. Inspired, he decided to do the work in its entirety with the Eaton Memorial Choir and Richard Tattersall's St Andrew's Choir. Elsie wryly recalled that 'Tattersall and MacMillan were Scots as well as youthful enthusiasts and they counted the liabilities together with the assets. They had no orchestra, no money, few choristers who had sung Bach, and, most serious of all, a public well satisfied with the standard Handel/Mendelssohn oratorio tradition and with little curiosity about other works ancient or modern.'[36]

The two men didn't rush the preparations; the choirs worked separately for a year. MacMillan's choir – and presumably Tattersall's – found it 'very uphill work to learn the music, and it was at first a struggle to keep them interested ... As the performance drew near they seemed suddenly to realize the greatness of the music and sang with a fervour that a great work should inspire.'[37] As anticipated, assembling two good orchestras was a major problem. MacMillan related how he 'often had to hang around the stage doors and plead with conductors to let this or that man off for an evening to take part in the *Passion*.' And in some cases the right instruments were just not available. 'We had our special problems, one of them being to secure two English horns to replace the *oboe da caccia*. I was rarely able to get more than one; the other part had to be played on a viola. The English horn player ... was wont to pawn his instrument, having no use for it in his regular work, and we had to supply funds to redeem it.'[38]

The resourceful MacMillan managed to engage Luigi von Kunits as concert-master for the first orchestra; Frank Blachford, former concert-master of the defunct Toronto Symphony, led the second. Christ was sung by baritone Campbell McInnes, who gave the role a rare dignity, intensity, depth, and, most of all, humanity, but there were risks in having him. According to Ernest, who knew him from his aborted elopement with Dorothy, McInnes could change from a Dr Jekyll to a Mr Hyde when under the influence of alcohol.[39] Tenor Alfred Heather, the Evangelist, 'delivered his lines with a simple directness of expression – sometimes with a certain impersonality, that contrasted effectively with McInnes's more intense style – but with that necessary touch of the dramatic that is demanded at certain points.'[40] He too was a drinker and had to be watched before performances. Willan was at the piano, since no harpsichord was available for the cembalo part, and Tattersall was organist.

And so Ernest MacMillan conducted Toronto's first complete

performance of the *St Matthew Passion*, entirely from memory, at Timothy Eaton Memorial Church on 27 March 1923.[41] The historic event was not treated as a concert *per se*. 'The principals wore morning coats and the choirs were dressed in black in keeping with the solemnity of the religious music drama.' Applause was forbidden.[42] When the work ended, everyone present, including the local musical press, knew that they had heard something extraordinary and wonderful, the first of what would become, under MacMillan's baton, an annual event in the city's musical life for the next three and a half decades.[43]

In 1926 the *Passion* moved to Convocation Hall, where MacMillan created the same religious atmosphere he had had at Eaton Memorial. Since Eaton Memorial's financial backing was no longer available, a group of private citizens led by Fred MacKelcan, a friend of MacMillan's, took over the finances and supported the performances for some years. Everyone associated with these early *Passions* – soloists, choristers, and instrumentalists, believers and non-believers – held a special place in their hearts for them and remembered them, for years to come, with reverence. The Canadian pianist Reginald Godden was at the 1928 performance: 'As the auditors, many with scores, quietly gathered to fill every seat, an uncanny electricity filled the air and one just knew this was to be an epic evening.' After the orchestra, choir, soloists, and keyboard players were in place, 'the source of it all, Dr. MacMillan' entered:

He had no score; it was all in his head and in his heart. A moment of absolute silence as his eyes scanned the ranks arrayed in a half circle and then the deep throb of the 12/8 opening began and we were transported on the heaving sea of the apotheosis of the Chorale Prelude and from there to the unfolding of the *Passion*. For days, we were lost in wonder at the mysterious power of that evening and the wonder was divided between the creator, Bach, and the projector of that creation, Dr. MacMillan. The *Passion* was to be for years to come the pinnacle of our listening lives ... That's how MacMillan made his mark in Canada. He created an impression on all of us at that period – the mystery, the totality of it all, his complete identification with it – this remains. Nobody else will ever do it as he did.[44]

5. Directing a School

By the 1924–5 season, Ernest MacMillan was becoming increasingly unhappy at Timothy Eaton Memorial Church. The elders accused him of doing too much German music and criticized his authoritarian ways with the choir. He countered by stating that they wanted 'the milk and watery stuff ... emanating from the United States.'[1] He pointed out that Handel, whose music was among the targeted, was really English. Opinionated and uncompromising, he let it be known that he thought church music much too serious a subject for ministers and laymen to rule upon. The complaints reminded him of the troubles he had as a youth at Knox, only now he knew for sure what he had only suspected then: that he was not, and never would be, cut out to be a church musician.

He resigned on 12 June 1925, the day after he had triumphantly led a large choir and Toronto's New Symphony Orchestra – soon to be the Toronto Symphony Orchestra – at the United Church of Canada's inaugural ceremonies.[2] With no comparable job in the offing, it took courage to give up the good salary, the fine organ, and the attractive concert site, but he was convinced that he had no alternative.

There had been two other setbacks that spring. One was a personal tragedy – Elsie's fourth pregnancy ending in another stillbirth. The other was a cut in his Academy earnings at a time when he could ill afford it. The Academy, with its 1,500 students, had recently been taken over by the Toronto Conservatory of Music (TCM), and Principal Vogt, a very good businessman, was cleaning house. Ernest was teaching piano (his sister Winifred was one of his best students), organ, and theory, but, despite his considerable reputation, he could not meet his guarantee, and Vogt had no recourse but to remove it. Ernest might have thought Vogt's action personal, since their relations were never warm. Vogt had left after Part One of the 1923 *Passion* performance and had stayed away from the 1924 and 1925 ones altogether, even though Ernest had sent him complimentary tickets.[3]

MacMillan did have several promising organ students, including Muriel Gidley, Charles Peaker, and Frederick Silvester. Gidley, for one, captured on paper what it meant to study with him in the 1920s:

There were no easily escalated steps to learning in the MacMillan studio. No subject could possibly remain tedious for long with brilliant, whimsical, and unpredictable Ernest MacMillan in command. A week's assignment might very well be to write a set of variations in different styles on a theme newly penned at the moment or, at the organ, one complete Bach Trio Sonata. Nevertheless, such was the power of his personality and his contagious enthusiasm that one felt impelled to tackle the impossible in order to measure up or give up ... During those early years, the MacMillan classes in score study, ear training, and diction were memorable. His wit and mimicry made these sessions irresistibly entertaining, as he previewed at the piano orchestral works to be performed at the next concert, embellished by his distinctive vocal instrumentation. For diction we might have a swing at Gilbert and Sullivan or some ingenious concoction of vowels and consonants. I was most impressed, however, by the practical possibilities of the study of phonetics to which we were introduced and which I used later on with my own choir.[4]

Another former student remembered him more for his humour, compassion, and considerate way of criticizing. 'Praise needs no special language; a student will always treasure compliments, but criticism received with shouts of glee and chuckled over for years – that's genius.' She illustrated his genuine kindness with a story. 'When a student from the West coast was taken ill, it was Sir Ernest who came tearing up three flights of rooming-house stairs with arms full of detective stories, and a cheerful assumption that there wasn't much wrong with the world, really.' Also, she wrote about what a taskmaster he was. 'He is allergic to human parrots and lessons often left one feeling rather like a puppy who has met a porcupine – full of little barbs of suggestion whose disposal was one's own affair entirely. His own enthusiasm kept him completely baffled by the laziness of this wicked generation; there was a period during his internment in the last war (his students were not allowed to forget) when he wrote a fugue a day. Was it by accident that these fugues kept being found?'[5]

Ernest put much effort into teaching and would often discuss methodologies with others. He and the gifted piano teacher Boris Berlin later made an important contribution to piano pedagogy by co-authoring a beginning text, *The Modern Piano Student*. It included photos and diagrams of hand positions, ear training and finger exercises, rhythms for clapping, guidelines for writing notation, interval work, and a good collection of beginning pieces. Its aim was to bring the student 'into touch with the living, inward spirit of music,' and so it did.[6] The authors recommended singing by rote and action songs before the child moved on to learning music *through* the piano. Once into piano study the student should not learn 'a series of pieces parrot fashion' but rather work towards 'the simultaneous development of fingers and brains.' Technique, he once explained, quite brilliantly,

does not mean merely the cultivation of mechanical skill – it does not mean slickness. For every possible musical effect, for every possible emotional shade, and for every kind of tonal colour that can be produced, there is a corresponding physical means of producing it. The theologian would say that 'the Word is the flesh' and, however grandiose our musical ideas, they must be expressed in physical terms, they must become flesh before they dwell among us so that we behold their glory. Technique consists in the analysis of every means of expression and the cultivation of the power to draw readily upon whatever resource is necessary ... The idea of separating technique from 'inspiration,' 'musical instinct,' or whatever we like to call it is foolish, for in the higher reaches of music one's musical conceptions grow side by side

with one's technique ... The breadth and variety of what one has to say
in music grows side by side with one's ability to say it, and any narrower
view of the term 'technique' is inadequate.[7]

On another occasion he talked perceptively about the teacher-
pupil relationship:

Every teacher knows what it means to be blamed because he hasn't been
able to kindle the divine spark in a willing and conscientious pupil. Do
remember – all you young students and all you fathers and mothers of
students – the best teacher in the world can only develop and foster
what is already there. He can't give a fine voice to someone who has
only a mediocre one (though if he knows his business he can enormously improve on nature); he can't bestow creative ability on a would-be
composer (though if he knows his business he can show him how to put
music together); he can't give a quick ear or an alert mind to one
whose aural and mental processes are slow (though he can show hundreds of interesting ways in which you can develop your technical skill);
he cannot bestow on you that faculty for commanding and holding the
attention of an audience, the faculty of establishing sympathy between
yourself and your audience, the faculty which, in one form or another,
must be present in the performance of anyone who hopes to succeed.
Yet, while you should not overestimate what a good teacher can do for
you, you should not underestimate it either. Many people don't get half
as far as they might along the road to musical excellence because they
don't give their teacher a fair chance.[8]

To return to the hard realities of 1925, MacMillan had to take
on two part-time jobs to supplement his meagre teaching income.
The first was teaching music and conducting an orchestra – in
reality just an ill-assorted group of mainly wind players – at the
senior school of Upper Canada College, an elite private boys'
school in Toronto. Ernest's friend Richard Tattersall taught music
in the lower school – perhaps he helped Ernest get the job. To
cope with his new duties, he had to learn the rudiments of each
wind instrument, no small challenge for a keyboard player, but he
took on the task conscientiously and in good spirit, although his
efforts to blow a clarinet drove his family to distraction. Ernest's

second job was at the University of Toronto's Hart House Theatre, where he composed and conducted music for dramatic
productions, much as he had at Ruhleben a decade earlier.

And then an unexpected twist of fate secured his future. Vogt
became seriously ill and the Toronto Conservatory's board was
faced, on short notice, with finding someone who could run the
school. Administration was not Vice-Principal Healey Willan's
strong suit, and so the board turned to MacMillan for help. He
agreed and soon was shining in this new role, keeping the school
on an even keel for the rest of the year and, in the process, taking the opportunity to study 'the administrative problems of a
large institution from the inside.'[9]

Vogt died a year later, in September 1926, and within a month
MacMillan was offered the job of principal. At first he hesitated,
since he knew that the post's demands might curtail his musical
activities, but, as he explained later, 'In the circumstances, I felt
I had little choice. My job at Upper Canada was gone; Hart
House Theatre had decided to economize and dispense with a
musical director; my special work at the Conservatory would cease
after a permanent Principal was appointed.'[10] And so, MacMillan
accepted the post, and, as it turned out, it was an eminently wise
decision, for it provided him not only with an excellent salary and
financial security but also with a site for concerts and festivals,
and a base of operations from which he could develop a first-rate
choir, a symphony orchestra, and an opera company.

Ernest put aside his personal feelings towards Vogt to write a
fitting tribute:

The wonderful feeling for musical colour which never failed to appear
in Vogt's performances, was compounded of an exceptional sense of
rhythm and an almost uncanny sensitiveness to vocal tone. I have often
wondered how he achieved his results ... Many who sang under his
baton have described to me his methods at rehearsal – his meticulous
attention to such matters as intonation, his illuminating orchestral
analogies, his clear mental conception of the effects he wished to obtain, and his rigorous discipline – but when all is said and done, any
artistic whole is greater than the sum of its parts, and there was a quality
in the man himself which counted for more than anything he did.[11]

He also made much of how the conservatory had prospered under Vogt's direction and how his sense of duty had kept him at his post even when his health said no.

Over a hundred letters from well-wishers arrived on Ernest's desk after his appointment was announced, an indication of the position's importance in the Canadian musical world and of the many admirers and friends he had already made. He answered every one of them, as he would, for the rest of his life, answer all letters received.[12] Proud Alexander MacMillan thought the post 'the premier place in music in the Dominion,' and wrote to his son: 'I was by no means surprised ... As things have turned out it is very fortunate that you were not committed to so many different kinds of professional work as last year. You can now concentrate upon the mastery of this great position.'[13]

But was it really that great a position? Granted the TCM was the best music school in Canada, but it was still, essentially, nothing more than a conglomeration of private studios and an effective national examination system modelled after Britain's. (Annual music examinations had not caught on in the United States.) There were no real courses, like those given by better schools in the United States and abroad. And there were no public subsidies or endowments. To cover operating costs, the school depended entirely on commissions extracted from teachers and revenues from examinations. Money and education lived together in an uneasy partnership.

The conservatory had started in 1886 in rented quarters on Dundas Square. In 1897 it became affiliated with the University of Toronto and moved to a new building, well located at the corner of College Street and University Avenue. The TCM operated as a private stock-bearing limited company until 1910, when Canada's revised taxation laws required it to become a non-profit school without share capital. Then, in 1919, by an act of the Ontario Legislature, its assets and property were vested in the University of Toronto. Two years later, the university took full responsibility for it and moved its new Faculty of Music into the College Street building.

At the time of MacMillan's appointment, the conservatory had about 7,000 pupils registered for private lessons and classes,

17,000 candidates taking conservatory examinations in over 100 centres nation-wide, a teaching faculty of close to 100 of the best musicians in the country, a 300–seat concert hall, plenty of studios, and a women's residence. There were also neighbourhood branches strung across the city so that small children need not travel downtown for lessons. In fact, most of the school's teaching was in the form of beginning and intermediate private lessons in piano. The TCM had neither an advanced program nor good performing groups – there was no choir and only a makeshift student orchestra which von Kunits had started in 1924. There *were* classes in ear training, rudiments, harmony, and music history, but few took them because of the cost. In sum, the self-supporting conservatory was little more than a musical department store where students studied whatever they wanted and with whom they wanted as long as they had the money to pay for it. Gifted young musicians had little choice but to leave the country to finish their training, many never to return.

One of the first things Ernest did on becoming principal was to set out on an extensive tour of American, English, and French music schools, to seek out ideas on how to improve the school.[14] His first stop was at the privately endowed and independent New England Conservatory in Boston, where he heard a full student symphony orchestra play a Brahms symphony at a near-professional level. Ernest was green with envy, since the TCM's small orchestra had to be beefed up with professionals to play even a Haydn symphony. He was further impressed with New England's opera department, which had staged *Madama Butterfly* at the Boston Opera House, its fine choir, its advanced conducting course whose members gained hands-on experience leading student groups, and its public school music program which prepared students to teach in Massachusetts schools. Toronto, needless to say, had none of these. To top it off, New England enjoyed high visibility in the community, thanks to its active alumni and publicity department.

At Harvard, MacMillan's next stop, he found music treated as a 'cultural subject, not as technical training.' Harvard granted a Bachelor of Arts with a specialization in music and had an agreement with the state department of education allowing qualified

Harvard music graduates to teach in the schools. (Colleges of education in Ontario had rigid entrance requirements and an iron grip on teacher certification.) To MacMillan's surprise, medieval and renaissance music, which he had always thought extremely difficult to teach, were brought to life by Harvard's Archibald T. Davison. He taught music history stylistically rather than in the traditional composer-based way still popular at the TCM.

Then it was on to New York's Institute of Musical Art, a part of the Juilliard School, but his visit there was extremely brief and perfunctory because he arrived just as the school was closing for the Christmas holidays. From New York he sailed to Liverpool, and made his way to Royal Manchester College. The two things which most impressed him there were the careful screening of students before admission, by auditions and written examinations, and the paying of teachers by salary rather than on a per lesson basis.

Ernest was able to fit in a visit to Edinburgh to see old friends, including Alfred Hollins and Peggy Maclean. Here he learned that Polly Lothian, who had died a short time before, had bequeathed to her beloved 'Dacey' five hundred pounds, a grandfather clock, an antique table and mirror, and a carved oak wardrobe, all of which he would get after the death of Peggy. He wrote to Elsie: 'It is simply amazing to think of what I owe to her and to Peggy ... May it be a long time before we fall heirs to them.'[15] He must have been thinking of Peggy and Polly's great hospitality on his many visits to Edinburgh, the many parcels they had sent to him at Ruhleben, and, especially, the grand piano which Polly had given him on receiving his doctorate from Oxford.

He also found time to visit Edgar Bainton, a former Ruhlebenite and director of the Newcastle Conservatory, and Benjamin Dale in London, who invited a number of Ruhleben alumni to hear 'Mac' give an organ recital at All Saints Church.[16] (Ernest seized every opportunity, through the years, to see former Ruhlebenites – enduring hardships together makes for lifelong bonding – although he never managed to attend their annual reunions. He maintained his close friendship with Dale until the latter's untimely death in 1943.) Ernest also met with two musical men of letters, Ernest Newman and Percy Scholes, and visited a few more music schools, from which he learned little.

His sister Dorothy, now married to Jack Hill, was living in London, and she and Ernest were able to spend time together. An old Toronto friend named Amice Calverley, a Canadian archaeologist, draughtsman, and composer, tracked him down. She had composed an opera and coerced the typically generous Ernest into playing it through on the piano for Sir Hugh Allen, director of the Royal College of Music and, coincidentally, one of Ernest's examiners for his Oxford doctorate. Calverley was hoping that the college would produce it. The opera was not as bad as Ernest had expected, and Amice was forever grateful to him for taking the time to do it. Then influenza struck, ruling out his scheduled visit to France and cutting his trip short. He returned to Toronto at the end of February to be reunited with his family, whom he had left alone for Christmas, and to get on with his work at the school.

Ernest gradually made improvements at the conservatory. He opened a small listening library, to meet the growing interest in recordings, and a cafeteria, which not only answered the need for a convenient eatery in a neighbourhood notably devoid of restaurants but also provided a central and informal meeting place for students and faculty. A 'Women Teachers' Clubroom' was approved, and an alumni association was organized. Soon the many students who made their weekly or twice-weekly visits to the College Street building for their private lessons could identify the new principal, for he made a point of being very visible – he seemed to be everywhere, in the foyers and corridors, and at lessons, classes, and rehearsals. He even had parties for students. Composer Louis Applebaum remembered, as a child, playing a noisy game of musical chairs in the Recital Hall, with MacMillan running the show from the piano and sons Keith and Ross joining in the fun.[17]

Some four months after becoming principal, Ernest was appointed dean of the Faculty of Music. The appointment was not unexpected – Vogt had also held both posts – but the university had deliberately delayed the appointment because it wanted to keep the two positions distinct from one another. As dean, he had virtually no duties for, while the Faculty of Music was the conservatory's parent body and authorized its diplomas and certificates, it did very little teaching and gave degrees by examination only, much like Oxford. He also had no salary, the principal's salary covering both positions. In addition to MacMillan, the Faculty of Music had three other lecturers: Healey Willan, F.A. Mouré – the university organist for many years – and Herbert Fricker.[18] Willan gave six lectures a year, the others four each. Willan was replaced in 1927 by cellist, composer, and writer Leo Smith.[19] MacMillan, very much wanting a full-time program of study for professionally oriented students, soon came to realize that the university, not the conservatory, was probably the better place for it. Little did he know how long it would take to come to pass.

Ernest did much soul-searching about the conservatory's examinations. Like many other musicians, he thought that examinations, by their very nature, limited rather than expanded musical training. Children might spend all year preparing three or four pieces to the exclusion of everything else. The end result was that instead of learning music for its own sake they focused their energies on earning high marks and certificates to make them and their parents happy. Teachers went along with it all, if for no other reason than the fear of losing students. That so few examination candidates continued to play their instruments after reaching adulthood suggested that the benefits were very limited.

However, there were practical – or moneymaking – considerations. The TCM depended on examinations for revenue, and their operation had been fine-tuned to insure that this continued. They were kept short so that the maximum number of candidates could be examined in a minimum amount of time, and examiners were trained to work efficiently, keep on schedule, and take on as many candidates as humanly possible. They heroically covered thousands of miles annually with marginal accommodation and indifferent food, and, for their efforts, received only the smallest of stipends.

Even if he had been tempted, MacMillan could not do away with examinations, and so, instead, he found what good he could in them. He wrote about how they helped average students, especially those in the lower grades, but always qualified his words by pointing out that they should be regarded as 'a means and not an end' and that 'candidates should not be hurried through them.' He was confident that the judgments of experienced examiners helped both the students and their teachers. Yet, on the other hand, he was quick to point out that the better the teacher the less the need for examinations, and that advanced professional students rarely need them.[20]

To help maintain uniform grading, Ernest gave workshops at which the examiners would all mark the same candidates, discuss various points arising from the marks, and agree on certain principles. The youngsters who served as guinea pigs usually did so quite cheerfully, and each would be rewarded with a box of chocolates. Ernest particularly cherished one acknowledgment from a rosy-cheeked chubby boy of about eight. 'Thank you very much for the candies which you sent me. I liked them very much and I shall be glad to play for you again any time.'[21]

Soon Ernest found ways to offer free classes in ear training, sight-singing, score-study, and choir training for all students taking private lessons, but, sadly, they were dropped several years later because of lack of funds. With more success he started a conservatory choir to perform with the conservatory orchestra. The momentous first concert was on 29 February 1928. Before intermission, von Kunits conducted the orchestra and soloists in several short works, concluding with Vaughan Williams's *The Lark Ascending*. In the second half, MacMillan led the choir and orchestra in the Mozart *Requiem*. Both the Vaughan Williams and the Mozart were new to Toronto.

The keen Edward Wodson of the *Evening Telegram* liked what he heard and reported that the orchestra was composed of forty students augmented by ten professionals, mainly in the wind section. Seventeen were 'young ladies' and several were 'mere children.'[22] Lawrence Mason wrote more effusively: 'It is almost unbelievable that a single year's training [more accurately six months] could have achieved such admirable results ... Dr. MacMillan is entitled to take deep satisfaction in the choir's astonishing showing, both technically and tonally.'[23] He praised the 'pre-

cision, certitude, unanimity, shading, real beauty' of both chorus
and orchestra and concluded by applauding the conservatory and
even comparing it favourably to English music schools.

The choir continued to progress and, within two years, was one
of the best in Toronto, second only to the Mendelssohn Choir.
Mason heard it do the Fauré *Requiem* at Convocation Hall on 29
January 1930 and called it 'a crowning miracle, a transformation
of a casual group of young students into an absolutely first-class
choir ... and only such words as "inspired" or "genius" could accurately be applied to the conductor. As for the youthful singers,
very possibly they may never arise to such a height again. But for
once in their lives they were entitled to feel that they achieved
perfection.'[24]

In 1929, MacMillan launched the Conservatory String Quartet,
with faculty members Elie Spivak and Harold Sumberg, violins,
Donald Heins, viola, and Leo Smith, cello. He even played Eugene Goossens's Piano Quintet with the group at its debut concert in the TCM foyer. From then on he frequently did piano
quintets with them, as did other pianists on the conservatory
faculty. On one occasion, the colourful Norah Drewett de Kresz
was to play the Franck Quintet but was stymied because the last
page of her score had vanished and no other copy could be
located in Toronto. Ernest heard about the problem and, thanks
to his astonishing memory, on the day of the concert sketched
out the missing page of music for all five instruments![25] Louis
Applebaum had another MacMillan 'memory' story from the same
period. He was having a piano lesson with Boris Berlin, when in
walked MacMillan to return some contemporary scores which
Berlin had received from Russia a week earlier. MacMillan handed
them to Berlin and then proceeded to play excerpts from memory,
talking all the time while Berlin looked at the actual music.[26]

Another notable innovation at the conservatory was opera. In
April 1928, the newly formed Conservatory Opera Company did
a week of Humperdinck's *Hansel and Gretel* and Gilbert and Sullivan's *The Sorcerer*, alternating them on successive nights. The
Hansel performances were preceded by the musical pantomime
Bluebeard, for which MacMillan had prepared an orchestral arrangement of Beethoven's Piano Sonata Op. 27, No. 2 (the *Moon-*

light). The singers were either students or graduates of the conservatory, and the delighted press lauded everything – MacMillan's conducting, the cast, the sets, and the costumes. Bridle raved about the Act II finale of *Hansel*.[27] Mason, equally pleased, observed that the audience had been 'spellbound' by *Hansel* and that, despite the theatre's acoustical problems (the performances were held in Toronto's Regent Theatre) and the lush orchestration, 'Dr. MacMillan did not make the mistake of sacrificing the many glories of the orchestra to the single glory of the singer.' Mason was, however, annoyed by the audience's bad manners – many came late and there was much talking during the *Hansel* prelude.[28] Sad to say, *The Sorcerer*, which Donald Heins conducted, did not earn similar praise. It is difficult to produce this early 'G & S' work, especially with inexperienced and poorly cast singers and inadequate staging. Fortunately, its failure did not detract from the triumph of the Humperdinck opera.[29]

The next year the more experienced company produced Purcell's *Dido and Aeneas* and Franz von Suppé's *Boccaccio*, the two alternating on successive nights as the year before. This time Hart House Theatre was the venue. *Dido*, a short masterpiece of its kind, was an excellent choice, and the young singers did themselves proud. Bach's *Peasant Cantata* preceded it on the program. *Boccaccio*, like *The Sorcerer* a year earlier, left the audience cold. It should not have been done, but Ernest was still a neophyte when it came to selecting, casting, and staging operas.

The Canadian Pacific Railway (CPR) helped make MacMillan's next operatic production his most memorable when it sponsored a five-day festival of English music in November 1929, in conjunction with the opening of its new Royal York Hotel in Toronto, the tallest, largest, and most costly hotel in the British Empire and the flagship of the CPR chain of Canadian hotels. The highlight of the festival was to be a Conservatory Opera Company production (and North American premiere) of Vaughan Williams's ballad opera *Hugh the Drover*. The CPR's interest in Canada's cultural heritage had begun in 1927, when John Murray Gibbon, its imaginative and dynamic publicity director, organized the first of several CPR-sponsored folklore festivals. Gibbon hoped that they would make Canadians more conscious of their diverse backgrounds, increase their sense of national identity, and encourage them to see more of their country – travelling on CPR trains and staying in CPR hotels. (Gibbon later wrote *A Canadian Mosaic*, a linguistic, religious, and racial analysis of Canada's population.)[30] The first festival was held in Quebec City, followed by sixteen others over the next four years in various locations country-wide – early examples of corporate sponsorship of cultural events of quality in return for indirect promotion.

MacMillan had struck up a warm relationship with Gibbon in 1927 at the first CPR Quebec Festival – of which more later – and may even have suggested the English festival. Gibbon and MacMillan jointly planned the event, which included the Vaughan Williams opera, lectures and concerts dealing with English music, English folk dancing done by dancers brought from England especially for the occasion, and English art and handicraft exhibits.

Hugh the Drover is redolent of English rural life and makes use of melodies based on English folk tunes. Alfred Heather was the inventive stage director. He had sung the Evangelist for several of MacMillan's *St Matthew Passion* performances and had recently directed the première of Healey Willan's ballad opera *Charlie and Flora* at Banff. Allan Jones, an American tenor who would later star in Hollywood films, was Hugh; the rest of the cast was Canadian. *Hugh the Drover*'s central event is a boxing match between Hugh and John the butcher, and the fight in Heather's production was done so realistically that reports of it made the sports pages of at least one Toronto daily. (Sir Thomas Beecham's production in England had avoided staging the fight by having the chorus surround the ring, leaving the actual combat to the audience's imagination.)[31] Toronto audiences were most impressed by the exertions of the two protagonists, who carried off their simultaneous singing and fighting in great style. MacMillan particularly enjoyed a line in sportswriter Lou Marsh's description: 'John, the battling baritone, hit the ropes so hard that he finished out the piece as a soprano.'[32] Edward Wodson wandered eloquently into *terra incognita*:

How the fighters could spar, undercut, left swing, right punch, leap, spit out a mouthful of teeth ... all in operatic form ... is still a matter of astonishment. Yet they did it. And roused the audience to thunders of applause, to wriggling on seats, to almost everything short of joining in the mill with each other! It was something to be seen and heard. Words cannot do it justice. And the singing ... was just as fine ... And you got every word they sang.[33]

Later, when portions of *Hugh* were broadcast, the fight was graphically described in sportscaster style by the well-known sports announcer Foster Hewitt.

Local critics lauded MacMillan's conducting, and they were not alone – a critic for New York's *Musical Courier* attended *Hugh* and extolled 'the masterful, vital conducting of Dr. MacMillan ... The chorus and orchestra were as one coordinated body, sensitive to the beauties of the music.'[34] However, it was Bertram Brooker, artist, novelist (he would win the first Governor General's award in 1937 for his novel *Think of the Earth*), and editor (of *The Year-book of the Arts, 1928–29*), who made the most prescient observation. He wrote:

[MacMillan] should have greater and more permanent opportunities to develop as a conductor ... As head of a conservatory he cannot possibly be of the same service to Canadian music that he could be as head of a big symphony orchestra, a big choir, or both ... [He] has convinced a great many that his ability to inspire and vitalize performers, both vocal and instrumental, amounts to nothing short of genius. Without minimizing other aspects of the festival ... the one salient thing which seemed above all to have a bearing on the future development of Canadian music was the conducting of Ernest MacMillan.[35]

MacMillan's two triumphs, *Hansel and Gretel* and *Hugh the Drover*, were revived in the spring of 1930 for a week's run, alternating performances nightly at the Royal Alexandra Theatre. The original casts were used and everything came off as well as or better than the first time around. These were the last Toronto Conservatory opera productions for many years to come. The Great Depression hit the school hard, and opera was one of the first casualties.

6. Canada's Musical Heritage

Interest in Canadian folk music had begun long before John Murray Gibbon's festivals. Marius Barbeau, one of the driving forces in this field, had already done much to research, collect, preserve, and publish Canada's indigenous – folk and aboriginal – music. A native of Quebec and a contemporary of Ernest Mac-Millan's, he had studied at Laval, Oxford (as a Rhodes Scholar), and the Sorbonne. In 1911 he had been appointed anthropologist and ethnologist at the Museum Branch of the Geological Survey of Canada (renamed the National Museum in 1927) in Ottawa, a post he would hold for his entire career. Barbeau was put in charge of North American Native studies, and proceeded to record the music of the Huron at Notre-Dame-de-Lorette near Quebec City, of the Salish of British Columbia, and others. He was soon collecting French-Canadian songs as well, and, by 1924, had deposited some 5,000 recordings and 5,000 manuscripts in the museum. A year later he co-edited a collection of forty-one songs, most of them previously unpublished. Indirectly, this book brought Barbeau into MacMillan's life and added a whole new dimension to the latter's multifaceted career.

It all started when Ernest reviewed the song collection for the left-of-centre intellectual monthly *Canadian Forum*.[1] His review broke new ground, for, until then, most serious musicians had ignored Canada's folk music. French Canadians, he wrote:

have been associated with our land longer than those of any other European people and have exercised a profound influence on almost every phase of our national life. No one guards his tradition more jealously. His songs are not, indeed, native to America except in a few instances, but in the three centuries during which they have flourished here they have played an important part in his life ... They lack the wealth of melody and sheer musical invention which distinguish the Celtic and especially the Irish, but in their place we find a rhythmic vitality combined with a wealth of expression which give it a very high place indeed. The music is full of sunshine and rarely leaves the listener in an unhappy frame of mind, even when the subject is a solemn one.

His perceptive and knowledgeable review also carried an important message for the future. 'We have been too much concerned with teaching the new arrivals our own ways and too little in discovering the contributions they are capable of making to our national life,' he wrote, and went on: 'If we have been negligent in the case of immigrants, what can we say of the people in whose eyes we are mere usurpers? ... [Native] folk-lore is a rich one and rooted deep in the soil ... A deeper interest in the real Indian – in his ways of thinking and feeling, rather than his outward circumstances – would no doubt bring revelations.'

MacMillan met Barbeau soon after the review's publication and, through Barbeau, he met John Murray Gibbon of the CPR. Together the three planned the first 'Canadian Folk Song and Handicraft Festival' to be held in Quebec City in May 1927. Given under the auspices of the National Museum, the National Gallery, and the Public Archives, with the CPR paying the costs, the event was a singular example of French-English collaboration. One of MacMillan's contributions was an arrangement of *Two Sketches for String Quartet Based on French-Canadian Airs.* The first sketch, 'Notre Seigneur,' about the legend of Christ disguised as a beggar, is meditative and modal in style and contrasts well with the lively and spirited second sketch, 'À Saint Malo,' the Breton port from which Jacques Cartier set sail. The Hart House String Quartet performed *Two Sketches* at the festival with much success. (The quartet had premiered it in Buffalo the previous January.) Later, MacMillan arranged the work for string orchestra, and it became his most frequently played orchestral work. He was, however, always embarrassed about its popularity, since he considered it a very minor effort.[2]

Several of MacMillan's vocal arrangements of French and English folk-songs were also sung at the festival. Prominent singers, including Campbell McInnes, were brought from far and wide, as were folk dancers, folk fiddlers, and handicrafters. The CPR's Château Frontenac Hotel even engaged several French-Canadian housewives to prepare traditional Quebec cuisine.[3] And throughout it all Barbeau played his Edison cylinders and showed his manuscripts to all who were interested.

It was thanks to Barbeau that MacMillan had an adventurous summer following the Quebec festival. Barbeau had planned a field trip of several weeks to study and record the music of the Tsimshian at Arrandale on the Nass River, sixty miles north of Prince Rupert in northwestern British Columbia. He asked Mac-Millan to join his party, and MacMillan accepted with delight. Working with Natives on their own ground was old hat for Barbeau, but not for MacMillan, who looked forward to what promised to be a new and unforgettable experience with real excitement. He was, after all, an urbane musician whose outdoor life had been limited to cottage stays and motor trips. Elsie, in fact, was the outdoor person.

Getting there was part of the fun, particularly the sea voyage from Vancouver, which was a visual feast. His boat wound its way up the coast, side-stepping countless small islands yet remaining within sight of the mainland with its heavily wooded shoreline and high mountains.[4] Eventually Ernest reached Arrandale to join the Barbeau team. In addition to Barbeau and himself, there were three others: Langdon Kihn, an American painter; Alex Gunn, a distant relative of Ernest through his aunt Christina; and a Dr Watson, a skilled amateur photographer from the Eastman Kodak plant. They were all quartered in a functional old government house next to an abandoned jail. No matter, the setting was enchanting, with a glorious view of hills up the river valley, an unspoiled countryside, tall hemlocks and red cedars, and wildlife everywhere. Barbeau called it a Paradise Lost.[5]

Ernest had hardly put down his bag when Barbeau, ready with manuscript paper and pencil, asked him to listen to a recording

of a Tsimshian song and transcribe it forthwith.[6] And that was just
the beginning. For close to three weeks, MacMillan listened to
songs almost non-stop, recording them on Barbeau's cumbersome
forty-pound Edison machine and then transcribing them as best
he could. It helped that Natives from all over the region worked
at a salmon cannery nearby, making it easy for them to visit Barbeau's camp to sing their songs and tell their stories and legends.
In turn, the Natives invited the visitors to their gatherings – feasts,
parties, and rituals – and to view their totem poles, masks, and
Chilkat blankets.

Tsimshian songs had, at one time, been highly developed, and
required special training to perform, but, by the 1920s, only a
very few older Tsimshians could still sing them. The younger folk,
converted Christians, would have nothing to do with such 'pagan'
music. As for the songs themselves, they were often rhythmically
complex and, on occasion, deliberately sung in a scale which did
not correspond to the notes of any Western musical scale. They
had originally come from Siberia and were indeed difficult to
transcribe into European notation. As MacMillan explained, 'One
song had a rhythm of successive 3/8, 5/8, and 4/8 bars, against
a 3/4 drum beat; another had a 6/8 drum beat against a 9/8
tune, the bars being evenly synchronized.' Pitch was also a problem. To notate the 'singing intervals between the cracks,' he put
plus signs before the written notes that were sharper than the
actual notes and minus signs before those that were flatter.[7] Barbeau, colourfully and, one suspects, with some licence, described
how absorbed MacMillan was with his work:

He abstractly marked time with his left hand while he bit into his sand-
wich of rye krisp and cold ham, and he kept humming a tune with a
look of tense concern over his face ... 'You seem to be in difficulties
with that tune' I remarked ... 'Wretchedly intricate!' he answered. 'The
song is alright. It is beautiful and haunting; it is grand! Yet I cannot
quite grasp it. The tune moves along at a marked pace, the drum accompaniment at another. Listen to this, the tune, one-two-three ... eight-
nine; it sounds like nine-eight. Against this the drum beats are something else, slower, quite different. No, listen to the melody itself, the
intervals. How plaintively the voice rises and falls, like the wind in a

storm. For modernity it goes beyond all the moderns; yet how strangely moving! Yes, a real song! Not only for the Indians, but for us. The voice of nature crying out! Yet those things can't be written down on our stave, they simply can't!'[8]

Barbeau went on to describe MacMillan's excitement when he finally sorted out the trouble with the cross-rhythms and the puzzling melodies:

'Eureka! ... Here I have it at last,' he exclaimed and went on to demonstrate how the nine-eight rhythm of the tune coincided with the six-eight of the drum. 'A tough job,' he exclaimed, 'Try it!' But we would rather not. We took him at his word. The spell of these songs was upon him, we could see, for their swaying appeal and their vocal fitness in the picture that still haunted him. They were human, they were alive, yet above all they were ... an art which challenged all his powers by its complex effervescence.[9]

The ever-observant MacMillan was troubled that Western influences at Arrandale did not always show up to advantage. With more than a tinge of sadness he described how badly the village band, of which the inhabitants were inordinately proud, had played as it accompanied a funeral procession. 'The sound of it floated over my ears in a most excruciating manner. After they had got beyond earshot, however, we heard an old woman singing to herself down on the shore. It was a wild, strange sound, something like the keening (Caoine) heard in parts of Ireland, but much farther removed from anything like European music ... It seemed part of the scene – as if, indeed, it were an essential part of Nature yet not part of humanity.'[10]

The Nass River expedition was captured visually in a short film sponsored by the CPR and released the following fall.[11] And Barbeau, MacMillan, and poet Duncan Campbell Scott set down three of the songs MacMillan had transcribed at Arrandale.[12] Ernest did the piano accompaniments, Barbeau did phonetic versions of the words, and Scott did the English translations. The first song, 'A Spirit Song,' begins with a declamatory syllabic introduction, 'I yo ho, hi ya hé,' followed by a short verse:

Behold the chieftain dancing for the first time!
Proud is he and noble, dancing for the first time.
High he lifts his lofty crest.
He inherits all the glory of his forebears.
Behold him dancing for the first time!

In the second song, 'Na Du – Na Du Du,' a mother sings a lullaby while holding her young son to her breast. She lovingly imagines him grown up, strong, and brave: 'I go to the streams for fishing ... to catch the spring salmon ... and find gifts for the Thunderwoman ... When I become a hunter ... I will set my bear traps, I will find food for my people, no one of you shall be hungry.' The third song, 'Stop All This Idle Chatter,' is the one MacMillan had struggled over with his 'rye krisp and ham.' Many years later, over seventy of MacMillan's Tsimshian transcriptions were included in a book by Barbeau and two other ethnologists.[13] The songs have a wide melodic range and some are of considerable literary interest.

The Quebec festival of May 1927 was such a triumph that it was repeated a year later. Ernest's arrangement of *Six Bergerettes du bas Canada*, a twenty-minute staged suite for voices and instrumental quartet – oboe, viola, cello, and harp – was a highlight.[14] It was modelled somewhat after the 'tableau,' which had some popularity at the time in French Canada. Ernest specified that the set should 'suggest a Watteau landscape,' that the cast wear early eighteenth-century costumes, and that 'the action be highly stylized and ... graceful.' The sensitively arranged songs deal with the lives and loves of shepherds and shepherdesses. Four are slow and relaxed in flavour and two are faster and more energetic. Ernest wrote well for the voices, using the accompanying instruments to provide colour, rhythmic interest, and tasteful *segues* from song to song. Ernest also arranged a series of French songs for male choir for the festival. One, 'Blanche comme la neige,' was later re-arranged for mixed voices and became a favourite of the Toronto Mendelssohn Choir.[15]

That same year, Ernest, now quite taken up with French-Canadian folk music, edited a volume of twenty-one songs and arranged nine of them himself.[16] Several of the songs in this rich

and varied collection are based on French melodies, and a few
date back to medieval times. (It has been said that French Canada helped France to rediscover its own folk music.) Many melodies are modal and can be sung without piano, yet the piano
arrangements are so subtle and, in a good many cases, so interesting that they help the melodies along, without endangering their
authenticity. Ernest's arrangements are particularly inventive, not
mere keyboard harmonizations. The piano weaves around the
melodies, reinforcing them or suggesting new patterns that juxta-
pose well with the singing voice.

One of the best songs in the collection, 'La prisonnière à la
tour,' is based on the English ballad 'The Gay Goshawk,' a tale
of a princess imprisoned by her father because he objects to her
choice of lover. Its simple yet haunting melody is complemented
brilliantly by Ernest's harp-like arpeggio accompaniment from the
keyboard. Two years later, Ernest arranged three spirited French-
Canadian sea songs, 'Le Long de la Mer Jolie,' 'Sept Ans sur
Mer,' and 'À Saint Malo,' for medium voice and strings; the set
is known collectively as his 'Three French-Canadian Sea Songs.'[17]

Another related project in the late 1920s was Ernest's *Canadian
Song Book*, commissioned by Canada's National Council of Education. He designed it to be 'of a comprehensive nature, including the best songs (whatever their origin) that have taken root in
Canadian soil.'[18] And it is just that, with its more than one hundred selections: national and patriotic songs, English and French
songs, Canadian and American songs, songs from other countries,
student songs, hymns, chorales, and carols. Used by countless
Canadian schools and other institutions over the decades, it is
one good reason why the name of Ernest MacMillan became so
widely known. The book, distributed in Great Britain as *A Book of
Songs*, led an *Observer* reviewer to say that MacMillan 'gives more
value for 7/6 [seven shillings and sixpence] than any other living
author, editor, or compiler known to me. He has also made of
this book of songs the most glorious and exciting jumble.'[19]

All of this transcribing and arranging of songs must have
sparked his creative – and romantic – spirit, for in 1928 Ernest
wrote a setting of Elizabeth Barrett Browning's 'Sonnet,' and
dedicated it to Elsie. The sonnet's difficult rhyme scheme was no

obstacle. The opening is simple, the piano quietly following the
singer 'If thou must love me ...'. The song gradually heats up –
the metre changes and changes again and the piano leads the
way as the song moves from C major to a brief section in A-flat
major. The reprise in C is more emphatic than at the start of the
song, the singer passionately exclaiming, 'But love me for love's
sake, that evermore Thou mayst love on, through love's eternity.'
As Frederick Hall has noted, 'the harmonies, rhythmic flow ...
and subtle musical underlinings of the text all combine to capture the emotional content of the poem.'[20]

The Quebec festivals and the Nass River expedition marked the
beginning of a lifelong friendship between MacMillan and Barbeau. The two men were as one in believing that folk-songs are
fundamental expressions of personal feelings, that they interpret
life, and that knowledge of them is essential to the understanding
of a people and their history. Despite their different backgrounds
and areas of activity, they shared a common commitment to serve
music in Canada. However, perhaps because of their differences,
their relations remained surprisingly formal. It would be more
than thirty years before MacMillan broke the ice by starting a
letter with 'My dear Marius' instead of the usual 'Dear Dr Barbeau,' and then suggesting that Barbeau do likewise. He did.[21]

Ethnomusicologist Kenneth Peacock, who worked with both of
them, described their contrasting personalities. 'Barbeau was the
ebullient visionary whose enthusiasms, one must admit, sometimes
went beyond the bounds of practicality; and MacMillan was the
equally enthusiastic pragmatist whose skilful diplomacy always
brought about a workable consensus.' And then somewhat wistfully Peacock added, 'Does this give any insight into the broader
aspects of the Canadian talent for cultural consensus? Perhaps.'[22]

By 1930, MacMillan had become something of an expert on
Canadian folk and Native music, and, although his active years in
this arena were virtually over, he campaigned vigorously, in talks
and papers, for their study and dissemination. And, from time to
time, he would transcribe and arrange folk-songs, which, thanks
to his composing and arranging skills and his ear for style, he did
with consummate ease. His attention to French songs fuelled his
thoughts about the relationship between French and English

Canada, thoughts which he had first mulled over in the summer of 1913 at Murray Bay. 'How wrong many a visitor to Quebec is when he admires the "picturesque" folk and their quaint, picturesque ways,' he said in 1930. 'It never seems to occur to him (the visitor), however, that in many senses these folk ... are decidedly superior to him. Their outlook may be narrow in certain respects and they may not have travelled far beyond the confines of their villages, but they are artistically, as well as economically, self-sufficient to an enviable degree.'[23] Ernest attributed French Canada's concern for preserving its culture to its minority status and reminded English Canadians that they too were a minority 'subjected to powerful influences, often unconsciously assimilated, that tend to make us almost indistinguishable from our southern neighbours ... We must, without closing our doors to the outside world, seek out and foster those elements that can best contribute to a truly Canadian culture.'[24]

Few musicians have had as many rich and varied experiences by age thirty-five as Ernest MacMillan. Consider his training and pre-war experiences in Canada and Scotland, his activities during his four-year imprisonment, his musical 'handyman' years in the early 1920s as church organist, recitalist, conductor, and examiner, and his rewarding excursions into folk music with Marius Barbeau. Now he was head of Canada's largest music school, dean of a university music faculty, and conductor of opera. To do all that he did without excessive stress and strain, Ernest needed a stable and supportive home life. Elsie provided it through her unconditional love, her attention to his every need, her concern that he have the privacy he needed, and her care of their two happy, bright, and robust sons whom he could enjoy when he had the time for it – which, all too often, he didn't. She usually kept them well out of their busy father's way so that he could work at home undisturbed.

In 1931, the family moved to a large custom-designed three-storey house on lovely Park Road in Toronto's fashionable Rosedale district. There they all had more space. Polly Lothian's majestic seven-foot Steinway grand piano was set in Ernest's study, which adjoined the large sunken living-room, the focal-point for the many receptions, parties, and musical evenings which Elsie would host over the years. By opening the study's sliding door Ernest could entertain his guests with piano accompaniments to his humorous rhymes and Gilbert and Sullivan verses – Elsie said that Ernest knew most of their works by heart. The grand was not, however, the only MacMillan piano: there was also an upright one, installed in the basement for Keith and Ross's use, with a blanket stuffed under its casing to ensure that it could not be heard elsewhere in the house!

Indeed, Elsie's zeal to protect Ernest from other music or just plain noise could go to extremes and led to some bizarre incidents. Once, when the eccentric Australian pianist and composer Percy Grainger was staying with them, Elsie asked him to use the upright, because Ernest had to rest before an evening concert. 'That was the day our sewer decided to back up,' Keith MacMillan related. 'We were mortified but Grainger was undaunted. I shall not soon forget the sight of him, his alarming shock of hair blazing in the gloom and his feet tucked up under him on the stool, playing our silent piano in a pool of fetid water, happy as a lark.'[25]

But the boys had few other restrictions imposed on them and, in fact, were often on the receiving end of substantial bonuses for being the sons of Ernest MacMillan. As they grew older, they happily attended rehearsals and concerts and accompanied their parents on trips to Europe and the American and Canadian West, times which they looked back on most fondly in later years. And, despite a certain formality at the dinner table – Elsie always dressed for dinner – mealtimes gave Keith and Ross a lively introduction to 'Stephen Leacock (who seemed to be associated with the dessert), Shakespeare, and Shaw, and, of course, to the Bible.'[26] Their father and mother would quote from memory 'large tracts of poetry and plays – Browning's *Pied Piper*, Shakespeare's *Twelfth Night*.' And all one had to do was mention 'the handbag?' and Ernest would take off on Lady Bracknell – he remembered every line she uttered. The boys were 'prisoners' during these long recitations but, wisely, valued them. There was much love in the MacMillan house, and, if their mother gave too much attention to their busy, illustrious, and often preoccupied father, Keith and Ross did not resent it – although they might have objected to her occasional dictatorial ways with them.[27]

The four MacMillans were fortunate to have many relatives close at hand. On Ernest's side there were his parents and two of his three sisters – Dorothy Hill was living in England. But there was always a certain degree of formality among them, that same formality which Elsie had felt during the years Ernest was in Ruhleben. Alexander MacMillan, friendly and affectionate as he was, was always a presence and could, at times, be quite formidable. On the other hand, visits to Elsie's spontaneous and fun-loving family provided them with many happier and more relaxed times. During holidays, the MacMillans would stay at 'The Park,' the Keith's house at Lorne Park west of Toronto on Lake Ontario, or at their island cottage on Lake Nipissing near North Bay. They particularly enjoyed being with Elsie's mother, who was strong, friendly, and hospitable, traits she had passed on to her daughter.

In short, Ernest's happy family life enabled him to carry on his many professional activities in high gear. Only one of his talents got short shrift – after 1925 he stopped composing seriously, other than a few songs and works for special occasions. It is hard to fault him on this. Canadian composers in the 1920s and 1930s earned little if anything for their labours, and there was no community of composers to whom he could turn for artistic and moral support. Healey Willan, English Canada's only important composer in the 1920s, was really a transplanted Englishman who composed as an Englishman. In French Canada, the most prominent composer was Claude Champagne, whose career in some ways paralleled MacMillan's. His music was influenced by Franck, Fauré, and Debussy, and received some small recognition. Still less recognition was accorded Rodolphe Mathieu, another Quebec composer, whose Wagnerian roots evolved into a style that showed the influence of Schoenberg and Berg.[28] There was neither a nascent school of Canadian composing nor a public that showed any interest in having one. Such a fundamentally unreceptive environment, combined with his own doubts about his composing talent, convinced Ernest that he could do much more for music in Canada, and, by extension, for himself, by conducting, organ playing, and directing music schools.

He wrote only three major compositions. After *England* came his String Quartet in C Minor, which he had started in the fateful summer of 1914 and revised and completed in Toronto after the war. In 1924 he composed an orchestral overture. Each work has an independent voice – albeit written in a traditional mode – and all three had at least temporary importance at a time when there was little new music in Canada. The quartet, first performed in full by the Hart House Quartet on 8 February 1925, is probably his best work and stands up well among early twentieth-century quartets of the post-romantic school. It contains, first of all, exemplary string writing, unfailingly idiomatic for each instrument and for the quartet as a whole. The sonata-allegro form of the opening movement is easy to follow. The first violin plays a fast and virile theme which circulates among the other three instruments, and is nicely contrasted by the lyrical second theme. In the development section, there is a dialogue between the instruments, an engaging scherzando section, and a short four-part fugue in close stretto. Then an inventive triple-metre treatment of the first theme leads to an accelerando at the coda. Altogether, it is a good example of MacMillan's skilful use of imitation and contrapuntal techniques, changing harmonies, varying tempi, rhythms, accents, and occasional but effective use of pizzicato.

The second movement, a Scherzo, opens with a simple and racy main theme that moves capriciously from loud to soft to loud and from arco to pizzicato and back again. Its second theme, still happier, is tossed about by each of the instruments in very rapid fashion; the technical demands are such that the players must take the lead precisely on cue. The Scherzo is followed by a third movement in ternary form, which opens with a slow, poignant, and extremely heartfelt theme on the viola. The harmonies are fine-tuned and there is a good, if obvious, transition to the second theme, introduced by the cello. Perhaps the most touching moments in the quartet are in this movement's quiet conclusion, reminiscent of the second subject of the first movement. It sets the stage for the last movement's slow introduction by prefiguring some of the material to come.

The zestful fourth movement, the longest of the quartet, is the most complex. The Allegro – which follows a slow introduction that shows Debussy's influence – consists of much melodic imitation, emphatic accented rhythms, and veiled recollections of earlier themes. (Robin Elliott reminds us that MacMillan gave a lecture on Debussy at Ruhleben and that he was evidently familiar with Debussy's String Quartet.)[29] The momentum builds until the movement's exuberant close. The first three movements, written when Ernest was in his early twenties, are more spontaneous than the final one, which he wrote some seven years afterwards. Nevertheless, the work is all of a piece, well-crafted and conservative in outlook and style, as to be expected from a musician with his background.[30]

The twelve-minute Overture – sometimes called Concert Overture – was written at the request of Luigi von Kunits for performance by his New Symphony Orchestra, the forerunner of the Toronto Symphony Orchestra.[31] Von Kunits's Violin Concerto and the Overture were performed together on 7 May 1924 at Massey Hall. Ernest conducted the première of his Overture and Frank Welsman conducted the Concerto with von Kunits as soloist. Both works were well received.[32]

The Overture is straightforward and, like the quartet, traditional in style and content. The introduction begins with a pentatonic five-note motive, played *pianissimo* by the celli. It is then copied in turn by the other strings, the woodwinds, and the brass, followed by a loud climax with the full orchestra. Then, after a grand pause, the Allegro section begins. The trumpets introduce a vigorous tune based on the motive of the introduction, followed by a contrasting second subject in the lower strings and then in the violins. The development and recapitulation use the material well and the coda is a stirring reminder of the introduction. All in all, it is a colourful work, with a variety of moods and tempi and some attractive harmonic changes, clear evidence of the composer's skill. However, it lacks a certain spontaneity. Its harmonies and melodic sequences, and their development and resolution, are nearly always anticipated; the introduction is more suggestive than it should be of Delius and Debussy, and the Allegro is too derivative of Elgar and Wagner.

Overall, Ernest MacMillan was a sound composer who, with his limited output of songs, choral and orchestral music, and the quartet, could have provided, if he had continued writing, a bridge for other English-Canadian composers eager to escape from the typically British school of composition exemplified in Healey Willan's work. Eclectic, even derivative, he was, nonetheless, seeking a middle road between British conservatism and the avant garde that would have given the next generation of composers a little more pride in their past.

When conductor Allard de Ridder planned on doing the Overture twelve years later with the Vancouver Symphony, Ernest said, with his usual ambivalence, 'It is, I am afraid, not a very original work. [It is] partly designed to give all the principal players a chance to be heard. It comes off not badly in performance.'[33]

7. Conducting a Symphony Orchestra

As 1931 got under way there was no inkling that by year's end Ernest MacMillan would be the permanent conductor of the Toronto Symphony Orchestra (TSO), a post he would hold for twenty-five years. The year started out well when London's Royal College of Music, one of England's two most prominent music schools, honoured him with a fellowship, a distinction held by only fifty living British musicians, including at that time such luminaries as Elgar, Vaughan Williams, Holst, and Stokowski. Much was made of it in the Canadian press. (Ernest would receive similar recognition from the Royal Academy of Music, England's other leading music school, in 1938.) In April he conducted the TSO in a joint concert with the Conservatory Choir. It was not the first time – there had been annual joint performances for the past two years – but it was special because it included his Overture.

Ernest's only worry in an otherwise happy spring was his mother's health; she had chronic circulatory problems, and the prognosis was poor. In May, Elsie left for Brittany with Keith and Ross, now ten and seven respectively, and Ernest joined them a few weeks later, after attending to year-end conservatory concerts and examining in western Canada. Leaving the boys happily ensconced in Dinard, Ernest and Elsie took a sightseeing jaunt through the cathedral towns of Normandy and then went to Paris, Ernest's first time there since the fateful summer of 1914. Alexander MacMillan, all the while, was keeping Ernest posted on his mother's health. One of his letters reported a slight improvement and described how 'she keeps your letter under the pillow, and I hear her murmur occasionally, "dear old Dacey."'¹ Following the Paris visit, Ernest attended the two international music meetings which had brought him to Europe.

The first one, on contemporary music, was held in London and Oxford in late July. Reporting on it later, Ernest commended Britain's composers and singled out for special praise Constant Lambert's now forgotten *Music for Orchestra.* (He had done Lambert's *Rio Grande* with the TCM choir and the TSO the previous year.) Ernest was, however, less pleased with Gershwin's *An American in Paris*: 'Plenty of ingenious colourful noise with some humour, with not much claim to being big music, and much too long.'² Ernest never fully understood American jazz and its popular offshoots, although he did conduct *An American in Paris* on 4 February 1936 with the TSO, and never conducted *Music for Orchestra.* Chalk it up to changing – or maturing – taste.

Then he went on to an Anglo-American music education conference in Lausanne, where he headed up the Canadian delegation, chaired the harmony and counterpoint section, and, as pianist, shared a short recital with violinist Géza de Kresz, leader of the Hart House Quartet (and husband of Norah Drewett). To round off the summer, he and Elsie set out on a short motor trip through Scotland. Alas, the trip was cut short because of a car accident at Inverness – Ernest fractured his right arm and needed an operation to repair the damage. The arm remained in a cast for several months, not a salutary state of affairs for any conductor but particularly not for Ernest at that particular time, in view of what awaited him on his return to Canada.

On his first day back at the conservatory in September, he ran into a visibly ailing von Kunits, who looked at MacMillan's cast and exclaimed 'This is a year of calamities.'³ A few days later, the TSO, aware that von Kunits was very ill, booked MacMillan to conduct the first two concerts of the season – the opening one was to be on 27 October. According to TSO manager H.P. Elton, MacMillan delayed his acceptance because of his broken arm but changed his mind when Elton told him that Sir Henry Wood, the founder of London's Promenade Concerts and the New Queen's Hall Orchestra, had once had a similar injury at the beginning of a London season and had 'bravely' carried on.⁴

Von Kunits died on 8 October. Many felt the loss. He had an
aura about him – his Viennese background, his close association
with Brahms, with whom he had played chamber music in his
early years, his continental manners, his personal style, and his
knowledge of seven languages. The orchestra players had been
particularly devoted to him, not only for his musicianship but also
for his human qualities, and a number of the violinists had
studied with him. Henry Saunders, secretary of the TSO players'
committee, wrote on the orchestra's behalf to Mrs von Kunits and
the family, describing how 'lovingly and intelligently' he had
worked with them and how he had been 'always courteous, gentlemanly, well-informed, and inspiring at the conductor's desk.'[5]

Almost immediately after von Kunits's death, rumour had it
that MacMillan would be the TSO's next conductor. It seemed
logical, for he had already shown his worth by having successfully
conducted the TSO at Conservatory Choir concerts. He was also
well liked by the TSO board and its chairman Colonel Albert
Gooderham, who also chaired the conservatory board, and it was
common knowledge that von Kunits had liked him too. MacMillan's heir-apparent status seemed assured, but the actual succession had its rough moments.

On 23 October, four days before the first concert, the TSO
formally offered MacMillan the conductor's post. The salary was
modest, $2,000 per annum, but adequate, since MacMillan would
retain his post at the conservatory. He accepted without hesita-
tion.[6] The local press proudly noted that, although there had
been a number of other qualified applicants, including some
from the United States, MacMillan was clearly the best choice.
There had been only one other serious local contender, Reginald
Stewart.

A great deal went on behind the scenes between MacMillan's
acceptance and the first concert. Usually discreet, MacMillan
behaved remarkably out of character when he recklessly blurted
out his plans for the orchestra's future at a players' meeting – he
threatened to make changes in personnel and to shift concerts
from afternoons to evenings. Such talk was untimely and disrup-
tive, and the musicians reacted badly, for they were not only
apprehensive but also resentful of his high-handed manner.

There was talk, too, that MacMillan and his influential supporters had been undermining von Kunits for several years in order to pave the way for his ascendancy to the TSO's leadership. Some, unaware that von Kunits's illness had been terminal, even blamed MacMillan for indirectly causing his death![7] Although there was no truth in any of these allegations, Ernest was, undeniably, remarkably insensitive to the orchestra's background and to the grief of its members.

Von Kunits had started the New Symphony Orchestra in 1922 at the behest of two Toronto musicians, violinist Louis Gesensway and flutist Abe Fenboque. Both hoped that playing good symphonic music would give them some respite from the steady grind of playing commercial theatre music for silent movies and vaudeville shows. Together with von Kunits they assembled an orchestra and, after much rehearsing, gave their first one-hour 'twilight' concert in Massey Hall on 23 April 1923 at 5:00 p.m., the only free time the musicians had between theatre matinées and evening shows. The public was told only that the early hour would allow businessmen and office workers to attend and still get home in time for dinner! The major work at this first concert was Tchaikovsky's Symphony No. 5, the top price was 75 cents, and the hall was half full.

The New Symphony was a cooperative: the players managed it themselves and divided the profits. Von Kunits got ten shares per concert and the rank and file each got one, with the concertmaster and principals getting something in between. Since attendance was often poor and profits small or non-existent, the orchestra soon enlisted the aid of a women's committee, but to little avail. After five years, Albert Gooderham and a group of community-minded and wealthy patrons proposed taking broad command of the cooperative's policies and finances. The players agreed, the new board went on to secure the charter of the long-defunct Toronto Symphony, and, in 1927, the New Symphony Orchestra became the Toronto Symphony Orchestra. With the change in governance, orchestra members began taking a more serious approach to concert giving. And, by the end of the 1920s, musicians were beginning to *need* the symphonic work because sound movies were fast making theatre orchestras redundant.

Their troubles were soon compounded by the Great Depression, which was wreaking havoc in Canada as everywhere else – theatres were closing, concert-goers were dwindling in number, and parents were curtailing music lessons for their children.

And so, when MacMillan took over, the orchestra's future looked gloomy indeed, which explains in part the uneasiness over his ill-timed remarks. In attempting to repair the damage, he prepared a long letter of explanation, but that only exacerbated the situation, for, instead of backing off, he became mired in details.[8] He started out by saying that he was satisfied with the playing of three-quarters of the members but wanted to hear the remaining quarter as soon as possible. This upset the *entire* orchestra, even though the better players knew that dead wood *was* holding them back. Then he went on at great length to justify his plans, saying that he was 'the last person in the world to wish the end of the old orchestra,' and that he fully realized how the orchestra's very existence

depends upon a special esprit de corps which has led its members to make sacrifices of time and money on its behalf ... But it must be realized that now, as never before, the very existence of the orchestra depends upon its gaining more and more public support, and ... this will be forthcoming ... if we leave no stone unturned to maintain the highest possible standard of excellence ... I have accepted the position of conductor in a very humble spirit, and I realize that I cannot look for any personal loyalty among the members until I have earned it. But I think that I may appeal not in vain to the devotion of the members of the orchestra, for it has a fine tradition to live up to.

Dealing with the issue of evening concerts, he wrote: 'There seems to be an impression that a series of evening concerts has practically been arranged, and that those tied up ... in the evening will, *ipso facto*, be excluded from membership. In point of fact, we are unlikely to be able to give more than two or three evening concerts this season.' But he stood his ground in principle: 'I presume we all look forward to the time when evening concerts will become fully established, but everyone must realize that, without more adequate financial support, this is not within the realm of practical politics.' He offered to meet with the orchestra committee to discuss matters further but asked that the meeting not be held until after the first concert and that 'no hint of dissention ... reach the public in the meantime.' It worked – the orchestra committee met almost immediately and prudently decided to respect the wishes of its new leader.

In those few days before his first TSO concert, Ernest showed that he did not understand the orchestral world – he had not 'grown up' as part of it, he had little actual experience with an orchestra other than at Ruhleben, and he certainly didn't speak its language. Dropping players or even talking about doing so – von Kunits had always recoiled from the idea – was a delicate matter and required an understanding of the shattering effect such dismissals could have. Given the depression and the scarcity of jobs, Ernest should especially have shown more sensitivity. He would have to learn that working with professional instrumentalists was altogether different from working with students and amateur choristers, whom he could command with impunity. Although he exuded authority and leadership, he should have realized that he must first gain the respect and loyalty of the players before taking such drastic action. The stakes were high – he wanted to conduct the Toronto Symphony more than anything else he had ever done. Looking to the future, he hoped for a permanent orchestra composed of the best musicians available, all earning enough money to devote their full time to playing in it. He knew from the outset that this was the only way for the TSO to become first class.

MacMillan did eventually learn to deal more diplomatically and positively with the orchestra. But he had a bigger problem. At thirty-eight, he still had had no formal conducting training, had never before conducted a fully professional orchestra on a regular basis, and did not play an orchestral instrument well, although he knew the fundamentals of nearly all of them. His conducting of choral music had shown that he had the talent and temperament to capture music's excitement, romance, and colour, but he had much to learn about *orchestral* conducting.

And so the day of the first concert arrived. The printed program included a tribute from the players, praising von Kunits as 'a man of culture, at once wide and profound, and of a kindliness of heart of singular grace and power of attraction.' It described him as a conductor who 'knew how to correct without causing pain; to guide, without creating resentment. He was an exceptional leader, because he was an exceptional friend.'[9] Were they telling Ernest what they expected of *him*?

At the start of the concert, audience and players stood in silence for two minutes. Then the funeral march from Beethoven's *Eroica* Symphony was played, which brought on many tears. Beethoven's Eighth Symphony and Chopin's Piano Concerto No. 1, with Ernest Seitz as soloist, made up the program proper.[10] As hoped, the tensions between MacMillan and the players subsided, thanks in large measure to the success of the first concert. There were no further challenges to his leadership style, and he did go on to audition players and dismiss a few, without any regrets on his part.[11]

The TSO's pattern of concerts continued that first year much as in previous years. There were fifteen in all – eight twilight, four evening, including one benefit and one special, and three for schoolchildren. Orchestral discipline improved and there was more diverse programming. Despite his still limited repertoire, Ernest did six symphonies, mostly without score: Haydn's Ninety-fourth (the *Surprise*), Beethoven's Eighth, Schubert's Eighth (the *Unfinished*), Tchaikovsky's Fifth, Brahms's Second, and Sibelius's Second, its first Canadian performance. In addition, he conducted major suites by Bizet, Falla, Holst, Rimsky-Korsakov, and Borodin, and concertos and other full-scale works for soloist and orchestra by Chopin, Rachmaninoff, Mozart, Lalo, and Tchaikovsky. He led many short works too, some difficult to learn and still harder to conduct – a Rossini overture or a Strauss waltz can tax a conductor's technical skill as much as a Brahms symphony.

MacMillan loved and responded to the rich sound of the orchestra as he did to the sound of the organ. His lush and suspenseful interpretations of Wagner, Tchaikovsky, Strauss, and Sibelius stirred Torontonians as they had been stirred in the past by only a few visiting orchestras. Now it was their own orchestra that brought them, cheering, to their feet. The press echoed the public's sentiments, unequivocally praising Ernest's exciting personality, vitality, and interpretive skills.

His two all-Wagner concerts that year – he augmented the orchestra from sixty to eighty-three – drew special praise. Hector Charlesworth attended the first one in December 1931 and wrote:

The organization has definitely stepped up into the ranks of symphony orchestras of the first class ... Even at the dinner hour, the audience stood and recalled Dr. MacMillan again and again after the program concluded. His gift of rousing not only his players but his audience to an exalted enthusiasm was never more clearly demonstrated ... Dr. MacMillan rose to his greatest heights in the *Tristan* music. Its sublime passion was expressed with a breadth of emotional exaltation that stirred every listener to an extraordinary degree. The writer had never expected to hear a locally organized orchestra play this music so beautifully and with such complete authority.[12]

At the second Wagner concert in April, the audience was so appreciative that Pearl McCarthy of the *Mail and Empire* feared that the TSO's 'magnificent conductor might be drawn to some larger centre.'[13] After all, she implied, why would he want to stay in colonial, provincial Toronto, which had so little self-esteem? Most Torontonians took it as a given that fine artists would move on to greener pastures.

Ernest's special affection for Sibelius was evident early on. His interpretation of the Symphony No. 2 moved the impulsive Bridle to call it 'the greatest work of its kind written in this century.'[14] Mason, who liked to remind his readers how sophisticated and informed he was, said that the TSO's performance was infinitely better than the London Symphony Orchestra's, which he had heard the year before.[15]

One of the most difficult concerts for Ernest in his entire career came on 20 January; it was an evening performance with Reginald Stewart playing the Rachmaninoff Piano Concerto No. 2. Ernest was beside himself with worry. His young son Ross was critically ill with a streptococcus infection and mastoiditis, and his mother was dying. Nevertheless, he proceeded with the concert and, as soon as it was over, dashed to her bedside. Ross soon recovered but Winnie died later that night. The orchestra sent Ernest its condolences, for which he thanked them: 'Probably most of you were aware that I was working under unusual strain. I felt throughout that every member was doing his or her best to support me and it was a wonderful inspiration. If, as I am told, the concert was an unusual success, every member deserves an unusual share of credit.'[16]

By the end of the first MacMillan season it was clear that, while von Kunits's memory was cherished, the TSO was now in more competent hands. Its players were growing to appreciate MacMillan for his remarkable musicianship, control, memory, and knowledge, and for the new vistas he was opening for them. As for MacMillan, he had found his true *métier*. *Saturday Night* spoke for all of the press when it attributed the TSO's 'most brilliant season in its history' to his 'amazing power' over musicians and audiences.[17] MacMillan's short message in the final printed program of the season showed what a firm grasp he had on the orchestra's future:

In the last analysis it is the public that decides whether a symphony orchestra shall exist in any community, and Toronto is no exception to that rule. The foundations of the orchestra must be laid on the broadest possible basis; ideally every citizen should feel that he or she has a definite and material interest in the orchestra as a civic and communal asset of the first rank.

Our future depends upon the orchestra itself, upon the conductor, upon the directorate and the women's committee – who have in the past given so fully of their time, their good advice – and upon all members and non-members of the orchestra who are contributing so generously to our funds. But above all, the future of the orchestra depends upon the public. If Toronto wants an orchestra she shall have one. In fact, she will have, broadly speaking, the kind of orchestra she demands – provided that the demand is backed by practical interest and support ... In spite of the world-wide depression we are looking to the future with confidence.[18]

Yes, in September 1931 Ernest MacMillan had been the right person in the right place at the right time. And, significantly, the orchestra's finances took a turn for the better under his leadership. The year before he took over, the twilight and school concerts had a deficit of $4,500, but, in 1931–2, the same number of concerts brought in a profit of $400. The school concerts had also improved in quality – Ernest took them very seriously from the outset, as one might expect given the importance he placed on musical education for the young.

Gooderham and Elton generously praised him at the TSO's annual meeting on 8 June 1932. Thanks to the season's success the board agreed to augment the orchestra to about eighty-five players and to increase the number of rehearsals for each concert from three to four. (The two all-Wagner concerts had each had a larger orchestra and four rehearsals, and their excellence had greatly impressed the board.) And, finally, twilight concerts were to be dropped.

As promising as Ernest's first year with the TSO had been, building an orchestra during the Great Depression was, no doubt, a larger task than he had reckoned on. The city had a shaky orchestral tradition, a limited number of good orchestral players, and a conservative public. Financing the orchestra had been a problem even in the prosperous 1920s; now the depression was providing the generally stingy Toronto rich with ready excuses not to support it. Furthermore, major companies such as Eaton's preferred funding *amateur* music organizations and drama festivals. Vincent Massey, scion of one of Canada's wealthiest families, was one of the few to understand and work to alleviate the plight of the orchestra.[19] He succeeded Gooderham as TSO president in October 1932 and did yeoman service for the TSO during his three-year term. Because of him, the Massey Foundation gave a $5,000 grant to the orchestra in 1932 and was a substantial contributor from then on.

Massey took on the urgent task of saving the acoustically superb Massey Hall, which was in disrepair and slated for demolition. His grandfather had given it to the city, and he now represented the family on the hall's board of trustees. MacMillan's success with the TSO and the promise it held for increased revenues helped to convince the trustees to renovate the forty-year-old building. Since Toronto's civic authorities refused to fund the renovations, the Massey Foundation provided the needed $40,000 as well as $8,000 to clear up outstanding loans and overdue interest payments. An improved Massey Hall reopened in the fall of 1933. It had an enlarged lobby and a new balcony foyer, and its seating was reduced from an unwieldy 3,500 to 2,765.[20]

When needed, Massey took a hands-on approach to his responsibilities as TSO president. For example, a month after taking office, he managed to get the work shift of postal employee R.H. Lodge changed from afternoons and evenings to late nights and early mornings. Why? Because principal oboist Lodge needed both jobs to make ends meet.[21] MacMillan and Massey developed a warm relationship which continued for three decades. Both men sought advice from the other on a wide variety of musical and cultural matters.

Ernest started his second TSO season with a complimentary concert at which he conducted samples of works to be included in the new ten-concert *evening* subscription series. Lawrence Mason, for one, was delighted with the turnout and with the sight and sound of the enlarged orchestra under the 'magnetic baton' of Ernest MacMillan.[22] In keeping with the orchestra's 'new look,' the players wore full formal dress. Women string players were relegated to inside positions so as not to upset the frontal appearance of the orchestra.[23] Massey explained to the audience that the one-hour twilight concerts had been dropped because their brevity had inhibited the inclusion of major works. (He said nothing about his hope that this time change would increase ticket sales.) Then he paid 'high tribute' to MacMillan, pointing out even more explicitly than McCarthy had the year before that 'the best way to keep in Canada an internationally eminent musician like Dr. MacMillan is to support an orchestra worthy of his steel.'

Another speaker at this complimentary concert was City Controller James Simpson, who spoke on behalf of the mayor (no doubt the mayor had more pressing affairs). Simpson sidestepped the issue of civic government support by asking the *audience* to support its orchestra. Toronto Board of Education representative A.M. Plumptre stressed the importance of children's concerts and the 'value of the orchestra in upholding standards of execution and taste for the schools.' In her far-sighted view, the concerts helped train children 'for leisure as well as for work ... and opened the gateway of beauty to the temple of happy and fully rounded living.' These good words did not alter the fact that the board of education did not fund the TSO children's concerts. Finally, TSO board member Rabbi M.N. Eisendrath of the prominent Holy Blossom Synagogue, one of the few Jews on any local cultural board, reminded the audience that, historically speaking, 'every nation's permanently significant contribution to human progress has been in spiritual values always, not in material things.' The orchestra, he said, 'was helping to melt all the city's diverse elements into a modern cosmopolitan community.'[24]

That season, Ernest, prudently, did mostly well-known works, including Franck's Symphony in D Minor and Brahms's Symphony No. 1. He was more adventurous with Bach, programming the *Second Brandenburg Concerto*, the Concerto for Two Pianos, with the young Canadian pianists Scott Malcolm and Reginald Godden, and several transcriptions of keyboard works and chorales. Bach was no favourite with symphonic audiences, but Ernest cleverly mixed Bach's works with more popular ones. Other major pieces that season were Elgar's *Enigma Variations*, Strauss's *Death and Transfiguration*, and two Tchaikovsky symphonies, No. 4 and No. 5. Except for a few mainstream contemporary works – Bloch's Concerto Grosso, short pieces by Holst, Delius, and Vaughan Williams, and Ravel's *Bolero* (always a hit) – short shrift was given to twentieth-century music. Ernest did give the North American premiere of a slightly abbreviated version of George Dyson's *Canterbury Pilgrims* for orchestra and chorus, but it received a poor reception – the music was nondescript and Chaucer's text failed to get through to the audience. Not one Canadian or American work was done.

It was at an all-Wagner concert in December 1932 that Ernest pulled off a feat that TSO musicians talked about for years. In cellist John Adaskin's words:

During one memorable performance we were to do the Overture or Vorspiel to *Parsifal* by Wagner. We didn't know the work and Wagner must have hated conductors when he wrote it because after five bars of a slow 4/4, the woodwinds are marked 6/4 while the rest of the orches-

tra stays in 4/4. Had it been a faster movement the problem could have
been overcome by beating a slow two. Those in 4/4 would count two to
a beat and those in 6/4 would count three to a beat. Unfortunately, the
movement is marked *sehr langsam* and of course we fell apart after the
sixth bar. Undaunted by mere technical difficulties, MacMillan said, 'all
players in 4/4 follow my right hand. All players in 6/4 follow my left
hand.'[25]

It was reminiscent of his work at Nass River, and the orchestra,
quite dumbfounded by this virtuoso display of rhythmic coordination and control, followed him without difficulty.

One improvement that year was the introduction of program
notes by Ernest's soon-to-be brother-in-law Ettore Mazzoleni.
'Mazz,' as he was known to family and friends, and Winifred
MacMillan were married in June 1933. He had studied at Oxford
and the Royal College of Music before coming to Toronto in
1929 to teach English at Upper Canada College and, later, music
history and conducting at the conservatory. He took over the conservatory orchestra after von Kunits died, and deputized for Ernest at the TSO from time to time. Mazz had an excellent baton
technique, which some thought surpassed Ernest's. He was slight
of stature with handsome, chiselled features and dark hair, and
had much personal charm, although, unfortunately, he could
often be biting and sarcastic with subordinates.

TSO fund-raising continued – modestly – during that second
season. In the 20 February 1933 program there was an 'S.O.O.S.
– Save Our Own Symphony' section, which pointed out that the
New York Philharmonic had raised $80,000 in three weeks, a sum
which would have carried the TSO for four years! The notice
implored readers to contribute so that the TSO could reach its
target of $20,000 – which it did. Happily, three concerts that year
were broadcast by the Canadian Radio Broadcasting Commission
(later the CBC). This gave the TSO wide exposure and generated
additional revenue for the orchestra and extra pay – $150 on
average – for the players.

MacMillan's second TSO season closed with a flourish: two
Beethoven symphonies, the Ninth (with the Conservatory Choir
and local soloists) and the First. Edward Wodson mirrored the

audience's enthusiasm when he called the concert 'the crowning triumph of a season overflowing with orchestral delights ... The orchestra played as though inspired and possessed of technique and unity that knew no bounds in the art of expression ... Dr. Ernest MacMillan is one of the greatest orchestral directors on this continent.[26]

8. The Depression Years

The Great Depression did not hit Toronto as hard as other Canadian cities. Nor did it have much impact on MacMillan's personal well-being. Like others with a steady income, he saw the drop in consumer prices by as much as 30 per cent make his own money go even further. The plight of the nation, with its relief lines and soup kitchens, its homeless and hungry, its protest demonstrations and pitched battles, did, however, affect his world of music enough to impede its growth for the entire decade.

In 1930 Toronto and its suburbs had a population of about 850,000, predominantly Anglo-Saxon and Celt, but with a substantial number of Chinese, Germans, Ukrainians, Italians, and Jews. Materially, it was clean, comfortable, and well-run. But its cultural life, although healthier than the rest of English Canada's, was developing only very slowly, and many felt that Toronto would never create artistic groups of international calibre. Torontonians still had a very colonial attitude. They lacked confidence in themselves and, by extension, in their artists, and looked to visiting performers for true quality. They believed that local professional groups should pay their own way, that the performing arts were a frill and a luxury for the few, not a necessity for the many, and that supporting them should go no further than the price of an admission ticket. Most professional musicians were managing to survive, but aspiring actors and dancers had to move to the United States or abroad, since there were no Canadian professional companies to employ them with any regularity.

The city *was* rich in amateur choirs. In addition to church choirs there were a number of good secular ones – the Mendelssohn Choir, the Toronto Conservatory Choir, Reginald Stewart's Toronto Bach Society, Healey Willan's Tudor Singers, the Jewish Folk Choir, and the Hart House Glee Club. For opera, there were the Toronto Opera Guild and the Canadian Grand Opera Association. Both were formed in 1936 and consisted of a mixture of professionals and semi-professionals who gave sporadic and often threadbare performances (the conservatory had stopped its productions). The Eaton Operatic Society, which performed at its own Eaton Auditorium, did Gilbert and Sullivan operettas.

The Hart House String Quartet, handsomely supported by the Massey Foundation, was clearly the best of the chamber music ensembles. Others included the Conservatory String Quartet, Samuel Hersenhoren's New World Chamber Orchestra, and Mona Bates's Ten Piano Ensemble. As for full-scale orchestras, there were, in addition to the TSO, Reginald Stewart's Promenade Symphony Concerts orchestra, founded in 1934 and composed mainly of TSO players, and the Conservatory Symphony, heavily augmented for concerts by freelance and TSO musicians.

Toronto took considerable pride in the Toronto Symphony Orchestra. Its conductor was as close to being a household name as any Canadian musician of the day, and its concerts attracted followers from all classes and nationalities.[1] Unfortunately, the orchestra needed more than enthusiastic audiences – it needed money to help pay its players more, lengthen its season, expand its repertoire, and engage more and better guest soloists. Its board was notably inept at fund-raising, and Toronto's civic government, unlike those of most North American cities, refused, out of hand, to grant funds to the TSO. And, since a good deal of Toronto's – and Canada's – corporate wealth was in foreign hands, Canadian subsidiaries often had to get head office approval to help the arts in their communities, and this was not always forthcoming. It was, therefore, money, or rather the lack of it, and not artistic excellence, that drove TSO policy. If it had not been for its admirable women's committee, which raised money by any and all means possible – ticket drives, rummage sales – the orchestra would have been in dire straits indeed.

The TSO, in order to develop a greater appreciation of sym-

phonic music and widen its audience base for the future, turned
its attention to children's concerts. MacMillan, following closely
on the heels of the American conductor Walter Damrosch, believed that children, if properly exposed to symphonic music,
would develop a love for it which would continue into adult life.
Accordingly, he directed three to five children's concerts annually, for which children paid twenty-five cents a concert, a tidy sum
for many families, although not enough to cover the orchestra's
expenses even when a concert was sold out.[2] Toronto's Board of
Education was less than cooperative, despite the great interest
and support of its music director Emily Tedd. The board not only
paid nothing towards the concerts but also, in its wisdom, would
not allow children to attend them during school hours, thereby
forcing the TSO to schedule them at the awkward time of 4:15
p.m. The board did, however, make one concession: the TSO's
women's committee, who managed the concerts, could advertise
and sell tickets in the schools. In fact, the very existence of the
children's concerts depended on the women's committee. There
were no children's concerts in 1935–6 because the women's committee had temporarily disbanded.[3]

Ernest worked hard to make these concerts successful. Knowing
that children have limited attention spans, he carefully chose
short works, preferably ones with a story that he could relate from
the podium in direct and simple language to help the children
focus on what they would hear. Excerpts from Tchaikovsky's
Nutcracker Suite, Saint-Saëns's *Carnival of the Animals* and *Danse
macabre*, and Dukas's *Sorcerer's Apprentice* were favourites. Yet few
knew better than Ernest that a formal concert in a large concert
hall, no matter how attractive the program and engaging the
commentary, is a difficult way to introduce good music to children. Wisely, he abandoned printed programs early on because
mischief-loving youngsters crafted paper planes from them and
launched them with ever-increasing skill from Massey Hall's balco-
nies to the main floor, distracting audiences and orchestra alike.[4]

And then, in December 1935, Ernest launched a new kind of
concert. It all began when TSO manager Jack Elton (son of H.P.
Elton) and several TSO musicians asked him to put on a special
Christmas concert that would include both seasonal music and 'a

certain amount of spoof.' They also suggested that Ernest dress
as Santa Claus to appear 'more human.' (He was becoming more
rotund in his forties, especially around the middle.) The musicians agreed to donate their services if the profits went to a special Players' Benefit Fund, and it was this that convinced Ernest
– if he needed convincing – to proceed.[5]

Such was the genesis of what became the annual 'Christmas
Box' concerts. They may not have been Ernest MacMillan's finest
conducting hours but they were certainly his funniest. This was
where his thespian talents took flight and where both children
and adults split their sides at his antics and at those of his musicians – a supporting cast who, like their zany conductor, abandoned their customary dignity to become uninhibited comedians
on the stage of Massey Hall.

Typically, the first half of a Christmas Box program would be
quite orthodox, with the last number before intermission acting
as a tipoff for what was ahead. Anything could happen in the
second half – and often did. Lawrence Mason, not noted for his
frivolity, reported that the first Christmas Box provided 'a laugh
a minute and the audience was rocked dizzy.'[6] The first half
wound up with Haydn's *Farewell* Symphony. During its last few
minutes, the players left the stage one by one, leaving the conductor alone and sound asleep. The second half included com-
poser-violinist Murray Adaskin rivalling the Marx Brothers at their
best with his *Impromptu* ('Concerto in Assorted Keys').[7]

The TSO boldly planned more fun for the next Christmas Box,
and it went from good to better or bad to worse, depending on
one's point of view. Augustus Bridle, who wrote in superlatives
compulsively, might be trusted when he said that the TSO 'improvised the jolliest musical show ever done here by professional
musicians disguised as amateur funmakers.'[8] In introducing
Haydn's *Surprise* Symphony, Ernest told the packed house that he
dreaded what was coming next, and with good reason. All was as
usual until the second movement, when a sudden *sforzando* from
the percussion, following a clearly ominous and excessively whis-
pered *pianissimo*, literally knocked four violinists right out of their
seats. From then on various instruments and sections brashly
interrupted the music's flow, as did 'Mae West,' the sultry movie

idol of the day played by TSO violinist Lillian Sparling, who moved seductively across the stage enticing a good many of the male members of the orchestra to follow her backstage. The helpless conductor did his best amid all of this confusion, only to be struck down at the end with a 'Stradivarius' violin and carried off on a stretcher playing his tin whistle – 'a martyr to symphonic duty.'[9]

The broad slapstick humour of the first years continued for some time and, according to Ernest, 'became crazier and crazier.'

Beethoven, I am glad to say, was spared, for he does not lend himself to burlesque, but we were able to include such numbers as '1812 and All That' and 'The Bolero to End All Boleros' – opening with Ravel's persistent rhythm on a noisy typewriter, including tap dancers, and ending with a rivetting machine and 'William Tells All' ... We seized on Mossolov's *Iron Foundry*, with its realistic reproduction of factory noises, to give a performance in which the entire orchestra was dressed in dungarees. I conducted with a monkey-wrench and started the playing by pulling a large switch. At the end, a factory whistle blew and the players knocked off work and opened lunch boxes, the contents of which were consumed on stage; our principal cellist, Leo Smith, kindly shared a banana with me.[10]

In later years there were more sophisticated Boxes – ones which anticipated Hoffnung and P.D.Q. Bach. Ernest's music appreciation lecture in 1950, entitled 'John Sebastian is Back,' brought down the house. Garbed in an academic gown and mortar board and sporting a severe-looking beard to enhance his dignity and impress the audience with the seriousness of the occasion, the straight-faced Ernest took issue with the learned Dr. Otto Pflumpheimer, who 'in that popular treatise "A Brief Prolegomenon upon Polyphonic Coordination" ... remarks that "Ordinary interchange of parts by an octave does not alter the roots of a harmonic structure, but a properly managed Double Counterpoint at the twelfth produces two markedly different harmonic effects besides changing the expressive ethos of the shifting theme."'

Ernest then reproached Dr Pflumpheimer for limiting his

research to the vertical shifting of themes. 'I myself spent a whole morning shifting themes from one corner of my study to another and spent the rest of the day carrying them from cellar to attic and vice versa, after which I carried them from attic to cellar and versa vice. Having done so, I downed a litre or two of beer, played through the 198 church cantatas of old John Sebastian Bach, and settled down to a good evening's work.' Still on the subject of 'shifting themes' – in a way – he went on to give a hilarious – and legendary – account of the origins of that popular tune of the day 'Good Night Irene, Good Night.' He related how it came from Bach's 'magnificent choralvorspiel "Gute Nacht, du Welt, Gute Nacht" – Good Night, Thou World, Good Night – the opening chorus of Cantata No. 165.'

It is not unlikely that this cantata was written ... in the spring of 1736, shortly after the birth of Bach's eighteenth child. It may be that the infant had just begun to add its voice to the general domestic polyphony, or perhaps one of the older olive branches had distracted his father's attention by climbing to the roof of the Thomaskirche in search of pigeons' eggs. Whatever the truth of the matter may be, there is a certain suggestion of agitation in the mood of this chorus.[11]

He went on and on, with impertinent musical excerpts interrupting his learned disquisition at appropriate and inappropriate moments until, finally, the whole orchestra rose up and played 'Good Night Irene.'

Another great hit was 'Wagnerian Lighter Motives,' which starred that madcap spoofer Anna Russell. She did three Christmas Boxes with Ernest in the 1940s and credits him with inspiring her 'musical' career. Above all, she admired his sense of timing, so indispensable to any comedian.[12]

Returning to the depression years, public-spirited Ernest Mac-Millan helped Toronto celebrate its hundredth anniversary in April 1934, by serving as chairman of the city's music and pageantry committee. The TSO, as befitted a civic institution (even though civic authorities did nothing for it), gave a resoundingly successful commemorative concert on 17 April at Massey Hall.

Wagner excerpts in the first half were followed by Beethoven's
Ninth, with the 200-voice Conservatory Choir. Then on 2 July at
the Canadian National Exhibition's grandstand on Toronto's lake-
shore, Ernest conducted a pageant, 'Milestones of a Century,' for
massed choir and philharmonic band. The fifty-year-old grandstand, built for elaborate variety shows, was filled to its 15,000-seat
capacity, with thousands more standing in the paddock and on
the lawn.[13] (It was a notoriously poor place to listen to music because of Lake Ontario's unpredictable winds.)

Evidently Ernest was having one of his sporadic bouts with
kidney stones, but he insisted on carrying on. When he mounted
the podium, the huge audience, knowing the pain he was in, gave
him a standing ovation. The pageant began with Ernest's own
arrangement of 'O Canada' followed by 'Hail Bright Abode' from
Tannhäuser, Beethoven's *Creation Hymn,* and several songs. Later,
the chorus and band combined forces with a troupe of flag-wavers
for another MacMillan creation, 'Hail to Toronto.' He had composed it expressly for the occasion, and the less said the better![14]
The choir (the *Star* said 1,000-strong, the *Mail and Empire* said
2,000) sang on a specially erected platform but, as expected, was
barely audible.[15] Years later Ernest admitted that he remembered
little of what happened that evening.[16] One wonders if he
shouldn't have put his time and energy to better use, but he still
hadn't learned to say no.

As for Ernest's more serious endeavours, in early 1935 he conducted the TSO in a concert of truly genuine merit honouring
three leading British composers – Gustav Holst, Edward Elgar,
and Frederick Delius. All three had died the previous year. Ernest
was partial to their music (his musical education, lest we forget,
was English to the core) and wrote a thoughtful and admirably
lucid essay about them.[17] Holst, he wrote, was the 'less exalted ...
His faults lie on the surface – notably a lack of consistency of
style. He tends now towards polytonality, now towards the extreme simplicity of folk song; he borrows his inspiration now from
a pseudo-orientalism, now from the Christian mystics, now from
Calvinistic psalmody.' On the other hand, Ernest countered, Holst
had a 'brilliant sense of instrumental and choral effect and the
intangible quality known as atmosphere.'

Next he turned to Elgar – he had been present when Elgar had conducted his Second Symphony in London the previous summer, his last public appearance. MacMillan called Elgar the British Empire's 'unofficial Musician Laureate' and defended his imperialistic attitude, which makes 'a profound appeal to the imagination and gives birth to noble conceptions.' It is 'too fundamental to be lightly dismissed, and no one can question its sincerity.' Ernest said that 'a mood of exaltation is natural' to Elgar, a devout Catholic; like all truly religious composers 'he had no need of writing *religioso* over particular passages, and his frequent use of ... *nobilmente* has in it none of the self-consciousness one might suspect in another ... One has only to think of the "Nimrod" Variation from the *Enigma* or the slow movement of the *Piano Quintet.*'

Lastly, Ernest addressed Delius. He pointed out the keen and perceptive harmonic sense and charm of his music and observed that he was 'something of the inspired amateur ... he ignores rather than defies many accepted methods of procedure, but unlike the ordinary amateur, he is never clumsy. He has the rare faculty of securing continuity; his music flows in a stream like that of Bach, though he secures this onward urge rather by harmonic than by contrapuntal texture; his music has in fact something of the nature of supremely fine improvisation.' Delius, Ernest believed, was at his best in forms 'which do not call for highly organized treatment.' He predicted that he would never be a very popular composer because his music is 'aristocratic in spirit and utterly lacking in sensationalism.'

The beautifully balanced concert began with Elgar's *Prologue to the Apostles*, with the Conservatory Choir assisting, followed by Delius's *Brigg Fair*, and then 'Mars,' 'Mercury,' and 'Jupiter' from Holst's *The Planets*. After intermission came Delius's musical setting of the Walt Whitman poem *Sea Drift*, with the English baritone John Goss as soloist (Goss later settled in Canada), and Elgar's *Enigma Variations*. Ernest conducted the entire program without score, and Goss, despite a cold, reached great heights in *Sea Drift*. The audience loved both the mysterious and evocative *Planets* and the romantic *Enigma*. As an encore, Ernest did – what else? – Elgar's 'Land of Hope and Glory.'

Without detracting from the concert's excellence, it is fair to say that its public success was in part due to English Canada's lingering view of itself as a cultural appendage to Britain. Yet, in fact, by the mid-1930s England's musical influence was beginning to wane while American influence, because of films and radio, was growing. Canadians were attending American music schools in increasing numbers, were staying on to build their careers in the United States, and were signing up with New York concert agencies, joining American orchestras, and singing in American opera companies. Canada's artistic ambivalence might only be resolved if its artists became less dependent on both countries. Still, many of Canada's English-speaking musicians looked to Britain for guidance and direction and to a large extent the public still believed that Canada's musical efforts, however good and well-meaning, were bound to be inferior to those of the old country.

By 1935 Ernest MacMillan had come to realize that the TSO, despite all of his efforts, was not a very good orchestra. Its violins were first class, but other sections – especially the winds and brass – ranged from ordinary to poor. And some instrumentalists were hard to come by in Toronto. Anglican minister C.V. Pilcher was Toronto's sole bass clarinettist, there was only one bassoonist of sufficient merit to play regularly (a cello often had to fill in on second bassoon parts), and mention has been made of the postal employee who was the orchestra's principal oboist.

The answer was to import players from elsewhere, but the TSO lacked the funds and the local musicians' union had stringent import regulations. The more Ernest heard other orchestras the more he wanted new and better players in the TSO. Luckily, local players of the first rank did appear from time to time. Nineteen-year-old Mary Robb, for one, was appointed principal horn in 1939 and, despite her youth, she compared favourably with top players in the United States and Britain. The year she was appointed, she married her horn teacher and TSO colleague Reginald Barrow. Ernest was organist at their wedding and, as a surprise, played his own improvised medley of orchestral horn solos, from Strauss to Mozart to Brahms.[18]

But finding good wind and brass players was only part of the problem. The repertoire, too, was too conservative. The TSO depended heavily on box-office revenues and, accordingly, Mac-Millan programmed mainly familiar eighteenth-, nineteenth-, and early-twentieth-century music. The few contemporary works were almost exclusively mainstream English. William Walton's music was actually considered too advanced! Notable for their absence were Schoenberg, Berg, and Webern, French composers later than Debussy and Ravel, and Hindemith, Prokofiev, and Shostakovich. For a while Ernest even passed up works by Rachmaninoff and Respighi, which later were sure-fire crowd pleasers. And he did very little American or Canadian music.

Ernest was no different from most conductors working with North American orchestras at the time. His favourite symphonic composers were Beethoven and Brahms, followed by Mozart, Schubert, Mendelssohn, Wagner, Franck, Tchaikovsky, and Sibelius. He did Franck's Symphony in D Minor seven times from 1931 to 1940, more times than any other symphony. According to subscriber polls it was the most popular. In the same period there were five performances each of Tchaikovsky's Fifth, Brahms's First, Beethoven's Fifth, and Sibelius's Second, and four each of Beethoven's Ninth and Tchaikovsky's Fourth and Sixth. It should be remembered that these large works were still comparatively new to Toronto's musical public. For variety, MacMillan programmed tone poems and overtures by Smetana, Rimsky-Korsakov, Debussy, and Ravel. The most popular shorter works were Wagner's *Die Meistersinger Prelude* (nine times), Tchaikovsky's *Nutcracker Suite* (seven), and Mozart's *Marriage of Figaro Overture*, Tchaikovsky's *Romeo and Juliet Overture*, and Sibelius's *Finlandia* (five each). Pleasing the public, however, wasn't everything. MacMillan boldly gave an all-Sibelius concert in 1935 to mark the composer's seventieth birthday. Sibelius was considered *very* modern.

It was disappointing that the TSO had only a few guest conductors in the 1930s. Although some blamed this on MacMillan's fear of competition, the overriding reason was lack of money. But even Toronto's charismatic and relatively inexpensive Reginald Stewart only conducted the TSO twice: a complete concert in

1933 and part of a concert in 1938. Perhaps the TSO management thought that Stewart was already overexposed to Toronto
audiences through his summertime Promenade Symphony Concerts at Varsity Arena and the Toronto Bach Choir's annual performances of the *St John Passion*. Furthermore, since many TSO
players worked with him, he could not provide the lift to the
orchestra that usually comes from guest conductors.

Other guests in the mid-1930s were Adrian Boult and Igor
Stravinsky. On 5 January 1937, Stravinsky did his *Firebird* and
Petrouchka suites (MacMillan conducted Brahms's Symphony No.
4 before intermission on the same program). Heinz Unger was
another guest. He had conducted in his native Germany and in
the Soviet Union, was now living in England, and would feature
more in MacMillan's life in the years to come. He shared a long
and demanding concert with MacMillan in November 1937. Unger
conducted the Berlioz *Symphonie fantastique* (its first performance
in Toronto since 1908) and the Mozart *Haffner* Symphony, and
MacMillan conducted the Tchaikovsky Violin Concerto with soloist
Mishel Piastro, concert-master of the New York Philharmonic.

MacMillan reported to Arthur Judson, Unger's New York manager, that Unger had given a 'superb' performance but that he
needed to adapt better to the limited rehearsal time allotted
North American orchestras. Unger had three rehearsals but had
wanted more, since the Berlioz is an especially demanding work
even for a virtuoso orchestra, which the TSO decidedly was not.
MacMillan also mentioned that Unger tended to talk too much
at rehearsals. He closed his letter by stating that it was 'a genuine
pleasure to have him here. Piastro will bear me out.'[19]

What MacMillan didn't tell Judson was the extraordinary reception public and press had given Unger. The audience 'cheered,
whistled, and stamped' at the conclusion of the Berlioz, and
Unger was recalled for bows five times.[20] Charlesworth wrote that
Unger had 'outstanding gifts ... His mastery of detail is amazing
and his beat authoritative and exacting ... He feels deeply every
nuance and has the faculty of making his musicians and auditors
feel them also.' He also raved about Unger's Mozart, 'exquisite
in detail and broad lyrical utterance.'[21] Wodson called Unger a
'miracle worker.' The TSO 'played as it had never played before

... It was a new orchestra – an orchestra utterly forgetful of the limiting adhesions of localism, an orchestra fired with an enthusiasm that matched its splendid technique.'[22] The grateful Unger thanked MacMillan profusely for having given him his first conducting engagement in North America.[23]

There were four guest conductors the next season, 1938–9, a clear departure from past practice, but not setting a trend since there were special circumstances in each case. The visit of Hans Kindler, conductor of the National Symphony, was by way of an exchange for a visit by MacMillan to Washington. The Rumanian composer, conductor, and violinist Georges Enesco conducted only part of a concert, at which he was also soloist. Similarly, the Czech conductor Henry Svoboda, in North America seeking refuge from his German-occupied country (as were many other European musicians), also conducted only part of a concert – several Czech works. And there was again Heinz Unger (now thinking of settling in Canada), who conducted a special concert. If MacMillan was jealous of Unger, as some suspected, then why had he invited him again, and to do a whole concert at that? In any event, Unger did a long and strenuous program: Brahms's Fourth Symphony in the first half and Wagner's *Siegfried's Rhine Journey*, Tchaikovsky's *Romeo and Juliet* Overture, and Liszt's *Les Préludes* in the second.

This time the press praised Unger even more. Mason wrote that 'the distinguished European visitor made the orchestra sing divinely' in the Brahms and the playing generally was 'taut, clean, unanimous, and sensitively responsive to the conductor's masterly leading.'[24] The elated Wodson called the TSO 'a recreated orchestra, marvellously quickened and inspired, using resources of tone and power and shade and rhythmic expression unsuspected before ... a sort of miracle.'[25] Following the concert, there was a lavish dinner reception in honour of Unger which was attended by Toronto's moneyed elite. Unger then returned to England.

Ernest MacMillan's years at the Toronto Conservatory of Music were characterized by administrative ups and downs, successes and failures, and a few persistent headaches. Because of his work at the TSO and his efforts to develop his own conducting career, or because the work at the TCM was simply not very interesting, he may not have given enough time to his duties as principal. It was a difficult balancing act and he worked hard to pull it off, for he did run the school, and, in the main, ran it well. He made the conservatory's ten-grade system and its 'practical' and 'written' requirements leading to the associateship more orderly and viable. He also revised the piano examination syllabus, stiffened its concomitant theory and ear-training requirements, and, in time, produced an excellent and pedagogically sound ear-training manual for examination candidates.[26] To underline the importance of ear training, he explained that it awakens the student's perceptive faculties and establishes in his mind 'a close association between the sounds and the symbols of music ... as natural in the case of music as it is with words ... We should learn to hear with our eyes – form an aural picture of the music from the printed page – and see with our ears – see imaginatively on paper the music we hear.' He admitted that some students have better ears than others, but few exploit their ears to capacity, and this often leads frustrated instructors to teach mechanically. MacMillan's outlook on this important branch of music study had a beneficial and lasting impact at the conservatory.

There were important administrative changes at the school in 1935. Sir Albert Gooderham, TCM chairman, had died and was succeeded by the well-known philanthropist Colonel Fred Deacon. Deacon shook up the conservatory's board and appointed several new members, including Floyd Chalmers, editor of the *Financial Post*. Assigned to head up the board's finance committee, Chalmers implemented sweeping economies in the school's operation and successfully persuaded the Province of Ontario to grant the Conservatory $15,000 to alleviate one of the school's periodic financial crises.[27]

Next, the new board tackled Healey Willan, who had been vice-principal since 1920. According to Chalmers, Willan had a long record of refusing to deal with 'trivial problems by locking himself in his studio and refusing to answer knocks on the door or rings of his telephone. His secretary was instructed to bring him no mail or problems. He spent his time – profitable for posterity – on composing.'[28] (Godfrey Ridout, a student of Willan's, remembered Willan's office as 'absolute chaos.') [29] It was an untenable situation, and, after much soul-searching, the board, using the pretext that it had to save money, eliminated the position of vice-principal and gave Willan a full year's salary as compensation. Willan did, however, remain at the university as organist and professor. Not unexpectedly, the MacMillan-Willan friendship cooled, but only for a short time.

Conservatory faculty member Norman Wilks was made executive officer – a new position. Wilks, who had won a Military Cross in the Great War, was an excellent administrator and far more interested in running the conservatory than Willan had been. As Ridout recalled, Wilks 'gave the impression, when you went to see him, that no one else was as important as you.'[30] Wilks's appointment made Ernest's crowded life more tolerable. No longer burdened with the conservatory's day-to-day business, he could devote more time to speaking and writing, to visiting teachers in their studios and helping them in their work, to writing teaching manuals, to assisting examiners at examinations, and to examining the upper grades. The TCM needed his high profile because there was now a rival examination system in the prairie provinces that was cutting into its profits. And he convinced Ontario's Department of Education to grant high-school credit to students who successfully completed an upper-grade practical examination and its theory and history requirements. Other provinces followed suit and, thereby, elevated the status of conservatory examinations immeasurably.

Ernest now had more time to adjudicate at competitive music festivals, which he enjoyed and did brilliantly. He believed that, at their best, festivals encourage better teaching and help to develop a more informed musical public. Keith MacMillan maintained that his father's adjudicating – and examining – across Canada enabled him to spot especially gifted students so that he could help them 'in their later studies and entry into the professional world.'[31] In a similar way, he identified talented teachers and enticed some of them to join the TCM staff.

Adjudicating at festivals was strenuous and exacting, but there were lighter moments, too. Cellist and composer Glen Morley recalled an 'atrocious' pun of Ernest's in Vancouver. 'He was hearing school choirs at the Kiwanis Festival. One group, singing about a little lamb, insisted on pronouncing it "Lawmb." In his summing up Ernest took issue with this, and said "You Mutton do that!"' Morley, outpunning the master, added that he 'wouldn't have minded so much if only he had looked a bit sheepish.'[32]

The conservatory celebrated its fiftieth anniversary with a re-soundingly successful concert at Massey Hall on 27 April 1936. Ernest conducted two works: his own *Te Deum Laudamus* for choir and orchestra, composed for the occasion, and *An Apostrophe to the Heavenly Hosts*, a major a cappella work by Willan written in 1921. The eight-minute *Te Deum* is spirited and festive – it features fine choral writing, rich harmonic changes, and, at times, reminds one of Vaughan Williams. The work's texture is leaner than *England*'s, with the orchestra effectively punctuating the choral text without distracting the listener. The overall result makes the listener feel uplifted indeed.

But such concerts, good as they were, did not hide the fact that the TCM was still the same limited and backward school it had been when MacMillan took office a decade earlier. He continued to press for an advanced school and other reforms. At last, in 1937, the university commissioned Ernest Hutcheson, a distin-guished pianist and president of the Juilliard School of Music, to report on the conservatory's work and its future.[33] Hutcheson's recommendations were a compendium of the school's needs: that it be funded by the province much as any other public education-al institution; that an endowment fund be established; that stu-dent fees be raised; that the faculty be smaller, salaried, better paid, and have no weak members; that there be a professional department distinct from the preparatory division; that profes-sional students be assigned to teachers by the school; that there be a summer school; that there be more scholarships; that the school have an employment office which would, among other things, help students to obtain concert appearances and CBC performances; that there be music classes for the community; that the school work closely with the department of education; and that there be more woodwind teachers. MacMillan had made many of the same recommendations at various times in the past, but Hutcheson's were listened to more carefully – an outsider's words usually carry more weight. Unfortunately, the Hutcheson Report was shelved for almost a decade because of the conservatory's resistance to change, the university's indifference towards musical education, the worsening depression, and then the war.

The university's passive attitude towards music made MacMillan's role as dean, by definition, low profile. The Faculty of Music's two degrees, the MusBac and the MusDoc, were based on the British system – final examinations and submissions alone determined success or failure. Students could attend lectures and tutorials or not, as they wished. The Faculty of Music had few students, and those it did have generally passed or failed their degree requirements with little fuss. There was one student, however, who caused MacMillan much distress. In 1934, Percival Price, the Dominion Carilloneur at the Peace Tower in Ottawa, had submitted his symphony, *The St Lawrence*, as the exercise for Toronto's doctoral degree. The work was subsequently rejected by a university committee which Ernest chaired.

Shortly thereafter a New York–based Pulitzer jury awarded Price a 'Travelling Scholarship' for being, in their estimation, 'the student of music in America that may be deemed the most talented and deserving in order that he may continue his studies with the advantage of European instruction.'[34] They were, of course, looking more for talent and potential and less for academic accomplishment, and were certainly not looking specifically at *The St Lawrence*. Price had also written a book on carillon playing which had nothing to do with the university's degree requirements but which may have impressed the Pulitzer jury. When Price informed the press of his scholarship, it appeared – or he *made* it appear – as if he had won the much more prestigious Pulitzer Prize. He failed to point out that the Pulitzer scholarship and the university degree were based on very different criteria.

The *Toronto Star*, eager to embarrass MacMillan in particular and academia in general, also failed, unforgivably, to pinpoint the differences. Instead it sought out several well-known musicians to malign the university and, by implication, MacMillan, whose sweeping influence many resented.[35] MacMillan's candid reply (from Vancouver where he was adjudicating) tried to set the record straight:

I don't remember much about the work. I recall, however, that it was an exceptionally neat manuscript, written evidently by a painstaking musician. On hearing the news I felt certain that the award had been given for Mr. Price's splendid book ... 'The Art of the Carilloneur.' This work should place him on a high level as a literary as well as a musical man. It is unique and, I feel sure, the only book of its kind ever published in Canada. It must have necessitated a tremendous amount of research.[36]

A few days later, sensing that he had not said enough, he explained the university's position in a letter to the *Mail and Empire.* 'Toronto degrees in music have in times past suffered from prejudice in the Motherland ... It will vanish entirely only if we maintain standards equal to those of any British university ... The degree of Doctor of Music is the highest distinction a musician may obtain by examination in any British country; it does not necessarily indicate the presence of genius and originality, but it at least demands an extremely high standard of craftsmanship.'[37] Obviously Price's symphony had not met this standard.

With MacMillan in an awkward position, Reginald Stewart saw a chance to score a few points and invited Price to conduct *The St Lawrence* at the summer Promenade concerts. The pro-Stewart audience, eager to support a Canadian wronged by MacMillan, loudly applauded Price. To calm troubled waters, MacMillan included the work on a TSO concert for the coming October and prudently asked Price to conduct it. This performance was received badly by both public and press. One reviewer declared that, while the St Lawrence River was a good subject for an orchestral work, Price's piece wasn't it![38] In the final analysis it was generally agreed that the university had judged Price's submission accurately. Five years later, Price left Ottawa to join the faculty of the University of Michigan and enjoyed a distinguished career as a carillon soloist and consultant in carillon construction.

In the year following the Price affair, MacMillan introduced formal lectures in orchestration and score study, and tutorials in counterpoint and fugue. Faculty students were also encouraged to attend conservatory courses taught by MacMillan, Leo Smith, and Healey Willan.[39] However, candidates could still earn their degrees without attending any lectures or tutorials.

MacMillan had long wanted music students to take other liberal arts subjects (he himself had taken another degree in order to get a broader education) and students in other departments to study music as part of their liberal arts component.[40] He had some success in 1937, when the university approved a four-year honours course leading to a BA in music. Since Ontario's colleges of education required a BA for admission, this degree made it possible for music students to become high school teachers. But other than this there was little change in the Faculty of Music over the next decade.

At the time of the Hutcheson Report, MacMillan also sought to establish a firmer link between the Faculty of Music and the advanced work given at the conservatory.[41] Looking to the future, he saw that the roles of the two schools needed clarification, for otherwise there would be unnecessary duplication of instruction and even conflict. In sum, although Ernest performed his decanal responsibilities satisfactorily, the Faculty of Music made little impact on Canada's musical life in the pre–Second World War era.

9. A Musical Knight

The eighteenth of May, 1935, was a red-letter day for Ernest MacMillan. It was the day the Right Honourable R.B. Bennett, Prime Minister of Canada, wrote him a 'personal and confidential' letter, which began: 'Although a young man, you have rendered great and conspicuous service in the many branches of human endeavour to which you have directed your efforts. Not only have you earned high commendation for the creations of your genius, but your skill as an organist and your ability as a teacher are widely known, and in my opinion merit recognition by the Sovereign.'[1] 'King George V,' Bennett went on, 'wished special recognition of Art, Music, Science, and Literature in his approaching Silver Jubilee birthday honors,' and, with Ernest's permission, Bennett would recommend to the King that a knighthood be conferred upon him.

The knighthood came as a complete surprise. The granting of royal honours to Canadians had been dropped by the Canadian government in 1919 but had been revived in 1934. Bennett, a royalist, had been the Conservative prime minister since 1930 and, after five years of ineffectual leadership in depression-ridden Canada, had launched a 'New Deal' similar to Roosevelt's in the United States – progressive taxation, minimum-wage laws, unemployment insurance, health and accident insurance, old-age pensions, and other social and economic benefits. Perhaps he thought that his new deal and the bestowing of royal honours a few months prior to a national election would help him politically, but they didn't – the Liberals routed the Conservatives, and

Mackenzie King became prime minister and would remain in that office for more than a decade.

Coincidentally – or perhaps not – two months earlier the governor general of Canada, the Earl of Bessborough, had asked Ernest to write a celebratory Silver Jubilee anthem to be sung by Canada's church choirs.[2] He agreed and, along with his publisher Frederick Harris, volunteered to donate all profits to the Jubilee Cancer Fund. With due dispatch, he had completed 'The King Shall Rejoice,' based on Psalm 21, and inscribed 'Dedicated by gracious permission to their Majesties, the King and Queen' on its title-page. Two Toronto church choirs performed it on 5 May, literally as soon as the publisher's ink was dry and just two weeks before Bennett's letter was sent. An attractive short piece, it moves along positively and joyfully in D minor, changing in the last few bars to D major as the choir proudly sings 'God Save the King!'

Bennett's letter had been forwarded to Ernest in Halifax, where he was adjudicating at a music festival. After digesting its contents he sought Elsie's advice, which she proffered in a charming and ingenuous note: 'La! La! We can't afford it of course, but do blow yourself to it darling. I am really terribly thrilled for you. *Nothing* is good enough, but this is the best your poor dear country can do about it ... But *don't* say "no" sweetheart ... What a thrill the TSO and the TCM will have, to say nothing of your friends.'[3] Elsie added that she had spoken with Vincent Massey, no doubt at Ernest's suggestion, and reported that he was 'delighted' and 'strongly urges yes.' Ernest also asked for advice from his close friend Fred MacKelcan, who wired a succinct and cleverly disguised reply. 'RECENT DEVELOPMENT NOT UNEXPECTED AND WILL BE EVERYWHERE REGARDED AS NATURAL AND SOUND STOP WILL BE REAL HELP FINANCIAL AND OTHERWISE BOTH INSTITUTIONS AND GENERAL SITUATION AND GIVE NEW ENERGY AND CONFIDENCE TO ALL INTERESTED AM FEELING TREMENDOUSLY BUCKED UP CHEERIO.'[4]

Convinced, Ernest wired his acceptance to Bennett on 23 May, and followed it with a letter, which in part reflected MacKelcan's advice:

As a merely personal distinction, however gratifying, I should be most reluctant to accept knighthood. As a recognition of the importance of music and the musical profession in the Dominion, however, I accept it with gratitude. If the status of my profession is enhanced in the public mind – and I think it will be – I shall rejoice as I should have rejoiced had the lot fallen on some other musician. I believe that those who have worked hard and faithfully on behalf of the institutions with which I am connected will be glad of my acceptance.[5]

The news was released to the press on 3 June. The royalist *Mail and Empire* enthusiastically filled a good deal of its front page with stories about Canada's new knights – nine in all – along with photos of Ernest and the other two artist-knights, portrait painter Wylie Grier and writer Charles G.D. Roberts. Edward Johnson, the internationally known Canadian tenor who had just been appointed general manager of the Metropolitan Opera Company, was made a Commander of the Order of the British Empire – one level below knighthood – on the same honours list.[6]

There were some negative reactions to the knighthoods in other Toronto newspapers. The *Daily Star*, the only left-of-centre daily in Toronto, allotted the news about one-tenth the space the *Mail and Empire* did, and asked in an editorial, 'What better are these men for having handles on their names – what better are they, for example, than other men of equal ability and distinction who have received no title at all? ... The whole business of a titled class as opposed to a non-titled class is an unwelcome return of a custom which Canada thought it had rid itself some years ago, and of which, if a popular vote were to decide the matter, it would very quickly rid itself today.'[7]

The *Globe* supported Bennett's choices but, by using an olfactory metaphor, questioned the wisdom of titles generally. 'Titles have an unpleasant odour in the nose of the Canadian public. Though pre-war in origin, the perfume owes its peculiar staying powers to the war years ... War titles were added to war profits for Canadian millionaires and politicians while wounds and death were being added to privation and suffering for Canadian soldiers ... No amount of care in the selection of their recipients will make them popular.' The right-wing *Evening Telegram* agreed with these sentiments.[8]

Whatever Ernest's motives – after all, knighthoods were and are a fact of life that impress all kinds of people – being *Sir* Ernest gave him more clout in his own country and, to an extent, abroad. (At least he didn't buy the coat of arms offered to all new knights!) The investiture was held in Ottawa on 26 September and he was, thenceforth, Sir Ernest MacMillan.

The future of music in Canada looked brighter the next year with the founding of the Canadian Broadcasting Corporation (CBC). Ernest, for one, had been anticipating it since the early days of radio and had first spelled out his views on music in Canadian broadcasting in 1932, in reply to playwright Merrill Denison's assertion that Canadian talent for broadcasting was 'practically negligible.'[9] Ernest had exhorted Canadians to support their performers, otherwise Canada would have no broadcasting life of its own. He continued, with what would become a Canadian leitmotif:

We seem to suffer in Canada from an inferiority complex – 'Can any good come out of Nazareth?' – and from a mistaken local pride which exalts home-grown products because they are home-grown and not because they are good ... Canada has abundant musical material of a high order ... Even if Canadian musicians were as mediocre as some Canadians assume them to be (on very inadequate grounds) they would have a plausible right on economic grounds for a reasonable measure of protection such as practically every industry in Canada now enjoys ... Under present conditions we are drifting towards the complete elimination of Canadian programs, and the prospects of hundreds of musicians in Toronto alone seem almost hopeless. The tragic thing is that they could do a large proportion of what we hear quite as well or better, and, given reasonable encouragement and support, the margin which lies between the best American and the best Canadian programs could certainly tend to diminish and possibly in time disappear.

Over the objections of private broadcasters, the CBC was created to operate in English and French, to span five time zones and ten million square miles, and to compete for listeners with 'the world's most clamorous broadcaster, the USA.'[10] User radio licence fees would be the main source of revenue to support its made-in-Canada shows. Ernest heartily endorsed one of the CBC's fundamental aims: to provide Canadian musicians with an outlet for artistic expression and a source of income.

A year later, in 1937, CBC general manager Gladstone Murray asked Ernest to be the CBC's music adviser, at an annual stipend of $1,000, and he readily agreed.[11] Before long he was helping to resolve disputes with the musicians' union over pay scales. Then he proposed an increase in live music programs, which led, in the 1938–9 season, to the TSO/CBC concert series, the 'Sunday Nine O'Clocks.' He also asked Murray to broadcast educational orchestral concerts, but this suggestion was only partially implemented at the time.

MacMillan gave up the CBC position after two years. He found it 'a bit of a sinecure; calls for advice were rare and, although I sent in reports of specific programmes from time to time, I never felt that I was of much use to the Corporation.'[12] He was, as usual, being overly modest, for he had played no small role in convincing the CBC to do good music programs in its early years when it was first finding itself. Even if he had done nothing, his mere presence would have deterred the CBC from turning its back on Canadian musicians and quality broadcasting. Late in 1939, the watchful Ernest wrote that the CBC must not yield to the temptation of relying too much on broadcasting American orchestras while cutting air time for less proficient Canadian ones.[13] 'Nationhood entails responsibilities as well as privileges,' he said.

Next, having severed his ties with the CBC, he lashed out at Gladstone Murray for neglecting serious music, and used broadcast figures from October 1938 and October 1939 to show that, in one year, there had been an *increase* of close to 50 per cent in live 'popular' music programs and a *decrease* of about 14 per cent in 'serious' music programs.[14] Acknowledging that much good *recorded* music was being broadcast, he wryly noted that recordings are 'good for the listener but of course rarely mean anything to the Canadian musician.' He wrote:

It is ... far more difficult for us in Canada than in most countries to build something musically worthwhile. If United States competition meant simply keeping us on our toes by the challenge of excellence all would be well, but, when we lack rich patrons to support musical activities on a scale commensurate with the generosity of many Americans, when no government subsidies ... are available for orchestras, when union conditions render it increasingly difficult to bring in first-class players for key positions and our music schools are given practically no assistance in training first-class young players to take the place of those who are getting on in years, finally, when we have to contend with that 'colonial complex' (I can give it no other name) which on the one hand pats home-town mediocrity on the back and on the other openly assumes that the home-made product will never measure up to what comes from outside, when such conditions obtain it is hard that one who has always endeavoured as I have to stand for quality in Canadian music should see the development of such tendencies as I have outlined in the one body that might save the situation.

Not surprisingly, Murray questioned MacMillan's interpretation of the broadcast figures, but Ernest's message had gotten through.

Ernest MacMillan's own career as a symphony conductor moved ahead rapidly in the 1930s. After two years as head of the TSO his reputation spread to Great Britain, and in July of 1933 he conducted the British Broadcasting Corporation's (BBC) symphony and chorus on its national program. These groups were among the best in Britain and conductors yearned to work with them. It was Ernest's first international conducting appearance, and, aware of its importance, he planned the program with great care: Brahms's Second Symphony (an audience favourite), Arnold Bax's *St Patrick's Breastplate* (Bax was a prominent contemporary British composer; Ernest had done the work with the TSO in the spring of 1931), and excerpts from Handel's *Solomon* (Handel was always popular).

The performance went well and London's press reviews, on the whole, were complimentary. The influential *Times* wrote that 'he showed a fine sense of light and shade, together with a keen appreciation of significant detail,' and the equally influential *Daily Telegraph* wrote that 'no one could have produced a more vivid reading of Bax's masterpiece.'[15] Nor did it go unnoticed that

Ernest conducted the entire program from memory. However, these same reviewers pinpointed publicly for the first time some of his fundamental conducting weaknesses: a ponderous and too solemn approach, overly slow tempi, an occasional lack of vitality, and a beat that was not sufficiently interesting, revealing, and precise. On balance, both reviewers thought that he had done well indeed. The forever self-deprecating Ernest could take heart that he had at least impressed, although not overwhelmed, London's knowledgeable press.

That a Canadian had been successful in London was important news in MacMillan's home town. The *Globe* said that 'Canadians will be delighted to learn of his signal success. This is regarded as a distinct honor to a Canadian conductor.' It reminded its readers with obvious pride that the most eminent artists at the 1931 Lausanne Conference had greeted MacMillan as 'an equal' and had honoured him with a place on 'one of the most important committees.'[16] So it went in colonial Canada.

Elsie was unable to accompany Ernest to Britain in 1933 and, as was his long-established custom when away, he wrote her frequently and revealingly about his activities. While in London he met Arnold Bax and Bax's close friend, the prominent pianist Harriet Cohen. He also renewed acquaintanceships with Arthur Beverley Baxter, his childhood chum from the Blakeley Trio days, and Davidson Ketchum, a fellow Canadian and former Ruhlebenite who would, years later, write the most comprehensive book about the Ruhleben camp. Ernest enjoyed the Ballet Russe de Monte Carlo and also the more plebeian show *Music in the Air*. And he told Elsie that the film *King Kong* was 'a super thriller calculated to give nightmares to the most sophisticated.' He even fell asleep at a performance of Sir Hubert Parry's *Job* – but who could blame him for that? Ernest was flirting with vegetarianism that summer and told Elsie – he thought she would be relieved – that he had abandoned it 'at least pro tem,' having dined at Simpson's on the Strand – 'the kind of place a vegetarian visits when he has a nightmare.'[17] (Simpson's is famous for its roast beef.)

After London, Ernest visited Bayreuth for the first time since 1914. He dismissed memories of that portentous August laconically: 'Here I am again, renewing my acquaintance with the

Wagner shrine under somewhat better circumstances than formerly.' His all-Wagner concerts had intensified his interest in how Bayreuth did the music of the man who had made it famous. As before, he enjoyed the orchestra more than the singers and found the settings greatly improved. 'The place itself casts a real spell upon one.'[18] He told Elsie that Adolf Hitler's presence at *Siegfried* had created great excitement. 'People outside of Germany have really no idea of the enormous effect he has upon the whole population.' How right he was.

Looking for inspiration, he next went to the Salzburg Festival and there attended performances of *Der Rosenkavalier, Tristan,* and *Così fan tutte,* and heard Bruno Walter – 'a fine conductor' – do the Beethoven Eighth and the Mahler Fourth. Ernest described the Mahler, which he was hearing for the first time, as 'more like ballet music than a symphony.' (It would be some years before he would take to Mahler.) He also attended a rehearsal of Brahms's Second Symphony but, disliking the tempi, passed up the concert to go swimming in the city's outdoor pool. To his surprise, the performance was piped to the pool from the Mozarteum! 'In the open air, lying in the sun with the castle and the hills standing out against a perfectly blue sky, one forgave much! Fancy hearing Brahms in a Canadian swimming bath.'[19]

He wound up his musical trip in Munich, where he saw *Parsifal,* and then, his batteries charged, he returned home to opera-less Toronto.

To Ernest's delight, the BBC invited him back for a second engagement the following summer. This time Elsie accompanied him. They landed in Plymouth and travelled by bus to Exeter to see the cathedral, where the ever-observant Ernest enjoyed the 'wonderfully varied bracery of its windows of the Decorated Gothic period.' Thanks to his prodigious memory, he later recalled browsing among the tombstones of a nearby graveyard and finding an amusing inscription on the grave of a ten-year-old girl: 'Into no sin did ever fall but what we mortals call originall.'[20]

They went on to visit his old Ruhleben comrade Percy Hull (organist at Hereford Cathedral and later knighted) and then to Stratford-upon-Avon, where quite by chance they met the young Canadian Robertson Davies, whom Ernest had taught briefly at

Upper Canada College. Together they went to *The Tempest* and
Love's Labours Lost, and Ernest enjoyed Davies's perceptive comments about the performances. Next, Ernest and Elsie flew to
France – their first flight ever – and wound up a busy summer
back in Britain driving from Cambridge to Aberystwyth with Ifor
Evans (another former Ruhlebenite) who was taking up a new
university post there.[21]

Happily, Ernest was again invited to conduct the BBC – for the
third summer in a row. Confidently, he programmed an all-Cana-
dian concert, including his *Two Sketches* and *Six Bergerettes*. In
addition, he participated in the first joint conference of the Royal
College of Organists (RCO) and the Canadian College of Organists (CCO). A number of other organists from Canada attended,
including Frederick Silvester and Maitland Farmer, who, while
there, both tried the RCO practical examinations. To their chagrin they both failed, and Ernest, who knew their playing, was
indignant.[22] And then he had his own moment of embarrassment.
In recognition of the high esteem in which he was held by the
organ world, the RCO asked him to perform in concert that
year's test pieces. He did them on a small two-manual organ, 'not
an easy assignment,' according to Muriel Gidley Stafford, who was
in the audience.

Playing from memory before an awesome assembly of British musicians,
examination candidates, students, and friends, the unthinkable happened – a sudden lapse of memory in the first movement of the Bach
C Major Trio Sonata, a moment of breath-taking suspense for all of us
'colonials,' including his father and sister Jean, until, with characteristic
aplomb and dexterity, he neatly recovered the sequential flow of the
movement and followed it through to its scintillating conclusion.[23]

At the conference, Ernest gave a paper on music in Canada, a
subject probably more meaningful to the Canadians present than
to the English. He said that Canada's musical life was freeing
itself of American influence (significantly, he said nothing about
English influence) although Canadian composers were still not
developing a national style. He noted with distress that music on
Canadian radio was catering to the lowest common denominator

and advocated a BBC-like government controlled network to help to remedy the situation. (The CBC was incorporated the next year.) And he singled out other Canadian problems. The country had no recognized centre of cultural life or satisfactory musical press, and musical interest was 'too localised because of the vast distances and poor communications.'[24]

Before leaving England for his next stop, Salzburg, he saw two old friends, Benjamin Dale and Antoinette Burgess, and attended the King's annual Buckingham Palace Garden Party. In Salzburg he visited the Austrian-born soprano Emmy Heim, whom he had met the year before when he had accompanied her in her first Toronto recital; it was the beginning of an extremely close musical partnership. The two artists loved to make music together, and Emmy, who had a distinguished performing career, claimed that she had never worked with a better or more instinctive pianist. And she admired unreservedly his devout approach to his *Messiah* and *St Matthew Passion* performances, calling them his 'annual confessions.'[25]

As for Ernest, he was enchanted with Emmy, perhaps first as a human being and then because of her voice (which admittedly was then past its prime), her musicianship, her loving approach to music, and her knowledge of languages (her 1934 Toronto recital had included a group of international folk songs in *six* languages). He marvelled at how she conscientiously made every note in a song 'a matter of special study' and every little phrase 'a miracle,' and how she covered such a wide range of moods in her programs.[26] Her human qualities, too, meant much to him. She looked at life with both irony and humour. 'Many will remember,' Ernest recalled years later, 'her group of three folk songs – French, German, and Yiddish – all on the subject of the girl who wanted a husband and rejected all the alternative suggestions offered by her mother. How completely she differentiated the characters of those three girls!' Emmy made Toronto her home after the Second World War, teaching at the conservatory and frequently visiting the MacMillans for informal musical evenings. It is unfortunate that there is only one recording of Emmy and Ernest playing together, an amateur one made at an evening get-together at Park Road.[27]

It was at the 1935 Salzburg Festival that Ernest heard Toscanini's memorable readings of *Fidelio*, with Lotte Lehmann, and of *Falstaff*. About the *Falstaff* he wrote, 'Never have I heard so perfect an operatic performance.'[28] It was standing-room only but, as he wrote to Elsie, it was worth it.[29] Toscanini, Lehmann, and two wonderful musical afternoons at 'Chez Heim' with Emmy 'singing for hours on end' all left him spellbound. Toronto seemed a million miles away.

His fourth and last BBC engagement was in the summer of 1937. On that visit he returned to Wales to see Ifor Evans and to adjudicate at the national Eisteddfod festival of music and poetry, whose origins date back to the seventh century. The festival left him with unforgettable memories of a 10,000-voice mass choir and fine orations, for which the Welsh are justifiably famous. Ex-prime minister David Lloyd George was one of the orators. Dressed in green Druidical robes, 'he was greeted with wild acclamation and I remarked to Ifor afterwards how popular he was with his own people; "Yes," said he, sagaciously, "but they don't vote for him."'[30]

Ernest MacMillan welcomed all opportunities to guest conduct. His first United States engagement was in 1936 at the out-of-doors Hollywood Bowl. He wisely selected a program which would show off his strengths: the Sibelius Second Symphony (one of his favourites), several shorter works, his *Two Sketches*, and his transcription of the Bach Prelude and Fugue in G Minor. The Los Angeles reviews were all complimentary and, in their way, very much on target. The *Times* described his reading of the Sibelius as 'definitely masculine ... without frills and furbelows ... straightforward without personal showmanship.'[31] The *Evening Herald* found it 'finished and all-ingratiating' and the program as a whole 'a steady buildup in the esteem of about 7,000 devotees, who seemed to receive something more than usual from his magnetic wand of direction. Conducting is a serious affair when you are a visitor with only one program in which to manifest your entire ability, but the sturdy Canadian showed himself a good neighbour and set out to lead and not to follow.'[32]

Ernest had chosen to travel to Los Angeles by car with Elsie and their teenage boys. Husband and wife had planned to share the driving but, after fifty miles, Elsie found his back-seat driving 'intolerable,' and he had to drive the remaining 10,000 himself.[33] On the way through Salt Lake City, Ernest visited the famous Mormon Tabernacle and was impressed with, among other things, its 'remarkable acoustic properties.' He had no inkling then that he would on three occasions in the future conduct *Messiah* in it. He was also overwhelmed by the natural beauty of the western states and marvelled at Utah's geological paradise:

Dinosaur Park, Bryce and Zion Canyons made us all wish that we had given more time to the study of rocks. Bryce Canyon in particular, with its multi-coloured assortment of quasi-architectural and sculptured shapes reminiscent of Gothic cathedrals, Indian temples, chessmen and statues of notable historic figures, all supplied in profusion by Nature, is a sight that no one should miss. Epics of Nature, however, are no more likely than humans to be heroes to their valets. An old settler to whom a portion of the canyon had been allotted as part of his ranch could see it only as 'a turrible place to lose a cow!' It doubtless is.

The MacMillan family sweltered through the great American desert. 'A strong wind blowing from the South was like the blast of heat from the engines of an Atlantic liner.' They arrived at Riverside, California, in 115-degree (Fahrenheit) heat to be provided with 'huge glasses of freshly squeezed orange juice at ten cents each. Never have I known anything more refreshing, except the swim in the ocean a couple of hours later. In all this heat our young sons insisted on wearing their flannel shorts and Upper Canada blazers.'

While in Los Angeles, the family visited the Disney studios, where fifteen-year-old Keith made a passing remark which became family legend. His proud father told it thus:

At that time they were experimenting with the idea of illustrating well known musical works. I remember Keith saying to our guide: 'Why don't you make a film of *The Sorcerer's Apprentice*?' The guide looked thoughtful and said, 'You've something there, sonny.' We have often wondered whether his suggestion may not have borne fruit in *Fantasia*, which appeared not long afterwards and in which Dukas's work figures so prominently.[34]

After his Hollywood Bowl concert, the MacMillans drove to Vancouver, where Ernest, already a favourite, conducted the fledgling Vancouver Symphony at the newly opened Malkin Bowl – also out-of-doors and modelled after the Hollywood Bowl – in Stanley Park. The concert's beautiful setting was somewhat marred by an 'Indian Pow-wow, which had by some oversight been timed for the same time as the concert 500 yards away. The sounds (to which were added the whistles of ships coming through the Narrows) hardly blended with the slow movement of Tschaikowsky's *Fourth Symphony* and my enthusiasm for Indian music was temporarily in abeyance.'[35]

It was Ernest's second visit to Vancouver that year; he had received an honorary degree – his first – from the University of British Columbia three months earlier. In his acceptance speech for the degree, he had pointed out how music had been neglected by Western historians, citing H.G. Wells's *Outline of History*, which had not *one* reference to music, and quoting Sir Henry Hadow: 'Our culture is like an ill-roasted egg, "all on one side." We are familiar with Spenser and Shakespeare but not with Byrd and Tallis, with Milton but not with Bach, with Goethe but not with Beethoven ... the Elizabethan sonnet but not the Elizabethan madrigal.'[36] Ernest ended by urging that music be studied 'as a literature – as the medium of expression adopted by some of the greatest men in history.'

This was the year, too, when Marjorie Agnew, a teacher at Vancouver's Templeton High School, started the first MacMillan Club, so that her students could *experience* the arts – listen to and make music, read and write poetry and prose, and study and make paintings and other works of art. Marjorie's enthusiasm was contagious and soon similar clubs were formed in other Vancouver high schools.[37] They were successful from the start. Collectively, the various clubs then got together to look for an appropriate umbrella name. With Marjorie's encouragement, the students rejected the idea of naming their clubs after a dead artist and chose instead to identify with a man they knew and admired. And so, with Ernest's blessing, the clubs became known as the Sir Ernest MacMillan Fine Arts Clubs. Their goals reflected Canada's cultural awakening: to raise the level of artistic appreciation of high school students, to familiarize them with artists and their work, to encourage their support of the CBC and their interest in its programs, to involve them in community cultural projects, to encourage their own creative work, and to foster among them a sense of Canadian unity.

Over the next three decades the MacMillan clubs flourished and spread throughout British Columbia and on into Alberta, the Yukon, and even a few as far east as New Brunswick. Their national newsletter included information about club activities and about Sir Ernest's comings and goings. They raised money for scholarships for gifted members; they sought out leading artists as guest speakers; they produced music quizzes for radio; and they formed a mass choir which sang for several summers with the VSO in Stanley Park. MacMillan himself conducted some of their concerts.

As a teenager in the 1950s, music critic William Littler was president of the Britannia High School Club in Vancouver. He recalled that Ernest MacMillan was never a 'glamorous figure' to club members, but 'more avuncular. When we met him there was nothing flashy, just reasonableness. His conducting was businesslike, methodical, an unselfconscious kind of performance. He was easy to like ... After all, Sir Ernest was our country's leader in music.'[38]

Marjorie and Ernest became good friends. She idolized him, and, at first, made him feel quite uncomfortable as she gazed at him with adoring eyes. Ernest was attractive to women and used to their attention, but he found this just a bit much. But, as their friendship grew, he could not help liking and admiring her for sparking the artistic consciousness and interest of so many young Canadians. Nor could he overlook the valuable personal services she performed for him – driving him about when he was in Vancouver, arranging hotel accommodations, and taking him to meetings. And, at times of stress, she gave him – and Elsie – much moral support. At their peak there were some sixty MacMillan clubs in Canada. Their numbers dwindled in the 1960s when Marjorie's health began to fail, and they eventually petered out.

To return to the 1930s, in December 1936 Ernest conducted in Montreal for the first time, and his popularity there soon equalled his popularity in Vancouver. Quebecer Wilfrid Pelletier, who was at the time conducting at the Metropolitan Opera, was trying to establish an orchestra in Montreal and had asked Ernest to guest conduct. Appreciating the difficulty of Pelletier's task, Ernest agreed to do so without fee.[39] The city greeted him with a civic reception and, by the end of the first rehearsal, the orchestra adored him. Following the concert, Ernest made a speech in French which drew as much favourable press as his conducting.[40] The next day, the Montreal Musicians' Guild made him an honorary member. Ernest conducted regularly in Montreal thereafter and was always paid for his services.

In July 1937, he was back in the United States to conduct the Chicago Symphony for four concerts at Ravinia, its summer home. This was his most important American engagement to date – Chicago had one of the top orchestras in the land. The brilliant and opinionated Claudia Cassidy, then reporting for the *Journal of Commerce* (she later moved to the more influential *Chicago Tribune*, where her reviews carried enormous weight in the musical world), said that Ernest was 'a conductor worth importing.' She was at the first concert and wrote:

It was Sir Ernest's evening and he made much of it, even to choosing the Sibelius *Fifth Symphony* rather than some more grateful work in which to display his gifts ... It is not his way to choose the easy path. He is a dogged man, though not a grim one, and he works without score in a manner soldierly, yet without the ramrod stiffness of the martinet. There is pugnacity in his method and he attacked the slashing finale of the Sibelius like a woodsman giving precisely the right amount of chop to a piece of recalcitrant wood. Not a bad method this for Sibelius, particularly when accompanied by the sweeping lyricism that takes account of the Tschaikowskian melody that sometimes emerges through the Finn's dourest pages ... Sir Ernest made the symphony a challenge to his listeners and I doubt that even those who disliked it found it dull. The performance was masterly.[41]

Senior Chicago critic Glen Dillard Gunn agreed with Cassidy about the Sibelius and said, after the second concert, that Ernest was also excellent in the Beethoven Eighth Symphony and 'had the score worked out to the last detail.'[42] Another critic, Cecil Smith, after hearing the Brahms Fourth, called him 'a careful reverent musician. He strives conscientiously to present the symphony as it is, confident that Brahms's ideas will achieve their effect if only they are adequately presented.'[43]

Six months later, in January 1938, he conducted the National Symphony in Washington. Kindler did an exchange with MacMillan by conducting the TSO in 1939. Washington's press, like Chicago's the summer before, was full of praise.

He was sure of his orientation and confident in the integrity of his beat ... He did not impose his will on the players but asked for consensus in his readings, and he obtained it with a readiness which resulted in eloquent playing. Sir Ernest is a musician whose assurance is tempered with modesty, whose ability is not vainglorious and whose taste prefers the noble and the beautiful in music. His command of the orchestra was firm but not arrogant, and his cues were timed with the certainty of collaborated response.[44]

Ernest's guest conducting also included the Philadelphia Orchestra, first on November 1937 for an American network broadcast and then in May 1938 at Massey Hall, where he did Pierné's *Children's Crusade* with the Conservatory Choir. At the final rehearsal for that event, he had a few anxious moments – a conductor's nightmare which hindsight makes funny.

My trousers were held up by a belt but had no belt-loops. The last part of the work depicts a shipwreck, and, though very absorbed, I could not fail to see that the women in the choir were looking apprehensive, the men (especially in the orchestra) decidedly amused, and the children expectant. When it came to the time 'the main-mast's going' I realised that this was exactly what was happening to me. I retrieved my trousers just in time – no doubt to the disappointment of many. [45]

The Philadelphia Orchestra, with its conductor Eugene Ormandy (Stokowski's successor), gave three other concerts during its visit to Toronto that May. Ormandy and Ernest hit it off well and the association led to a warm friendship between them.

Ernest made other visits to the United States that spring and summer. In Detroit he conducted a series of five Ford Sunday Evening Hour broadcasts for CBS, with five leading soloists: Kirsten Flagstad, Lily Pons, Giovanni Martinelli, José Iturbi, and Nino Martini. He also spent a week at New York University as lecturer and choral teacher and followed that with a visit to Tanglewood in western Massachusetts, where he mixed with other American musicians, thrilled to the Boston Symphony Orchestra at its Music Shed, and entertained friends and family, including Winifred and Ettore Mazzoleni, at a rented cottage nearby.

10. Personal Problems – Resolved

The 1938–9 TSO season consisted of ten subscription concerts, four school concerts, a Christmas Box concert, two special concerts, and two Opera Guild performances – nineteen in all, about the same number as in preceding years. The budget was only $62,000 – a mere $4,000 more than, for example, in 1933–4 – and there was an accumulating deficit. The CBC weekly series of nine 'Nine O'Clock,' concerts for which the CBC paid the TSO an additional $20,000, was the one new development. Of the $82,000 total, $3,500 went to MacMillan (an abysmal fee for a ranking conductor) and $54,500 to the eighty-five players. It is not difficult to estimate how much the average player earned. To put it bluntly, the TSO season was too short and the players were paid too little. And to compound the orchestra's problems, some sections were terribly weak and its board was as ineffective as ever.

Ernest was growing more and more despondent about the TSO's future, and also about his own conducting career, which he felt was stagnating. Where were the American offers? He had had excellent press yet no American orchestra had sought him out to be its conductor. He began to doubt his ability. Was he as good as Unger, Ormandy, Stokowski, or Kindler? His 'Memoirs' reveal how well he understood the fundamentals of conducting. 'A conductor must know the score, have an ear that can detect errors, exercise diplomacy in engaging and seating his men,' and know when to be patient and 'when to wield the whip.' He must also be 'something of a showman without sacrificing the intentions of the composer.'[1] No conductor, he went on, 'has a right to interpose himself between audience and composer – especially a great composer. It is not necessary to follow the original score slavishly ... but the interpretation should never violate the essential elements of style.'

Generalities, yes, but all were true. He went further in replying to a questionnaire sent to him by Lazare Saminsky, a prominent American musician who was planning a book on conducting:

Every conductor develops his own style of gesture; provided he achieves the desired result, the means are secondary. Ideally his every movement must assist in conveying his meaning to the orchestra ... Extravagant gestures may be justified in a climax but, if persistent, can become very irritating. However any member of an audience who is disturbed by the antics of the conductor can close his eyes and let his ears alone be the judge. Perhaps the best results can be achieved *by this particular conductor* only by these means, so let us be tolerant.[2]

To Saminsky's question about the influence of tradition on a conductor's choice of tempi, Ernest replied that there were no 'correct' tempi as such. The conductor should know what the traditions are in regard to a work but unless a tradition has been firmly established – he suggested that recordings would eventually do this – the conductor should follow his best instincts. The conductor must be steeped in the musical style of the period from which the music emanates, but not be 'too meticulous, too purist,' for then the music might lose its vitality. Interpretations may vary with the times, but vitality is always a must.

Good as all of this reads, in practice, Ernest's baton technique could be clumsy and his beat sluggish. He responded to the sound of the orchestra instead of anticipating it. He tended to beat through bars unnecessarily, which slowed down the ends of phrases. And his stick, although expressive, was not always in accord with the music and often lacked vibrancy and sensitivity. He also had trouble making the orchestra sound cohesive, like a real ensemble. This may have been because he did not tune the orchestra carefully enough, rehearse it in sufficient detail, or isolate parts of a work for intensive review.

On the other hand, MacMillan had a fine feeling for orchestral sound and balance, 'from the bottom up,' said conductor Victor Feldbrill, a former protégé of Ernest and the TSO's resident conductor from 1973 to 1977. If he had 'focused his rhythm to match his concept of sound it would have led to great things.'[3] Like Stokowski, also an organist, he 'wanted the sound to wash over you, and that creates good orchestral texture with often incredible results.'[4] In addition to achieving good orchestral balance and allowing the listener to hear what was going on, his interpretations were always stylistically appropriate. To sum up, Ernest MacMillan was a supremely gifted musician who lacked the conducting ability to inflame an orchestra with a flick of the stick, a movement of the eye, a grimace, a smile. He excited, but he didn't transport.

By the fall of 1938, MacMillan had become so frustrated with the TSO's chronic shortage of funds that he donated $250 (no small sum then) and offered to surrender his fee entirely if the players would get more. He even suggested stepping down. 'If it might ... be thought best for the welfare of the organization that another conductor should be appointed ... I should willingly retire. I have always felt that it is dangerous to tie up institutions too closely with personalities.' (There was no contract to break. A handshake had always sufficed between him and the TSO board.) Of course, the board ignored him as it had three years earlier when he had, for similar reasons, tried to resign. Now, with things no better, he was more than ever determined to leave the TSO, but, with Reginald Stewart waiting in the wings ready to take over the day he left, he had good reason not to cut his Toronto ties too hastily, for once that was done there would be no turning back.

Ernest had been in touch with Sir Adrian Boult (Boult had been knighted in 1937) about jobs in England, and had also contacted his American manager Arthur Judson. Judson was president of New York's Columbia Artists Management and had impressive credentials. Musically trained, he had been manager of the Philadelphia Orchestra, was still the manager of the New York Philharmonic, and for a time had managed both. He placed most of America's leading conductors and more or less controlled the American conducting world. Furthermore, his judgment about conductors was respected and valued.

In a letter to Judson, Ernest wrote of the TSO board's persistent complaints about his 'modern' programming, of its refusal to authorize more concerts and better pay for the players, and of how it measured the orchestra's success 'by its ability to soothe the tired business man – a worthy enough function, but hardly an exclusive one.'[5] Hoping to impress Judson with the urgency of the situation, he wrote that this would be his last TSO season and that it 'may mean taking up some academic position elsewhere ... or simply living a retired life as a teacher and perhaps taking up again a church organistship.' Naturally, he went on, he would prefer to stay in conducting and, to help his case with Judson, pointed out that Philadelphia Orchestra musicians were pressing him to conduct in their city. 'You know the members of the orchestra are the most critical of one's critics, and it is always gratifying when one can win their confidence.'

Finally he got to the point. 'Do you still think I have a career as a conductor? I passed my 45th birthday last month so I have not by any means unlimited time ahead.' He asked if he should advertise his availability more extensively (artists paid for their own advertising costs), how he should follow up personal contacts, and how he could get invited to conduct New York's Lewisohn Stadium summer concerts and the NBC Symphony. He even told Judson how disappointed he was not to be asked back to conduct the 'Ford Sunday Evening Hour' broadcasts, despite his apparent success with them in 1938. 'If you think I am crying for the moon, tell me so, and I shall look around for a quiet spot where I may practise the maxims of Lin Yutang. The only prospect I can see so far as Canada is concerned ... is a National Orchestra under the control of the CBC. But that seems far away at present.'

Judson replied sensitively.[6] He reminded Ernest that it takes time to build a conducting career and that, having put in the 'foundation' in Toronto, he should 'continue to build on that foundation.' As for taking a teaching or organ position, Judson thought it a backward step. Then he gave Ernest sound advice about coming to terms with Toronto's musical taste:

As far as orchestral music is concerned, Toronto is a comparatively new city ... You are in the position of educating your public. Most of your programs, even of older music, present such music for the first time to your public. You will have to be patient until your public has a chance to grow up to what you want to give them. Boards of directors are notoriously conservative. You will have to handle them carefully and get as much as you can. Do not take it as a personal affront when you find it impossible to perform certain works. If they are not done this year, they can be done next year. After all, the main thing is to keep on establishing the orchestra on a sounder basis and increasing the audiences. After a certain point, you can go further and faster with your programs. Just now, you can go only as far and as fast as your public will follow you.

He added that Toronto's problems were not unique, that Ernest's continuing success with the TSO would open doors for better jobs, that moving now 'would wreck everything you have worked for during the past years ... It may be hard and you may have to shut the door of your office and swear occasionally but in the long run, it will pay dividends.' Judson made sense but, however veiled, he was implying that, in his estimation, the great orchestras of the United States were not for Ernest. Ernest had not got the answer he wanted.

In January 1939, Ernest, increasingly dissatisfied, formally asked the TSO board to commit itself to more concerts and better salaries for the players so that they could give up other work and devote more of their time and energy to the TSO. And then, to force the board's hand, he added, 'If it is found impossible to extend the activities and enlarge the general scope of the orchestra, I should prefer to know it in time so that I may plan accordingly.'[7] The board did not reply. Finally, at the end of March he prepared a letter of resignation to TSO chairman Colonel Bishop – but set it aside at the urging of Elsie, Fred MacKelcan, and his Canadian manager Wilfred James, who all feared that he might be acting too impulsively and didn't really want to leave the TSO. They knew Ernest better than he knew himself.

Two weeks went by, with no word from the board. Finally, on 11 April, Ernest posted the March letter and enclosed a conciliatory covering letter. 'I am no longer able (my doctor, Trevor Owen, will bear me out on this) to carry on under the nervous strain of present conditions.'[8] Medical excuses were out of character for Ernest. He was not one to complain of illness, even if family and friends *had* hovered over him all his life, but he was caught up in a mid-life crisis. His covering letter repeated the conditions under which he would reconsider his resignation and introduced an important new one: 'In the event of our being at war, of course, all arrangements would be subject to change.'[9] Quite naturally, with such an escape clause, board members wondered if Ernest was really serious about resigning. They knew him well and suspected that his threat to leave was a ploy – 'showdown tactics' without a showdown. And few doubted that war was imminent.

Ernest's ultimatum to the board demanded firm seasonal, not weekly, contracts for the players and ample funds to import new players, particularly winds. He also asked that the board take over negotiations with Toronto's musicians' union and its despotic president Walter Murdoch. Ernest was tired of dealing with Murdoch, who, without giving thought to the implications behind his protective stance and its effect on the TSO's artistic development, was against importing players. And last, Ernest wanted a minimum of twenty concerts annually and full control of programming. He was also tired of fielding complaints from board members about his 'modern' programs – too much Sibelius and Richard Strauss.

With the die cast – almost – Ernest left for British Columbia to adjudicate at a festival, give an organ recital, and visit some of the MacMillan Fine Arts Clubs. He found his first transcontinental flight very tiring – the weather was bad and there were frequent landings and take-offs – and a few days later he had a kidney-stone attack. It was all very depressing but he was cheered up a few days later by Elsie's news that the TSO board had actually formed subcommittees to address his concerns![10]

His optimism soon waned. He heard nothing from the board and, at the end of April, wrote to Elsie that he hoped to effect a smooth retirement from the TSO: 'It seems very ungracious, but I just *can't* feel differently.'[11] But he *was* regaining his spirit. Adjudicating at the Penticton festival in the Okanagan Valley, one of his favourite places, must have had something to do with it. In Edmonton following the festival, he wrote a most entertaining 400–line poem which makes great fun of adjudicators – himself included – and the whole adjudicating process. Here are some of the lines of 'The Song of Winnie-Ha-Ha (With apologies to Longfellow)':

> Came the stern Adjudicator
> Of the tribe of the MacMillans,
> Came in feathers and in war-paint
> Utt'ring wild, blood-curdling war whoops,
> Came with eye severe, forbidding,
> Came with predatory scalp-knife,
> So that altos and sopranos
> (To say nothing of the Basses
> And still less of throaty tenors)
> Trembled at his very presence,
> So that all the lads and lasses
> Were afraid they would be eaten,
> Killed and fricaseed and eaten
> By this fearsome, savage ogre.
>
> Came the pianists and fiddlers
> And a solitary cellist,
> Came the chubby boy sopranos
> Wearing spotless Eaton collars
> Topped by rosy, shining faces.
>
> Came the dainty little maidens
> In their well-starched party dresses
> With bewitching smiles and dimples,
> Came the Donors of the Trophies,
> Came the most important people
> Of the City of Penticton.[12]

And further on, after describing the playing and the grading and the anxiety of candidates and audience, he came to his young Penticton assistant, 'the lovely Winnie-Ha-Ha,' who had

cheered him, brought order out of chaos, assembled his many
mark sheets with their many comments, and, most of all, made
him smile.

> And her gracious, charming presence
> And the sunlight on her blonde hair,
> Her unostentatious guidance
> Through the mysteries of adding
> Had completely counteracted
> All his baser, Lower Nature,
> Had quite tranquilly effected
> This most strange transfiguration.
>
> From that moment on, the Ogre
> Was comparatively human,
> And competitors were treated
> With a tolerable mildness.
>
> Praises therefore give to Winnie,
> To the winsome Winnie-ha-ha,
> Saviour of the Okanagan!
> Let the singers and violinists,
> Let the pianists and cellists,
> Let the choirs and their conductors,
> Raise a psalm to her who saved them,
> From the sad Fate hanging o'er them.

He gave some thought to becoming the permanent conductor
of the Vancouver Symphony Orchestra (VSO). Its incumbent,
Allard de Ridder, was leaving, and the job was his for the asking.
However, the VSO was still a very young orchestra, and would be
quite a comedown from the TSO. He then turned his thoughts
to the Seattle Symphony (a better orchestra than Vancouver's) –
he could have taken it on along with the VSO – and went to
Seattle to investigate. The University of British Columbia's newly
created chair in music might also fall to him if he settled in
Vancouver. Ernest, a bit out of character, asked Elsie to leak these
possibilities to the TSO board to help his bargaining position.[13]

In June, MacKelcan and Hahn sent Ernest wires urging him not to act hastily. He heard no more and returned east in July in time to conduct the Montreal Symphony at the chalet on Mount Royal. From there, he and Elsie visited Rudolf and Irene Serkin at their Brattleboro, Vermont, hilltop home, where Ernest had a few piano lessons with Serkin. Several years before he had asked the pianist for lessons but Serkin had refused, saying that Ernest didn't need any. This time he agreed. At the first lesson, Ernest asked the generous and self-effacing Serkin if he played too much like an organist, to which Serkin replied, 'You play like a very good pianist who hasn't kept up his practice.'[14] The MacMillans had a delightful time with the Serkins, and with members of the Busch family as well – Irene Serkin was the daughter of violinist Adolph Busch and niece of the conductor Fritz Busch.

They went from Brattleboro to Philadelphia, where Ernest conducted members of the Philadelphia Orchestra outdoors at the Robin Hood Dell. The press praised him, but modestly. The *Record* thought his Mozart G Minor Symphony (No. 40) 'too deliberate' and the Enesco *First Rumanian Rhapsody* attractive and interesting but not necessarily distinguished. It did, however, acknowledge that Ernest's reception from both orchestra and audience 'approached an ovation.'[15] The review of *Evening Bulletin* critic Henry Pleasants (who would become a prominent author) was better. Ernest's reading of the Mozart 'was the work of an admirably equipped musician. It was well-proportioned and tastefully phrased. The tempi were rather deliberate but they were consistently sustained and might have been completely effective had the performance had as much of vitality and temperament as it had of restraint and good judgement.' Commenting on the second half of the program, which, in addition to the Enesco, included Ravel's *Mother Goose Suite*, Pleasants said that 'Sir Ernest handled everything with authority, although again with the inevitable Anglo-Saxon temperance and respectability.'[16]

The rest of the summer was all holiday. First he and Elsie went to Tanglewood, where they stayed at the same cottage he had rented the previous summer, and from there they visited the New York World's Fair. 'Nation vied with nation to express its friendship with the United States. Even the comparatively restrained exhibit of Great Britain included the family tree of George Washington emphasising his British origin ... The Japanese "Friend-Ship," on which Japanese and American girls played together with evident enjoyment, struck us, even then, as rather ironical.'[17] Ernest thought little of the Canadian exhibit. 'No doubt it had its striking features, but it was certainly not memorable; many other countries were more lavish and imaginative.' While at the fair, the MacMillans heard the news of the Hitler-Stalin pact. They returned home fearful and apprehensive. Canada declared war on 10 September 1939.

The onset of war was a catharsis which made Ernest look outward instead of inward. It resolved his angst about his conducting and led him to put aside his personal aspirations and frustrations and face up to a larger and more pressing task, – helping his country and its allies defeat a tyrannical foe. The war brought him back to fundamental issues and responsibilities, to serving his fellow man and his institutions in a time of need. It also meant being artistically responsible, as he made clear when discussing an 8 October program with the VSO.

I was distressed that a cry against German music as such should have been raised at this early stage. Nazism has attacked the cultural and intellectual life of its own, as of other lands; for that reason amongst others we are fighting it. If it is going to be considered unpatriotic to perform German music during the war it seems to me that we are surrendering to the thing we are fighting. To perform music by living composers like Richard Strauss and others who are more or less in accord with the Nazi regime might be debatable, but it will be quite impossible for any orchestra or any other musical organization to carry on without the German classics. I can see no earthly reason why they should. Should such a question become acute here I would certainly change my mind about continuing as Conductor for the present season. Germany was jingoistic enough, Heaven knows, during the last war, but, having read the Berlin papers almost throughout that period, I can testify that there was very rarely a time when some theatre in Berlin was not performing Shakespeare. This matter may require a little propaganda to clarify the public mind, but I think the sooner it is done the better. Any attempt to omit the standard classics would, in the long run, diminish the popular appeal of the orchestra.[18]

The principal work on the program was Brahms's First Symphony. Significantly, he also included two British works, Sir Alexander MacKenzie's *Britannia* and Vaughan Williams's *Fantasia on a Theme by Thomas Tallis*.

While he was in Vancouver to conduct the VSO, he also awarded conservatory graduation certificates and gave a talk to the Vancouver Institute on 'Hitler and Wagnerism,' addressing in it Wagner's influence on Hitler and its resulting effect on Germany.[19] The paper, coming so soon after the outbreak of hostilities, shows how quickly Ernest had emerged from his bout with the TSO and his self-indulgences of the previous year.

First, he described how *Lohengrin* had 'captivated' Hitler at an early age and how, later, when he became a friend of the Wagner family, Wagnerian theories and concepts had coloured his mind. Ernest explained how important music was in Wagner's scheme of things:

Wagner is strongest when he frankly subordinates words and action to music. The weakness in certain works, particularly in certain parts of the *Ring*, are found precisely where the musician temporarily loses control and the voice of the preacher or philosopher is heard. Yet the words in such passages are by no means always inferior as poetry to other passages which, in their musical setting, give us great delight. Wagner's self-deception in this respect is mentioned only as a particular instance of a fundamental egotism, amounting practically to self-hypnosis, which permeates his entire attitude to life.

Wagner, the egocentric philosopher, fascinated Hitler most, said MacMillan, quoting the Wagner scholar Ernest Newman to make his point. Wagner, 'from the beginning to the end of his career, laid down, for universal acceptance, ideas and theories that were purely personal to himself, and he was unable to conceive how the whole world, when it came to its senses, could think differently from him ... His faith in his own philosophical ideas, his belief in their importance for the regeneration of the universe, would surely be grotesque if it were not so pathetic.'

MacMillan enumerated the ways in which Hitler resembled Wagner: how he had a 'passionate conviction that he was always right,' how he believed without question in the 'importance of his message to the world,' how he was 'utterly unscrupulous in making use of his friends or anyone else to further his purposes,' and how he was 'sublimely disdainful of the rights of others.' Both men believed in the superiority of the German 'race' and, to MacMillan's disgust, were violent anti-Semites – MacMillan's views, throughout his life, were profoundly egalitarian and without prejudice towards others. But, he reminded his audience, Wagner was withal a great composer, while Hitler was a failed artist who found an alternative and deadly way of expressing himself:

Hitler felt a perverted Wagnerism in almost all his actions and speeches. Like Wagner, he must always be explaining himself, and his speeches suggest a parody of Wagnerian music, with their fluent spate of sound, their constant reiteration of the same leading motifs and their continually rising climaxes. Furthermore, his elaborate staging of those speeches is Wagnerian in its splendour, and, in the monumental party rallies and similar national occasions, the artist in him is seen in its most impressive and most dangerous aspects ... Wagner presents us with the picture of the artist who found in his art a fulfilment that makes his personal failings and confused thinking unimportant; whereas Hitler appears as the supreme perversion of the romantic imagination, the frustrated artist, not lacking in elements of greatness, but pursuing his aims regardless of any considerations save those dictated by his own dangerously vivid imagination.

How could the German people subscribe to such a 'threadbare philosophy' and deliver themselves 'body and soul into the hands of such a sorry mountebank crew,' asked Ernest? He attributed this to their 'strange faculty of self-hypnosis' and speculated that under 'similar circumstances we, too, might succumb to so hollow a system.' He ended with a graphic scenario. 'Hitler sees himself as a knight in shining armour, appearing like Lohengrin at the most critical moment of Germany's history to rescue her as Lohengrin rescued Elsa, from slander, torture and death ... When he departed with heroic gestures to lead his injured nation against the treacherous Poles, can we doubt that the militant sword-motif of the *Ring* sounded continuously in his ears and that he saw himself as Siegfried setting forth to slay the dragon?' And then, almost precisely foretelling what was to come, he said, 'Premonitions of his approaching death ... lead one to suppose that he may regard the present holocaust in the light of a sort of *Götterdämmerung* with the whole of Europe afire as a funeral pyre for Adolf Hitler.'

Canada's enigmatic Prime Minister Mackenzie King heard about the paper and asked MacMillan for a copy. In a letter to MacMillan he pronounced it 'a valuable contribution to an aspect of Hitlerism the great significance of which should be widely known and appreciated.'[20] He made no mention of how impressed he had been with Hitler just a few years earlier. An American diplomat reported that King had called Hitler 'a very sincere man ... sweet ... although he was clearly a dreamer and gave the impression of having an artistic temperament.'[21] King had written in his diary at that time that 'Hitler might come to be thought of as one of the saviours of the world. He had the chance at Nuremberg, but was looking to Force, to Might, and to Violence as means to achieving his ends, which were, I believe, at heart, the well being of his fellow-man; not all fellow-men, but those of his own race.'[22]

When MacMillan sent his Hitler paper to King, he enclosed a copy of a memorandum he had prepared, on 'Music in War Time,' which spelled out ways in which music could aid the war effort.[23] Hoping for King's support, he asked him, gently, to consider 'a consistent plan for the exploitation of music as a factor in war and for the incorporation in all plans for Post-War reconstruction of a more definite policy with regard to music and the arts generally. Great Britain and other countries have done a great deal ... but our efforts in Canada have been somewhat sporadic and lacking in coordination.' It was Ernest's first attempt to persuade top government officials to support the arts.

Skilful politician that he was, King skirted Ernest's suggestions
with gratuitous words: 'I feel the same about the importance of
preserving natural beauty at a time of war – parks, flowers, music.
The need that all of Nature and the fine arts have to contribute
toward uplifting the soul of man is greater, I believe, at a time of
war than at any other time, if for no other reason other than that
war goes so far toward the destruction of *everything*, including that
which is highest and best.'[24]

Fifteen months after giving his paper on Wagner and Hitler,
Ernest spoke to American music teachers in Cleveland on a related theme, the Nazis and artistic freedom. His thoughts about the
playing of German music were similar to those he had first aired
in his September 1939 letter to the VSO:

If the Nazi view of life were to prevail, not only music but all the arts
would wither and die. This can be asserted in full consciousness of the
fact that Germany, which has given to the world its greatest musicians,
has been a model to other countries in publicly subsidising musical
organisations. It can be stated, too, in full consciousness of the fact that
music may flourish apart from democratic institutions; the history of the
18th century shows this, though the case might have been different if
the 18th century patrons of music had been dictators on a 20th century
scale and with 20th century facilities for interfering with their subjects.
The Nazi system has proved terribly efficient in strangling true culture.
Its attack on the human mind has been more disastrous even than its
attack on life and property.[25]

And he went on to talk of Nazi book burnings: 'Any country
that drives from her borders her Einsteins, her Thomas Manns,
her Sigmund Freuds, and, in general, her most distinguished
thinkers is impoverishing herself incalculably ... Not only does she
lose them, but, by making an example of them, she suppresses
the moral courage of those among her younger sons who might
have taken their place.' He condemned the Nazis for banning
music by Jewish composers and for their 'savage determination to
stamp out all that is most characteristic of each nation. When we
hear that Smetana has been banned in Czecho-Slovakia and
Chopin in Poland, can we doubt that England under their con-

trol would be forbidden Purcell and Elgar, and that America would no longer hear MacDowell, Stephen Foster, or George Gershwin? No musician can afford to be indifferent to the outcome of this struggle.'

II. *Music and the War Effort*

Ernest MacMillan was fearful that activities and organizations not considered vital to the war effort, such as symphony orchestras, would be neglected or abandoned. In the Great War, Toronto's orchestra had limped along for four years and then folded, not to be revived for five years and not to regain its prestige and audiences for still another decade. Now it was a more substantial organization, and Ernest was determined that it not go under again.

And so in those first horrendous days of the war, as Hitler successfully invaded Poland and the Western powers stood helplessly by, Ernest, who had already put his plans to resign from the TSO behind him, set about countering any moves that threatened the orchestra's existence. TSO board member James Hahn, for one, pressed the board in early September 1939 to return the orchestra to a 'share' plan, as in von Kunits's New Symphony Orchestra days. The prescient Ernest told Hahn how wrong he was: 'The less disruption there is in the general economic life of the country the better. Every organization that folds up creates an additional problem for its employees, and hence for the country.' Canada, he said, would prosper, as would the TSO: 'People need music and need it badly in wartime.' He argued that his work of the past eight years must not have been in vain.[1] It worked. Hahn backed off and the TSO went on as in the past. To everyone's delight, ticket sales gradually increased. Few knew that both Ernest and concert-master Elie Spivak quietly gave up their salaries for the season.

The winter and spring of 1940 was a terrible time for the Allies. After Dunkirk the entire free world feared the worst, and when Paris fell, Ernest dejectedly wrote to Elsie from Vancouver, 'Seriously, after this spell is over I must get out of music. It is quite impossible to keep one's mind on it under present conditions, and there are things to do, surely, that a reasonably intelligent person can accomplish.'[2] But he put aside such thoughts and was soon caught up with tending to the needs of his sister Dorothy, who had returned to Canada after many years abroad. She and her eleven-year-old daughter Jocelyn were English evacuees. In mid-June, after a perilous ocean crossing (Gracie Fields had been on the same boat), they arrived safely in Toronto and moved in with Alexander and Jean on Elgin Avenue.[3] Dorothy had a history of heart trouble and was quite unwell with another unidentified ailment. Ernest took matters in hand and, with some difficulty, found a doctor who diagnosed and successfully treated her thyroid. Dorothy was also without financial resources and desperately needed a job. Ernest made widespread enquiries on her behalf – she had an MA in Philology from the University of Toronto and had also studied at the Sorbonne in Paris.[4] She finally became a diction teacher at the Toronto Conservatory, where, through the years, she taught many fine singers.

In Toronto young Jocelyn felt for the first time that she had a family – and a distinguished one at that. But it wasn't easy to know it intimately. She found that her illustrious uncle was never really at ease with her or, for that matter, with children generally. Elsie, on the other hand, was warm, thoughtful, and hospitable, and made her feel very welcome. Jocelyn remembered visits to the Keith's Lorne Park home (which Ernest called his Shangri-La) and their tramps through the woods, with Ernest methodically singing themes from *Hansel and Gretel*. This was his bright side, but she also remembered his black moods, when he would erupt in a temper at the slightest provocation. Ernest was not the only one with mood swings. His three sisters were much the same. At times, according to Jocelyn, brother and sisters seemed bottled up, as if they were nursing secret feelings and frustrations. They carried a lot of baggage inside them, which they were disinclined to share with others.

And, Jocelyn felt, the MacMillans mixed family pride with feelings of superiority. She recalled studying piano with volatile and impatient Winifred and being told, when pupil confessed to teacher that an assigned piece was too difficult, 'You're not a MacMillan if you can't do it.' When Jocelyn finally talked back to Winifred, she was dismissed and told never to return. She also remembered, with amusement, an 'essential' favour her mother did for Ernest as the war continued. The wartime liquor ration did not cover the demands of hospitality as well as personal intake, and so Ernest would drive Dorothy to the government controlled liquor store where she would sign for her allotment – his choice – and then turn the purchase over to him![5]

Ernest used every opportunity to remind others that musicians best served their country by doing what they knew best – making music. In an address to a group of Toronto businessmen in December 1940, he described how a Prom concert to a full house in war-torn London's Queen's Hall had been prolonged because of a particularly vicious bombardment. 'Musicians and actors took to the platform and played, sang, and recited until four in the morning to keep up the audience's spirits.'[6] The British flocked to concerts with unflagging enthusiasm and, when the Promenade Concerts were halted temporarily in September 1940, it was because of London's transport problems, not the bombings. Musicians, Ernest proudly proclaimed, 'are as capable as anyone else of rising to an emergency and doing their jobs with perfect *sang-froid* under extreme difficulties.' He practised what he preached. The TSO and smaller groups from the orchestra played at bond rallies and similar events for the duration of the war.

And concert attendance did grow. In the 1940–1 season, TSO subscriptions increased by three hundred, and increases continued each year until the end of the war. One of Ernest's responses to this happy state of affairs was to start TSO secondary school concerts in the 1941–2 season. They were given in the evening at Massey Hall and broadcast on the CBC, much like portions of the subscription concerts. Thanks to the efforts of musically minded students from across the city, attendance was so good that soon each concert was repeated. The first president of the student's council was conductor Victor Feldbrill, and one of its first members was composer Harry Somers.[7] Students paid forty cents admission to hear much of the same music that was being played for TSO adult audiences. To help publicize the concerts and raise money, schools had 'tag days,' and the TSO's women's committee conducted 'talent searches' for soloists. In his 'Memoirs,' Ernest looked back with great satisfaction to those concerts and to the end-of-year get-togethers, when student council members would assemble at Park Road for a short business meeting, followed by a program by the teenage musicians. Then the floor would be cleared and there would be dancing on into the night.[8]

Unfortunately, the TSO children's concerts ran into difficulties in 1942. Wartime fuel shortages necessitated cancelling the chartered buses which brought the children to and from Massey Hall. For a while they used public transportation, but this created unmanageable chaos on the city's already overburdened streetcars at the height of the evening rush hour. Toronto's transit officials, in desperation, urged the TSO to suspend the concerts for the duration. Rather than do this, the TSO, with the help of the CBC, continued them as a radio series entitled 'Music for Young Folk.' Ten forty-five-minute broadcasts were given in the first series, from 20 January to 24 March 1943. The TSO performed for four of the programs and small ensembles for the other six. Ettore Mazzoleni, recently appointed associate conductor of the TSO, led the orchestra and shared the narration with MacMillan and Roy Fenwick of the Ontario Department of Education.

Now Toronto school authorities were more cooperative – an estimated 14,000 children in the Toronto area listened to the concerts in class, assisted by handbooks prepared by the CBC and music educators. Programs were built on what had gone before, and there were follow-up discussions in class. There is no doubt that, from a learning point of view, they were a great improvement over live concerts in Massey Hall.

What with all the TSO's various concerts and the summer Promenade Symphony Concerts, Toronto was experiencing a musical high. In the summer of 1942, the Proms (the biggest drawing card) had 12,000 more listeners than in any previous season, and Ernest predicted that overall attendance at Toronto orchestral concerts in 1942–3, summer and winter, would reach almost 250,000.[9]

Our indefatigable musical warrior's diary was packed full. In 1940, in addition to the TSO, he guest conducted the Montreal Symphony, gave organ recitals in Toronto, the Atlantic provinces, and British Columbia, and even adjudicated in Kingston, Jamaica. Inspired by Winston Churchill's tenacity and courage, Ernest and his sister Dorothy wrote the words and music for a patriotic song entitled 'It's a Grand Life If We Don't Weaken,' which the TSO and a choral group performed for the Christmas Box concert on 17 December 1940. The song's lyrics read, in part, as follows:

> When Winston says 'We can take it'
> He knows the bulldog breed,
> And his voice rings out round the Empire
> With the very words we need.
>
> We're with you Winston Churchill
> We'll hold on, grim and gay,
> And we'll fight it through to a finish
> For that's the British way.

On 21 January 1941, the TSO and the Mendelssohn Choir did MacMillan's *England*, its first performance in twenty years. It was, furthermore, the first time *he* had conducted it. The work was well received, as much for the text's unabashedly flagrant flag-waving as for its music. Also in January, Ernest took on an important non-musical wartime task when he agreed to chair the Canadian branch of the War Prisoners' Aid Committee of the Young Men's Christian Association (YMCA), the body responsible for providing adequate facilities for study, recreation, and worship for German prisoners of war in Canada. Ernest's own first-hand experiences a generation earlier had made him well aware of the importance of these things. Doing the job well, he hoped, would encourage the enemy to provide similar facilities for Allied prisoners of war.[10] He conscientiously chaired committee meetings several times yearly, kept in close touch with the prison camps, and visited them from time to time. Generally conditions were similar to those he had endured at

Ruhleben. At Lethbridge, Alberta, Ernest attended a camp concert where he found the orchestra to be 'somewhat better' than the Ruhleben orchestra. He was amused by the way in which the man who announced the program goose-stepped to the front of the platform and gave the Nazi salute (he was forbidden to say Heil Hitler). 'He would announce a work of Mozart, Köchel Verzeichnis number and all, in the voice of a sergeant-major, salute once more and retire until the next number.'[11]

In a related context, Ernest sought the release of German-born anti-Nazi youths of military age who, when war broke out, had been interned in Britain and then sent to Canada for imprisonment as enemy aliens. Most were young and Jewish.[12] Negotiations moved slowly, and Ernest wrote to F.C. Blair, the Director of Immigration and a notorious anti-Semite, to try to speed things up. Blair never replied![13] The Canadian Cabinet finally approved the release of the young men, many of whom became leading Canadians in the next quarter-century.

Meanwhile, Ernest's feelers of 1939 to find a new position bore fruit when, in early March 1941, Edinburgh University invited him to succeed the brilliant musician and scholar Sir Donald Tovey as Reid Professor of Music.[14] No doubt the invitation stemmed from Ernest's inquiries to Sir Adrian Boult. Honoured by the invitation and mindful that his first music history teacher, Frederick Niecks, had been the Reid professor, Ernest was tempted indeed. The prestigious post called for six months each year of lecturing, administering, and conducting the university's Reid Orchestra in Edinburgh, with – most important – the other six months free to follow one's own pursuits.

But the Edinburgh post also had its drawbacks, and Boult warned Ernest about them.[15] It was unpromising financially (the salary was a mere 1,000 pounds per annum), the smaller Reid Orchestra was not as good as the TSO although 'a live-wire conductor could help,' and Ernest was more in the 'centre of things' in Toronto than he would be in Edinburgh. Boult had spoken to Vincent Massey, the Canadian high commissioner in London, who was of the opinion that it would be a 'calamity' if Ernest left Canada and that Edinburgh wasn't a good enough appointment for him anyway.

And so, with Toronto, the TSO, and Ernest himself much changed after two years of war, he declined the offer. He wrote candidly to Edinburgh that building the TSO into a first-class group was 'exceptionally interesting. Nevertheless, I have always felt that it is possible to get into a rut. The TSO's activities in recent years have not expanded to the extent I should have wished. Now, however, there seems to be a greater interest in the orchestra. The boards of the Orchestra, University, and Conservatory were so urgent in wishing me to remain and so cordial in their professions of support that I finally made up my mind to remain.'[16]

Alexander MacMillan was very disappointed. As Ernest told it, his father 'divided the cities of the world into two categories – Edinburgh (his birthplace) and the rest. Naturally he urged me to accept and I doubt if he ever forgave me for declining.'[17] Alexander had indiscreetly told Augustus Bridle about the invitation when it had first arrived and, when Ernest said no, the three local newspapers made much of it, saying how proud Canada should be that he was asked to Edinburgh and how proud it should be that he had said no.[18]

Not two months later, Reginald Stewart, Ernest's longtime rival for Toronto's conducting crown, got into a serious squabble with the Toronto Musicians' Association, sponsor of his Promenade concerts, and he resigned in a huff. The resignation was immediately accepted by high-handed union president Walter Murdoch and Proms manager and violinist Ernest Johnson, who both thought that Stewart's programs were getting too heavy for summer fare and were hurting the box office.[19] Within weeks, Stewart left Toronto to become the director of the Peabody Conservatory in Baltimore, one of America's finest music schools. The following year he was made conductor of the Baltimore Symphony. A *Globe and Mail* editorial spoke for many: 'It should be a matter of widespread regret and of heart-searching among the parties responsible for it that Canadian culture, which is none too rich in devoted servants of first-rate calibre, is to lose his notable talents.'[20]

Following conducting engagements at his two favourite summer haunts, Vancouver's Stanley Park and Montreal's Chalet, MacMillan gave a series of six half-hour piano and violin sonata recitals on the CBC with Canadian violinist Kathleen Parlow. Parlow had returned to Toronto after a distinguished international career and, with Ernest's enthusiastic approval, was teaching at the conservatory. They did varied – and difficult – repertoire: Grieg's G Major Sonata, Beethoven's *Spring* Sonata, John Ireland's Sonata No. 2, Dohnanyi's Sonata, Op. 21, Brahms's D Minor Sonata, and Mozart's A Major Sonata (1787).

The tape of the Grieg performance reveals that Ernest was an excellent partner – Charles Peaker called him a 'musician's pianist' – who coped well with the work's technical demands.[21] Parlow's rich tone overpowered his more pallid sound, but he, more than Parlow, took advantage of the work's intrinsic interest and humour. The two musicians, pleased with their collaboration, asked the twenty-two-year-old Winnipeg cellist Zara Nelsova to join them to form the Canadian Trio. Nelsova was a great asset, since she knew the literature well, having played trios from childhood with her sisters. A few months earlier Ernest had appointed her principal cellist of the TSO. Although she had no previous orchestral experience, she played so much better than any of the other local cellists that Ernest gladly took the risk.

The Canadian Trio made an auspicious debut at Eaton Auditorium on 28 November 1941, playing Schubert's Trio in B-flat Major, Haydn's Trio in A Major (revised by Tovey), and Tchaikovsky's Trio in A Minor. The press was overwhelmed with the group's ensemble playing, which clearly eclipsed other local chamber groups. Ernest welcomed these excursions into trio and sonata playing, for he loved the music and relished the demands made on his musicianship. Sad to say, the groups disbanded the next year when Nelsova, after a New York debut at Town Hall, left Toronto to pursue a solo career and Parlow moved on to string quartet playing. Thus ended Ernest's brief spell as professional chamber musician.

The fall of 1941 was busy in other ways too. Queen's University awarded him an honorary LLD. And on 5 December, one week after the Canadian Trio's debut, MacMillan conducted the conservatory's choir and orchestra in a Convocation Hall performance of Mozart's *Requiem* and Symphony No. 39 to commemorate the 150th anniversary of the composer's death. However, neither Mozart nor his music attracted anything like the attention they would receive fifty years later for the 200th anniversary.

A few days after the *Requiem*, he left for New York. The long-awaited opportunity to conduct there had finally come. He would do two broadcasts with the National Broadcasting Company (NBC) Symphony, an orchestra hand-picked for Arturo Toscanini and considered one of the very best in the United States. (Reginald Stewart had conducted it the previous April.) Over its seventeen-year life, 1937 to 1954, it gave weekly broadcasts, with Toscanini conducting from twelve to twenty of them annually and guest conductors doing the rest. Toscanini also made many recordings with the group.

Before leaving for New York, Ernest had been in an irritable mood and, on the day of his first concert, apologized to Elsie by letter.[22] 'It is,' he wrote, 'good for my soul to spend Christmas away from home for once so that I shall realize how much I miss being with you.' He told her that the NBC Symphony was 'superbly responsive' and described a performance he had attended of *The Marriage of Figaro* at the Metropolitan Opera and another of *Watch on the Rhine* on Broadway, which he thought not as good as its reviews.

NBC relayed the concerts to the CBC and, judging from the many congratulatory wires and letters Ernest received, most of musical Canada heard them. He did Schubert's Ninth Symphony for the first broadcast and Tchaikovsky's Fifth for the second. Alas, despite the fine orchestra, Ernest had his usual problems. He conducted slowly and stodgily, acceptable perhaps in Europe, but not in New York and especially not with this orchestra, which was accustomed to Toscanini's driving and much faster tempi.

Sensing that he had not overwhelmed the orchestra with his readings, he was somewhat cheered by a letter from Samuel Richard Gaines, an American composer who had known Tchaikovsky. Gaines told him how much he had enjoyed the horn solo in the second movement of the Tchaikovsky and how much the composer would have liked it too.[23] Ernest had taken the solo so slowly that Harry Berv, the hornist, was close to exhaustion by its end, though he played it beautifully. Ernest admitted that he had persuaded Berv to play it in 'a leisurely, dreamy fashion; he had always been accustomed to taking it faster.'[24]

Hyman Goodman, TSO violinist and – for almost a decade – its concert-master, tells a waggish story about Ernest's rehearsal of the Schubert. After the first run-through, the NBC's concert-master, Mischa Mischakoff, hoping to cut short the preparation of that very long work, rose and congratulated MacMillan for his fine reading. Whereupon Ernest, quite missing the point, told the orchestra to turn back to the beginning to start strenuous re-hearsing.[25] These were Ernest's only appearances with the NBC.

There were more engagements in the United States – the Phila-delphia Orchestra at the Academy of Music in February and Washington's National Symphony at the Watergate Pavilion in June. Bad luck befell him on both occasions. In Philadelphia he had an inflamed and painful right arm, probably due to tension, and in Washington the first of his three scheduled concerts was rained out. He didn't conduct in the United States again until 1946.

As the war continued, the CBC responded to Canada's growing interest in serious music with increasingly imaginative program-ming. In 1942, it produced a series of 'British Ballad Operas,' most of which Ernest conducted. There were performances of *Acis and Galatea* (Handel), *Dido and Aeneas* (Purcell), *The Beggar's Opera* (in the Austin version), *Merrie England* (German), *The Bohe-mian Girl* (Balfe), *The Immortal Hour* (Boughton), *Hugh the Drover* (Vaughan Williams), *The Devil Take Her* (Benjamin), and *Transit through Fire* by Healey Willan and librettist John Coulter, the CBC's first commissioned opera. *Transit through Fire* is about 'youth in search of a purpose in life,' and its subtitle, 'An Odyssey of 1942,' places it firmly in the 1940s. A Canadian soldier and his wife, as MacMillan describes it, 'look back from 1942 at the period of chaos and frustration of the 30s.'[26] The whole panorama of life in Canada is depicted, as the young man strives to succeed at university, lives through the stock market crash, the ensuing depression, and the early days of the war. The opera concludes with a marching song 'full of hope for the future.' (The CBC commissioned a second opera by Willan in 1946, *Deirdre of the Sorrows*.)

Of course, the title of the series was a misnomer, since only a few of the works were ballad operas. To explain the rationale for the series, CBC general manager Gladstone Murray said that the Met's Saturday broadcasts were 'not everybody's meat. The Anglo-Saxon temperament does not on the whole take to the themes and declamatory style of grand opera. The Briton, on the whole, prefers musical comedy or light opera with its simple emotions, catchy tunes and words that can be appreciated.'[27] Murray's views reflected the low level of his musical sophistication, taste, and outlook. He considered English-speaking Canada to be Anglo-Saxon only – and he was the *head* of the CBC. But, his views aside, the quality of the productions was superior, and with *Transit through Fire* there was something new in the air – the CBC's recognition of Canadian music.

On 27 April 1942, after several years of soul-searching, indecision, and frustration, Ernest resigned as principal of the Toronto Conservatory, although he continued to be dean of the Faculty of Music. The resignation was not unexpected. Many felt that he should have left the post sooner, for he had done all he could for what was fundamentally a hopeless situation, a school completely dependent on teaching and examination income. Ernest said none of this in his letter of resignation. Having recently become the conductor of the Mendelssohn Choir, he gave 'increased pressure' from his outside activities as his reason for stepping down.[28]

The conservatory board, especially its guiding force Floyd Chalmers, welcomed MacMillan's departure. While full of admiration for MacMillan's musical and executive talents, Chalmers believed that he held too many leading positions in Toronto's musical life and was not devoting enough time to his conservatory post.[29] (Chalmers had for a long time favoured Reginald Stewart in the MacMillan/Stewart contest.)[30] To force the resignation, the board, with Chalmers as the *éminence grise*, had offered MacMillan unacceptable salary terms for 1942–3.[31] It did, however, give him a generous separation allowance.

The conservatory honoured Ernest at a farewell dinner party, although it came a year after his resignation. Teachers humor-

ously and affectionately acted out highlights of his life and un-
veiled a portrait of him in his doctoral robes by the noted Canadian painter Kenneth Forbes – Elsie's cousin. Ernest called the
portrait conventional, yet well done, and said with a smile that it
would probably be on view long after he was forgotten. He envis-
aged it hanging in a twenty-second century salon entitled 'Portrait
of a Man in Academic Costume, Early 20th Century.'[32]

Ernest had been asked to take over the Mendelssohn Choir
because its retiring conductor, the seventy-four-year-old English-
born Herbert Fricker, had been in poor health for several years.
Fricker had come to Canada in 1917 to succeed the choir's
founder and conductor, A.S. Vogt, but it was not until after the
Great War, when enough male voices were once more available,
that he restored the choir to its former eminence. The establishment of MacMillan's Conservatory Choir in 1927 had spawned a
healthy rivalry between the two groups that continued until the
Second World War, when once again the inevitable shortage of
male singers resulted in poorer quality and curtailed schedules
for both choirs. Fricker, in failing health, was unable to face such
difficulties a second time. MacMillan's appointment as his successor was artistically sound *and* practical.

Almost immediately, MacMillan merged his Toronto Conservatory Choir with the Mendelssohn group to found the Toronto
Mendelssohn Choir. All members were asked to reaudition. There
was much pruning, and the end result was a better choir than
either of the other two had been. The conservatory gave the new
choir rehearsal and office space at minimum rates.

Always on good terms with Fricker, Ernest paid him a warm
tribute at a Canadian College of Organist's dinner on 2 November 1942. In praising Fricker's taste in choral music, he altered a
line from the Book of Proverbs: 'His works rise up and call him
blessed.' Ernest noted the many enduring choral masterpieces
Fricker had done in his twenty-five years as the Mendelssohn
Choir conductor, especially Fricker's favourite, Bach's *B Minor
Mass*. He also spoke of the many fine American orchestras –
Pittsburgh, Chicago, Philadelphia, Cincinnati, Detroit – which had
played with the choir. Clearly, the two men admired one another.
MacMillan, it was said, had learned much about choral technique

from Fricker, and Fricker thought MacMillan the finest organist he had ever heard.[33]

Soon after MacMillan's appointment, the CBC invited him to conduct an ambitious series of Handel's less-frequently done oratorios – *Joshua, Saul, Samson, Solomon,* and *Judas Maccabaeus* – and several of his secular choral works – *Acis and Galatea, Alexander's Feast,* and the *Ode for St Cecilia's Day.* The programs, more imaginatively presented than those on the opera series, showed how the CBC was broadening the country's musical taste. They also revealed to many a sceptic that Ernest MacMillan not only had an immense choral repertoire but also knew the difference between choral and orchestral conducting. He wrote tellingly on the subject:

The choral conductor should be thoroughly familiar with the words as well as the music of the work he is directing. Inasmuch as the singers have usually the complete vocal score in front of them, it is not always essential in *a cappella* singing to give a decisive down-beat – or even any type of conventional beat – to indicate the rhythm. Facial expression counts far more with a choir than an orchestra; the singers, if they have learned their work thoroughly (and perhaps memorized it), are able to watch the conductor more closely than can members of an orchestra and feel a stronger emotional rapport with him.[34]

In a word, Ernest believed that choral conducting is far more personal than orchestral conducting. Eye contact is paramount. A skilled conductor rehearses a choir much like a sculptor works with a chisel, painstakingly carving out each syllable, note, phrase, and stanza until satisfied. On the other hand, an orchestra plays music without words and in addition expresses itself through difficult instruments. Orchestral players, therefore, look for clear beats and other basic directional aids. Eye contact is rare, the setting more impersonal, the conductor more objective, his gestures more controlled and precise. At his best, the orchestra conductor, as Vaughan Williams has said, 'plays on the orchestra,' the orchestra is *his* instrument.[35] When choir and orchestra perform together the conductor must carefully balance his treatment of these two disparate musical groups.

How a conductor rehearses a choir tells us much about how he arrives at the finished product. Maud McLean, a Mendelssohn Choir chorister and choir historian who had joined the choir as a school-girl in Ernest's first year, recalled that 'his rehearsal methods were a genial blend of humour, courteous concern, and scholarly musicianship, harmonised with the skill and genius of a man completely familiar with the capabilities of both a choir and an orchestra.'[36] He was 'a veritable tower of strength ... who inspired us to new heights we would not have dared tackle without him.' She also remembered how he used imagery to teach the choir to sing 'Their Sound Is Gone Out' from *Messiah*, by suggesting they visualize 'a lighthouse with its sweeping beams of light piercing the darkness.'

But Ernest also had his problems with the Mendelssohn. He could be impatient when rehearsing new works, not unusual when a gifted musician works with amateurs. And then, he was so busy with other commitments that he left many of the preliminary rehearsals to chorusmaster Frederick Silvester. This meant that when choir and orchestra were brought together doubts could arise in the choir as to what was wanted. And because financial considerations limited orchestral rehearsal time, Ernest often concentrated too much on the orchestra at the final rehearsals before a concert, at the expense of the choir.

Ernest even had the occasional temper tantrum when the Mendelssohn failed to cope with difficult music. McLean remembered two such incidents. In one, in January 1944, Ernest walked out of a rehearsal of a new work, Healey Willan's *Brébeuf.* In his defence, he was in a highly agitated state because his younger son, Ross, a fighter pilot in the RCAF, had just left for Europe to fly with the famed Johnny Johnson squadron.[37] (Keith, an RCAF aerial photographer, had already been overseas for three years.) In the other incident, also during the war, he became so distraught with the choir's work that he threw his music in the air and flung his music stand across the room. From time to time after that, Elsie would attend rehearsals, and there were no recurrences. In more temperate moments, when the choir sang sluggishly, he would tell them with a twinkle in his eye that he felt as if he were trying to take 'a jellyfish for a walk on the end of an elastic band.'[38]

All in all, the Mendelssohn's members remembered MacMillan's days most fondly. His first concert with the revamped choir and the TSO was a grandiose *Messiah* at Massey Hall on 29 December 1942, preceded by a CBC broadcast of Part One only, on Christmas Day. The choir had 184 voices and, as if that wasn't enough, 100 additional singers from four Toronto churches were stationed in different sections of the Massey Hall balcony to sing in the 'Glory to God,' 'Worthy is the Lamb,' and 'Hallelujah' choruses.

No choral work is closer to the hearts of English-speaking people than *Messiah*. 'Going to a performance is as immutable a Christmas institution as going to church or eating a slice of turkey.'[39] And no one was more thrilled by MacMillan's first *Messiah* than the astute Hector Charlesworth, who said that the choir had 're-emerged in the aura of its former glory.'[40] He praised MacMillan's approach to the work, his execution of the choruses, his handling of the orchestra, and Ellis McClintock's superb rendering of the trumpet obbligato in the 'The Trumpet Shall Sound.' McClintock, like a number of other Toronto musicians, was a member of an armed forces band, and Ernest had arranged for his release from military duties to play the concert.

The choir did *Messiah* annually at Christmas from then on, and like the *St Matthew Passion*, it became Ernest MacMillan's 'property.' He believed that its libretto presents 'the great drama of Divine Love and Redemption with a breadth of vision and universality of application that far transcend mere narrative.' Choruses such as 'For unto Us' and 'His Yoke is Easy' are 'largely adaptations from a book of duets set to Italian words ... and call for a comparatively light bel canto style ... Thus, great climaxes like those associated with the words "Wonderful, Counsellor, the Mighty God" ... are thrown into high relief.' Ernest stressed the need for 'delicate grace' in 'His Yoke Is Easy,' and for frivolity in 'All We Like Sheep,' which 'heightens greatly the tremendous coda set to the words "The Lord Hath Laid on Him the Iniquity of Us All." What dramatic work,' he asked, 'offers a more startling contrast than the snarling mockery of "He Trusted in God; Let Him Deliver Him," followed by the poignant "Thy Rebuke Hath Broken His Heart," the finest recitative in the oratorio and perhaps in any Handelian work?' As for the 'Hallelujah' chorus, 'from its very first chord,' it is 'laid out in such a way as to suggest a blinding glory – and what a pity it is that so many conductors hurry over it without giving it a chance to produce its full effect! Still greater, perhaps the greatest piece of sheer choral virtuosity in music, is the final "Amen"; it is comparable only to the "Sanctus" of Bach's *B Minor Mass* in its continually mounting affirmation of faith.'[41]

Years later when MacMillan reviewed a newly published facsimile of Handel's autograph score, he addressed *Messiah*'s controversial accompaniments and pointed out that their very sketchiness should allow conductors to take liberties with them.[42] As a 'non-purist,' he defended using the large orchestra and chorus, so different from Handel's much smaller forces, believing that performances of great works should be stylistically in accord with the times. His conception of the work was grounded in the Victorian era, which, in his view, contemporary audiences and choirs raised in the Protestant tradition preferred, and he may have been right. Having large forces sing out the words of the Lord meant much indeed to Ernest the Presbyterian.

The inevitable loss of TSO musicians to the armed forces had not been as calamitous as Ernest had first feared. On the contrary, the orchestra's quality had remained stable for a time and then had gradually improved. As already noted, some who joined the forces remained in the Toronto area and continued their TSO work if only on an occasional basis. Two fine wind players were hired: principal oboist Perry Bauman in 1940 and principal flutist Gordon Day in 1941. Together, they substantially elevated the quality of the TSO woodwinds. Then, in the fall of 1942, Ernest stuck his neck out by auditioning and reseating the string section. It led to the 'resignation' of about eight players of considerable seniority, although a few were later reinstated. The result was an outstanding string section.

In 1942–3, the TSO made several recordings for RCA Victor, the first commercial recordings of a Canadian orchestra made by an American company. The major work was Holst's *The Planets*. Ernest showed an uncharacteristic lightness of touch in 'Mercury,' relentless drive and splendid management of large forces in 'Mars,' and fun and jollity in 'Jupiter.' He had a rare sense of communion with Holst's music. The 'Haydn Serenade' (now usually attributed to Romanus Hoffstetter), was equally well done and shows off the fine TSO strings. Both readings are collectors' items.[43]

In December 1943, after years of unsuccessful lobbying, the City of Toronto stingily granted the TSO $1,500. Jack Elton, hardly ecstatic, pointed out acerbically that nearby Buffalo gave its orchestra $7,500 for only ten concerts. (The TSO gave thirty-eight that year.) Fortunately ticket sales were so good in the 1943–4 season that players, conductor, and staff all received bonuses. And then Elton confirmed that, for the 1944–5 season, wages would be almost doubled – to $40 weekly.[44] Nor was Ernest forgotten. Although not stated publicly, his annual salary went up to a munificent $5,000. In that season subscribers made up a staggeringly high 80 per cent of ticket holders for the twelve subscription concerts, five of which were sold out! These good times led to increases in the number of concerts – the Christmas Boxes and each of the five secondary school concerts were repeated, and Friday evening Pops concerts, patterned in part after Toronto's Prom concerts and in part after the famed Boston Pops series, were revived. (There had been Pops concerts in the 1920s and even one in the 1933–4 season.) Toronto was on a musical high.

The BBC had tried to get Ernest to conduct again after his 1937 visit, but the war presented insurmountable travel problems. The BBC did, however, honour him in a very special way on the evening of his fiftieth birthday, 18 August 1943, when they aired a half-hour broadcast dedicated to 'one of the ten outstanding musicians of the Empire.'[45] The program, announced as 'a birthday present from the English people,' was sent by short wave to North America and parts of Europe. Ernest heard it at Lorne Park.

Like most Canadians, Ernest knew that Canada's interests during the war were bound up with the Soviet Union's, and that Soviet citizens 'were putting up a fight that won our wonder and admiration.'[46] He also admired how well that country supported its artists, even though he worried about how it curbed artistic freedom. On 26 January 1943, after six frustrating months spent trying to track down the score and parts of Shostakovich's Seventh Symphony, the *Leningrad*, written during the siege of that great city, Ernest finally conducted its Canadian première with the TSO. Toscanini and the NBC Symphony had performed the North American première the previous July, and Koussevitsky and the Boston Symphony had done it at Tanglewood in August; both performances had gotten extraordinary attention in the press. Massey Hall was filled to capacity, and, according to Ernest, the performance was greeted 'with enthusiasm strange in retrospect. The acclaim ... was probably not for the composer, who has written much finer music, nor for the performers; it was a tribute to the heroism of the Russian people.'[47] Ernest wrote to Shostakovich after the performance to tell him of its success and received back a warm note of thanks.[48]

A few months later Ernest spoke at a 'Salute to our Russian Ally,' sponsored by the Canadian Writers' Broadcasters' and Artists' War Council.[49] Thwarted for so many years by Canada's indifference to its artists, he could not help but admire the Russian approach:

In Soviet Russia, the artist has a recognized public position and is expected to fulfil public responsibilities. The ivory tower has vanished yet he does not feel himself restricted; on the contrary in serving the people he is set free for self-expression on the broadest lines. He is set free ... by having made available to him educational facilities proportionate to his natural abilities, for Soviet Russia freely recognizes the one aristocracy that has a legitimate place in education – the aristocracy of capacity. He is set free ... by being given the best available tools of his profession – again in proportion to his proved ability to use them ... He is set free by the warm and increasingly intelligent appreciation of his public ... Finally he is set free by being made to feel that the best he has to give can be and must be part and parcel of the great civilisation that he ... is engaged in building.

Ernest admitted that he was drawing a picture of an 'artist's Utopia' and that Soviet artists undoubtedly had 'their mental trials, tribulations, and disappointments there as elsewhere. Frankly, some of the accounts I have been given of musical life in present day Russia have been too rosy to convince entirely a rather sceptical Scottish-Canadian.' Nonetheless, he applauded the Soviet Union and asked that Canadians 'be pardoned for looking a little enviously at a nation that so consistently and publicly maintains a consciously formulated ideal for its artists as for all its citizens.'

On 13 November 1943, the TSO, under the auspices of the National Council for Canadian-Soviet Friendship, did a special concert of Canadian and Russian music. It provided an unusual opportunity to do *four* Canadian works: Ernest's own Overture, John Weinzweig's fanfare *Salute to the USSR*, Claude Champagne's *Danse villageoise*, and Robert Farnon's *Ottawa* Symphony. The Russian part of the concert included Khrennikov's *Much Ado about Nothing Suite* and Shostakovich's Fifth Symphony, one of Ernest's favourites. In the next few years, Ernest gradually became disenchanted with the National Council and found it harder and harder to go along with its uncritical attitude towards the Soviet Union.

Ernest performed another patriotic service when, in February 1945, he gave three talks in German that were sent by short wave to Germany over the newly established CBC International Service and the 'Voice of America.' They were titled 'Music in Canada,' 'Musical Education of Canadian Youth,' and 'Canadian Musical Development.' In introducing Ernest, much was made of his internment in Ruhleben during the Great War.

As the war drew to a close and travel became easier, the TSO stepped up the number of guest artists. Among the more memorable appearances were those by the great Russian violinist Nathan Milstein. His two visits in 1944 were given under difficult circumstances – for different reasons – yet both came off well. In January, because of a train delay, he arrived with only minutes to spare for the concert and played the Tchaikovsky Concerto and the Bach A Minor Concerto without rehearsal. In the following December, his appearance coincided with one of Toronto's worst snowstorms in living memory. Conductor, guest artist, players, and the small and loyal audience all trudged to Massey Hall through the snow. Both Milstein and MacMillan wore tweeds, the orchestra was in street clothes, and ten of its players never made the concert. Yet Milstein, as always, played beautifully.

Australian pianist Percy Grainger's visit in November 1945 saw the renewal of his friendship with Ernest that had begun when Grainger first appeared with the TSO in 1938 to play the Grieg Piano Concerto, a piece long associated with him. On that earlier concert, he had also done several of his own shorter pieces, which he alternately played or conducted, with MacMillan going to the piano when Grainger took the podium. Grainger had even played a Hammond organ, which he was experimenting with at the time. (That earlier visit had been the occasion of the already-described sewer backup during which an unconcerned Grainger had merrily continued to practise.) Grainger's rare talent and broad interests paralleled those of his Canadian friend. Like MacMillan, he was a composer, pianist, and conductor, and was very involved in folk music – only in his case it was English and Scandinavian.

For the 1945 visit, Grainger's wife, Ella, a Swedish poet and artist, accompanied him, and they stayed with Elsie and Ernest. It was not uncommon for the MacMillans to host visiting artists, but having the Graingers was special because the four were so congenial. Yet the two men, despite their professional similarities, looked at life very differently, and it was this difference that must have appealed to Ernest. He would have seen in the more free-spirited Grainger the sort of person *he* might have been had he placed less emphasis on responsibility and service. Unlike MacMillan, Grainger refused to tie himself down to a performing career or an academic post, although he did teach piano off and on at the Chicago Musical College and had headed the music department at New York University briefly in 1932–3. 'My life,' he wrote, 'has been one of kicking out into space, while the world around me is dying of good taste.'[50] Along the way he had developed an interest in what he called 'free music,' based on 'continuous gliding tones, whose melody, rhythm and texture were liberated from the traditional constraints of scale, beat and harmony,' and for which he invented and built 'a series of mainly electronic composition machines.' Ernest may never have completely understood or sympathized with Grainger's inventions, but his respect for the man and his gifts – Grainger was a true 'original' – never wavered. Grainger, a longtime naturalized American citizen but still very Australian, wrote Ernest a few days after the 1945 concert to express his admiration and affection for his colleague and to compliment him on what he was doing for Canada:

It was generous indeed to give us such a very good time, both musically and humanly. The rehearsals and concerts were a sheer delight. The orchestra – so skilful, mellow, balanced, responsive, vital – is a mirror of your own musical soul, so sane and yet so emotionally expressive. It fills me with pride (as an Australian-born musician) that Canada has produced so superlatively great a musician as yourself, and it is an added satisfaction to think that you have been able to rise to these heights in your native land, rather than to be doing your great work amongst strangers.[51]

12. Canada's Musical Ambassador

With the end of the European war imminent and his sons safely back in Canada (both returned home in early 1945), Ernest welcomed an invitation from the Australian Broadcasting Corporation (ABC) to do an extended conducting tour of Australia in the spring and summer of 1945. Other than a brief trip to Jamaica in 1940 and guest conducting in the United States in 1941–2, he had not been out of Canada since before the war.

An Australian tour had been in the wind as far back as 1937, when Ernest and his Australian counterpart, Bernard Heinze, a prominent conductor and director of the Melbourne University Conservatorium, had explored an exchange.[1] At that time, Ernest had not pursued the engagement with particular zeal because Arthur Judson had told him that conducting in Australia was a 'mere job' and would do nothing for his reputation in North America.[2] But times had changed. Engagements in the United States were not pouring in and Australia was eager to have him.

ABC proposed a fourteen-week country-wide tour of twenty-one concerts (ten different programs), sixteen to be evening performances with broadcasts and five to be young people's matinees.[3] In addition, it asked Ernest to give a series of organ recitals. Eugene Ormandy had done an ABC tour the previous year, so Ernest conferred with him about programming and related matters, only to find out that there were very few truly professional orchestral players in Australia, and they were mainly located in Sydney and Melbourne. Ormandy urged Ernest to be firm in seating players and cautious in programming concerts in the three smaller cities,

Adelaide, Perth, and Brisbane. And then he closed with a bit of personal advice: to take warm clothing and underwear – Australians didn't heat their homes.[4]

Ernest sent off his programs to ABC but turned down the proposed organ recitals, pleading that he was out of practice – which he was.[5] As the departure date drew near he realized, more and more, how much he needed a change after five and a half busy years in wartime Canada. Furthermore, the trip to Australia would give him a chance to spread his conducting wings in virgin territory and promote goodwill and fellowship with Canada's sister nation and staunch wartime ally. He said later that 'the nations of the Commonwealth were like younger members of a large family who wrote home pretty regularly to mother but did not make any great effort to keep in touch with each other.'[6]

Unfortunately, Elsie could not accompany him, because of an ear problem, which was aggravated by air travel. It was just as well, since the air trip was strenuous – it spanned forty-eight hours, thirty-three of which were in the air. Sydney, Australia's largest city, gave him the full celebrity treatment, complete with press and radio interviews. Ernest enjoyed it all, and, as the tour progressed, he became more and more attractive to the media, making astute observations about Australia and informative and evocative statements about Canada.

As he had hoped, there was ample rehearsal time with the Sydney Symphony for his first concert on 22 April. The program included Sibelius's Second Symphony, Beethoven's Fourth Piano Concerto (with the Australian Eileen Ralph as soloist), Rimsky-Korsakov's *Russian Easter* Overture, and a Bach transcription. Neville Cardus, the music critic for the *Sydney Morning Herald*, was in the audience. Formerly with the *Manchester Guardian*, where he had also been a distinguished writer on cricket, Cardus was known for his informed, colourful, and outspoken reviews. Obviously, a good Cardus review could mean a great deal to Ernest internationally.

Anticipating Ernest's arrival in Sydney, Cardus had listened to and justifiably praised the TSO recording of Holst's *Planets* and had concluded that Australian orchestras were not in the TSO's class.[7] Unfortunately, Cardus, who had a very personal conception of the Sibelius Second Symphony and read a great deal of external meaning into it, was thoroughly displeased with Ernest's reading. He wrote how Ernest conducted like a 'patient schoolmaster,' that his interpretation lacked the necessary theatrical temperament, and that 'for the first time in my experience ... I found it sounding dull. There was little of legendary awe and gloom; even in the slow movement where the brass instruments should seem to emerge from the mists and primeval slime making their dinosaurian noises – even here we remained in the temperate zone of things.'[8] He went on to say that 'the noble second subject of the *Andante* was without drama ... I found no imagination in it; the accumulative drive of the finale, where a special army seems to advance from a void of history, was always too precise with calls and echoes of brass too near us; there was little grip of orchestral perspective.'

At a subsequent concert, Cardus heard MacMillan conduct the Franck Symphony and liked it more; and then, after MacMillan's broadcast of Beethoven's *Eroica*, he made a complete about-face and, perhaps by way of apology, congratulated him on his 'magnificent' conducting. 'Why didn't you give it in Sydney? It was painful to me to write an unfavorable notice of your first concert – a difficult work with a strange orchestra ... You gave us in the "Eroica" the great *wheel* of the first movement, inevitable yet unforced. You achieved the difficult task, in the slow movement, of concentration without rigidity and, best of all, you brought sweetness and pathos out of strength.'[9] He also admired the 'drive' of the Scherzo and the firm handling of the Finale. 'How masterfully you attended to the incomparable writing for the bass instruments.' And then came the highest praise of all: 'The interpretation, in its arch and wealth of symphonic detail, took my mind back to Richter.' (Richter was Wagner's *Ring* conductor and, for many years, headed the famed Hallé Orchestra in Manchester.) Cardus, still trying to make amends, promised to express his appreciation in the *Manchester Guardian* and *The New York Times*, since he was a stringer for both papers. And, finally, he hoped that he would meet Ernest when he returned to Sydney at the end of the tour.

Ernest's reply was cordial:

I fancy that most conductors would rather be successful in interpreting Beethoven than any other composer; and in such a work as the 'Eroica,' one feels an uncommon sense of responsibility. Naturally, I was sorry that you felt as you did about the Sibelius, but, when one is on the firing line, one must be prepared to be hit from time to time. I didn't realize that it sounded so dull. Perhaps I was more tired than I realized, having left home immediately after a heavy season and having had little time to get my second wind after a tiring journey.[10]

Almost twenty years later Ernest recalled his reaction to Cardus's two reviews. 'I subjected myself to some soul-searching and, while unable to account for the difference, realized that he might well be right in both instances. One is not necessarily a good judge of oneself.'[11]

With Cardus's bad review the one exception, Ernest enjoyed the entire trip. He was impressed mightily that ABC flew several players from eastern Australia to Perth to bolster its orchestra for his concerts, that unlike Canada every city had a good concert hall, and that the halls in Sydney and Melbourne had good organs. But, on the other hand, he found Australians rather stiff when it came to concerts for young people. He had one of the children shoot him with a pop gun in 'Pop Goes the Weasel' – in typical Christmas Box style – and was amused when he learned that such behaviour was thought inappropriate for a symphony conductor. The Australian press made a few other interesting observations. One interviewer said that, when Ernest talked about music, he assumed a 'pontifical air,' but a 'bright twinkle in his eye' would signal 'his short upper lip to disappear into a puckish grin.'[12] In one newspaper he was described as 'forceful' and 'indomitable'[13] and in another as 'having quiet humor, a fondness for epigram, a reluctance to express dogmatic opinions. He looks a little like Charles Laughton – without the histrionics.'[14]

Ernest was aware of the strong British influence in Australia. Although an independent spirit was growing, Australians still looked to Britain as home, and, according to Ernest, their speech reflected this, resembling cockney but with words 'drawled' rather than 'clipped.' For him, Melbourne seemed more British in ambience than Sydney, and Adelaide more so than both of them.

As if wishing to prove the strength of its links with the old country, Australia had little or no central heating, and Ernest, as Ormandy had warned, shivered his way through June and July, the country's winter months. He stayed in clubs rather than hotels in Adelaide, Perth, and Brisbane because hotels tended to be cold, as well as uncomfortable and noisy.[15]

His personal contacts with Australians were particularly gratifying. More than a decade later he would write, 'I cannot think of a soul I met in Australia whom I didn't like; if the Australians didn't like me, they must have been expert in concealing their feelings.'[16] While there, he saw several former Ruhlebenites, including Edgar Bainton, who had left Newcastle to become the head of the Sydney Conservatorium, and he made friends of long standing with ABC people, Australian and Canadian government officials, and countless musicians. He also had a visit with C.V. Pilcher, former TSO bass clarinettist and his collaborator on 'Hail Toronto,' and now the Bishop Coadjutor of Sydney.

MacMillan ended his Australian tour in Sydney, and after his final concert Cardus credited him with conducting one of the best performances of Debussy's *Nuages* and *Fêtes* he had ever heard. And the two men did meet and spend time together, unusual since many critics think it unethical to mix socially with performers. Either Cardus did not have this concern or he was so eager to meet an interesting musician from abroad after six years in Australia that he was ready to overlook it.

ABC gave him two farewell gifts. One was a scrapbook of reviews and press clippings about his visit and the other was an elegant ebony baton circled with silver, probably inspired by the fact that he had broken three batons early on in the tour, a most unusual streak of bad luck. There were other gifts: books, paintings, recordings of Aboriginal music, and a boomerang. A group of schoolchildren sang 'The Maple Leaf Forever' for him and he reciprocated by singing 'Waltzing Matilda.'[17] He flew home from Sydney at the end of July. On the plane were two charming young fans who kept him cheerful during the long hours in the air, and he thanked them with a short poem. His return was a happy one, indeed. A few weeks later the Japanese surrendered. The war was over.

Canada's musical ambassador of goodwill, for that was what he was in Australia, did his stuff again the next year, when he conducted in Rio de Janeiro. The arrangements leading up to it were nightmarish, but, in the end, the benefits accrued made it all worthwhile. The first proposal to conduct came from the Canada-Brazil Trust Fund in May 1944.[18] Ernest's noncommittal reply said that he knew little about Brazil's musical life other than that it had produced a number of distinguished composers and that its music 'had taken on a decidedly distinctive stamp.'[19] He heard nothing more for over a year, and then – it was just after his return from Australia – Canadian composer Claude Champagne wrote to tell him that Jean Desy, the Canadian ambassador to Brazil, had confirmed (!) that he and MacMillan were to share the podium for two concerts in Rio de Janeiro in 1946.[20] MacMillan, who had not yet agreed to go, was astonished at Desy's presumption. He was also put out for being put on a double bill with Champagne, who was not a conductor. Then, to add insult to injury, Champagne informed him that there would be no fee, just expenses.[21] Clearly, Champagne's involvement was already a *fait accompli* and Ernest was expected to accept the proposed scheme. Although Ernest's days of conducting gratis, other than for benefits and charity, were over, he agreed to the plans for the sake of Anglo-French amity, and began program discussions with Champagne.[22]

Negotiations with Brazil moved ahead with increasing uncertainty. Ernest discovered an interesting new wrinkle – José Siqueira, Brazilian conductor, composer, impresario, and general factotum of musical affairs in Rio, expected Ernest to get engagements for him in North America in exchange for his 'hiring' of Ernest for Rio.[23] Next Ernest heard that Desy had booked him for *four* concerts on condition that four concerts be found in Canada for the resident Rio opera conductor, Eugene Szenkar![24]

There were more letters, and then in March 1946, Desy informed Ernest that the concerts would be in August, not June, as originally planned.[25] Champagne, unlike MacMillan, was undisturbed by this merry-go-round and scolded MacMillan for being so fussy and bureaucratic. He reminded him that he, Champagne, would be conducting the Canadian works while MacMillan would be conducting 'the *British* [his italics] ones.'[26] By this time Ernest had turned over the booking arrangements to Arthur Judson's deputy, Bruno Zirato, who was used to dealing with South Americans and who knew when to apply pressure and when to sit back and wait for developments. Zirato finalized everything: Ernest would give six concerts, do almost all of the conducting, and receive a fee of $2,400; Champagne would only conduct his own symphony.[27] Zirato's assistant also reminded Siqueira that he must not forget – as he often did – to attend to such niceties as meeting MacMillan at the airport and providing good accommodation and personal attention when needed.[28]

Although it would have been comparatively easy to fly directly to Brazil, Ernest wanted Elsie to accompany him, and this meant travelling by sea. Elsie, who was enchanted with the prospect of seeing Rio, decided to keep a diary of the trip. They travelled by freighter, the *White Swallow*, which left Montreal on 9 July, was delayed for several days near Chicoutimi on the Saguenay, and didn't reach New York until 19 July. From there they sailed on to Savannah, enjoying the voyage immensely. While at sea they usually kept to themselves, relishing the quiet times together like so many long-married and too-busy couples in similar situations. Ernest sunned himself on deck, where he diligently studied Portuguese, so that when several Brazilians boarded in Savannah, he was able to try out his new language with them. Unfortunately, by the time they got to Trinidad, the boat was so far behind schedule that Ernest had to fly the rest of the way, several thousand miles more, in order to reach Rio in time for rehearsals. In due course, Elsie joined him there. She described her arrival:

soon after breakfast [we] saw the first mountains, some misty in the distance, some post-card sharp beside us ... we could not leave the sun-deck as the matchless panorama of the beach and mountains unrolled before us. Tense with excitement we watched the city take shape, gazed at the sky line of rugged crags and wooded peaks, the Christ figure on towering Corcovado, the surf breaking on the great white beach of Copacabana. The climax came when at last we sailed between the famous Sugar Loaf and the fortress and entered the main harbour – that incomparable basin backed by mountains, ringed by boulevards that is the front lawn of the wonder city of the Western world – Rio de Janeiro.[29]

Some days later, she made some trenchant observations about Rio itself. She called it

a city of extremes and contradictions, of great wealth and abject poverty, of incredible achievement and maddening unreliability, of gracious kindness and self-centred egotism, of sensitivity and obtuseness, of dramatic contrasts in every sphere of life. 'God was a Brazilian,' they say, and surely to no other people has nature been so lavish with her gifts ... God is still a Brazilian but with feet and legs of clay. You find yourself wondering how much of this is just shop window. The enchanting mosaic sidewalks – that are laid in sand, the spectacular and impressive buildings – that are mildewing at the corners, the plaster carvings – that are peeling off. You ask yourself: Is it beauty truly blest? Will it endure wind and weather? And, above all, is this instability symptomatic of a lack of quality in its builders? ... Rio is a city built both on the enduring rock of natural and man-made beauty and on the shifting sands of Brazilian temperament ... The purpose of governments is to govern and of public services to serve the public ... Here they are expected to enrich the office-holders.[30]

Rio's active musical life put Toronto's to shame. The Orquestra Sinfônica Brasileira gave over one hundred concerts annually in Rio alone, including several for young people, and there was also an opera orchestra with completely different players.[31] Most of Ernest's concerts were held at the ornate and acoustically fine opera house, the Municipal Theatre, which closely resembles Paris's Palais Garnier on the Place de l'Opéra. (Toscanini had made his very first conducting appearance with *Aida* at the Municipal Theatre on 30 June 1886, eight years before Toronto's Massey Hall was built.) However, much to Ernest's annoyance, the rehearsals were often held at another location because the theatre was so busy. And, to make matters worse, rehearsal and concert times were often changed, even at the eleventh hour. Yet musicians and public took such changes casually. Once, because of a disturbance in the city, fifteen musicians failed to appear for

Sir Ernest MacMillan rehearsing the TSO. (KMFC)

Ettore Mazzoleni conducting soloists Gordon Day, flute, Eugene Kash, violin, Greta Kraus and Arnold Walter, harpsichords, in a 1941 CBC broadcast. (CPFC)

A cheerful Ernest photographed with three koalas during his
Australian tour. (ECMF)

OPPOSITE:

Claude Champagne and Sir Ernest sharing a happy moment in
Rio de Janeiro. (ECMF)

The TSO conductor bicycling in June 1942 in order to save fuel and help the war effort. (ECMF)

Metropolitan Opera mezzo-soprano Gladys Swarthout accepting
flowers at a TSO Pops Concert. (ECMF)

OPPOSITE:

Ettore Mazzoleni, Healey Willan, and Edward Johnson discussing a
Willan score. (CPFC)

TSO concert-master Elie Spivak and Sir Ernest, shortly before Spivak
left the orchestra. (TSOA)

The TSO as it appeared from the Massey Hall mezzanine in the
1949–50 season. Sir Ernest conducts. (TSOA)

OPPOSITE:

top: The TSO's conductor with his 1951–2 horn section. Left to right:
Reginald Barrow, Leonard Hale, Sir Ernest, Clifford Spearing,
Kenneth Godwin, and (seated) Mary Barrow. (ECMF)

bottom: Concert-master Hyman Goodman and principal cellist
Rowland Pack with Sir Ernest in his final year with the TSO. (TSOA)

Sir Ernest blissfully strumming a guitar at a Royal York Hotel
square dance in 1950. (*Toronto Globe and Mail*)

Wearing a coonskin hat, Sir Ernest chats with his grand-niece Carol
Griffin at a 1955 Christmas Box concert. (ECMF)

Proud Elsie and Ernest with their grandchildren. They used this
photo as their 1959 Christmas card. (KMFC)

Four generations of MacMillans in 1955 – Alexander, Ernest, Keith, and Keith's son, Ian. (KMFC)

Father and son in the Scottish highlands in the summer of 1952. (KMFC)

Ernest, Elsie, and Marius Barbeau at Mount Allison University, where Ernest received an honorary doctorate. (ECMF)

Keith MacMillan explains the intricacies of his tape recorder to his father, while Isabel Pierce of the Mendelssohn Choir looks on. (KMFC)

The Royal Conservatory of Music on College Street and University
Avenue before it was demolished in 1963–4.
(University of Toronto Archives)

Healey Willan and Ernest banter over drinks at the Arts and Letters
Club. (SOCAN Archives)

Ralph Bunche, Nobel Peace Prize winner, with (left to right) CBC chairman R.L. Dunsmore, composer Godfrey Ridout, and Sir Ernest, in New York, United Nations Day, 24 October 1961 (TSOA)

Duke Ellington meets Sir Ernest at a 1968 CAPAC reception.
(York University Archives)

Sir Ernest with Seiji Ozawa, the TSO's new conductor, and Ozawa's wife, Kyoko Edo, in October 1965. (ECMF)

Noted Indian musician Ravi Shankar visits Sir Ernest MacMillan at Park Road. (KMFC)

Sir Ernest with five other leading Canadians on the Scarborough bluffs, Toronto, in centennial year. Left to right: Morley Callaghan, Sir Ernest, Kate Reid, A.Y. Jackson, Glenn Gould, and Marshall McLuhan. (York University Archives)

an actual concert! Player fatigue was Ernest's biggest problem for, although orchestral playing was a twelve-month job, the pay was so low that the musicians had to play in dance bands late into the night to augment their incomes. Many of their Toronto counterparts, particularly wind players, did the same but showed its ill effects less, perhaps because they were spared Rio's warm and enervating climate.

Despite all the booking problems and the loose organization of rehearsals and concerts, Ernest was nearly always cheerful and his programs, on the whole, came off well. After all, the engagement was sufficiently prestigious – other conductors that season included William Steinberg, Eugene Ormandy, and Charles Münch – for him to tolerate Rio's idiosyncrasies. He made sure that each program included at least one Canadian composition or arrangement, but the score and parts for Champagne's symphony arrived too late and his *Danse villageoise* was substituted. By this time MacMillan and Champagne were fast friends.

Ernest made such a hit with Rio's audiences that, shortly before it was time to go home, he was asked to do two extra concerts on top of the original six, even though his contract was still not ready for signing. And, when he attended a concert conducted by Siqueira on 19 August, the orchestra broke into 'Happy Birthday' in his honour. He enjoyed speaking Portuguese with orchestral players, government officials, and the high society he met at endless parties, although most upper-class Brazilians preferred French, and, incidentally, expected English Canadians to be fluent in it.

To coincide with Ernest's visit, Ambassador Desy had mounted a display of Canadian paintings and handicrafts at the Canadian Embassy to publicize Canada's artistic achievements. Among the exhibits, Ernest found a handbook on Canada in Portuguese which was 'well illustrated and included a chapter on the fine arts. The fine arts, however, don't seem to include music, for there was not a word of it. The attitude of my country toward music just makes my blood boil.'[32]

While Ernest and Elsie were returning to Toronto – by boat – a Toronto newspaper quoted Maestro Siqueira: 'Sir Ernest's concert meant for us the golden closing of a golden season. His conducting was simply wonderful and the final concert was one of the biggest musical triumphs this city has ever experienced.'[33] This praise was on top of the effusive accolades which had appeared in Rio's Portuguese and English-language press after each concert.

Ernest brought back to Canada a better knowledge and understanding of serious Brazilian music. While in Rio he had attended an impressive new ballet, *Yara*, by Francisco Mignone, and at a Toronto press conference he promised to do a work by Mignone with the TSO, as well as one by Siqueira.[34] And Eugene Szenkar, the opera conductor who had arbitrarily wanted engagements in Canada in exchange for Ernest's in Brazil, had turned out to be, in Ernest's words, 'one of the most distinguished conductors now resident in Brazil and one from whom I heard some very fine operatic performances.'[35] With Ernest's blessing, Szenkar conducted several TSO concerts the following February.

To top off a good year, Toronto's city fathers gave Ernest a civic reception on 10 October and presented him with an illuminated address and an inscribed silver tray. In his thank-you address Ernest said how impressed he had been in both Australia and Brazil with the 'public recognition accorded to musical activities,' inferring that Canada had some way to go in that area.[36] Elsie received another kind of recognition. She loved hats, the more daring the better – 'a hat was either an adventure or a catastrophe,' she used to say. Apparently she found a purple creation with large feathers in Rio and wore it to a Prom concert on her return home. When she entered the large arena, the audience rose and applauded her![37]

Both the Australian and Brazilian engagements had boosted Ernest's morale and his prestige in Canada. Between his two trips, the National Film Board did two short films of the TSO, featuring his *Two Sketches* and Kabalevsky's *Colas Breugnon* Overture on one, and the third movement of Tchaikovsky's Sixth Symphony on the other. Although the sound is poor, Ernest and the orchestra come across well in the rather dated but nonetheless attractive setting of the film, which was widely distributed internationally.[38] Laval University in Quebec City presented him with an honorary DMus in 1947. In conjunction with the academic ceremony he conducted the Quebec Symphony, first at an afternoon children's concert, where he spoke in his carefully prepared French to the young audience, and then at an evening program that included Dvořák's *New World* Symphony and his own *Two Sketches*. French Canada's English-speaking musical hero paid tribute to the city of Quebec, 'the very essence of Canadian civilization,' and to Laval, 'with great institutions like Laval, Canada can achieve the place it deserves among the nations.'[39] Seven months later, in October, he received another honorary doctorate, a DLitt from McMaster University in Hamilton, Ontario.

The TSO began having guest conductors again after the war, including three who exchanged podiums with Ernest: Hans Kindler of Washington's National Symphony in 1946 (they had already done an exchange before the war); Fabien Sevitzky of the Indianapolis Symphony in 1946 and 1949; and William Steinberg of the Buffalo Philharmonic in 1950 (Ernest had also conducted the Buffalo orchestra in 1945). The most enjoyable exchange from MacMillan's point of view was with Kindler, for he was not only a fine conductor but also a cellist of note, and at their occasional meetings, he and Ernest would play sonatas together to their great mutual satisfaction.

MacMillan's press was good in all three cities. Washington said: 'Authority and benevolence mingles in his manner towards the players, and solicitude for fine phrasing alternated with a dominating command for power. He was not a placid wielder of discipline, but an exciting stimulator of vitality.'[40] The *Indianapolis Star* in 1946 called Canada's musical knight 'a delightful personality, with a beguiling elfin charm besides. His attractive stage presence suggests a particularly genial character out of Dickens ... a fellow you would like to have "a miniature of" for a mantel piece ... a rare blending of solid directorial assets and executive ability of the first order.'[41] The Indianapolis Symphony had just returned from a strenuous tour – twenty-two concerts in twenty days – and the critic thought Ernest all the better for doing the concert with minimum rehearsal time, to the obvious satisfaction of the orchestral players. His programming was also praised and the reviewer added that 'Toronto audiences are well-served.' And his two

Buffalo concerts were also well received; his 'courteous and gentlemanly demeanour warmed the audience' as did his 'quiet authority.'[42]

The TSO was becoming a veritable success story. For the 1945–6 season, it boldly increased the number of Friday pops concerts from eight to twenty-four, and the Robert Simpson Company began sponsoring the broadcast of a one-hour portion of each one on CBC's coast-to-coast network of thirty-nine stations.[43] Then, in the next season, four more pops concerts were added. The principal conductors were MacMillan and Mazzoleni, with Arthur Fiedler of the Boston Pops a frequent guest. Players' salaries were raised again – the minimum to $60 weekly – and a retirement benefits plan was established. Ernest's salary was now $13,500, still not much for a leading North American conductor, but reasonable nonetheless. In the 1947–8 season – subscription sales had been going up annually – the TSO made a daring and successful move by repeating twelve subscription concerts on successive nights instead of scheduling fourteen single ones, as in previous years. The result was a considerable gain in revenue at little extra cost. The two 1947 Christmas Boxes were completely sold out and three Boxes were planned for 1948. The CBC's children's broadcasts, begun during the war, were discontinued in 1947 when, with the help of the indomitable women's committee, live concerts at Massey Hall were revived.[44] Always looking for ways to improve these concerts, Ernest changed the pattern and repeated *one* finely honed program for five different audiences. It was a good plan, but there was a negative side to it: children who had previously enjoyed going to several concerts now attended only one.

As the orchestra's season expanded so did the demands on its players, and this forced Ernest to make some painful decisions to maintain the orchestra's quality. A particularly difficult one involved Elie Spivak, who had been with the TSO as long as Ernest himself had. Spivak was an innately musical violinist with an especially warm tone, but he had never been an assertive concertmaster, as much because of his gentle and sensitive personality as his restrained playing. But by 1949 his playing was seriously deteriorating, as the result of an undiagnosed illness. Spivak and Mac-

Millan had been good friends as well as associates, which made it still harder for MacMillan to bite the bullet and ask Spivak ever so gently to resign. Spivak, hurt, fought back and wrote that he felt an 'overwhelming heaviness of spirit ... My admiration for you as a great musician and a great man has never wavered – almost for a lifetime.'[45]

But MacMillan was adamant, and Spivak wrote again. 'I hope that the next few words will give you as much musical comfort as they give me personal sadness. Will you please accept my resignation as concertmaster.'[46] To which Ernest replied with a handwritten note accepting the resignation and adding, 'It will be a genuine pleasure to have you as guest artist in the coming season.'[47] (To sweeten matters and alleviate whatever guilt feelings he may have had, Ernest had promised Spivak solo appearances the following year.) Jack Elton told the press that Spivak was leaving in order to pursue a concert career.[48] MacMillan kept his promise and Spivak played Lalo's *Symphonie Espagnol* four times in the next season – at pops, school, and out-of-town concerts, but not at a subscription concert. There was an emotional overtone in this choice. MacMillan and Spivak had done the piece in their first season together, in 1931.

To cope with the large number of pops concerts, the orchestra engaged TSO violinist Paul Scherman as assistant conductor in 1948. Scherman, who held the position for eight years, handled the diverse repertoire of the pops concerts well, and his clean baton technique enabled the players to prepare concerts quickly and efficiently in limited rehearsal time. Mazzoleni, who had been associate conductor since 1942, had found that his TSO work interfered excessively with his conservatory commitments, and Scherman's appointment allowed him to make an easy exit. Scherman, who admired Ernest's extraordinary memory and scholarship, said years later: 'I'll never forget his first performance of Bartók's Concerto for Orchestra – a difficult score to memorize. Ernest was fantastic, so prepared for the first rehearsal that the whole orchestra burst into applause.'[49] When Keith MacMillan reminded him of his father's occasional memory lapses in the spring of 1952, Scherman quickly retorted: 'It's our virtues that give us stature, our faults that make us human beings.'

In 1948, there was another development – Heinz Unger re-appeared and took up residence in Toronto. MacMillan was far from pleased. When Unger had been in Toronto in 1938, he and some avid supporters had heard rumours that MacMillan might be leaving the TSO (it was the time of MacMillan's despondency with the orchestra) and had made some inappropriate and taste-less proposals to the TSO that he be MacMillan's successor. Mac-Millan had gotten wind of this, and from then on was wary of Unger. Unger had written to MacMillan from England during the war to try and clear himself, but MacMillan's responses had been guardedly cool.[50] He rarely judged people unkindly, but thought Unger a flagrant opportunist and, worse, an ingrate. He had, after all, given Unger his first chance in North America.

Unger formed an amateur community orchestra in Toronto and waited for other opportunities. On one occasion, when ill, he had Victor Feldbrill conduct for him, and then spread the word without any basis in fact that Feldbrill, who was enjoying Ernest's support and encouragement as a budding conductor, had signed on as his assistant. Ernest, in view of his own experiences with Unger, was more than a little annoyed with Feldbrill, who, he thought, had 'deserted' him. Feldbrill clarified matters quickly with MacMillan, but tension mounted between MacMillan and Unger.[51]

The next episode in the MacMillan/Unger saga – not an adversarial one – occurred in June 1949. Unger was to have con-ducted two Promenade concerts, but he took ill again and this time asked MacMillan and Scherman to take his place, one for each Prom, which they did. Following the engagements, MacMil-lan and Scherman generously forwarded the conductor fees to Unger, who thanked them profusely and offered to assist them in like fashion![52]

After the war, the TSO had many fine soloists. In the 1946–7 season Fritz Kreisler and Lawrence Tibbett appeared on the same police benefit concert at Maple Leaf Gardens. The unforgettable Kreisler was to play the Mendelssohn Concerto. When he arrived at the rehearsal he said to conductor and orchestra, 'Gentlemen, you know this concerto and so do I. I'll see you tonight.' Other soloists that season included a Toronto pianist, fifteen-year-old

Glenn Gould. It was Gould's first appearance with the TSO, and he did the Beethoven Fourth Piano Concerto at two school concerts under the baton of Bernard Heinze, who was 'exchanging' with MacMillan following the Australian tour of 1945. Wodson wrote that Gould played Beethoven like a master. 'The grace and understanding of the boy were never at fault ... He sat at the piano a child amongst professors, and he talked with them as one with authority. It was a joy to hear his beautiful playing and to see him so modest and self-forgetful.'[53] Pearl McCarthy was equally enthralled but warned that 'the young artist showed some incipient mannerisms and limited his self-control to the periods when he himself was playing. As he approaches adult status he will undoubtedly learn to suppress this disturbing fidgeting while his collaborators are at work.'[54]

Gould's first appearance was somewhat overshadowed two months later by another brilliant young Toronto pianist, nine-year-old prodigy Patsy Parr, who played shorter works and several of her own pieces at a pops concert with MacMillan conducting. The next year she was soloist with the New York Philharmonic and gave a Town Hall recital. Gould and Parr would each appear several times with MacMillan on Massey Hall's platform in the years to come.[55]

Each season from then on had an impressive list of soloists, but the 1948–9 season stands out particularly. Guest artists from abroad included violist William Primrose, soprano Eileen Farrell, pianists Artur Rubinstein, Witold Malcuzynski, and Clifford Curzon, and violinists Jascha Heifetz – he crankily insisted on more rehearsal time and got it – and Joseph Szigeti. Canadian artists were pianist Ida Krehm and violinist Géza de Kresz, who had been a founding member of the Hart House Quartet in 1923. De Kresz had recently returned to Toronto after twelve years in Budapest. On 11 June 1950 Ernest led the TSO and a massed choir of 1,000 voices at Maple Leaf Gardens, to celebrate the twenty-fifth anniversary of the founding of the United Church of Canada, as he had done at its founding. The next night he led choir and orchestra in a benefit concert for the Winnipeg Flood Relief Fund. The Red River had overflowed and destroyed a considerable part of the city – a major catastrophe.

13. A Spokesman for Music

As expected, Norman Wilks succeeded Ernest competently as conservatory principal. Two years later, the conservatory had a financial bonanza: Frederick Harris, president of the thriving Frederick Harris Music Company, which published the conservatory's examination material, willed his company shares and its considerable annual income to the TCM.[1] Then, in late November 1944, Wilks died unexpectedly at fifty-nine. The board appointed the witty and affable organist Charles Peaker as director (a new position) and Ettore Mazzoleni as principal. But it soon became apparent that Peaker was a poor administrator, and Mazzoleni took over, assuming his new responsibilities with ease. Floyd Chalmers had, in the meantime, successfully persuaded the Ontario government to erase the conservatory's $200,000 debt – a second bonanza.[2]

And so, by the end of the war, the conservatory was back on a reasonably secure footing, much as it had been in the 1920s. In 1947, after almost ten years of behind-the-scenes manoeuvering, King George VI granted it the privilege of being known thenceforth as the *Royal* Conservatory of Music of Toronto (RCM). The year before, it had launched its Senior School for gifted post-secondary school musicians, patterned after Juilliard's program, and its Opera School to train singers, coaches, conductors, and stage directors, the first of its kind in Canada. Both departments were headed by Arnold Walter, a rather short, blond, German-speaking Moravian pianist, composer, and critic. He had fled Germany after Hitler's rise to power and had come to Canada in

1937 to teach music at Upper Canada College. Walter had impressive credentials: he held a doctorate in law from the University of Prague and had studied musicology at the University of Berlin and piano with Rudolf Breithaupt and Frederic Lamond.

Walter engaged Nicholas Goldschmidt as the Opera School's musical director, and, two years later, Herman Geiger-Torel as its stage director. The Opera School thrived, and its early productions, first at Hart House Theatre and then at Eaton Auditorium and the Royal Alexandra Theatre, were the forerunners of the Toronto Opera Festival (later the Canadian Opera Company). It was the kind of opera school that Ernest MacMillan had long wanted, but he had lacked the know-how and the personnel, knowledgeable central Europeans like Walter, Goldschmidt, and Geiger-Torel, all of whom had grown up with opera. The man who could have been one of the great operatic conductors of his generation now stood by and watched Canadian opera grow without him.

Opera added glamour to the RCM, as gifted musicians from all parts of Canada flocked to Toronto. Postwar RCM students included singers Lois Marshall, James Milligan, and Jon Vickers, conductors Mario Bernardi, George Crum, Victor Feldbrill, and George Hurst, stage director Irving Guttman, and prominent instrumentalists too numerous to name. Composition also thrived, both in and out of the conservatory, stimulated by a new generation of composers – John Weinzweig, Godfrey Ridout, and Louis Applebaum, who had begun their work in the 1930s, and John Beckwith, Harry Freedman, Clermont Pépin, and Harry Somers, who followed them.

The Faculty of Music of the university also mounted a new program in 1946: a three-year MusBac course to prepare students for teaching secondary school instrumental and vocal music. Known as School Music and later as Music Education, this program had its students study string, woodwind, and brass instruments, conducting, choral music, and music theory and history. Although aware of its potential benefits, Dean MacMillan would never have gotten it under way without the urging of Arnold Walter, who knew how school music teachers were trained in the United States and was intent on having similar training in

Toronto. After convincing MacMillan that it was feasible and
getting the university's go-ahead, Walter and MacMillan engaged
Eastman graduate Robert Rosevear, a young American school
music teacher and accomplished conductor and horn player, to
run the program and be its professor of instrumental music.[3]
Leslie Bell, a well-known Toronto choral conductor who taught
at the Ontario College of Education, was put in charge of choral
music, and, a year later, Richard Johnston, another Eastman
graduate, was brought from the United States to teach harmony
and related subjects Eastman-style. His teaching methods contrasted sharply with those of the English-oriented Willan and Smith,
which meant that, for a time, there were two distinctly different
kinds of theory instruction at the Faculty of Music, one for the
'old' MusBac and one for the 'new.' This split made for interesting debate.

Rosevear was an efficient administrator and, thanks to him, the
course was a success from the outset. Twenty-one students enrolled in the first year, mostly war veterans who were older and
generally more serious, practical, and career-oriented than typical
first-year undergraduates. They learned to play all instruments,
however sketchily, in the conservatory's limited and poorly sound-
insulated practice space. Squealing clarinets and blaring trumpets
could thus be heard throughout the school. The hopelessly small
library was housed in a room no larger than the dean's office,
and there was little rehearsal and storage space. MacMillan now
had to deal with purchasing instruments, sheet music, instruction-
al and reference books, and the like, and with allocating rooms
for practice and rehearsal. Although Rosevear attended to all the
details, Ernest was, in effect, administering a fair-sized university
music department and wasn't sure that he wanted the job.[4] The
space problem was alleviated, in the second and third years of the
program, with the acquisition of two new buildings immediately
west of the conservatory. School Music moved ahead. Within ten
years high schools all over Ontario had bands and orchestras with
University of Toronto graduates as their directors.

Late in 1948, Ernest wrote candidly to university president
Sidney Smith that enrolment in General Music numbered only
thirty-six, a drop of 15 per cent from the previous year.[5] However,

enrolment in School Music had grown to seventy-two, even though it was making 'greater demands on students – or at any rate on their time ... due in great part to its vocational nature.' Ernest wondered if General Music didn't need younger professors. Yet he was reluctant to force early retirement on Willan and Leo Smith, who were both in their late sixties, as long as keeping them on did not 'handicap the Faculty in its operations.' General Music needed revision, he pointed out, and the Faculty of Music's 'entire setup' needed reform. 'I shrink from making myself responsible for such changes and, if the University thought that my own retirement would facilitate matters, I should be more than happy to tender my resignation ... I have heavy responsibilities elsewhere and my work as Dean has of late years grown far beyond what it was when I resigned directorship of the Conservatory.' Sidney Smith took no action.

Willan and Leo Smith retired in 1950, and Ernest, fearing that Toronto was being 'Americanized' by the School Music program, advertised for their replacement only in the British press, but sought only one 'senior post' to cover the work done by both men. The salary and rank he offered were higher than those of Rosevear and Johnston, which annoyed them considerably, for it appeared that MacMillan considered English-trained musicians superior. True or not, MacMillan wanted to retain at Toronto the kind of training he had had as a youth. In actual fact it is questionable whether MacMillan ever really believed in the School Music program, although later he spoke of its results with pleasure. When he discussed it with Harvey Perrin, a Toronto high school teacher and later director of music for Toronto elementary and secondary schools, he said, 'Harvey, you should know that there is only one MusBac, the kind you have.' (Perrin had the General Music degree.)[6] Elsie MacMillan, no doubt influenced by Ernest, often referred to the General Music program as 'our course.' Ernest's appointee, George Loughlin, stayed for only two years and then went on to Glasgow University in 1953.

Interest in serious music was growing rapidly in postwar Canada. Orchestras were appearing across the country, concerts of increasingly higher standards were being given in small as well as large centres, and the CBC was producing more and more live music broadcasts. Canada's growing independence as a nation had much to do with all this, but Canada also had Ernest MacMillan to give its musicians confidence and direction in developing a musical life of their own. Undoubtedly, Ernest's visits to Australia and Brazil had sharpened his interest in government subsidies for the arts. Noting that Australia funded its orchestras through ABC while Brazil funded its opera companies, orchestras, and composers directly, he said in a press interview that 'the ideal solution for the problem of financing a first-rate orchestra lies somewhere between the extremes of no subsidy at all and full subsidies provided by the State.'[7] Australia, he said, relied too much on subsidy and not enough on public interest; it had nothing equivalent to the Toronto Symphony Association, its board, or its women's committee, all of which forged links between the orchestra and the community. (Did he really mean this, in view of the TSO's financial difficulties over the previous fifteen years?) Ernest favoured a typically Canadian compromise with both government *and* broader-based private support, the latter to come from corporations, the rich, and the music-loving public at large. In this same interview he said that Brazilian composers appeared more productive than their Canadian counterparts because they received generous subsidies and opportunities for performance of their works by subsidized ensembles. Would Canada do the same? he asked.

MacMillan had already done some informal lobbying for federal arts assistance in his 1943 letter to Mackenzie King on music in wartime. In 1944 he had spoken with Vincent Massey on the same subject. Always one to encourage the arts, Massey had asked Ernest to set down in a letter his vision of music in postwar Canada and had promised to bring it, unofficially, before appropriate government bodies. Ernest complied in short order and urged the establishment of a public body or bodies similar to Britain's Council for the Encouragement of Music and the Arts, the forerunner of the Arts Council of Great Britain. Definite policies were needed – 'first in the field of education; secondly in stimulating creative effort and ensuring the cultivation and judicious use of its best performing talent; thirdly in disseminating knowledge and appreciation of native [he meant Canadian] art both at home and abroad.' Composers needed more and better incentives, he went on, acknowledging all the while the encouragement given by the Canadian Performing Rights Society and the CBC. As for disseminating knowledge, he himself had been acting 'as a sort of unofficial clearing-house for information about Canadian music' while the CBC was preparing 'a catalogue of Canadian music.' But more ambitious and comprehensive undertakings were needed.[8]

In view of ensuing events that spring, his letter to Massey had probably found its way to high governmental circles. Through the efforts of Member of Parliament Dorise Nielsen, a delegation of representatives from Canadian arts groups was asked to appear before the House of Commons Special Committee on Reconstruction and Re-establishment (the Turgeon Committee). Elizabeth Wynn Wood, a prominent Canadian sculptor who was organizing the delegation, invited Ernest to join it. She also asked him to prepare a brief on Canadian music and to comment on her recently published article, 'A National Program for the Arts in Canada,' in which she proposed a Ministry of Fine Arts.[9]

He responded positively to Wood's piece, although he doubted that the time was ripe for such a ministry, believing that it would bring about 'an atmosphere of officialism that has not been entirely conducive to a healthy artistic life, and this we must at all costs avoid.'[10] He had sensed intuitively, even before conducting in Australia and Brazil, that Canada was better suited for arm's-length cultural agencies, such as the CBC.

To deal practically with Wood's request for a brief and, since there was 'no body of musicians really representative of the whole country,' he formed a Music Committee with Norman Wilks as chairman. The brief it prepared was endorsed by the Canadian Performing Rights Society and the Canadian Federation of Music Teachers, and was forwarded to the Turgeon Committee along with fifteen others from organizations of visual artists, writers (French and English), landscape artists, handicrafters, potters, and dramatists. It asked for an International Exchange and Information Bureau much like the British Council's, for better musical education, for more scholarships for the gifted, for assistance to music publishers to publish Canadian music, for more music festivals, and for more large concert halls.

On 21 June 1944, Wood's delegation of arts representatives appeared before the Turgeon Committee, the first such delegation in Canada's history. Ernest was there with Wood, Marcus Adeney, John Coulter (who read the submission), and several others – ten people in all.[11] The group asked the government to set up a body 'for the supervision of all cultural activities' and to build a network of community centres across the country as hubs of artistic activity. The National Gallery, the National Film Board, and the CBC would serve them. The delegation said that about $10 million would be needed to establish the centres and recommended that, initially, a survey be undertaken to ascertain community needs. The delegation also asked for a national orchestral centre, to 'train players, composers, and conductors, and to give financial assistance to provincial orchestras on a pro-rata basis with local grants,' and for a state theatre for musical and dramatic productions, a national library, an enlarged National Gallery, and an enlarged National Archives.

Nothing came out of the Turgeon Committee, but the hearing showed the government that artists were a power to be reckoned with. The committee praised the briefs, their presentation, and the delegates' responses in the question period. As one Toronto newspaper put it, 'They were frankly heralded as a "long-haired" delegation and came with as tight and tidy a brief as ever has been submitted to the committee.'[12] Ernest was concerned about the implications of the word 'supervision' in the delegation's first recommendation, but it became a non-issue as the submission disappeared into the parliamentary archives. The whole event did, however, lead to one substantive outcome: the formation of the Canadian Arts Council (CAC), an amalgam of the various groups which had made up the delegation. The Music Committee became a CAC affiliate but remained moribund until 1946, when Ernest asked Charles Peaker to reactivate it. Peaker convened it on 2 July, and the eleven present – Ernest was conducting in Montreal and couldn't attend – renamed themselves the Canadian Music Council (CMCl).[13] John Cozens, a Toronto choral director and later chief of protocol for the government of Ontario, was 'endorsed' as secretary-treasurer, a post he held for three decades.

Little happened for another year. Then Peaker resigned and the CMCl balloted for a successor. Ernest MacMillan, who had not been asked if he wanted to stand for the post, was elected president. He accepted under certain conditions: that annual dues be increased (from $1!), that a budget be struck, and that more Canadian musical organizations be urged to join. Several meetings were held in the fall of 1947, in the course of which a constitution was drafted and surveys were undertaken. In 1948, the CMCl entered nine Canadian compositions in the arts competitions of the XIV Olympiad in London. John Weinzweig's Divertimento No. 1 won a silver medal, and another work by Jean Coulthard received honourable mention. The CMCl was formally incorporated and received its letters patent on 30 July 1949. Ernest remained its president for the next seventeen years.

Just two months earlier, on 8 April 1949, after five years of sporadic lobbying by the CAC, other arts groups, and individuals, a parliamentary Order in Council had established the Royal Commission on National Development in the Arts, Letters and Sciences, better known as the Massey Commission after its chairman, Vincent Massey, who was now back in Canada. It was a momentous event in Canada's cultural history. The commission was charged with addressing a number of fundamental issues: Canada's radio and television policy; the operation and future development of federal agencies such as the National Film Board; Canada's relations with UNESCO and other international cultural organizations; government relations with national voluntary bodies in arts, letters, and sciences; ways of disseminating information on Canada to other countries; and measures for the preservation of historical monuments. To carry out this enormous assignment, the commission processed 462 written briefs, held hearings in every major city in Canada, listened to over 1,200 witnesses, and delivered its report to the governor general just two years after its formation.

MacMillan, Mazzoleni, and Walter prepared the CMCl's brief to the commission. It concentrated on the plight of Canadian musical composition and the need for mechanisms – a directory

of Canadian composers, a library of selected scores, and a catalogue of available works – to foster performances of new works.
It proposed a bureau of information to promote Canadian music
and musicians and endorsed the CAC proposal for a National
Arts Board modelled after the Arts Council of Great Britain and
the British Council, Britain's vehicles for state patronage of the
arts.[14]

The commission also asked Ernest MacMillan to prepare his
own background paper. Carefully written in measured prose, it
made a case for more support for Canadian composers, but its
main thrust was musical education and performance.[15] Professional training of Canadian musicians was improving thanks to
Quebec's provincial conservatory and the University of Toronto's
Senior School, but it had not yet reached the level of the best
schools in the United States and abroad. More money was needed
to improve the schools and to give students financial assistance.
With some irony MacMillan pointed out, as he had in the past,
that Canadian concert artists had to use New York managers to
get Canadian bookings, since these managers controlled the
Canadian concert field. Some Canadian concert clubs, he explained, were trying to operate independently and book Canadian
musicians, but needed help.

Moving on, he urged more support for the CBC for better
promotion of Canadian composers, performers, and performing
groups, and for more effective dissemination of information
about music in Canada. He proposed a yearbook (he was probably thinking of Britain's *Musical Yearbook*), a national scholarly
journal, and a national music library. Not surprisingly, he made
a special case for more aid for symphony orchestras, lamenting
that Canada had only four professional ones, that none had year-
round seasons, and that all were too dependent on box-office
returns. Such help would, he said, encourage innovative programming, provide orchestral musicians with better employment, and
encourage recording. He gave choral music and opera positive
ratings, especially opera, which was doing very well in Toronto
but lacked a suitable venue for its productions, and supported the
creation of a national arts board. His paper could have been
written with more passion, yet – and few realized this at the time

– how penetrating was his analysis of music's needs and how farsighted were his proposed remedies!

The CMCI was elated when the Massey Report became public in May 1951.[16] It clearly outlined the needs of performers and, especially, composers. The report recommended a stronger CBC with more geographically dispersed Canadian content in its programming and an expansion of its International Service, the establishment of a National Library which would collect not only books published in Canada and those published elsewhere by Canadians or with Canadian themes, but also other materials, including 'Canadian music in printed or manuscript form, and ... records,' and an expansion of government funding – scholarships, fellowships, grants – for study both at home and abroad.

Last and most important, the report recommended the establishment of a council 'to advance the arts and letters, the humanities and social sciences in Canada' and 'to promote a knowledge of Canada abroad.' Such a council would grant funds to orchestras, underwrite tours by concert artists and groups, commission music for events of national importance, give awards to young people of promise, and sponsor foreign engagements. The report spoke for cultural nationalism, its response to Canada's newfound prosperity, pride in its wartime achievements and 'new international status and a feeling that the nation was in the process of discovering itself.'[17] Canada's intelligentsia were realizing that, even if the country were to awaken to culture, if that culture were not its own, it would not be long before the country was swallowed up by its neighbour to the south.

There was still another development in Ernest's busy life. The Composers, Authors and Publishers Association of Canada (CAPAC) appointed him honorary president in 1947, a position he would hold for twenty-two years.[18] As president, he could direct funds towards performances of Canadian music, scholarships for young composers, and other worthy musical causes, and represent CAPAC at international conferences on performing rights matters. In 1949 he attended his first conference in London, a city he had not seen in twelve years, and while in Great Britain he took the opportunity to visit his beloved Edinburgh. There he attended the third annual Edinburgh Festival and heard music performed at a standard which raised his sights, sharpened his ears, and prompted him to note how Canada needed a festival like Edinburgh's.

With CAPAC funds Ernest planned and conducted in January 1948 a TSO concert of Canadian music: Healey Willan's Symphony No. 1 and shorter works by Godfrey Ridout, Leo Smith, Claude Champagne, Maurice Dela, and John Weinzweig's Divertimento No. 1, which had already been played that fall at the opening concert of the subscription series. Prior to the concert Ernest beseeched Toronto's music lovers to attend, 'not on the grounds of public spirit, patriotism or the support of a "worthy cause" (though such motives are worthy enough), but rather because the quality of the music justifies such a response ... Ultimately musical works of any age or any nationality stand or fall by their own quality ... and if they are not heard under favorable conditions they may prove still-born.'[19] It didn't help much. The public applauded the concert and press reviews were good, but box-office receipts came to a paltry $631; the concert's final deficit of $2,965 was borne by CAPAC. It was clear that contemporary music did not easily appeal to a public immersed in the classics.

Nevertheless, public or no public, Canada's composers moved ahead. In March 1950, student composers at the Faculty of Music and the Royal Conservatory jointly hosted the fourth annual symposium of the Juilliard chapter of the International Federation of Music Students, with participants from Toronto and five other leading North American schools. Each school put on its own chamber concert; there was also an orchestral concert at Convocation Hall which featured student works from all six schools. MacMillan, sympathetic with the meeting's aims, chaired a panel on the problems of music publishing. It was refreshing to hear symposium attendees discuss and openly criticize one another's works, and disturbing to hear how eager some were to abandon the past. One young composer said that he hoped 'nobody ever again writes like Liszt and Rachmaninoff' and another that Hindemith was now an 'old master' whose influence should not 'warp' the creative progress of young composers.[20] It made Ernest wonder.

Canadian composers took another step forward a year later, in

1951, when John Weinzweig spearheaded the formation of the Canadian League of Composers (CLC) and was appointed its first president. The league aimed to promote Canadian composition, to advance the professional interests of Canadian composers, to fight the resistance to Canadian music of publishers, managers, and a conservative and apathetic public, to foster communication between composers, and to establish composition as a recognized profession.[21] MacMillan was *not* asked to join the league, nor was Champagne, Walter, or Willan. According to Weinzweig, the league was primarily for the younger generation of composers.[22] Four years later Willan would be appointed an honorary member. MacMillan, whom the league did not consider an active composer, never was, despite a substantial list of compositions to his credit.

Ettore Mazzoleni conducted the first league-sponsored concert of Canadian music for small orchestra in May 1951. The following year, the league engaged the TSO for a concert of Canadian music for large orchestra and asked CBC music director Geoffrey Waddington to conduct it. The likeable Waddington was, at best, only a competent conductor, but it was the league's way of thanking him for commissioning and performing Canadian works on the CBC. The program included one outstanding work, Harry Somers's *North Country*, and two very good ones, the Violin Concerto of Alexander Brott (with soloist John Dembeck), and the Nocturne of Harry Freedman.

Ernest attended the concert and, evidently, grumbled throughout about the music, with Elsie admonishing him frequently to keep quiet. In fact she had all she could do to keep him from leaving at intermission.[23] Untypically, he was rudely voicing his contempt for music he thought lacked craft and/or inspiration, two musts in his book of compositional rules. Then too, it must have upset him that the league seemed to be snubbing him in spite of all his efforts on behalf of composers at CAPAC, the CMCl, and the TSO. Since taking over the orchestra in 1931, MacMillan had programmed works by twenty-four Canadian composers on subscription concerts alone. By 1956, when he would leave the TSO, this total would increase to thirty-two, with many represented more than once. By then he would also have included works by some of them on pops, school, and special concerts, as well as works by eighteen other Canadian composers. Considering the TSO's dependence on box-office earnings and the city's conservative audiences, it is an impressive record.

Ernest MacMillan may have had his problems with composers, but, on a brighter note, the Toronto Mendelssohn Choir moved from strength to strength under his leadership after the war. The *St Matthew Passion* and *Messiah* were annual events and the choir usually did at least one large-scale additional concert each year with the TSO. The *Passion* in particular had a long history in Toronto, starting with Ernest's first performance in 1923 using church choirs, then with the Toronto Conservatory Choir, and finally, after 1942, with the Mendelssohn. The CBC, recognizing the unique contribution of MacMillan's quarter-century of *Passions*, broadcast the 24 March 1948 performance nationwide from Convocation Hall. It was a milestone in Canada's musical life. Each of the CBC's radio stations had the option of airing the three-and-a-half-hour broadcast or staying with its regularly scheduled programs. Significantly, only two turned down the option. After the broadcast, Canada's establishment newspaper, the *Financial Post*, commended the CBC 'for its courageous decision to make this whole work available, not just to metropolitan concert audiences, but to almost everybody in Canada.' And then it lauded MacMillan: 'Bach's music, for the great majority, is an acquired taste, the result of much listening to the best. No one has done more to make Canadians Bach listeners than Sir Ernest.'[24]

Two years later the Mendelssohn sponsored a three-day festival to commemorate the 200th anniversary of the death of the great composer. The programs were of sufficient variety to please any Bach lover. The American organist E. Power Biggs opened the festival on 19 April with a brilliant but poorly attended matinée program at Eaton Auditorium, the lovely art deco hall in the T. Eaton Company's College Street department store. That evening, the choir and the TSO under Ernest's baton performed the *B Minor Mass* at Massey Hall; Ernest had done it with the choir the preceding year, its first performance since Fricker's day. The next afternoon Mazzoleni conducted the Conservatory Chamber

Players in several smaller works, with Greta Kraus as harpsichord soloist, and in the evening MacMillan conducted the *St Matthew Passion*, its second performance that spring; the first had been given at its usual location, Convocation Hall. The festival preferred Massey Hall because it had more seats and better acoustics. The results were so favourable that future *Passion* performances were given there. Yet, good as it was at Massey Hall, Ernest had lost something too, the quasi-religious and intimate setting of Convocation Hall, which helped so much to make *his* reading such a uniquely moving experience for his audience.

The audience at Biggs's second recital the next afternoon was much larger than at his first, news of his prowess having spread among the organ community. The festival's tribute to Ernest's favourite composer concluded that evening, when he led an exhausted choir and orchestra in Bach's Overture in D Major, Cantata No. 53 ('Schlage doch') with contralto soloist Herta Glaz, the *Peasant* Cantata, and the *Magnificat*.[25] It was a difficult yet truly comprehensive program, but Ernest would have been wiser to spread the concerts over four days.

Family matters continued to play an all-important part in Ernest's life. Keith married a fellow student, Patricia Dustin, on 17 May 1949 at Trinity College Chapel. Proud father Ernest celebrated the happy event in a way only he could by sitting at the chapel's organ and improvising on Bach's Little Fugue in E Minor and several of Keith's tunes from student musicals he had written while at Trinity College. A month later he was convocation speaker at the college. And when Patricia MacMillan presented him with his first grandson, Ian, in September 1950, he was as thrilled as any grandfather could be. Keith, with his penchant for electronic recording, had made a tape recorder for his father, and when he arrived at Park Road to share his happiness with his parents, Ernest promptly turned it on and out came Ernest's voice singing 'For unto us a child is born, a son is given.'

On 24 September MacMillan gave his last public organ recital at Toronto's Grace Church on-the-Hill. The program consisted of selections from Bach's *Clavier-Übung Book III*: the opening E-flat Prelude, seven other preludes, and the concluding *St Anne* Fugue. In the 1930s and 1940s he had given over fifty programs in Canadian churches, concert halls, and on radio, even though he was frustrated at not being able to meet his own exacting standards because of insufficient practice time. He even did a successful series of recitals on the CBC in 1938 and on the private Toronto radio station CKEY in 1945. This 1950 career-ending concert was, according to Keith, 'superb.' However, Keith said that his father had had enough. 'He felt he had to decide either to devote much more time to "keeping up" the instrument or, at the age of fifty-seven and with the heavy pressure of other duties, to abandon the effort to rekindle the old virtuosity and fire. He chose the latter.'[26]

Out of the blue in July 1951 CKEY offered Ernest a pleasurable job – a weekly one-hour broadcast of classical and semi-classical recorded music.[27] 'Sir Ernest Plays Favourites' was first aired on 5 November 1951, and the programs continued for several years. He was in his element, making clear, concise, and attractive comments about all kinds of music – other than jazz and popular. A year later the series won the Ohio award (the radio equivalent of an Academy Award) and a Canadian Radio Award for best non-network music program (classical).

14. A Question of Power

By 1951 fifty-eight-year-old Ernest MacMillan had reached the peak of his career. The TSO and the Mendelssohn were continuing to improve, the Faculty of Music was growing, and his work at CAPAC and the CMCl was stimulating and rewarding. Soon there would be a national arts council to fund music and the other arts, and he had played no small role in its creation. The future of music in Canada looked bright indeed.

Thus he was ill-prepared for the events of the spring of 1952. A major confrontation unfolded at the University of Toronto. As the RCM had developed in the 1940s, so had the rivalry between Mazzoleni and Walter, with Dean MacMillan a wary observer. MacMillan and Mazzoleni were bound by long professional association, friendship, and family, while Walter was alone, an unwelcome newcomer in a city suspicious of central Europeans. MacMillan freely admitted that Walter was a genuine idealist who loved music and dreamed, as he did, of the great days ahead for music in Canada. He also credited Walter with the knowledge and ability to get things done quickly and efficiently. But at the same time, MacMillan disliked Walter's outspoken and overbearing manner and the way he played politics. Although neither MacMillan nor Walter suffered fools gladly, MacMillan hid his feelings better.

Arnold Walter did have one important and influential ally who both respected and trusted him, Floyd Chalmers. Chalmers felt that the conservatory had stumbled along for too many years without strong direction. Now, with Walter, he had at last found

a dynamic leader and a visionary much like himself. The aggres-
sive Walter, egged on by his wife, Maria, who shared many of his
confidences, inevitably raised hackles and, at one point in 1948,
so exercised university president Sidney Smith that Smith feared
Walter might cause a crisis at the conservatory.' Smith wrote of
Walter's 'overwhelming ambition, Teutonic mentality, and an
individualism to the extent of failing to work with others ... To
my mind, Mr. Mazzoleni has shown the patience of Job in his
endeavors to work with Dr. Walter.' His letter was to Edward
Johnson, RCM board chairman and manager of New York's Metropolitan Opera Company. Johnson would feature prominently
in the events to come.

Johnson, a native of Guelph, Ontario, had had a distinguished
international career as an operatic tenor and had been awarded
several honours, including an honorary doctorate from the University of Toronto in 1934 and a CBE from Buckingham Palace
in 1935. Ernest had met him in 1934 on the occasion of the
Toronto doctorate and, two years later, had given him a warm
introduction in New York at a Canadian Club dinner fêting Johnson on his appointment as general manager of the Met. In 1945,
the University of Toronto had appointed him to its board of
governors and to the chairmanship of the conservatory board.
However, these appointments may not have been made solely on
the basis of his professional accomplishments, for his son-in-law,
George Drew, was premier of Ontario, and Toronto was a provincial university. A year later he was appointed honorary president
of the Toronto Mendelssohn Choir. By this time, MacMillan knew
him well.

Johnson had handsome features, snow-white hair, and an erect
carriage that made him look taller than his five feet seven inches.
He spoke well and with great charm, if not always with much
substance. He was neither a particularly good administrator nor
an inspired innovator – it was said that his lieutenants at the Met
really ran the company – but he had, nonetheless, managed to
keep the Met afloat and healthy without compromising artistic
standards during the difficult years of the Great Depression and
the Second World War.

As chairman of the conservatory board, Johnson hoped to

rationalize the conservatory's activities and goals with those of the Faculty of Music, but his efforts were sporadic because of his Met commitments. Chalmers would often have to go to New York to discuss conservatory business with him, as did Walter, who gradually won Johnson's confidence. In 1950, Johnson was winding up his Met career and beginning to focus more of his attention on the conservatory. He struck the Reorganization Study Committee to unify the RCM and the Faculty of Music and asked MacMillan to sit on it. But after a year of non-productive meetings, Johnson told President Smith that his enthusiasm was waning.[2]

Then, in October 1951, Smith met with MacMillan, Mazzoleni, and Walter, and they tentatively decided on a single new university music school, with two divisions – the School of Music, formerly the Royal Conservatory, and the Faculty of Music. The new two-division body would take over the name of the Royal Conservatory of Music, a name too good to give up. The Faculty of Music would become responsible for the Senior School to ensure provincial funding for its students; and the School of Music would keep the Opera School. Furthermore, the School of Music, presumably to strengthen the quality of its instruction, would make contract renewal for teachers conditional on a satisfactory volume of teaching. Each body, the school and the faculty, would be headed by an assistant dean reporting to a *full-time* rector in charge of the entire operation. (Ernest, who had no intention of giving up the TSO, had agreed to surrender the faculty deanship when the reorganization was completed.) Since Walter was the obvious choice to head the enlarged Faculty of Music, the senior of the two divisions, insiders wondered if the position of rector was only being proposed to prevent him from becoming top dog.

Tensions mounted and gossip was rampant. At the end of February, MacMillan heard a disquieting rumour – that Mazzoleni (his choice for dean – the title 'rector' had by this time been dropped) would not get the top job. Ernest was undoubtedly influenced by family considerations. Mazzoleni needed help. His wife, Winifred, was terminally ill and there were two young daughters, Andrea and Clare, to care for. Smith, aware of MacMillan's partisanship, avoided him as much as possible during the winter of 1951–2. He didn't want Mazzoleni *or* Walter as dean, since either choice would invite conflict – it was common knowledge that there was no love lost between them. An additional reason for not giving Mazzoleni the position was that, although he was a formidable musician and a good conductor, he had no driving interest in musical education and insufficient understanding of North American professional music schools. And, as an administrator, he often spent too much time on minor issues. Edward Johnson also didn't want Mazzoleni. He was troubled by the MacMillan/Mazzoleni alliance and feared that if Mazzoleni were dean, MacMillan might rule the school by proxy. Johnson, who had a sizeable ego, was jealous of MacMillan's importance in Canadian musical life. In fact, some said that he was still smarting over not having been knighted with or instead of MacMillan in 1935.

Walter, who certainly merited the deanship, never had a chance. Smith and several other university officials disliked him, and conservatory teachers distrusted him. When he had appointed teachers to the Senior School six years earlier, he had bypassed and, thereby, alienated some prominent teachers of long standing in favour of several relatively new ones, most of whom had emigrated from Europe and were considered 'foreigners.' Indeed, Walter was still thought of as a 'foreigner' even though he had been in Canada for fifteen years. Teachers referred to him as the 'The Prussian,' yet, if truth be known, few disliked Prussianism more than Walter. Then, too, diplomacy plays an important role in the Anglo-Saxon world, and Walter didn't know the fundamental rules.

At the beginning of March there were rumours that the new dean would be none other than the seventy-three-year-old Edward Johnson. MacMillan couldn't believe it. Apart from being too old, Johnson knew next to nothing about musical education. Indeed, the only arguments for the appointment were his international reputation and his political connections. MacMillan wrote forcefully of his concerns to Smith on 6 March, but without mentioning Johnson:

I have always expressed my willingness to fall in with any plan that would improve present conditions. From the first I recognized that such reorganisation might very well involve my resignation ... While for many reasons I should find it a relief to relinquish that office, I should not like it to be assumed that I am prepared to resign voluntarily, irrespective of what the proposed set-up might be ... Many other considerations are involved in this matter and I should like to discuss them with you before a final decision is reached ... I have no desire to delay matters, but as all discussions in which I have taken part have only dealt with generalities, I am in the dark as to what solution is contemplated. I should not wish to be presented suddenly with a *fait accompli* which might prove very embarrassing to me and others.[3]

Aware of MacMillan's veiled threat and its implications, Smith replied the next day.[4] He dodged a confrontation by writing that 'questions relating to personnel have not been settled' and reminded MacMillan that 'the success of the reorganization will be better assured by men who can give their full time to teaching and administration.' And then Smith tried to divert him. 'The foregoing has, of course, no relation to your capacity, talent, and prestige, which the University craves ... I have been hoping that we could find for you in the Graduate School a position that would not take too much of your time but, on the other hand, would enable us to promote and develop our graduate work in the field of Music, for which you would have direct responsibility ... As soon as the personnel situation becomes clear I will seek the opportunity to discuss matters with you.'

Smith was playing for time. The news had leaked prematurely – the reorganization and the appointment of a new dean had not yet cleared the university's board of governors. Nor was Smith ready to face the fuss MacMillan might make when the new appointee was announced publicly. But MacMillan was in no waiting mood. He thanked Smith for promising to meet with him soon and then flexed his muscles: 'I hope I may assume that no irrevocable decisions will be taken without my knowledge ... I have no desire to interfere in matters outside my own sphere, but I do feel very strongly about some aspects of this change, and as long as I remain in office I should welcome an opportunity of making my views known.' He turned down Smith's offer to head up a graduate department and then warned him petulantly not to rely on him in further reorganization plans.[5]

Mazzoleni wrote Smith on the same day pointing out that he had to confirm next year's contracts with the many RCM teachers and that if any were to be let go he needed to tell them 'at the earliest possible date. However, I feel strongly that no contracts should be terminated or negotiated until we have given a full and clear explanation of the reorganization plan ... to the entire faculty.'[6]

Obviously, Smith had to act. He immediately wrote to Johnson in New York asking that the appointments – his as dean of the conservatory, Mazzoleni's as principal of the school, and Walter's as director of the faculty – be submitted for approval to the board of governors at its next meeting the following week, along with the reorganization plan.[7] Smith told Johnson that MacMillan 'might not be ready to leave the deanship in such a happy mood as he indicated in earlier conversations or as I had reason to anticipate. I have not discussed the matter of personnel with him. On the other hand it may be that he might have some anxiety about Arnold Walter becoming the administrative head directly in charge of Sir Ernest's present colleagues in the Faculty of Music.' He did not let on to Johnson that MacMillan was dead set against him – Johnson – as dean. He may have cleverly used the reference to Walter to spare Johnson.

Of course Smith was wrong to consider Johnson as dean in the first place. Two days later, MacMillan, now certain of his information, pulled out all the stops and protested to Smith.[8] He pointed out that Johnson was already past retirement age and that, because of his lack of academic background, 'Dr. Walter would be in control of the situation.' He reminded Smith that the new appointment was to be full-time, which was why *he* was leaving, and that Johnson could not possibly give it his undivided attention either, having just been appointed chancellor of the Chicago Musical College. The Chicago school was in poor financial shape and, MacMillan pointed out, Johnson's office there was 'obviously no sinecure.' He feared that if Johnson were dean there would be resignations of 'valuable subordinate members of the Conservatory staff.' Then, in a last ditch attempt to get his way, MacMillan offered to stay another year until an appropriate appointment was made. He went on:

I have one and only one personal interest in this matter. The proposed scheme ... would mean a demotion for Mazzoleni. In ordinary circumstances I know that he would not accept it but offer his resignation forthwith. However he is not in a position to do so. His wife (my sister) is dying of cancer, and, apart from the personal grief and anxiety, his medical and other expenses ... have been formidable. He would never tell you this himself ... and has never suggested that I interfere in this whole matter ... This new arrangement will mean a very severe blow to him and, in view of the excellent job he has done since taking office, I for one think it grossly unfair.

Ernest suggested the delay to enable Mazzoleni to 'reconsider his whole position. We might lose him to the States – we in Canada seem to have an unfortunate habit of losing our best men – but at least we should not be inflicting additional pain on one who – and here I speak as a brother-in-law – has behaved splendidly throughout a time of trial.'

If MacMillan hoped that Smith and Johnson would back down for compassionate reasons, he was wrong indeed. On 29 March the three men had a meeting at which, according to MacMillan, Johnson said that he had no wish to be dean and, further, did not feel qualified for the post.[9] Then MacMillan proposed postponing the reorganization for a year and appointing Mazzoleni as acting dean in the interim. Johnson refused out of hand and on 3 April informed Mazzoleni with finality that he would be the principal of the new School of Music effective 1 July, at no change in salary.

On 7 April, Winifred died. She was only forty-nine, the youngest of Alexander and Wilhelmina MacMillan's four children. Two evenings later, following the funeral, Ernest led the TSO and the Mendelssohn Choir in the *St Matthew Passion*. It was a sad evening for the family. Winifred's older daughter, Andrea, who had not attended the funeral, mourned with her uncle at Massey Hall.[10]

The day after the funeral, the university's governors approved the conservatory's reorganization scheme. MacMillan again told Smith that the university was pushing it through 'at all costs, irrespective of the personalities involved or of the views of many who are more conversant with the situation than those exerting the pressure.'[11] He reiterated that he would not, voluntarily, resign 'without being made aware of the full details of the proposed setup ... I hope that I am not going to be put into the somewhat embarrassing position of being asked to resign, but matters seem to be drifting in that direction.'

Smith replied evasively. He regretted that MacMillan couldn't accept the deanship because of 'obligations to the Symphony and other organizations,' repeated his offer to make MacMillan head of graduate studies, and cleverly added a new one – 'I would like to propose to the Board of Governors that you be appointed Dean Emeritus of Music as from July 1st, 1952.'[12] Within the week, frustrated and outflanked, Ernest turned down both offers and retired from the university.[13]

A few days later, in an open letter to the Faculty of Music, he announced that he would be leaving on 30 June and described the reorganization and the forthcoming appointments of Mazzoleni and Walter.[14] Smith, after reading it, sent a more temperate and encouraging statement to the Faculty about the proposed organization, but with no mention of who would be the new dean. In fact, it suggested that there would not be a dean and that Mazzoleni and Walter would each head a department. By implication, they would, in future, be doing battle without an umpire. Almost immediately Mazzoleni wrote a letter to Johnson, declining his appointment as principal,[15] and another to his conservatory staff, informing them of the reorganization and telling them that he and Walter had each been asked to lead a department without any mention of a dean being appointed. 'Since this represents a basic departure from the original plan which called for a unified control and since I was not consulted or officially informed of the change, I at once replied that this would endanger the whole plan of reorganization and I would have no part in it.' Mazzoleni said, emphatically, that he could not accept a plan that was 'damaging to the Conservatory and to those having any part in its widespread activities.'[16] It was hard to disagree with him.

The unfortunate events which followed could have been avoided if Smith and the conservatory board had acted sooner and more decisively. But university presidents have many things on their mind, and boards of non-profit institutions are notoriously dilatory. Mazzoleni's letter precipitated a meeting by conservatory teachers on the following Sunday. Many attended, not so much out of affection for Mazzoleni, although he had many supporters, but more because they feared 'The Prussian.' Then the fracas hit the press, and Ernest issued a lengthy statement explaining his position and why he supported Mazzoleni. One front page carried the sensational headline, 'MacMillan Retires, Mazzoleni Resigns, Discord Rocks Royal Conservatory.'[17] The next night, a standing ovation and the dazzle of flash cameras greeted Mazzoleni at Massey Hall when he came on stage to conduct the conservatory orchestra and chorus in Godfrey Ridout's new oratorio *Esther.* Was it spontaneous? Earlier that same day, conservatory secretary-treasurer Roy Loken had delivered a handwritten note to Sidney Smith telling him that Mazzoleni's office had asked that press photographers be on hand that evening because there would be some special excitement. Loken's note said that 'outside groups' were behind it.[18]

The press was having a field day. Colonel Eric Phillips, chairman of the university's board, responded to a reporter's query about the controversy by snapping, 'a tempest in a teapot.'[19] And so it was! On 1 May, the conservatory board called a teachers' meeting and officially announced the reorganization plans and the appointment of Edward Johnson as unpaid coordinator until a dean was chosen.[20] John Weinzweig, vice-chairman of the Conservatory Faculty Association, the closest thing there was to a teachers' protective organization, was in the chair, and, thanks to him, the conservatory teachers took the news calmly.[21] Actually, they had no alternative, since they were engaged only on an annual basis with no job security. Many were so apprehensive about offending the administration that they insisted on anonymity when speaking to the press. It occurred to only a very few that the conservatory teachers, or at least their association, should have been consulted during the reorganization deliberations. This lack of respect and concern for teachers' views underlined the anomalous relationship between teachers and the conservatory's administration. They were not employees and had no say in determining the school's policies or future.

Loken wired Mazzoleni on 3 May to ask if he still refused to accept the principalship, and Mazzoleni stuck to his guns.[22] But his resolve was weakening, since now the only reason left for resigning was his 'demotion.' On 6 May, without telling Ernest, he went to see James Duncan, vice-chairman of the conservatory board. The next morning Ernest opened his *Globe and Mail* and was shocked to read that Mazzoleni had withdrawn his resignation and was now supporting the reorganization and Johnson's role as interim coordinator.[23] Ernest had fully expected Mazzoleni to refuse the demotion.

It was the last straw in a nightmarish spring. In addition to the strain of the controversy and the grief over Winifred's death, he was dealing with the death of his old friend and colleague Leo Smith and with added responsibilities and work brought on because TSO assistant conductor Paul Scherman had had a heart attack. Ernest was having memory lapses while conducting, which his physician attributed to overwork and worry. For these many reasons, the TSO granted Ernest a much-needed leave for the first part of the 1952–3 season.

Elsie described his desolation in a letter to their good friend Dalton Wells.[24] (Wells was married to Kay Irwin, who had had a two-piano team with Winifred in happier days. Kay and Ernest also shared the same passion for writing 'fun-poems,' and often exchanged them with one another.) She was puzzled as to why Mazzoleni hadn't talked to Ernest before making up his mind and attributed it to a 'psychological collapse.' She told Wells that Ernest really wanted to be dean emeritus but had to refuse because of the stance he had taken. Now there were no thanks, Elsie went on, in spite of his twenty-five years as dean. She had never seen Ernest so 'down' but was 'proud of him.' He was keeping his 'self-respect' and doing 'something for standards of decency in the conduct of public affairs.' In fact, she wrote, Ernest had even offered to resign from the TSO because of the bad publicity connected with his name, but the TSO chairman had 'pooh-poohed it,' reconfirmed his leave at full pay, and given him a bonus!

Ernest felt betrayed, especially by the university – he had served it as organist, composed hymns for its prayer books, earned his

BA from it, and been its dean of music. Yet, his statement to the press revealed just how much *he* missed the point: 'One could wish ... that those who direct so admirably the destinies of the University, but whose knowledge of the musical world must in many cases be very limited, would pay greater heed to the counsel of those who do know about such matters.'[25] He failed to realize, or didn't want to realize, that he had become too used to power, too used to *his* opinions being supreme. He had, in a word, lost his objectivity. He should never have expected to play a role in selecting his successor and had overreacted when Mazzoleni said yes to the principal post. After all, Mazzoleni really had had no choice but to say yes – he had two motherless children, no financial resources, and no other job to go to. Finding a new post for the coming year on such short notice would be wellnigh impossible. (Ernest did write unofficially to a leading Vancouver Symphony patron asking whether the VSO, which was looking for a new conductor, would be interested in Mazzoleni, but the post had already gone to Irwin Hoffman.)[26] Mazzoleni may have shown bad judgment in not consulting Ernest before accepting the new post, but he, like Ernest, was under great stress. After this trying time, their relations cooled forever, although they kept up appearances in public and at family gatherings.

The university fracas resulted in MacMillan leaving under a cloud of his own making, and ended forever his role in academia. But, personal considerations aside, just how well did the new structure realize *his* goals for musical education? Certainly, he had to admit that the Faculty of Music was much better off; it had been strengthened by the addition of the Senior School, which now offered an artist's diploma, and Walter was an excellent director. But what about the School of Music? MacMillan had long abhorred its system of commission-based lessons, yet this would continue with the reorganization. Nor was there any plan to develop a closely integrated preparatory and senior program for gifted teenage students, with permanent teachers who could work for both the Faculty and the School. Instead, the Faculty and the School would each go its own way in the years to come, with conflicts from time to time. In truth, Ernest should have left the Faculty when he left the conservatory in 1942. Instead, he had spread himself too thin and, in the end, had failed to provide the strong leadership and clear direction needed to bring about a truly effective reorganization.

15. A Matter of Morality

Although the TSO's popularity had reached new heights by mid-century, it was still underfunded. It paid its players inadequately, had a limited budget for soloists and guest conductors, was unadventurous in its programming, and did not tour. Compare it to the Minneapolis Symphony, for example, which had a similar length of season (twenty-six weeks) and served a population of roughly similar size. Minneapolis and St Paul together were, at that time, slightly smaller than Toronto, yet its symphony was larger – it had eighty-eight regular players compared with Toronto's eighty-three – and its basic weekly wage was $90 while Toronto's was only $70.[1] It spent over $100,000 a year more than Toronto on salaries and contributed to a players' pension fund, which the TSO did not, even though plans for one had been in place for some time. In 1951-2, Minneapolis's private and corporate donations and civic grants totalled $200,000, while Toronto's came to a paltry $56,000. Even Canada's Vancouver Symphony, with its shorter season and smaller community, raised almost $10,000 more than Toronto that year. Was it any wonder that MacMillan wanted government subsidy so badly?

Yet, because of extra earnings from the CBC, some of the TSO players were not as badly off with regard to income as their weekly wage suggests. In addition to the regular broadcasts of TSO concerts, the CBC had organized its own Toronto-based symphony and many TSO members played in it. In addition, the CBC produced live concerts with smaller ensembles and used music as an adjunct on other programs, such as radio dramas. In fact, opportunities for CBC freelancing were so lucrative in the early 1950s that several leading TSO players left the orchestra.

Nevertheless, despite its fiscal problems and the loss of players to the CBC, the quality of the TSO was better than ever, and it was eager to gain wider recognition. Touring was one way, but so far it had failed to develop a 'tour circuit' – out-of-town concerts were at best limited to nearby cities. Another potential outlet was commercial recording. The CBC had recorded the TSO in a fair number of Canadian works, but only for its International Service, not for commercial distribution. In fact, no *commercial* recording company had shown any interest in the TSO since RCA Victor in 1942–3. Minneapolis is a good comparator here, too. It was busy recording for both RCA Victor and Mercury; but, then, its conductor was the gifted and internationally known Antal Dorati.[2] Perhaps record companies didn't think the TSO and MacMillan good enough, or perhaps they disliked Toronto's recording sites, recording equipment, or technicians, or thought the orchestra's recording contract with its players too inflexible.

And so change was in the air when Ernest proudly announced that on 27 November 1951 the TSO would play for the first time in the United States, one of five orchestras on a Detroit concert series, the others being the Philadelphia, Boston, Chicago, and Cleveland orchestras.[3] The TSO hoped that this engagement, to be given in such distinguished company, would lead to more invitations to the United States. To ensure the concert's success, Ernest decided to include an American work, Herbert Elwell's *Pastorale*, and to introduce the young Canadian soprano Lois Marshall in its solo part. Ernest had first thrilled to Lois's unique and radiant lyric soprano voice, with its extraordinary range and purity of sound, four years earlier. Her vocal gifts, musicianship, and intuitive expressiveness added up to rare artistry. From 1947 on, a devoted Ernest had engaged her at every opportunity, and especially for *Messiah* and *St Matthew Passion* performances. She admired him, too, and, although she sang these great works with many other conductors throughout her career, she maintained that Ernest's interpretations were supreme.[4]

The entire Detroit concert, which also included Elgar's *Enigma Variations*, a work with which Ernest had much affinity, came off very well. The press praised Marshall, the TSO, and MacMillan. Only one thing clouded the event: the TSO had to replace seven of its members for the concert because the United States Immigration Department had, for undisclosed reasons, refused them entry. Given the times, it was not hard to guess why – they were thought to be communists or communist sympathizers. After the Detroit concert, the six players resumed their places in the TSO for the rest of the season, but the TSO's compliance with the American decree would come back to haunt the orchestra and its conductor.

Six months later, on 21 May 1952, Toronto's three daily newspapers reported that the TSO had not renewed the contracts of six of its musicians for the coming season because they had been refused entry to the United States and would thus be unable to play with the orchestra for the return engagement in Detroit in December 1952. The musicians, three double-bass players, two violinists, and the principal flutist, were six of the seven who had been replaced the year before.

TSO manager Jack Elton had first brought the problem of the six players to the TSO board meeting on 21 April.[5] MacMillan did not attend. It is not clear whether Elton acted on MacMillan's instructions or on his own initiative when he told the board that for artistic reasons there could be no substitutes for such an important concert, leading, as it might, to other American engagements. (Years later, MacMillan said that he left the decision to the board.)[6] The board agreed with Elton and, by extension, MacMillan, and left Elton to handle the matter. He took it to the Toronto Musicians' Association (TMA), which agreed to support the TSO's management.[7] The six players then appealed to the TMA, but their appeal was turned down because, according to TSO contracts, the players must fulfil *all* of the orchestra's out-of-town engagements.[8] The American Federation of Musicians (AFM), of which the Toronto union was a member, barred communists and their supporters from membership, but TMA president Walter Murdoch insisted that his union's position had nothing to do with politics. 'It is a straight contractual matter. The Federation has always been keen on keeping contracts, but there is nothing wrong in the orchestra's not rehiring musicians.'[9] With little hope of success, the musicians appealed to the AFM in New York.

The 'Symphony Six,' as the six musicians were called, fought back on the home front too, denying that they were members of any 'subversive organization' and saying how disappointed they were that their orchestra was letting them go because of *one* concert in the coming season. They cited Amsterdam's Concert-gebouw, one of the world's great orchestras, which had recently cancelled an entire American tour because several of its members had been barred from the United States.[10] The press, at first sympathetic to the plight of the Symphony Six, indignantly demanded explanations from the American government and asked why the Canadian government had not intervened. But, almost immediately, their indignation lessened and one newspaper even said that under the circumstances the TSO had acted 'reasonably.'[11]

Still, the obviously bad feeling generated by the firings in the community prompted the TSO board to review its decision on 26 May. Twelve members – double the usual – attended the special meeting. Again MacMillan was absent.[12] At the meeting, Rabbi Abraham Feinberg read a letter protesting the TSO action from R.S.K. Seeley, provost of Trinity College and president of the Civil Liberties Association. After discussion, the board voted nine to three to uphold its decision, but with the proviso that if the six players were cleared by the United States by 1 September they be rehired.

The 'Assembly For Canadian Arts,' a group of concerned Canadian writers, artists, and musicians, invited the Symphony Six and the TSO management to a meeting at the Arts and Letters Club on 29 May and urged the TMA to attend. The TMA responded by advising the six not to attend the meeting and not to discuss TMA and AFM business with the assembly or similar organizations. The same instructions were given to TMA members of the assembly's executive who, upon hearing this, promptly resigned. The TMA even assigned several of its members to go to the meeting to enforce the edict.[13] Morry Kernerman, a local violinist but not a TSO member (years later he would be its assistant concertmaster), attended and was waylaid outside by two zealous fellow musicians who told him, 'We are under strict instructions to

forbid you to go to the meeting.' Once inside, Kernerman identified only one other musician. The TMA had done its job
well.[14]

The *Toronto Evening Telegram* called it a 'communist meeting!'
The less-biased *Globe and Mail* quoted from the assembly's formal
statement: 'The refusal to renew contracts may indicate an
infringement of Canadian artists' right to employment.'[15] It also
quoted an assembly spokesman who denied accusations that the
assembly was a Red front: 'Our plans have only been aimed at the
promotion of art and entertainment in Canada.' Intimidated, a
good many assembly members resigned for fear of being labelled
communists.

On 4 June the United Church of Canada resolved by a 'slim
majority' to urge TSO directors to reconsider their decision to
fire the six members.[16] It questioned, as the assembly had, whether Canada should 'allow another government to say whom we
should employ.' The church, however, did not influence the TSO
board. As for other TSO players, most agreed with the decision
and shunned the Symphony Six. Those who commiserated with
them said nothing publicly for fear of being ostracized, fired from
their jobs, expelled from the union, and prevented from entering
the United States. There was fear in the air in Canada as never
before. In the past, a few well-meaning liberals had protested
when prominent Canadians had been barred from the United
States or when others already there had been detained and de-
ported back to Canada. There was the occasional flurry in the
press when such things occurred, but nothing more. It took a
symphony orchestra to bring McCarthyism out into the open and
make it a national issue.[17]

People were wondering during those days in late May 1952 how
Sir Ernest MacMillan felt about the Symphony Six issue, but he
remained silent. He had had an exhausting spring in so many
ways and may simply have been too whipped psychologically to
muster the strength to justify his action publicly on such a difficult issue. But how he disappointed the Symphony Six. Nearly all
of them were from immigrant families and proud to be members
of Canada's leading orchestra. They had grown up revering Sir

Ernest MacMillan and what he stood for and were hurt beyond belief that he did nothing and never uttered a word of concern about them. They had expected more.

A glance back in time sheds some light on MacMillan's orientation to the whole affair. Five years earlier, he had resigned from the National Council for Canadian-Soviet Friendship because he doubted that the Soviet Union was really interested in friendship and believed that Canada's efforts were 'decidedly one-sided.'[18] Subsequently, he had refused to support other left-wing groups. On 5 July 1950 he had written to the *Globe and Mail* complaining that the 'Canadian Artists Assembly For Peace' had used his name in a drive for membership. He knew nothing of the organization and viewed with 'suspicion any group that in the present crisis raises its banner under such slogans. Naturally everyone wants peace, but the present Communist enthusiasm for it in countries on this side of the Iron Curtain is really too transparent.'[19] (The Korean War had broken out that June.) He had concluded by saying that if the group was 'lending its weight to the policies of the United Nations, it has my full sympathy.'

Perhaps his feelings about the importance of the United Nations reached UN headquarters, for in December 1950 he conducted at a celebration of the second anniversary of the United Nations Universal Declaration of Human Rights at New York's Metropolitan Opera House. Ernest was in distinguished company. Eleanor Roosevelt gave the principal address and said unequivocally that 'human rights must be applied to all human beings, regardless of race, creed or colour. When they are applied, it will mean a growing understanding among the peoples of the world. Freedom can never be absolute, because it must be consistent with the freedom of others.'[20] Fritz Busch, musical director of the Dresden Opera before Hitler came to power, conducted the New York Philharmonic and the Schola Cantorum, with Marian Anderson and Claudio Arrau as soloists. Ernest's turn came after intermission when he led the same groups in excerpts from *Messiah*, with John Brownlee as soloist. It was his first conducting assignment in New York since the NBC broadcasts in 1941. United Nations Secretary Trygve Lie thanked Ernest by letter the next day, and Ernest, moved indeed by the celebration, replied, 'it seemed to me a most valuable reminder of the ultimate values that we must keep in mind in these troublous times.'[21]

Shortly before the UN engagement, Ernest had become concerned that some Canadians were, without warning, being denied entry to the United States, usually because of present or past affiliation with left-wing groups. Fearing that this could well happen to him, despite his change of heart, he wrote to the American consul in Toronto confessing that he had once been a member of the Council for Canadian-Soviet Friendship and expressing the hope that this would not jeopardize his admissibility to the United States in the future. 'I need hardly say that I am not a Communist and have no sympathy with present Communist aims and that I have disassociated myself with the Council.'[22] A consul officer phoned him promptly and assured him that American officials at Toronto Airport would extend him every courtesy.[23]

A year later, prior to the first Detroit concert, he had unsuccessfully sought the help of the Canadian ambassador in Washington to remove the ban on the seven barred musicians. He may have expected that their clearance would be pro forma as his had been the year before. And in January 1952, he had written to American immigration authorities on behalf of Steven Staryk, one of the seven (later, one of the six), to try to clear his name. 'He is an exceptionally talented violinist and valuable member of the orchestra. I have no reason to doubt that he has no Communistic affiliations other than that he played from ages twelve to fourteen with a Ukrainian orchestra that is under some suspicion.'[24] Staryk remained barred.

Ernest was silent throughout the spring and summer of 1952. But, the following November, in response to a letter from Dan Cameron, president of the Canadian Federation of Music Teachers, he opened up. Cameron, who lived in Regina, had talked about the TSO's action with bass player Ruth Budd, one of the Symphony Six, and had asked MacMillan for more information.[25] MacMillan told Cameron of his initial attempt to clear the six musicians with American authorities and went on:

with the political question the orchestra is not immediately concerned. The six, being unable to fulfil the terms of the contract, have been replaced by six other Canadian musicians, and the orchestra, far from suffering musically, has in some respects improved. I am told that the six themselves have found other adequate employment; this is likely, as good orchestral players are in great demand, but I have no first hand information ... At the present time morale seems to be excellent.

The tumult and the shouting have pretty well died here ... We for our part have no wish to brand our ex-players with any political label, but the very vehemence and persistence of the campaign is in itself suspicious and, as in so many cases, the liberal instincts of some of our best citizens have been successfully exploited.

Having dutifully brought the plight of the six to the attention of the Canadian ambassador in Washington, having been assured that they had found 'adequate employment,' and having noted that the orchestra had even improved since their departure, Ernest was left with a clear conscience. It was in some respects a replay of his thinking when he took over the TSO in 1931 and threatened to release some players *for the good of the orchestra.* For Ernest, the group as a whole was more important than individual members, and this may help to explain his dispassionate attitude to the entire Symphony Six affair. However, he *was* undervaluing the substance of the questions raised and the protests made. They are worth reviewing.

In August 1952, the annual Couchiching Conference held a panel entitled 'The Outlook for Freedom in the Garrison State.' Panellists included R.S.K. Seeley, chairman of the conference, and Eugene Forsey, director of research for the Canadian Congress of Labour.[26] In response to questions about the Symphony Six, Seeley, who had protested the TSO's action in May, said that the TSO had not given the musicians a chance to defend themselves and added that, while the TSO had acted legally, it was 'putting money before the making of music.' He, for one, intended to deprive himself 'of the pleasure of listening to the orchestra' the following winter. Forsey went a step further when he said bluntly that the TSO was 'putting money before self-respect.' Later in the discussion Seeley pointed out the disturbing trend in Canada towards 'guilt by association' which could lead to 'loss of liberty.'

John Moscow, a violinist member of the Symphony Six, took heart from such pronouncements and said to a *Toronto Star* reporter, 'We had given up hope. Now we know we have not been forgotten.'[27] When the *Star* asked Jack Elton for his views, he explained that if the TSO refused to accept engagements in the 'major leagues ... it would not be able to build up the prestige of the orchestra and the city. It's all very well for Dr. Seeley to take the position he has, but we must consider the other 80 or 90 members of the orchestra and whether the TSO is to become a truly international orchestra or not. Does Dr. Seeley think we should refuse to play in the U.S. and allow six members of the orchestra to control its whole destiny?'

More than a week later, a lengthy *Star* editorial supported Seeley.

Dr. Seeley fears that the TSO directors have, by their action, set the dangerous precedent in Canada of making employment contingent upon a person's ability to obtain a border crossing card from the U.S. Immigration Department ... Significantly, Dr. Seeley's statement last week was followed by an Ottawa dispatch reporting that the Canadian External Affairs department is deeply concerned about the large number of Canadians who have been refused permission to cross our 'invisible border' even for short visits ... It is strongly felt here that the regulations contained in the McCarran Act are so vicious that an opportunity should be found to make the Canadian viewpoint known.[28]

The editorial then pointed out that a person can be refused admission to the United States on the flimsiest grounds, and concluded, 'The prestige of the TSO is being jeopardized in Canada and the United States among people who place high value on moral responsibility and loyalty between employers and employees.'

Two of the most prominent, long-standing, and hard-working members of the TSO board, Mrs Edmund Boyd and Mrs R.B. Whitehead, resigned at its first meeting in September because of the Symphony Six.[29] Neither resignation was accepted initially, but two weeks later they reaffirmed their resolve, and Boyd asked that her reasons be put on the record, although there is no evidence

that they were. Both women, however, agreed to remain on the
women's committee. Rabbi Abraham Feinberg sided with Boyd
and Whitehead but said he felt he could 'serve the orchestra best
by remaining on the board.' At the TSO annual general meeting
which followed, President W.G. Watson 'glanced at a telegram
then set it aside. It was learned later that it was from a group of
"interested Toronto citizens" urging that the matter of the six
musicians be brought up for discussion.' There was no discussion.[30]

A week later the board struck a 'personnel committee' to 'continue investigations' concerning the Symphony Six and to handle
'continuing representations if at any time such a situation should
again occur.'[31] The *Globe and Mail* gave this development front-
page attention, suggesting that all new players would in future be
screened to make sure they could get into the United States. This
was promptly denied by Watson. An inside page of the same
paper gave Lester Pearson's account of Canada's unsuccessful
efforts to have the decision overturned in November 1951. Pearson, Canada's minister of external affairs, said that it would not
'serve any useful purpose to take the matter up again.' He defended the American action by saying that there had never been
any 'implicit' right for people to cross the border and that 'entry
to either country was always subject to immigration laws and
security.'[32] Pearson blamed the present situation on the Cold War
– even Canada, he said, had stopped people from entering the
country 'to attend meetings of Communist organizations or because it thought these people might stir up trouble.' Pearson,
who would later be prime minister, admitted that 'security information' was shared with the United States and added that 'there
is nothing out of the way in that.'

It had become clear that the Symphony Six would not be reinstated. A few professional groups, including the Federation of
Canadian Artists and the Canadian Arts Council, resolved to
support them.[33] Others did not. The Canadian Congress of
Labour turned down a proposal of support on 26 September. The
Symphony Six's appeal to Toronto's Mayor Lamport came to
nothing as did their appeal to the AFM. The six musicians slipped
out of sight, eager to have the incident forgotten so as not to

have their future employment jeopardized more than it already had been.

Steven Staryk, the youngest of the six and the one on whose behalf Ernest had written in January 1952, had been a member of the first violin section. He was later concert-master of three of the finest orchestras in the world: the Royal Philharmonic (under Sir Thomas Beecham), the Concertgebouw, and the Chicago Symphony. Needless to say, by the time he joined the Chicago orchestra, he had been cleared by American authorities. He returned to the TSO as concert-master from 1982 to 1986. To his credit, in 1953 Ernest wrote again to U.S. Immigration on Staryk's behalf. 'I know nothing of his political affiliations and was genuinely surprised and distressed to learn that he should have been refused a border crossing card ... I would be very happy if he were able to clear himself in this regard ... for he is young and at the beginning ... of a distinguished career.'[34] But, despite this second effort, Staryk never got over the feeling that Ernest had let him down.[35]

What became of the three double-bass players? Ruth Budd rejoined the orchestra in 1964, William Kuinka remained a freelance player, and Abe Manheim became librarian of the VSO and then of the Rochester Philharmonic, in the United States! Dirk Keetbaas, the principal flutist, joined the Winnipeg Symphony, also as principal, and later became a CBC producer. The other violinist, John Moscow (he later returned to his Ukrainian surname Moskalyk), taught at the Royal Conservatory and the University of Toronto until his sudden and untimely death at age fifty in 1966.

Ernest MacMillan was a staunch believer in individual freedom and democracy. Yet he was party to depriving six musicians of one of democracy's fundamental rights, that one is innocent until proven guilty. He disappointed those who thought that Canada's national musician should not allow the United States to decide who should or shouldn't be in the TSO. Many agreed with his action, a few didn't, and it was with those few that his reputation was tarnished.[36]

In the four seasons following the Symphony Six affair, the TSO gave only seven concerts in the United States, all in Michigan. An eighth was cancelled because of a snowstorm. So much for the TSO's developing American market. At Massey Hall, subscription sales dropped an unprecedented $7,000 in 1952–3, accounting for about 85 per cent of the year's deficit.[37] Thirty-one subscribers openly gave the Symphony Six as their reason for cancelling, but others may also have cancelled for the same reason.[38] The TSO board blamed the drop in subscriptions on Canadian television, which had just completed its first year in Toronto. According to President Watson, comparable American cities had had even larger drops in attendance when television had first been introduced, but, in fact, American television had been available in Toronto for several years.[39]

In July 1952, Ernest, putting his Toronto problems behind him, sailed with Elsie from Quebec City for a four-month European holiday. When the trip was first planned, he had tried to line up some conducting engagements in England but had not followed up leads, preferring, it appears, a complete break from musical assignments. The spring had sapped his energy and damaged his pride. He was frustrated at not having gotten his way with the conservatory appointment, and he was angry with Mazzoleni. As for the Symphony Six affair, he had no doubt that he had acted in the best interests of the orchestra, but it had taken its emotional toll, nonetheless. And he was still grieving his sister's death.

Europe was to be a no-work holiday, with one exception. MacMillan had agreed to write a series of articles on the Edinburgh Festival for *Saturday Night*. He had been to the 1949 festival and wanted a second look to convince himself that Canada should hold a similar festival at Niagara Falls, a tourist hub for Canadians and Americans. Before his departure, he had heard that Stratford, Ontario, would hold a world-class Shakespearean festival during the summer of 1953 with the leading British director Tyrone Guthrie as its head. Music – and Ernest MacMillan – must not be left behind. The *Saturday Night* pieces would help his game plan.

They debarked at Liverpool, where Ernest had fun playing the great organ in the city's new cathedral, 'which, though still incomplete after fifty years, demonstrates as does no other building

I know that our generation is still capable of producing genuinely great Gothic architecture.'[40] They visited other cathedrals that summer, and his spirits soared – life seemed more positive in the presence of these magnificent monuments. He was thrilled with floodlit Canterbury, especially the crypt 'with the light from outside filtering through the windows and throwing lights and shadows on the magnificent Norman arches and columns.' And how he relished the singing of the Canterbury boys. At Canterbury the MacMillans enjoyed a reunion with retired Hart House warden Burgon Bickersteth, an old Toronto friend and an ardent supporter of Ernest's early *Passion* performances. They also had a week at nearby Haslemere attending the Dolmetsch Festival of old music.

Two weeks in Scotland followed. Again, it was much like a homecoming for Ernest, so strong was his sense of belonging there. Even the pouring rain which greeted them on arrival 'seemed quite natural and in no wise dampened our spirits.' Alexander MacMillan, now in his eighties and as bouncy as ever, joined them for a trip in the Highlands, and, according to Ernest, 'there was not a town, village, mountain, or glen about which he could not give us historical information or quote apposite lines of poetry.'[41] The trip took them to the Isle of Skye and to the far northeast, from where many MacMillans had come.

Then came Edinburgh. Not surprisingly, his first *Saturday Night* article contrasted Canada's and Great Britain's summer musical activities. Canada had Montreal's opera festivals, Vancouver's Theatre Under the Stars, Toronto's Melody Fair, and summer drama groups in resort areas such as Muskoka, Ontario – but they were mainly light fare. By comparison, Britain had its Edinburgh and Dolmetsch festivals, the contemporary music festival at Cheltenham, and the Three Choirs Festival, which in 1952 was at Hereford. Ernest reminded his readers of John Murray Gibbon's music festivals in the late 1920s, which might have continued had it not been for the Great Depression. Now, he wrote, was the time for Canada to revive what Gibbon had started.[42]

In a later article he described a memorable Edinburgh performance of Mahler's *Das Lied von der Erde,* with the magnificent contralto Kathleen Ferrier, tenor Julius Patzak, and the Concert-

gebouw Orchestra conducted by Eduard van Beinum.[43] One wonders if Ernest appreciated the irony of hearing this great orchestra, which had *cancelled* its American tour under circumstances
not unlike those of the Symphony Six, and in his beloved Scotland of all places. If he did, he said nothing. And the irony would
have been even greater had it been known then that some years
later this same orchestra would go to the United States with
Steven Staryk, who still had no official clearance from U.S. Immigration, as its concert-master.[44]

Ernest heard, for the first time, Hindemith's opera *Mathis der
Mahler*; he had done the popular *Mathis* Symphony with the TSO
the previous April. Rather disappointed with the opera, he wrote
that 'it takes Wagner to build an operatic masterpiece largely on
an instrumental foundation.' Opera depends on its 'lyrical qualities, and the problem of the artist's relation to political events of
his time might be dealt with more satisfactorily in a spoken play.'
Nevertheless, he thought moments of *Mathis* were of 'overpower-
ing intensity.'

The opera is about the German Peasants' Revolt in 1524. There
is irony here too, if one looks for it. When Wilhelm Furtwängler
had scheduled its première at the Berlin State Opera in 1934,
Adolf Hitler had banned it because he found its theme of defi-
ance of authority objectionable. Furtwängler wrote Hitler a strong
letter protesting the ban and stating unequivocally that the State
Opera's music director must have the authority to select repertoire without interference from the state. Hitler retaliated by
removing Furtwängler from his post and forcing him into temporary retirement. Hindemith went into exile. Both Hindemith and
Furtwängler were men of conviction and did not hesitate to defy
government edicts, although some of Furtwängler's subsequent
actions in Nazi Germany have been questioned. The opera was
finally premièred in Zurich in 1938.

Another group that Ernest heard at Edinburgh was the National Youth Orchestra of Great Britain, conducted by Walter Susskind. It played 'with a verve and enthusiasm that I have never
seen surpassed and with a degree of finish that would have done
credit to many a professional orchestra ... I stress the importance
of this orchestra because I feel that we in Canada could offer

similar opportunities to our gifted young people through the creation of a summer camp on the lines of the camp at Inter-lochen, Michigan.'[45] Ernest couldn't foretell that Canada would, within a decade, not only have several fine summer music camps of its own but also its own National Youth Orchestra conducted by the same Walter Susskind, and that, in due course, Canada's youth orchestra would rival Britain's in excellence.

A visit to continental Europe was next on the itinerary. Ernest, who had love-hate feelings about Germany, said that Hitler's legacy of devastation in his own country 'must even shock those who look on it as retributive justice ... Symbolically the Cathedral of Cologne still raises its great spires towards the heavens, soaring above the ruins as does the dome of St. Paul's in London.' He was enthusiastic about Germany's cultural revival. It is, he wrote, 'as ever, finding its soul in music ... Berlin, emerging by mighty efforts from its ashes, divided between two apparently irreconcil-able worlds and a pivotal point in the Cold War, is carrying out a programme of festivities during the month of September that can scarcely be paralleled throughout the world.'[46] While in Ber-lin, he visited Ruhleben, the old racetrack he knew so well. An-other visit that moved him greatly was to Canadian sculptor Wal-ter Allward's Vimy Ridge War Memorial honouring those who had fallen in the Great War. Ernest said that it 'should convince the most sceptical that Canada can produce great art.'[47]

The MacMillans were back in Toronto in early November and found the TSO in good form, thanks to the brilliant if slightly off-centre Otto Klemperer, the first guest conductor of the season. Klemperer had made a great hit with Toronto's *cognoscenti*. Sir Bernard Heinze and Paul Scherman conducted in November, and Ernest mounted the TSO podium in early December. There was the controversial engagement in Detroit later that month fol-lowed by three Christmas Box concerts. And, just after Christmas, he conducted *Messiah* with the Salt Lake City Oratorio Society in the famed Tabernacle, where he made such a good impression that he was asked back the next year and again two years after that. The *Salt Lake Tribune* said that he directed 'like a shepherd bringing a precious flock home to the fold' and that, in the final chorus, he 'played his master hand as he built tender and sublime tones into great resounding chords. A time tested audience remained under the conductor's spell until the final "Amen."'[48]

January came and went, Ernest fitting in guest appearances with the Calgary Philharmonic, still a semi-professional orchestra but moving ahead, and the Vancouver Symphony. In March, the Italian conductor Victor de Sabata conducted the TSO in a special concert featuring the Brahms Fourth Symphony. It was his second appearance with the orchestra. Two years earlier local impresario Walter Homburger had sponsored him and the TSO in a concert in which the main work was Brahms's First. On both occasions he was dazzling. Four decades later, players and listeners still remember vividly those dynamic and gripping performances, at which, incidentally, de Sabata stole a leaf from Ernest's book by conducting *rehearsals*, as well as concerts, from memory.

Unquestionably, TSO audiences had an unprecedented year of fine guest conductors, starting with Leopold Stokowski in the spring of 1952, continuing with Klemperer, and then de Sabata. They were, it seemed, hearing their orchestra with new ears and perceiving previously unknown qualities in its playing. This musical revelation came hot on the heels of a doubtful if not downright unfavourable article about MacMillan in February's *Mayfair*, a general-interest magazine that had articles on the arts from time to time. It was his first really negative press in all his years in Toronto.[49] Provocatively titled 'The Elegant Enigma of Sir Ernest,' its theme was blazoned in large bold type: 'THROUGH THE TWENTY YEARS OF SIR ERNEST MACMILLAN'S REIGN AS CROWN PRINCE OF CANADIAN MUSIC, CONTROVERSY HAS WOVEN AN INSISTENT DISCORD INTO THE SYMPHONY OF HIS SUCCESS. HIS ADMIRERS ARE CERTAIN HE HAS PUT CANADA ON THE MUSICAL MAP; HIS CRITICS ARE JUST AS SURE HE'S A STUMBLING BLOCK ON THE PATH TO OUR CULTURAL MATURITY.'

The piece enumerated his assets and liabilities, virtues and vices, and peppered them all with clever journalistic tricks – some truths, some half-truths, some misinterpretations, and some inaccuracies. The author, Leslie F. Hannon, wrote: 'MacMillan is variously criticized as being stuffy; of failing to exercise progressive artistic leadership; of being basically antagonistic to contemporary music – particularly that of Canadian composers; of moulding the

TSO into an aggregation of court players existing to provide a musical and social setting for an inner circle of Toronto rich; of being overly concerned about his personal profit and renown; and of being fearful, because of awareness of his own limits, of direct competition on the podium.'

Hannon implied that MacMillan had frozen out his two local conducting rivals, Reginald Stewart and Heinz Unger, and that his knighthood served 'as a seal upon his stubborn conservatism.' He criticized MacMillan's role in the conservatory fracas but defended his role in the Symphony Six episode. He called Ernest's Canadian Music Council 'a walled-off preserve for the ruling clique, because it lacked a practical grasp of how to translate ideals into hard work.'

Like many such pieces, it said a great deal that was uncorroborated. And, of course, Ernest couldn't fight back. Even if he had, he could not have undone the damage. One never can. The wise reader knows that prominent people are at the mercy of ruthless journalists and that they must take what they read with a grain of salt. But not everyone is wise, and there are kernels of truth in even the most biased writing. Those close to Ernest said that he was offended and hurt by the article, but he took a deep breath and tried to forget it.

The University of Toronto hoped too that he would forget about the conservatory fracas and his dispute with the university. Later that spring, University College principal F.C.A. Jeanneret asked Ernest if he would help the college celebrate its centenary by writing a short work for organ to be played at the commemoration ceremony at Convocation Hall.[50] But Ernest still had the fracas on his mind – the *Mayfair* piece hadn't helped – and turned Jeanneret down.[51] Soon, however, he received a personal invitation from the university asking him, as one of University College's most distinguished graduates, to accept an honorary LLD in conjunction with the celebrations. Ernest, pleased, said yes to both the degree and the organ piece.[52] The degree was awarded on 16 October, and two days later he played his new four-minute-long *Cortège académique* at Convocation Hall. It is in three-part form and, unlike most academic processionals, rather frisky, as if Ernest wanted to lighten the mood for such events and stress their happy aspects. One can surmise, too, that the work even pokes fun at the university in the final section – in fact, the penultimate chord is jarringly dissonant. It was puckish Ernest at his best.

16. Successes and Failures

In a life which seemed to be increasingly prone to ups and downs, Ernest had an 'up' when the Mendelssohn Choir recorded his two favourite choral works, *Messiah* and the *St Matthew Passion*. The recordings were done by Beaver Records, a company which Fred MacKelcan had founded in 1950, primarily to record the Mendelssohn. MacKelcan was one of Canada's great patrons of the arts at the time and as good a personal friend as Ernest ever had. Beaver was the first commercial *Canadian* company to record serious music. It released *Messiah* in 1952 and the *Passion* in 1953 – each release was on three long-playing discs. A single disc of *Messiah* highlights was also produced.[1]

The choir's soloists at the time were especially fine: soprano Lois Marshall, whose Naumburg Award recital in December 1952 at New York's Town Hall earned her new and extraordinary acclaim and led to her being selected by Arturo Toscanini as a soloist for his performance and recording of Beethoven's *Missa Solemnis*; tenor Jon Vickers, who would, in a few years, be singing at Covent Garden, Bayreuth, and the Metropolitan Opera, and be one of the great *Heldentenors* of his generation; and baritone James Milligan, whose rich voice would bring him leading roles in oratorio and opera – including the Wanderer in *Siegfried* at Bayreuth. Ernest gave all three their first major performing opportunities.

Shortly after the *Passion* sessions, the CBC recorded the Mendelssohn Choir and the CBC Symphony Orchestra, with Ernest conducting several Handel excerpts – 'In the Lord Put I My

Trust,' movements from the *Water Music,* and 'The King Shall Rejoice' – for airing just prior to the Queen's address on Coronation Day, 2 June 1953. Beaver later obtained the master tapes from the CBC and released them on a disc titled *Tribute to Her Majesty Elizabeth II.*[2]

MacKelcan, delighted with the pressings, insisted on paying the typically reluctant Ernest $2,500 for the Bach *Passion* and Handel *Messiah,* and $500 for the Coronation music.[3] Sales were brisk. By the end of 1954, over 9,600 sets of *Messiah* (2,200 in Canada and 7,400 in the United States), over 6,000 copies of the highlights (in the United States only – it was not yet for sale in Canada), and over 2,000 sets of the *Passion* (1,500 in the United States and 500 in Canada) had been sold. *Messiah,* which was also distributed in Britain and Australia, remained a strong seller for several years.

The success of the *Messiah* recording suggests that MacMillan's 'time-worn' Victorian interpretation pleased many, both in Canada and abroad. The *Passion* recording was less successful, because of some spotty solo singing, a dry Evangelist, and MacMillan's notoriously slow tempi in Part One, as is particularly evident on disc. Put simply, in giving Bach's lyrical lines lots of space he tended to drag them. Yet the devotional feeling is there, the weight and intensity of the words and phrases meaningfully pushing the story on. In Part Two, MacMillan comes into his own. The drama builds and builds until one sits on the edge of one's seat, such is the tension. There one finds the essential MacMillan – the lifelong student of Bach, the lover of Jesus, the Presbyterian, the son of Alexander MacMillan – deeply involved in the pathos of the tale.

Beaver made one other recording in the spring of 1953 – MacMillan conducting the TSO in Tchaikovsky's Fifth Symphony. It was poorly produced and there was some quite unacceptable out-of-tune playing in the winds. The dirge-like character of the introduction is intense, but the Allegro which follows is slow and heavy, because of Ernest's wayward approach to tempo changes. Thus the recapitulation and coda lose their interest and leave the listener behind. The second movement is not overly slow, as it had been when Ernest did it with the NBC Symphony, but it is too dark and gloomy, more Dostoevskian than Chekhovian. The third movement sparkles, and the string playing is bright, clean, and warm. But the final movement is too fast – perhaps the third movement is too – and the general feeling is one of rushing headlong to the finish. Hardly Ernest's finest effort, it in no way compares with his excellent *Planets*, recorded ten years earlier. It is troubling that he was so matter-of-fact in recording such a brilliant work. One wonders why and how he let the pressing go through.

With an ever-growing market for long-playing records, a second Canadian company, Hallmark Recordings, began operations in 1953, with Keith MacMillan as one of its heads. As far back as 1949, Keith had been recording TSO concerts for his own and his father's use, and this served as a training ground for his work with Hallmark and as a music producer at the CBC, which he joined in 1952 after giving up doctoral studies in biology. Hallmark made several recordings of Ernest MacMillan and Lois Marshall, including Elwell's *Pastorale*, Bach's Cantata No. 51 ('Jauchzet Gott'), and Mozart's *Exsultate Jubilate*. Keith did them with filial care and the discs have stood the test of time. Alfred Frankenstein, a leading San Francisco-based critic, wrote in *High Fidelity* that Marshall's performance in the Elwell was 'superb' as was 'the work of the conductor, the orchestra, and the recording engineers.'[4] A few months later in the same journal C.G. Burke praised 'Jauchzet Gott' but said that the court paganism of Mozart's motet 'is chastened by the conductor's beat into primness, nothing pagan about it.'[5] Whatever, Beaver and Hallmark recordings helped build the reputations of MacMillan, the soloists, and the choir. If Toronto was no longer the choral capital of North America, as it had been thirty years earlier, its undertakings still stood for quality in the musical world.

The Mendelssohn's successes in the early 1950s sparked plans for a New York appearance. Ernest, particularly, was eager to show off the *Passion* – his *tour de force*, his homage to Bach. And so, on 27 April 1954 in Carnegie Hall, the choir, assisted by members of the TSO, sang *Messiah* and, on the next night, it did the *Passion*. The choir had not been in New York since 1924, long before MacMillan's involvement, and on that earlier occasion, noted critics Henry T. Finck, Olin Downes, and Deems Taylor had all praised its Beethoven Ninth, Finck going so far as to say that he had not heard it done as well since the days of Anton Seidl before the turn of the century.[6]

The 1954 press response to the *Messiah* soloists – Marshall, alto Margaret Stilwell, Vickers, Milligan – was especially good. However, the critics had mixed views about the choir and MacMillan. Olin Downes of the *Times*, still reviewing concerts, had little good to say of *Messiah*, preferring

the sum of the soloists' efforts to those of the chorus – admirably drilled, sure in attack and treatment of minor parts, but rarely more than routine in its very polite and discreetly shaded transmission of Handel's flaming music. The most expressive passages were those of the slower tempi and the darker or quieter moods, such as the fine delivery of the opening lines of 'Surely He hath born our griefs.' In general there was a pedestrian spirit and little of dramatic variety or power in evidence. It was not thus with the inspired and impetuous Handel, when, in his passion of creation he penned this rapturous, poignant, triumphant masterpiece.[7]

The faults Downes ascribed to Ernest were of course nothing new, but words like 'pedestrian spirit' rankled. Fortunately there were good reviews too. Louis Biancolli, of the *New York World Telegram and Sun*, thought it was the best *Messiah* he had heard in years, with 'fine singing ... and playing ... and a wondrous sense of the beauty and poetry of Handel's music from everyone.'[8]

There were, on the other hand, *no* good reviews of the *Passion*. The New York critics neither liked nor understood MacMillan's performance and his devotional approach. They had been conditioned to more 'exciting' *Passions* with clearer contrasts in mood, tempi, and dynamics. MacMillan's reading neither engaged nor transported them. New York valued the sensational – in the best sense – more than the overly temperate and controlled.

Ross Parmenter, another *Times* critic, found the *Passion* too slow: '[It] did not seem to lift quite to the realms that were implicit in Sir Ernest's conception ... The work ... clearly had been expounded rather than intensely performed.'[9] A second critic, Robert L. Bagar, said that the score came through with 'spruce cleanness but considerably restrained. Our Canadian cousins, apparently, match their English brethren in the department of reserve.'[10] Still another, Miles Kastendieck, wrote that 'the responsiveness of the choir to MacMillan's direction suggested that it was smouldering with dynamic possibilities. That he did not avail himself of these made the difference between a satisfactory and an inspired performance.'[11] A fourth (unnamed) critic thought it 'more a pious ritual than a live performance' and felt that the choir was in a rut from doing the piece annually for so long; it needed to restudy it, otherwise 'all features musical, the bad as well as the good, find themselves tyrannically perpetuated from season to season ... It lacked freshness ... It was an amiable, good-natured performance, more concerned with propriety than elevation of spirit, more wedded to choral ease than to dramatic vigour. Thus heard, the "Matthew Passion" tends to seem somewhat fossilized, somewhat benumbed and rigid.'[12]

The reviews were remarkably similar, which made their impact even greater. Toronto critics had become so accustomed to MacMillan's readings that they listened with only half an ear and rarely spoke negatively of them. Yes, his *Messiahs* and his *Passions* had been great achievements, but they needed these discriminating appraisals, however harsh, from the undeniably important and knowledgeable New York press, which had such fundamentally different views about the work's interpretation. It was a bitter pill for Ernest to swallow.

And so, realizing that both he and the choir needed a change, MacMillan did the *St John Passion* instead of the *St Matthew* the following Easter in Toronto. He studied the *St Matthew* anew and then did it again in 1956 and 1957. He may have freshened his outlook, but his approach didn't change. The same faults, if that is what they were, were still there. But the experience of those later performances was, as always, extraordinary for everyone. Robertson Davies's well-chosen words about MacMillan's 1953 performance remain valid: 'It is fully as important that Canada has a musician capable of such an interpretation as it would be if we had an actor capable of a very great production and personal interpretation of *King Lear*; it is a circumstance for which we may be nationally grateful, and in which we may take national pride.'[13] If Ernest MacMillan was not the conductor he could have been, he came closest to it when he brought Bach's masterpiece to reverent Toronto audiences.

The 1953–4 TSO season was Ernest's twenty-third as TSO conductor. He had not had an easy time in the early years, when he had had to learn his craft and win the confidence of his players. He had done both, and, in the process, had transformed the orchestra from a casual group of players into a first-class ensemble. During the Great Depression the board had paid him and his players poorly. The war brought more personnel and money problems, but he had coped with them successfully. Prosperity followed – larger audiences, longer seasons, more concerts, more-frequent CBC broadcasts, and improved salaries and artistic quality. By around 1950 the TSO was ranked among the top twelve orchestras on the continent even though Toronto contributed far less money towards its well-being than comparable cities in the United States. And the man in great measure responsible for this was Ernest MacMillan.

Then came the university fracas, the Symphony Six, the poor press of the Mendelssohn's New York concerts, and the *Mayfair* article, all of which made him more vulnerable. His public wondered. A generation of Torontonians brought up on Ernest Mac-Millan's TSO began to realize that few things in life are forever and that a change in TSO conductors was possible, even desirable. The *Globe and Mail*'s youthful music critic John Kraglund inadvertently underscored this realization. Unlike most Canadian critics, who were primarily interested in educating their public by bringing music to life in their reviews, Kraglund demanded high standards of performance in the first instance. He unfailingly detected flaws in the TSO's intonation, tone quality, and ensemble playing, and in Ernest's shortcomings in maintaining tempi and rhythm. On the other hand, Kraglund admired Ernest's taste, general control, and choice of repertoire. His reviews of the TSO were candid, sometimes patronizing, and on occasion cruel. On balance, they were more favourable than not, but some were devastating and those that were were usually aimed at the conductor.

Consider these biting excerpts from Kraglund's review of the first subscription concert of the 1954–5 season. 'There was little about the audience to mark a gala opening, and, much worse, the performance disappointed most of our fond hopes.' About the *Roman Carnival* Overture of Berlioz, he wrote, 'Sir Ernest's valiant efforts gave the overture a vagueness quite foreign to Berlioz, and *fortissimo* passages were just plain noisy,' and then, about the Tchaikovsky Sixth Symphony, 'The composer's romantic melodies held our interest during the first part of the opening movement. Then came the dramatic development and once again we were swamped by the volume of sound.' About the Scherzo he said: 'It got off to a quite delightful beginning. Then came more *fortissimo* passages that eventually concealed the emphatic marching rhythm, and a finale that seemed inordinately depressing.'[14]

We'll never know how much Kraglund's reviews bothered Ernest, but they probably contributed to his growing perception that the TSO neither wanted nor needed him any more. And, as this sunk in, came the realization that *he* no longer needed the orchestra either. It had been both his strength and his weakness to take on too many jobs, but now these jobs provided him with attractive alternatives to an increasingly unpleasant situation. Ernest also sensed – and this might have been closer to the bone than bad reviews – that some of the players, especially the younger ones, were critical of his stick technique, his rehearsing style, and his dragging tempi, and believed that he was holding back the orchestra from recordings, summer seasons, international tours, and the like. There was also a growing number of mature music listeners who, if they didn't object to Ernest's excellent programs, did object to his heavy-handed and soporific approach to some of the brightest music in the repertoire. John Kraglund in good part expressed their feelings. In a word, Toronto was tiring of Sir Ernest MacMillan.

And so on 12 January 1955 Ernest wrote his letter of resignation to TSO president Trevor Moore.[15] (Moore was the brother of the great English accompanist Gerald Moore.) His letter, published in the March issue of the *TSO News*, showed a fine sense of time and place. It began: 'On two or three occasions ... I have mentioned to you that I felt the time was approaching when it would be in the interests of both the orchestra and myself that I should relinquish my post as Conductor. Much as I enjoy the work, I feel in it an increasing sense of strain, especially when combined with the many other activities in which I am involved.' He went on to say that, if a satisfactory successor could be found, he wished to retire at the end of the 1955-6 season to round off twenty-five years as head of the TSO. Vladimir Golschmann of the St Louis Symphony would retire the same year, also after twenty-five years. His length of service would also match Serge Koussevitsky's, who had conducted the Boston Symphony from 1924 to 1949, and surpass Leopold Stokowski's, who was with the Philadelphia Orchestra for twenty-four years (1912-36). The North American record would still rest with Frederick Stock, who was the Chicago Symphony's conductor for nearly thirty-eight years (1905-42). Ernest suggested that the TSO engage five or six guest conductors for his last season and, because he would do less conducting, proposed that his salary be reduced. 'I am very well aware of the financial difficulties that confront you – difficulties only too familiar to the governing bodies of orchestras.'

With style and elegance he thanked Moore, past-president Watson, the board, the women's committee, Paul Scherman ('who has been a tower of strength'), and Jack Elton ('an admirable manager and such a good friend'). And then he added, 'Of the work of our Concertmaster Mr. Goodman and of all of my colleagues in the orchestra I cannot speak too highly. The spirit of friendly cooperation which has prevailed is not by any means always found in similar organizations ... It has been a privilege accorded to few musicians to work under such happy conditions and I am most grateful to all who have contributed to the success of our efforts. Long may the Toronto Symphony flourish.'

The TSO board met the next day and, perhaps hastily, voted that his 1955-6 salary be $14,000, only slightly less than originally budgeted, and that his pension be an extraordinarily generous $9,000 per annum.[16] The board met again on 26 January and nominated four of its members to a conductor's selection committee and three others to serve as advisers. It never dawned on the board to add the concert-master and perhaps a player or two to the committee, but, in 1955, North American musicians did not take part in such matters. In less than three months Elton brought the selection committee's recommendation to the board for approval, and, forthwith, forty-two-year-old Walter Susskind, former conductor of the Scottish National Orchestra and currently with the Victoria Symphony in Melbourne, was offered a three-year contract.[17] Ernest was relieved. The difficult decision was behind him, his resignation had been handled well by the board, and an eminently suitable successor had been appointed promptly.

A month after his resignation, the League of Composers sponsored another concert of Canadian music and, this time, had MacMillan conduct. The *Serenade Concertante* of Murray Adaskin, François Morel's *Esquisse*, Robert Fleming's concert version of his ballet *Shadow on the Prairie*, and Godfrey Ridout's *Cantiones Mysticae* all came off well. They were mainstream works to which Ernest could relate. Less successful were pieces by Andrew Twa, Udo Kasemets, and the Italian composer Adone Zecchi – the performance of his *Two Inventions* was part of an exchange agreement worked out between the league and the Italian section of the International Society for Contemporary Music. John Kraglund's review was temperate, although he hoped – and rightly so – that the time would soon come 'when Canadian compositions can be doled out more intelligently, one at a time, on regular concert programs.'

It was a different story when Yehudi Menuhin played the Mendelssohn Concerto on the final pair of subscription concerts that season. He was rewarded with Kraglund's blistering words: 'This performance proved to be one of the most disappointing we have ever heard, at least on the professional level.' He described it as 'carelessly matter of fact, phrases were blurred; the tone thin, brittle and scratchy; and pitch not always accurate.' (Although Menuhin did receive an ovation when he finished the concerto he did indeed play it poorly.) Kraglund described Ernest's accompaniment as 'restrained' and 'quite commendable' and his reading of Brahms's Fourth Symphony as 'excellent ... although a lack of distinction made it seem excessively long.'[18] Is it any wonder that Ernest could hardly wait to leave the TSO?

Once the concert season was over and he was less busy, Ernest felt as if a new life had already begun, even though he still had twelve months more with the TSO. He and Elsie planned to drive to Chester, Nova Scotia, to visit Winthrop Bell and his family. (Bell was an old Ruhleben friend with whom Ernest had kept in touch. Bell often wrote Ernest about his CBC broadcasts, which he never missed.) But before setting out on the long drive – Ernest loved long drives – there was son Ross's wedding to attend. Ross, now a chemical engineer, was marrying concert pianist Gwen Beamish at Toronto's St Paul's Anglican Church on 2 July, and Ernest, of course, was to be at the organ. Then it was on to visit the Bells. Ernest and Elsie had their own small cottage at nearby Mahone Bay and liked it so much that they planned to return the next summer. It was their first extended stay in maritime Canada.

Now for the final TSO season! Ernest would have a lighter load, for, even though his successor had been chosen, the TSO had followed through on his suggestion to have several guest conductors. Thus, with such luminaries as Sir Thomas Beecham, Pierre Monteux, Heinz Unger, and, of course, Walter Susskind helping to share the load, he had more time for other things. Early in October, he met with a group at Niagara Falls to discuss ways and means of implementing a festival there, but no one took it in hand. That same month he played a prominent role as conductor and commentator on a CBC broadcast honouring the seventy-fifth birthday of his old friend Healey Willan, and in December he conducted three Christmas Box concerts. The admiring John Kraglund wrote that they might be Ernest's last, but 'we refuse to believe it any more than we believe that Santa Claus will fail to show up at the end of the concert. Besides, where else can the TSO find a conductor with the spirit of eternal boyhood and a talent for straight-face comedy?'[19] Immediately after that he flew to Salt Lake City to conduct his third and last *Messiah* there, and, in March, he did *Elijah* with the Winnipeg Philharmonic Choir. It was April all too soon and his final pair of subscription concerts as conductor of the TSO.

Events and gifts were planned to thank and honour him, and the local newspapers gave him much coverage. The *Telegram* ran a feature story with the headline 'Sir Ernest the Musician Retires

– 25 Year Reign As "Little Titan" of the Toronto Symphony.'[20] Ernest might well have been peeved to be called little – since he was somewhat taller than the five feet seven the article said he was, and he had never before been called a 'titan!' But, as if to make up for these minor impudences, several attractive photographs from his childhood, youth, and Ruhleben accompanied the article. It also quoted Ernest on one of his favourite subjects: Canada's need for cultural independence. 'Where would broadcasting be without the CBC? We have such a vast quantity of New York and Hollywood material, so much American influence, that we soon won't have any national life of our own.'

The *Toronto Star* also interviewed him, and he was uncommonly frank as one often is when leaving a position.[21] When the *Star* reporter, George Bryant, challenged him about his own conservatism, he replied somewhat defensively, 'My conscience is clear. I've given an awful lot of first performances here. I've always believed you can't live in the past, a musician must chew on something new to keep up to scratch. But a conductor must consider his audience and in Toronto the audience is conservative … Of course,' he went on somewhat sadly, 'there is a smaller group, a minority, interested in the new, and I've been hit in the crossfire.'

Yes, he couldn't please everyone. In 1936, his first performance of Sibelius's Fourth Symphony, perhaps the composer's most radical, was not well received. He had expected the audience to be more tolerant of the new and experimental. Even when he did it again in 1948, most listeners continued to wonder what it was all about.[22] If this was the reaction to Sibelius, one wonders what audiences would have thought of Schoenberg, Messiaen, or Ives. Conservative or not, Ernest MacMillan *had* brought to Toronto the music of the post-romantics and the impressionists, of the early Stravinsky, of the neoclassic Canadians, and of other early- and mid-twentieth-century composers from other countries. He had taken his audiences no further than the limits of his own taste, for better or for worse.

Bryant alluded to Ernest's work prospects in the future. 'There may be another position coming up, but he can't say anything yet. He will not however be sitting on his hands.' To which Ernest added, 'After an active life like mine, that would be an awfully uncomfortable position.' (A year before, a *Globe and Mail* editorial had speculated 'that more than one important appointment within Canada merely waits his acceptance.')[23]

The *Globe and Mail* wrote generously about his wide influence. 'During his tenure with the Toronto Symphony, Canadian culture has begun to come of age. We are a much less self-conscious people culturally than we were when he began ... He has played an important part in that process of maturity.'[24] It applauded his efforts to win recognition for promising young Canadian musicians and ended with: 'Sir Ernest's vigour seems undimmed. His departure from the podium at Massey Hall will not mean, we hope, his withdrawal from the other activities in which he is occupied. There is still a need for the wisdom of his experience and the occupation of his many talents.'

The Mendelssohn Choir assisted MacMillan in his final TSO concert. The program opened with the *Te Deum* he had composed for the conservatory's fiftieth anniversary concert in 1936. Next came *Francesca da Rimini* by Tchaikovsky, and then the *Schicksalslied* ('Song of Destiny') by Brahms. Was there some sort of personal statement behind these choices? Both are based on turbulent themes. The Tchaikovsky, inspired by Dante's *Inferno*, deals with the horrors Francesca endures in Hell as the result of an illicit love affair, while the Brahms contrasts the aloof Olympian gods with the restless and unhappy destiny of the human race. But the Beethoven Ninth Symphony, after intermission, was the high point. His orchestra and choir played and sang their hearts out for him. The fine quartet of soloists – Mary Simmons, Maureen Forrester, Vickers, and Milligan – were the icing on the cake. As the great work ended the audience rose to its feet as one and cheered.

The tributes included a 'Valedictory' in the printed program thanking him for his achievements with the TSO, and a speech to the audience at intermission by Trevor Moore. A portrait or, more precisely, a surrogate of a portrait of Ernest by Canadian artist Cleeve Horne was also presented – the work had not yet been completed. Eventually it would hang in the lobby of Massey Hall. That was not all. A wire with Walter Susskind's best

wishes arrived just as Ernest was about to go onstage for the
Te Deum.

There was also a significant tribute from Toronto's 'Mayor of
All the People' Nathan Phillips.[25] After years of benefiting from
the prestige the orchestra brought and giving little in return, the
city's attitude was finally changing. Phillips spoke with warmth
about 'a great Torontonian who has just completed a vital chapter in his career and an important chapter in the cultural history
of the community. Many of you have come to think of Sir Ernest
as a personal friend ... He made Toronto a better place in which
to live.'

Yes, he had indeed met Toronto's musical needs and deserved
its tributes. He was its very own 'town musician,' a twentieth-
century Johann Sebastian Bach to whom all turned for music.
The city and its people respected Sir Ernest, and the feeling was
mutual. He appreciated and even enjoyed the temperament and
life-style of the stiff, starchy city, which now numbered 1,350,000
inhabitants. If he had left Toronto years before he might have
achieved more with his great talent, been a better conductor, and
perhaps even been more at peace with himself. Instead he had
taken a different path. Toronto and Canada were the beneficiar-
ies. The TSO had several better conductors in the future, but
never one who captured the hearts and minds of the city as Ernest MacMillan had. It was a milestone, the end of an era for him
and for Toronto.

To be sure, this TSO departure was not in any way like his troubled exit from the university four years before. Now, he was simply relieved to be leaving a job that he no longer wanted and
which no longer wanted him. A summer of honours followed.
The University of Rochester's Eastman School of Music awarded
him an honorary Doctor of Music on 10 June (Rochester had
given Mazzoleni a doctorate a decade earlier) and New Brunswick's Mount Allison University in Sackville awarded him an
honorary Doctor of Laws on 11 August. They were, respectively,
his sixth and seventh honorary degrees. Predictably, his departure
from the TSO had sparked them. More were to come – from the
University of Ottawa in 1959 and the University of Sherbrooke in

1962. The carefully crafted Rochester citation showed much insight when it said, 'In the classical English mode of discretion
and control, he combines with unique distinction the qualities of
musical learning, creation and performance which the University
of Rochester is proud to honor in keeping with the ideal that
long has guided its own musical tradition.'[26]

The New Brunswick honorary degree ceremony was aptly scheduled for the third and final day of the 1956 Mount Allison Summer Institute on 'The Arts in Canada.' Ernest, in addition to
giving the convocation address and serving on one of the conference panels, covered its proceedings for the *Globe and Mail.* The
Toronto newspaper was busy addressing Canadian culture and
was especially critical of the CBC for doing too many American
television shows.

Walter Herbert, head of the Canada Foundation, was the conference theme lecturer. He began the proceedings by urging
Canadians to 'feel more acutely' about the arts, and he chastised
the federal government for its 'indifference' towards the arts.[27]
His remarks set the tone for the lively, informative, and, at times,
heated discussions which followed. Governments, television, the
CBC, the Canadian people, and the national inferiority complex
were, in turn, blamed for the slow progress of the arts in Canada.

The theme of Ernest's forum was 'What Can Everyman Do
about the Arts in Canada?' and he chose to speak about the
increasing numbers of music graduates teaching in the schools
and how important their work was.[28] Clearly, he had overcome his
doubts about the value of Toronto's school music program. His
rather bland convocation speech at the end of the conference
underscored the need for amateurs to *make* music, and not to
leave it solely to professionals. Personal involvement – playing,
singing – best develops musical ears, he said. Ernest also reproached Canadians for not honouring their own artists until
they proved themselves abroad. He singled out Glenn Gould and
Jon Vickers to make his point.

The Mount Allison conference was one of the first to address
the arts in Canada. It provided a platform for the movers and
shakers in the arts world to awaken the Canadian people culturally. Canada's population had grown by almost a third since the

beginning of the Second World War, and in 1956 nearly a third of the population was under fourteen years of age. Immigration was up, cities were growing, the quality of life was improving. Canada had become a country of eager, energetic, and optimistic young people and, although it was still essentially conservative in outlook, it was ready for change.

Following the conference, Ernest and Elsie set off for a two-and-a-half-month sojourn in Europe. When they returned to Toronto in the early winter, it hit Ernest, perhaps for the first time, that he was no longer the principal player in its musical world, that his successor, Walter Susskind, now held centre stage. He contemplated retreating to his handsome Rosedale house, to enjoy his grandchildren, compose, write, relax. But he was only sixty-three, still in good health, and thriving as the senior musical statesman of Canada. What began to bother him, however, was that, although there were certainly some good conducting years left in him, where were the invitations? Was their absence *his* fault?

Since the end of the war MacMillan's American conducting career had been, more or less, on hold. After Brazil, Arthur Judson barely gave him a nod – exchange dates only in Washington, Indianapolis, and Buffalo. In 1954 he had conducted in San Antonio, where one newspaper said innocuously that he led the symphony 'calmly – a likeable, unpretentious master of music whose merits became gradually apparent as he unfolded his program.'[29] Another described him as 'the grey haired maestro who conducts with plump dignity' and who speaks with a 'deeply British accent.'[30] Was this the best he could do?

Inevitably one asks: why didn't he contract another New York manager more eager to find work for the veteran conductor of the TSO? Was it because of loyalty to Judson? Or because he refused to push himself? Or because it went against the proud MacMillan grain to actually look for work?

Even more puzzling: why didn't he pursue a European career? Before the war, he had made a good impression with the BBC and with Sir Adrian Boult. During the war, transportation difficulties ruled out European engagements but, as soon as the war was over, a BBC memo discussing potential conductors mentioned MacMillan's 'senior position in Canada' and his recent success in Australia, and put him 'high on the list.'[31] And then, for almost a decade, Ernest played a cat and mouse game with the BBC. He would tell the BBC that he was available for concerts, and then that he wasn't, and then that he was, until it was too late to fit him into its schedule. (Most concert dates are best booked at least a year to eighteen months in advance; Ernest seemed to work six months or less in advance.) Ernest Bushnell, a CBC executive, told the BBC in December 1946 that Ernest might be available for English concerts in the summer of 1947, depending on whether he toured South Africa. Nothing came of the tour; Ernest simply stayed home. A tour of South America was also in the wind and also came to nothing. In mid-1947 Ernest engaged Harold Holt, one of England's leading concert managers, to book him for the summer of 1948. But Ernest stalled on citing available dates and Holt gave up.

He didn't stop trying. After entertaining BBC executive K.A. Wright in Toronto in 1950, he wrote to him about conducting at the 1951 Festival of Britain, which, among other things, would include the opening of Royal Festival Hall on the South Bank. But, again, he was too late. Then Jack Elton tried to fix some BBC concerts for Ernest for February–March 1952 when the TSO was having guest conductors, and mentioned a Scandinavian tour around which other dates could be set. The BBC replied with an offer of engagements with its Northern (Manchester) and Scottish BBC symphonies, the London BBC Symphony already being booked. Once again, nothing happened. Instead, Ernest remained in Toronto that winter to fight the conservatory battle. He didn't even try for summer concerts, although he knew he would be in Europe and had told the BBC he would be available. Instead, he took a four-month European holiday. (One could argue that conducting would have been more therapeutic than wandering around the continent at that bad time.) It was the same pattern the next summer. Holt arranged a booking with the RIAS radio orchestra of West Berlin and asked the BBC to fit in concerts for him *en route.* Ernest eventually backed out. He did two Montreal concerts that summer and nothing else.

Clearly, if MacMillan had really wanted to conduct in Europe he could easily have done so, but, whenever concerts seemed imminent he found ways *not* to do them. He never conducted in Germany, in Scandinavia, in South Africa, or – after the 1946 Rio visit – in South America. Granted, fees in postwar Europe and on other continents were not as good as those in North America, but, with Ernest, fees were never a major issue. Perhaps he was afraid of resentful players, unpleasant managers, and bad reviews. Or was it something more subtle and elusive?

17. Good Statesmanship

With the publication of the Massey Report in 1951, the Canadian Music Council (CMCl) could finally see the light at the end of the tunnel – a national organization that would fund the arts. But when? No one knew. In the meantime, the council did the best it could with its limited resources. It sent selected Canadian scores to the 1952 Helsinki Olympiad, and the CMCl's John Cozens began a library of sorts with 700 Canadian pieces. The council provided the Department of External Affairs with information about Canadian music to send to its embassies around the world, but when MacMillan asked Lester Pearson for money to send CMCl delegates to UNESCO meetings, Pearson said there wasn't any.[1] Delegates went at their own expense or, if fortunate enough to work for an obliging institution, at the institution's expense.

Arnold Walter, one of the more diligent conference-goers, was elected the first president of the International Society for Music Education at its inaugural meeting in Brussels in 1953. Walter's growing international prestige and MacMillan's CAPAC-sponsored appearances at CISAC (the parent international performing rights organization) generated in other countries increasing curiosity about Canadian musical life. The next year, the ever-patient John Cozens and the Department of External Affairs began working towards placing selected Canadian orchestral scores in Canadian embassies for study and, it was hoped, performance. After two years and much correspondence, External Affairs reproduced only five Canadian works for the purpose.

Meanwhile, CMCl membership grew and diversified to include composers, conductors, heads of conservatories and university faculties, and representatives of Jeunesses Musicales du Canada, of the CBC, and of associations for teachers, composers, organists, publishers, performing rights groups, and festivals. Under MacMillan's guidance it prepared a brief for the Ilsley Royal Commission on Patents, Copyright, Trademarks and Industrial Design in 1954.[2] According to John Mills, CAPAC's general manager for many years, some people who appeared before the commission were eager to strip composers of copyright protection, and it was MacMillan and his CAPAC colleagues who fought a most convincing and successful battle to prevent this.[3] Following CAPAC's lead, the CMCl, with MacMillan wearing his other hat, proposed to the same commission that composers be given more control over how their works were performed, recorded, and marketed, but this fell on deaf ears. Since copyright laws governing composers' royalties from record sales were based on the 78-rpm recording as the unit, the CMCl also proposed new rules for long-playing records which would take into account the length of the work recorded.

The CMCl next directed its energies towards three specific projects: a lending library for Canadian music, a book on the state of Canadian music, and a Canadian musical quarterly. Of the three, the book was the most immediately feasible, since MacMillan had managed to get the University of Toronto Press to agree to publish it. The council elected him editor and designated Arnold Walter to help him select subjects and contributors – Ernest often said that Walter never ceased having good ideas. All went smoothly from start to finish, thanks to Ernest's diligence and care. He hounded contributors to meet their deadlines and, to the delight of the publisher, carefully polished their prose.

Music in Canada was published in April 1955.[4] The rather drab looking volume of about 100,000 words begins with a short foreword by Governor General Vincent Massey, followed by a substantial introduction by MacMillan. He set the stage by noting that Canada had passed the 'pioneer stage' of satisfying her physical needs and that it was now time to turn 'to those things of the spirit that have so greatly enriched the life of older nations.'

Then he expressed the need for a Canadian arts council and warned that if Canada was not more generous in funding music its musicians and musical groups would not flourish. 'Music, the most social of the arts,' he declared, 'possesses supremely that unifying power which, given due support, will play a unique part in fostering and preserving the spirit of devotion that welds together a great nation.'

The book's eighteen chapters, all written by leaders in the field, deal with a wide range of topics about Canadian music, covering the fields of history, composition, performance, and education. Ernest did the chapter on choral music, in which, incidentally, he said almost nothing about himself, paying tribute, rather, to the amateur music maker whose activities foster 'a healthy communal life' and produce intelligent audiences. He wrote that people best understand and appreciate music if they sing and play it themselves, but, he observed, the distractions and social obligations of modern life were making inroads into choir singing.

William Arthur Deacon, a leading book reviewer, called *Music in Canada* a key book. 'It brings the accomplishments and problems of this major art into clear focus. Its importance far exceeds that of any other book published this year.'[5] Other readers and reviewers were, like Deacon, impressed that the contributors had amassed so much information about Canadian music. William Krehm of the CBC, however, was one of the few to say that, despite the book's good intentions, it could have done a lot more. He observed that its stress was 'on inventory rather than evaluation,' that it lacked personal points of view, and that, by avoiding them, all that was left was a 'dreary array of facts, names and figures that occasionally read like a mail order catalogue.'[6] He observed astutely that, because many chapters were written by professional musicians, a 'certain etiquette' had been imposed

that makes formal politeness triumph over frankness of judgement. Too often instead of assessment what predominates is a stiff and courtly bowing from the waist ... There is endless mention of notable, distinguished, performers and performing groups, and rarely a clue as to how good or bad they are or may have been and just what is the manner of their excellence. And still that sort of thing is of decisive importance to the chronicles of music as to its contemporary practice.

Music in Canada was indeed flawed. It raised few questions and provided still fewer answers. Yet for more than two decades it was a useful reference for scholars and laymen alike. And Ernest Mac-Millan had done the lion's share of the work. By 1960, 1,600 copies had been sold.

When MacMillan had written his resignation letter to the TSO in 1955, the CMCl was already beginning to make plans for a badly needed musical quarterly. A serendipitous encounter in New Brunswick that summer gave these plans impetus. Ernest and Elsie were passing through Sackville *en route* to Mahone Bay and, experienced travellers that they were, were seeking ice cubes for their evening drinks (alcoholic beverages were not available in hotels and restaurants). They stopped to ask a young man, who was out walking with his son, for directions. The young man was Geoffrey Payzant, an organist and aesthetician who taught English, philosophy, and music at Mount Allison University. He recognized the MacMillans and promptly introduced himself and directed them to a local service station for the ice.[7]

Payzant, who had already read *Music in Canada* and made note of Ernest's plans for a quarterly, used the encounter to initiate an exchange of letters with him. Getting right to the point, he offered his services as editor. They met again, and Ernest, having assured himself of Payzant's suitability, invited him to Toronto to meet Arnold Walter, who would chair the editorial board, John Cozens, who would supervise the business details, and other members of the board. The meeting went well, and Payzant got the job. Walter and Payzant kept in close touch by mail, and the first issue of the *Canadian Music Journal* (*CMJ*) came off the press a year later – in October 1956, the fifth anniversary of the publication of the Massey Report. The following year fate again played a role when Payzant was offered a teaching position at the University of Toronto, and all *CMJ* work was subsequently done in Toronto.

Payzant's scholarship, editorial skills, and practical approach to journal business pleased both MacMillan and Walter. Each issue included several substantial articles, accounts of musical events, and reviews of recordings, music, and books. The first began with a short piece by MacMillan about the CMCl, followed by four long articles – 'Johnson's Two Musical Friends – Burney and Hawkins' by Percy Scholes, 'The Dodecacophonist's Dilemma' by Glenn Gould, 'Music and the University' by Harry Adaskin, and the first half of a two-part article, 'A Century of Musical Periodicals in Canada,' by Helmut Kallmann. There were also reports on musical events at Stratford, Montreal, Banff, the University of British Columbia, Otter Lake, and Mount Allison.

There was a mixed response to the first issue. To some CMCl board members it was too heavy, to others too light.[8] Some wanted more articles about the Canadian musical scene, a daunting task for Payzant and the editorial board, since they were already having difficulty finding good writers on music. Others debated, expertly and not so expertly, about the journal's cover design, paper, and typography. One journalist said it was too limited in its appeal; another dismissed it as having no value for intelligent readers. Thanks to substantial advertising and the purchase of subscriptions by CAPAC and BMI Canada Limited (the two Canadian performing rights organizations) for their members, the journal's finances were sound for the time being.

The Massey report's proposal for a national arts council was still on the drawing-board as late as the spring of 1956, even though informed arts aficionados were unfailingly confident that its formation was imminent. The *Globe and Mail* had hinted in 1955 that Ernest MacMillan had a new job waiting for him after leaving the TSO. A year later, it asked him point blank if he would like to be head of the Canada Council (CC), as the proposed body was now being called. Almost coyly, Ernest replied that he wondered whether he was 'fitted' for the job, 'even if they offered it to me, which is by no means certain.'[9] He felt his command of French inadequate, and then with patently false modesty said, 'it may be that I am too engrossed in my own field of music to see the arts in perspective.' He predicted that giving out money would be the council's most difficult job and warned that it must not 'spread the butter too thin.' Moving on, he bemoaned the fact that a German orchestra had had the money to tour Japan the year before, but Canada, a rich country, couldn't or wouldn't underwrite such trips.

At long last, in the summer of 1956, Prime Minister Louis St Laurent proposed using the $100 million in succession duties from the estates of two recently deceased and wealthy Canadians, Isaak Walton Killam and Sir James H. Dunn, to launch the Canada Council.[10] Economist John Deutsch and J.W. Pickersgill, St Laurent's secretary of state and close confidant, then proposed that the sum be split – half to universities and half to start a council for the arts, the humanities, and the social sciences. This was the proposal that St Laurent unveiled at the National Conference on Higher Education in Ottawa on 12 November 1956 with these stirring words: 'The world today needs abundant sources of intellectual and moral energies. Canada wants to be one of those sources ... With that purpose in mind, we must further develop and enrich our national soul.' It was one of St Laurent's finest hours.[11] The announcement establishing the Canada Council was included in the Speech from the Throne on 8 January 1957, and royal assent was given on 28 March. St Laurent had already invited Ernest, who was vacationing at Mahone Bay, to be on the board of the council. Of course he agreed forthwith but saw immediately that the CMCl would have no direct involvement in the CC's operations.

Albert Trueman, former president of the University of Manitoba and of the University of New Brunswick, and commissioner of the National Film Board, was appointed director. Nothing more was said about Ernest's candidacy, which was just as well, for it was hardly the right job for a practising musician. The chairman of the first council was the minister of national defence, Brooke Claxton, who had put his considerable influence behind its founding. The vice-chairman was the Very Reverend George Henri Lévesque, who had been second in command on the Massey commission. Ernest was one of only two or three artists out of twenty-two council members, the others being academics, university presidents, businessmen, and wealthy patrons of the arts. It was clear that the council had no intention of letting artists play too big a role in setting policies or funding individuals and artistic groups. It planned instead to seek out their advice through panels, conferences, and juries.

The Canada Council met for the first time on 30 April 1957 at the Parliament Buildings in Ottawa.[12] It struck a five-member executive to transact council business between meetings, and in August it appointed three representatives to the UNESCO commission. Ernest was not a member of either group. After broad consultation, the council formulated procedures and policies. Claxton and Trueman did their jobs superbly and the CC moved ahead, winning much respect. The government may have backed into public support for the arts, thanks to the Killam and Dunn windfalls, but its new council was soon a source of national pride.

By the end of its first year, the CC had granted $230,000 (36 per cent of its annual income) to music. The Toronto Symphony and the Montreal Symphony received $25,000 each, while six other professional orchestras, including one chamber orchestra, were given smaller grants. It was, indeed, a heady time for Canada's professional orchestras. Council grants increased their incomes by over 10 per cent, and, as MacMillan had predicted, this injection of funds led to more performances, better players, more innovative programming, more touring, and, ultimately, increases in attendance and private support. To demonstrate its scope the CC supported arts festivals in Vancouver and Montreal, and community arts councils in Calgary and Vancouver. And, at the end of its eighth month of operation, it held a three-day conference on the arts in Kingston, Ontario, to which it invited about fifty persons, representing the various artistic disciplines from across the country, for strenuous navel-gazing and group discussions. Ernest was, of course, an active participant.

Meanwhile, the CMCl had not been sitting on its hands, especially with its president on the Canada Council. Back in November 1956, before Ernest had been invited to join the CC, he had asked leading composers, performers, and music educators to contribute to a CMCl brief to the incipient CC.[13] In the spring of 1957, as the founding of the CC drew closer, the *CMJ* devoted an entire issue to it, including two trenchant pieces by Arnold Walter on government patronage of the arts and related matters. The CMCl brief went to the CC in the autumn of 1957, and it produced a CC grant of $5,000 to the *CMJ* and funds for a feasibility study for a centre for Canadian music.

In the council's second year, Peter Dwyer, a wartime British MI5 officer and cultivated lover of the arts, was appointed its arts supervisor. Dwyer had a special feel for dealing with artists and arts groups and showed rare judgment in deciding when to help them and when not to. It was, in fact, his insight and clear-headed views that played a key role in shaping council policies. In February 1960, Dwyer said provocatively that the million dollars assigned to the arts for 1959–60 would benefit 'comparatively few people. But by origin the money belonged not to the few, but to the many; it came in a sense from every Canadian taxpayer. I do not think it wrong that the many should have assisted the few. For it may well be that in centuries to come it will be by those few that the many will be remembered.'[14]

'The problem is this,' said Dwyer, 'should the funds be devoted primarily for the benefit of those already devoted to the arts, or should it be used in a way best calculated to carry the arts to those in whose lives the arts at present play little or no part? In other words, should it be used for the established church or for missionary work.' Believing that the latter course would open the floodgates to hundreds of amateur groups and seriously drain the council's funds, he advocated that the council support the professional and leave amateurs to their own resources. Further, he believed that council awards must be large enough to be meaningful – don't spread the butter too thin, to use Ernest's metaphor.

Ernest was, understandably, eager for orchestras to receive substantial grants, but he was careful not to let his personal bias affect his judgment during his tenure at the council. One example of his fairness concerned Heinz Unger, who asked Ernest to help him get a grant for the York Concert Society. Ernest told him to write to Trueman, which Unger did.[15] Then Trueman consulted Ernest, who replied that on artistic grounds the York was surely worthy of support although he would be more enthusiastic about funding it if it gave its concerts outside of the TSO season – not an unreasonable view, since many TSO players were in Unger's orchestra.[16]

Albert Trueman recalled years later how much the council benefited from Ernest's 'experience, knowledge, personality, and musical genius available, especially in those early, crucial, formative days.'

He was, of course, the obvious choice for the role of music counsel, although, believe me, his talents and abilities and the help he gave us were by no means restricted to music ... I recall him as a quiet, though by no means retiring member of the Council, a gentle and understanding compassionate man, who talked reason, never with lifted voice, never in passionate argument. Sir Ernest was a strong man, secure in the eminent position he occupied, learned and wise, but never using his strength to beat down opposition, and never using his learning and wisdom to embarrass others.[17]

Trueman also found Ernest realistic when confronting problems. He understood that 'not all things are possible for the administrator, that the *practical* concerns and the *practical* limitations of an organization must be recognized and may not be casually ignored.' But 'he never took the fatal view that good actions should be attempted only if they caused no inconvenience to the management.'

It was Ernest MacMillan who was behind the successful realization of the third of the CMCl's projects – the creation of a Canadian music centre. In 1957, John Weinzweig and John Beckwith, on behalf of the Canadian League of Composers, provided the CMCl with a plan for a centre that would circulate and promote unpublished Canadian music. It was their version of what Ernest had been talking about for ten years, and Ernest included an outline of it in the CMCl's rather sketchy brief to the Canada Council.[18] Although sympathetic, the CC decided to reserve judgment pending the outcome of a feasibility study by business consultant Kenneth L. Carter, whom it hired for the purpose. After investigating similar service-oriented bureaus in the United States and Canada and discussing his findings with the CMCl board, Carter recommended to the CC that it fund the centre through the CMCl as it did the *Canadian Music Journal.* Less than a month later, in early May 1958, the Canada Council granted the CMCl $60,000 over a three-year period to launch the centre. Ernest's personal prestige and the fact that the CMCl, under his chairmanship, would control it had much to do with the council's speedy approval *and* its largesse. At the same time CAPAC granted the new centre an already promised $30,000, also over three years, again thanks to Ernest.

The objectives of the new body were after Ernest's own heart: to encourage publication, recording, and distribution of Canadian music; to keep in touch with individuals and groups concerning the centre's activities with a view to the securing of donations; to disseminate information about Canadian music; to maintain a library of recordings and copies of scores available to conductors, musical organizations, Canadian missions abroad, exhibitions, and conferences; to stimulate the playing or other use of Canadian music by orchestras and other groups and individuals; to issue an annual booklet containing a survey of the year's music in Canada; and to undertake such other activities as may from time to time prove expedient on behalf of Canadian music.[19]

The centre was to have its own eight-member board, appointed by the CMCl, and three of its members were to be businessmen. There was an irritating incident in connection with the composition of the board. Jean Papineau-Couture had written to Ernest to state bluntly that he wanted the majority of the centre's board to be League of Composers members and that the league should be consulted in the selection of the centre's director. He took the liberty of copying his letter to Walter and to Claxton, Trueman, and Lévesque of the Canada Council.[20] Ernest calmly replied that the Canada Council had already laid down its guidelines for the board's composition.[21] Then he continued: 'The League does not include all of the composers in Canada and is only one of many organizations affiliated with the Canadian Music Council. However, I can assure you that it will be adequately represented on the board.' Further, he went on, the board must be approved by a full meeting of the CMCl and, subsequently, by the Canada Council. Two league composers, Papineau-Couture and John Weinzweig, did become members of the centre's first board. Jean-Marie Beaudet, a CBC conductor and executive, and a member of the CMCl board, was appointed the centre's first executive secretary.

With the CMC in place, Ernest could finally rest – the CMCl had accomplished its three major objectives, in establishing *Music in Canada*, the *Canadian Music Journal*, and the Canadian Music Centre. In the depression-ridden 1930s Ernest had often felt that Canada was his prison, that it cared little if at all for the arts, that his efforts to keep the TSO and conservatory alive were draining him of his energy, impeding his musical future, and even damaging him psychologically. Now, a generation later, Canada had come through with what he had been seeking. It had been worth the effort. It *was* important to be Canadian and to live in a country that was recognizing its artistic potential for the first time and doing something about it.

18. The Busy Sexagenarian

To return to the winter of 1956–7, Ernest conducted *Messiah* at Massey Hall on New Year's Day and, as usual, John Kraglund disliked his slow tempi, his 'contemplative interpretation [which] does nothing to stress its inherent excitement and joy.'[1] Kraglund even suggested that some in the audience were falling asleep in their seats because of the dull performance! A week later Ernest resigned from the Mendelssohn. The choir's board, in appreciation, voted him a gift of $2,000 and, on his recommendation, appointed chorusmaster Frederick Silvester his successor.

Now, without winter commitments for the first time in twenty-five years, the MacMillans packed up and took off for a January-to-March stay at Mahone Bay to escape Toronto's cold and inhospitable winter weather. Ernest loved both the Atlantic and Pacific coasts but preferred the Atlantic. When asked about his *favourite* vacation spot, he named Mahone Bay. 'As I make this choice, the Rockies seem to rise up in all their grandeur to reproach me; the woods and lakes of Northern Ontario, the fascinating contours of the Laurentians, and the delightful old churches and manoirs of the Île d'Orléans all exercise a powerful attraction, as do many other spots in this vast Canada of ours. Yet ... it is a picture of the South Shore of Nova Scotia that first flashes into my mind.'[2]

And so, Ernest settled into a quiet and isolated stay at his Atlantic retreat. He and Elsie set up housekeeping at the home of their absent friends, Ray and Hazel Colwell, whom they had known since 1940. They had a superb view of the bay and its 365 islands – one for every day in the year, it was said. Ernest, thinking of his place in history, began writing his 'Memoirs.' The fifteen short typescript chapters (about 140 double-spaced pages in all) are his selection of 'incidents, pictures, and persons fished up from my sea of memory.'[3] He probably typed them himself – the nature of the overtyping and interlinear insertions suggest this. There is also handwritten editing – a word or phrase changed here and there. The 'Memoirs' are easy reading, never prosaic, and even lyrical at times, as in the first words of the Introduction:

The No-Man's Land that lies between sleeping and waking borders on a dark sea of oblivion – now lazily, now darting past too swiftly to allow one to identify them. Long forgotten incidents – memory's flotsam and jetsam – come to the surface now and then. Sometimes they take on recognizable shapes; sometimes they are so covered with the seaweed of many years that, after a vain effort to identify them, I throw them away. When I am wakeful enough to cast a fishing-line into the sea, strange creatures emerge. To one I can give a name – to another I cannot, though I am dimly aware of having known it some time in the past. Often the most vivid memories are those of early childhood and the least so those of yesterday. Fishing in the sea of memory is on the whole a pleasant pastime but now and then it brings a pang of regret.

His use of the sea as his metaphor reflected his love for it, which shone through at different times in his life: his ocean voyages, his *Three French Canadian Sea Songs*, his 1941 TSO and Conservatory Choir 'sea' concert which had included Vaughan Williams's *Sea* Symphony and Debussy's *La Mer*, and even a short article, 'Music and the Sea' written the previous year, in which he had noted that 'the sea itself is music. It has rhythm and melody and its motion never ceases.'[4]

Most of the chapters deal with periods in his life. The first three – on his childhood, the stay in Scotland, and his college years – are followed by ones on Ruhleben, his homecoming, and the 1920s. He also devoted chapters to the conservatory, the TSO (the early years only), the knighthood, and the trips to California and Australia. In the final chapters he reminisced about vacations, wartime, folk music, his ancestors, and the Christmas Box

concerts. Thus the 'Memoirs' are a mine of observations, reflec-
tions, and anecdotes that reveal his personal views, his modesty,
and his exemplary fairness in judging others (if he judged them
at all). His fundamental kindness comes through too, as does his
deep affection for his close friends and family and fondness for
people generally. It is also evident that travel greatly enriched his
life. His keen eyes saw things that many a mortal misses, and he
could set down what he saw in clear and vivid prose. Now in his
sixties, he had few regrets, at least most of the time, about what
he had and hadn't accomplished, and about not having immersed himself more exclusively in one or another area of music.

It is interesting to note that his unhappy departure from the
university is glossed over and there is no mention of the Symphony Six. But Ernest may have thought that he had said enough
during the fracas for the record, and, as for the Symphony Six,
his silence was simply a continuation of his silence throughout
the entire episode. Or were these events still too painful to write
about? He must have thought of the Symphony Six when Adrian
Boult wrote him that spring about a group in which he was active
– Musicians For Peace. 'I hope you'll be interested ... and support
this international peace organization. While we must in a friendly
spirit have differences of opinion on world politics there is a
great deal of common ground for aspiration and endeavour.'[5]
One suspects that Boult knew that he and MacMillan held different views on the merits of international peace groups – many
were left-wing – but he may not have known that MacMillan had
been scrupulously shunning affiliation with all such organizations
in Canada.

Ernest replied politely that he was pleased to know of the
group and then continued rather formally, considering that he
was writing to an old friend:

Music as an international language transcends political barriers and can
surely play a significant part in promoting international understanding.
I shall be most interested to learn in detail how the new organization
proposes to function ... All musicians must surely rejoice at the increase
in the frequent exchange of artists and orchestras between the Eastern
and Western worlds. We in Canada have been especially delighted

recently by hearing of the very cordial reception accorded in the USSR to our young pianist Glenn Gould. Orpheus with his lute has performed countless miracles in the course of past centuries. Perhaps it is not beyond his power to melt an iron curtain.[6]

At the end of March the MacMillans drove back to Toronto by way of Ottawa, where Ernest showed his old colleague and friend Marius Barbeau accompaniments he had written for Barbeau's collection of *jongleur* songs. In early April, safely home, he was toastmaster for a dinner honouring union president Walter Murdoch, who had prevented him from importing musicians of quality in the 1930s but had supported the TSO throughout the Symphony Six affair. Did MacMillan know that many Toronto professional musicians abhorred Murdoch's autocratic rule and that he made and broke union laws as it suited him? (To Murdoch's great surprise and chagrin, he was voted out of office the next year, thanks to a group of TSO and freelance musicians who mobilized the silent majority into action.) Ernest conducted his last *Passion* with the Mendelssohn Choir in April, and choir members gave him a television set and an engraved cigarette case as parting gifts. Never a heavy smoker, Ernest had given up pipe smoking after the Second World War and had, instead, taken to cigarettes.

In the spring he continued to be busy. At the end of April he attended the first meeting of the Canada Council. Then, on 13 May, the CBC's 'Assignment' series did an interview with him about his life and aired it in five fifteen-minute segments on consecutive days in June. Because of his work on copyright protection as CAPAC president, GEMA, CAPAC's West German equivalent, awarded him the Richard Strauss Medal. Not to be outdone by its northern neighbour, Austria formally presented him with a facsimile of the autograph score of Mozart's *Ave Verum*. The presenter was none other than Kurt Waldheim, the man who went on to become secretary-general of the United Nations and president of Austria (and was later alleged to have been a war criminal).

In July, Ernest and Elsie did another of their trans-Canada motor trips – Ernest had conducting dates in Vancouver and

Victoria. Back again in Toronto, he gave a few speeches, attended meetings, conducted the CBC Symphony Orchestra, and on 29 September was at the organ of St Andrew's United Church to play at a special thanksgiving service honouring the frail but still active Alexander MacMillan, who was celebrating his seventieth year as an ordained minister. Ernest then conducted a Bach concert with the choir and soloists of St Paul's Anglican Church, the first of annual appearances there over the next decade. The St Paul's organist and music director was Ernest's old friend and admirer, Charles Peaker, who had begun a biography of Ernest earlier in the year. Peaker had already interviewed people who had known Ernest as a boy and young man, and had drafted two chapters, but the enormity of the task soon overwhelmed him. After a publisher responded negatively to an early submission he laid the project to rest.[7]

The 1957 fall calendar was taken up with a bit of this and a bit of that, but they were all things he had done in the past *in addition* to his major symphony and choir commitments. It could have, should have, been a time for creative work – composing, writing, studying new music; or even for indulging in some over-due recreation – crossword puzzles, which he loved doing, or reading detective stories. But Ernest was having inner problems which were tying him up in knots, so that he avoided the very projects one would have expected him to enjoy. For example, for over a year he had been corresponding with Alexander Brott, conductor of the McGill Chamber Orchestra. Brott had offered him the first commission from the Lapitsky Foundation: a fifteen- or twenty-minute work for string orchestra, with or without a soloist, to be performed by the McGill Chamber Orchestra.[8] Not unreasonably, Brott surmised that having just left the TSO, Ernest would have time to compose again, albeit more for joy, as in this case, than for money, since the commission was not overly generous.

However, Ernest turned down the offer, explaining with unusual candour: 'I am suffering from a certain amount of mental fatigue, which makes concentration difficult, which is one reason why I am shedding some of my responsibilities. I hope that this is only a passing phase and that after a period of rest I shall be able to work again at composition.'[9] How truthful was he? It was just after his departure from the TSO, and he would be at Mount Allison later in the summer. Perhaps he doubted that he could still compose, or feared that anything he did compose would be labelled old-fashioned? Or was it something deeper, harder to pin down? Did he feel inadequate in a more general sense?

Undaunted, Brott tried again a year later. Again Ernest procrastinated. He was 'not sure enough to promise,' and he expressed the hope that 'one of these days' he would send Brott an 'uncommissioned' work to include on one of his programs. Brott encouraged him, and this time Ernest, 'much touched,' promised to try, although he said that he still found himself 'very rusty.' Two months later, Ernest apologetically wrote to Brott to extricate himself from the commitment. 'I seem to be dried up for the time being at least and I would on no account be willing to offer you an inferior work.'[10] Brott asked him for the last time in 1959, and again Ernest politely said no.[11]

The problem could have been physical as much as mental. In 1957, his physician, Dr Ian MacDonald, noted that he was suffering from high blood pressure and signs of vascular or neurological complications.[12] Arteriosclerosis (hardening of the arteries) was also evident and was the cause of a slight stroke that year, which had stiffened Ernest's fingers and prevented him from playing organ and piano with his usual dexterity. He bore this affliction stoically, but Keith noticed that his father was drinking more heavily, perhaps because of his stiff fingers or because he was spending too many evenings idly at home.[13] Although Ernest had a few drinking sprees through the years, he was not an alcoholic, as some people feared. MacDonald, for one, assured Keith that Ernest did not behave like one. In any event, he soon brought his excessive drinking under control.

The second year of Ernest's retirement was much like the first, although less busy. Again, he broke Toronto's winter with a two-month stay at Mahone Bay. And, after an uneventful spring and summer, Ernest and Elsie sailed from Quebec City for two and a half months in Europe – Holland, Belgium, Germany, Austria, Switzerland, and France. The one work-related stop was to the Brussels World's Fair on behalf of CAPAC. Later, in Lucerne, while they were enjoying the scenery and appreciating the off-season prices and absence of other tourists, news of a new grand-child, Keith and Patricia's fourth child, Kevin *Ernest*, caught up with them. Elsie wrote about how they loved the Oktoberfest in Munich, 'overflowing with beer and sausages ... Everybody singing and sweating and eating and drinking and making love.'[14] On they went to musical Vienna, with its four opera houses and many concert halls, and to Salzburg, where they visited 'the white and gold music room of the Mirabel palace, where Mozart often played. On the program was Mozart's own arrangement of the *F Minor Fantasy* for mechanical organ which Ernest used to play – I hope he will soon do so again.'[15]

All his life, Ernest had enjoyed a solid support system, provided first by his parents and sisters and later by Elsie and his sons. Family support was still there during this trying time in the late 1950s, but now he also had an admirable secretary at CAPAC, Maria Baumeister, who managed both his business and personal affairs. Maria sensed that he hit a low point in 1958. He was not busy enough in those first two years after leaving the TSO, de-spite occasional conducting, his Canadian Music Council and Canada Council commitments, and dealing with the birth pains of the Canadian Music Centre. Even the motor trip to British Columbia in the summer of 1957 and the European trip the next year were not the tonic they should have been.[16] Such a range of activities would have been enough for most people in their mid-sixties, but not for Ernest MacMillan. Dr MacDonald implied years later that Ernest might have been suffering from 'burn-out' or 'loss of purpose,' not uncommon in active people, who, having borne demanding responsibilities, find themselves with time on their hands and nothing new on the horizon.[17] But given the quantity and variety of Ernest's commitments in this period, all of which he met with his usual thoroughness, this diagnosis is questionable.

Things took a turn for the better in 1959. In January he had fun being a guest on the popular CBC television quiz show, 'Front Page Challenge.' In mid-March he started a busy three weeks of conducting. First it was with the Edmonton Symphony, where morale was low because there had not been a permanent conductor for some time. Ernest rehearsed the group thoroughly, which helped restore its confidence, and then graciously conducted a morning program and a concert at nearby Camrose, in addition to the scheduled evening performance.[18] He went on to British Columbia to conduct the Victoria Symphony and a Vancouver radio concert, and then flew back to Toronto to do a joint concert of the Toronto Bach Society and the Festival Singers. The next month he heard that the TSO had fallen on hard times and he proposed – seriously – that his pension be reduced from $9,000 to $7,000 for that year – which it was.[19] Ernest may have felt uncomfortable with his large pension, when players' pensions were next to nothing, but it was, nonetheless, an extremely generous act.

In early May, he received yet another honorary doctorate – from the University of Ottawa. The citation there likened him to 'a ray of divine splendour.' Ernest, with Elsie, then geared up for another trans-Canada drive to British Columbia, where they spent two rejuvenating months. John Avison, conductor of the CBC Vancouver Chamber Orchestra, was taking a short leave, and Ernest not only replaced him as the group's conductor, but, thanks to a tip from Marjorie Agnew, also stayed in the Avisons' lovely home while Avison and his wife were away. The orchestra gave weekly broadcasts, ideal for Ernest since he enjoyed being under pressure to learn new works. He even squeezed in a flying trip back to Toronto to conduct Handel's *Utrecht Te Deum* on CBC radio. Keith, now a senior producer, was in charge of the program.

MacMillan concluded his stay in the beautiful western city by conducting the Vancouver Festival Orchestra at the inauguration of the city's new civic auditorium, a gala event attended by Queen Elizabeth and Prince Philip. The first half of the concert was devoted to Handel's music and concluded with his *Coronation Anthem*, 'The King Shall Rejoice,' with Lois Marshall as soloist. At intermission, the Queen and the Duke of Edinburgh took their places in the royal box. Ernest then conducted a brass fanfare he had written especially for the occasion, followed by his own impressive three-stanza arrangement of 'God Save the Queen.' To top things off, the president of the festival announced that Her

Majesty had approved naming the hall 'The Queen Elizabeth Theatre.' It was a truly royal occasion and there was much cheering. Ernest, an unregenerate anglophile and royalist, enjoyed the event immensely. (The Queen Elizabeth Theatre was designed to serve orchestras, opera, and drama, but it had poor acoustics for orchestral music. Similar dual- or triple-purpose halls – Toronto's O'Keefe Centre, the Salle Wilfrid-Pelletier in Montreal – were completed in the early 1960s. The O'Keefe served neither opera nor orchestral music well, and the Pelletier was a much better opera house than orchestra hall. Good new *orchestra* halls finally appeared in Winnipeg and Saskatoon in the late 1960s.)

The most exciting development in this period of Ernest Mac-Millan's renewed activity was the CBC's invitation to conduct a new twenty-six-week radio series, the CBC Talent Festival. It was to be aired from different cities across the country and would, each week, feature two carefully selected young Canadian artists, usually a singer and an instrumentalist. On the basis of these broadcasts, a jury would choose four artists to appear again on a final broadcast. There would be cash prizes for all four finalists and additional performances, at later dates, for the two grand-award winners. The CBC stressed that the Talent Festival would not be a popularity contest but a thoroughly professional career-launching event.

Ernest played a major role in the Talent Festival's success. According to Carl Little, one of the producers of the festival, he brought to the series 'his wide experience as a conductor together with a very keen interest in musically-gifted young people and an understanding of the perils as well as the challenges of precociousness.'[20] As a high school student, Little had heard Ernest adjudicate at a music festival in Saint John, New Brunswick, and recalled how 'constructive and encouraging' his remarks had been. It was these qualities, along with 'his ability to be sympathetic and supportive,' which were such great assets to the Talent Festival. He was 'a man of much charm and wit, and he was able to put nervous young performers at their ease. His relaxed benign approach gave them a sense of confidence, and his wide musical knowledge helped him to anticipate and avoid pitfalls.'[21]

Indeed, the Talent Festival could not have come at a better time for Ernest. Here he was, a long-time advocate of creating opportunities for young Canadian artists, and now young Canadian artists were creating an opportunity for him. And how it pleased him that the programs prompted Canadians to sit up and take notice of the talent in their own backyard! He personally had tired of tackling the great symphonies and oratorios; festival programs of short solos and movements from concerti were much more to his liking at this stage in his life. Moreover, the trips across the country, with their weekly concerts to live audiences, brought him before the public, which he had always enjoyed, and reinforced his reputation as Canada's 'national' musician, just in case anyone had forgotten. And, social being that he was, he relished the opportunities to renew old friendships and start new ones. The winners of the first competition were pianist Gordana Lazarevich, who later became head of the music department at the University of Victoria, and Cornelis Opthof, later a leading baritone with the Canadian Opera Company for thirty years. Not all of the winners have been as successful, and many of those who did not win went on to have brilliant careers. Such is the way of competitions.

Ernest was festival conductor from 1959 to 1965, with some assistance from John Avison. He then shared the podium with Wilfrid Pelletier for a year before leaving it to chair the jury. The 1965 finals, the last ones he directed, were held in Montreal. He gave a fine bilingual introduction and presentation of prizes, but he had obviously slowed down musically – the first movement of the Sibelius Violin Concerto and, especially, the final movement of the Mozart Clarinet Concerto, dragged interminably.

Consider the many tasks this energetic sexagenarian was filling in 1960: conducting the weekly Talent Festival programs, chairing the CMCl and the CMC, sitting on the Canada Council, doing miscellaneous conducting, and giving occasional speeches and papers. Two talks, in particular, stand out: one on Mahler for the centenary of the composer's birth, and one on Calixa Lavallée, the nineteenth-century composer of the music for 'O Canada.'

Ernest was a fan of Lavallée's (the previous December he had played the role of Lavallée on a CBC television quiz show 'Live a Borrowed Life') and had long wanted 'O Canada' to be the country's official anthem, with 'God Save the Queen' redefined as the Commonwealth anthem. He pointed out that 'O Canada' was well within the vocal range of most people and reasoned that, because of its popularity in French Canada (its original text is a French poem by Adolphe-Basile Routhier), giving it official status would be 'one small step in the direction of bi-culturalism which many of us think should give Canada its distinctive character but which we are still so far from achieving.'[22] In Canada's centennial year 1967, 'O Canada,' with its French text, *was* approved as the Canadian national anthem and a year later an amended English version of a somewhat free translation by Robert Stanley Weir was also adopted. 'God Save the Queen' was made the official *royal* anthem. (Legislation officially confirming 'O Canada' as the national anthem was not passed until 1980.) Ernest had no personal interest in one over the other. His choral arrangements of both had long been favourites of English-speaking choirs throughout the country. Interestingly, he was known to dislike the playing of national anthems at concerts, a popular practice until the late 1960s.

Ernest MacMillan ventured into a completely different arena in March 1960, when he appeared before Canada's Board of Broadcast Governors. This board had, for several years, been reviewing submissions from private companies seeking a Toronto television franchise. All of them promised that if they were given the coveted franchise they would use Canadian artists, focus their efforts on Canadian content, and, most of all, improve Canada's cultural life. Ernest represented 'Upper Canada Broadcasting,' a corporation established in 1956 specifically to win the franchise. Fellow board members included architect Anthony Adamson, comedians Johnny Wayne and Frank Shuster, and playwright-actor-director Mavor Moore. This extraordinary excursion into uncharted waters brought Ernest face to face with the hard realities of the world of commercial media, where promises are made but rarely kept, and where corporate earnings matter more than anything else.

At the hearing, he pointed out that both serious and light music have a role in any broadcasting station. However, he was

particularly advocating his company's proposal since, in cooperation with the conservatory, it planned to present promising
young artists to TV audiences. MacMillan, humorously, told the
board: 'I am known as a "long-haired musician." Although my
present appearance may belie the fact [he kept his hair short,
and, as always, it stood straight up] ... I can also on occasions let
my hair down.'[23] Then he told them about his work on *Don't
Laugh* at Ruhleben and assured them that he had never lost his
'taste for the music of light entertainment – providing it is good
of its kind.' He said that his TV station would play the music of
Canadian composers, opera and ballet would be presented, and
there would be educational shows to compare favourably with
those presented by Leonard Bernstein, only with a local musician
(perhaps himself?) directing them. The board, in all its wisdom,
awarded the franchise to the *Toronto Telegram* group, which already owned an AM radio station in the city, 25 per cent of a
Hamilton television station, and a film distributing agency. As
they say, the rest is history.

A more rewarding involvement, although it lacked the long-
term promise of a television station, was with the planning committee of the 1960 International Composers' Conference at the
Stratford Festival. It was the brainchild of Ernest's long-standing
admirer and colleague, the festival's music director Louis Applebaum. Delegates representing twenty countries from all over the
world attended the week-long conference in early August to
discuss such varied topics as serial and electronic music, training
composers, aesthetics, sociology, and composer-performer-audi-
ence relations. Works by Canadian composers were given at the
conference's five concerts, and Canadians made their views
known on their country's music to the delegates in the ten panel
discussions. Elsie MacMillan's Christmas letter to friends described it as 'a most stimulating and heady affair. No wonder,
with the extremists among the electronic engineer-composers and
the serialists declaring the three B's as obsolete as battleships now
that they had exploded the musical atom, and Russia holding the
Party Line of "Music for the People"!'[24]

On that visit to Stratford, Ernest heard Walter Susskind conduct the embryonic orchestra of young players that would be-

come the National Youth Orchestra a few months later. He was later asked to conduct its first formal session in Toronto during the next Christmas holiday, but other commitments ruled this out. He and Elsie did, however, put on a typically delightful party for the young players just before the New Year.

And there were other new involvements. Ernest had long been an honorary patron of Jeunesses Musicales du Canada (JMC), but it wasn't until the summer of 1960 that he took on an active role. Substantially funded by Quebec's Ministry of Culture, JMC's goal was twofold – to present concerts by talented young performers and to develop young audiences for good music. Its imaginative programming had set an example for concert-giving groups nationwide. (The National Film Board had made a documentary on JMC in 1955 directed by the brilliant Claude Jutra.) JMC had grown rapidly under its resourceful founder and director Gilles Lefebvre, and, in addition to concert-giving, it was now operating a summer camp for teenage musicians at Mount Orford in the Eastern Townships of Quebec. Following the Stratford composers' conference, Ernest headed to Orford to conduct the inaugural concert of the camp's new chamber music recital hall.[25] Clermont Pépin's *Hymne au vent du nord* was the featured work, with the internationally known Quebec tenor Raoul Jobin, JMC president at the time, as soloist.

It was an evening to remember. The CBC planned to televise the concert, but the excessive demands of the TV equipment caused a power failure just as the program was about to begin. The duo-pianists Victor Bouchard and Renée Morriset valiantly came to the rescue, making their way through the dark concert hall to the platform and playing impromptu music by candlelight *à la Liberace* to entertain the audience for a full hour until power was restored and the concert and the televising could begin.

Ernest became president of JMC in 1962, and during his two-year term did extensive fund-raising and helped to start a JMC chapter in British Columbia. Initially, he put Lefebvre in touch with Marjorie Agnew, but, because Marjorie was sceptical about its chances for success, J.J. Johannesen, a Vancouver businessman and visionary like Lefebvre, launched it instead. No doubt it was Ernest's work with JMC that earned him yet another honorary doctorate (his ninth and last) in 1962, this time from the University of Sherbrooke, near Orford. Two years later he was elected honorary life president of JMC.

Following the 1960 Orford visit, he went on to Quebec City for a Canada Council meeting hosted by Father Lévesque in the fine old Maison Montmorency, a Dominican guest house haven for rest and contemplation in a setting of great natural beauty. Then he made a short trip to Europe with Elsie, to take in the Edinburgh Festival again (the MacMillans had become patrons of the Toronto Edinburgh Festival Committee) and a CISAC meeting at Lake Lucerne. They were back in Canada in time for the CBC Talent Festival in Winnipeg, where Ernest had the pleasure of visiting his former protégé Victor Feldbrill, now conductor of the Winnipeg Symphony. The rest of the fall was taken up with criss-crossing the country for the Talent Festival and meeting friends and colleagues along the way. In early December, he was off to Winston-Salem, North Carolina, to conduct a local production of *Messiah*. Lois Marshall was the soprano soloist.

The affairs of the CMCl and the new Canadian Music Centre kept Ernest busier than anticipated. As CMC president (he had been elected to the post in 1959) he was much involved in the appointment of a successor for the centre's executive secretary, Jean-Marie Beaudet, who had resigned at the beginning of 1961. MacMillan's choice was CBC radio producer and former TSO cellist John Adaskin; the board, after much discussion, concurred. Adaskin did well at the job, initiating a number of new and useful projects, especially the laying out of guidelines for a graded list of Canadian music for use in the public and high schools. With the centre in order, Ernest then found time to play a special role as vice-president of the Inter-American Music Council (CIDEM), an organization of music councils of countries in North, Central, and South America funded by the Organization of American States (OAS). Since Canada did not belong to the OAS, the CMCl was granted special permission by Ottawa to join CIDEM. In the 1960s, CIDEM sponsored conferences and concerts of music by Western Hemisphere composers. Political conditions in South America prevented many of its other projects from getting off the ground.

Alexander MacMillan died on 5 March 1961, just two weeks short of his ninety-seventh birthday. He had been a major force in Presbyterian church hymnology in his long and fruitful life and had been honoured first by the Presbyterian and then by the United Church. And, like his son, he had been awarded an honorary doctorate by the University of Toronto. It would be fair to say, too, that, despite his many long absences when his children were young, he had been a good father and very much a family man. In his later years, he had exuded friendliness and warmth to his grandchildren and great-grandchildren in spite of his formal bearing. He never lost his rich Scottish accent and never tried to hide his pride when talking about his distinguished son. Although Alexander had always had a small income, he had inherited funds from a wealthy brother in the United States, invested wisely, and, thanks to his Scottish thrift and prudence, left a fair-sized estate.

Marius Barbeau and Ernest MacMillan continued to work together on occasion. Eventually, the efforts of Barbeau and other ethnomusicologists in bringing to light and disseminating Canada's immensely varied folk music led to the formation of the Canadian Folk Music Society in 1957. Soon afterwards, the society became an affiliate of the International Folk Music Council, which held its first meeting in Canada at Quebec City in 1961. Over two hundred scholars from Europe, Africa, the Americas, the West Indies, and the Middle East read papers, played music, visited historic sights and archives, and were entertained by the two old friends who charmingly re-enacted their 1927 experiences on the Nass River.[26] MacMillan conducted a conference orchestra in a program which included Native songs, folk-songs from Newfoundland and French Canada (his own sea songs were among them)[27], and Claude Champagne's *Danse villageoise*. Things had come full circle. Barbeau and MacMillan were again key players at a folk music meeting in Quebec City. It was too bad that John Murray Gibbon had not lived to be there with them.

In June 1961, Ernest again approached the TSO to reduce his pension because his income had increased. This time he asked that payments halt for the rest of the year. Then, in December, he proposed that the size of his pension be *permanently* reduced to $6,500 per annum. The board agreed.[28] And, he still refused to take a fee for conducting a TSO school concert in February 1962. Yet he was far from rich.

There was one major disappointment in store for him. After thriving for several years, the *Canadian Music Journal* began to flounder and ceased publication in 1962.[29] Poor sales, not enough advertising revenue, and insufficient subsidy were the reasons for its demise. Although international circulation had grown, national circulation had fallen with a corresponding drop in advertisers. Payzant's departure as editor because of other commitments and the difficulty in finding an appropriate successor hadn't helped. Ernest wondered if the CMCl had been too optimistic 'about the probable public response to, and support of, a magazine of this nature.'[30] There was no doubt that the *CMJ*'s editorial format hadn't worked. Nor could anyone suggest a satisfactory alternative. In 1963, the CMC launched another periodical, *Music across Canada*, which expired after six issues, and, in 1967, *Musicanada*, which lasted until 1970. Since 1965, the CAPAC-sponsored *Canadian Composer* – Ernest may have had a hand in it – has filled some of the void, although it is more of a newsmagazine than the *CMJ*.

Two years before the *CMJ* ceased publication, editor Payzant had written a scathing article on the ill effects of the more than 150 annual Canadian competitive music festivals.[31] 'Festivals,' said Payzant provocatively, 'were a peculiarly British institution [and] only the British could make a virtue out of music-making in public under the conditions of an athletic contest.' He criticized how festival committees prepared contest lists, and how teachers were pressured into training their students for festival appearances and were judged by the number of winners they produced, at the expense of more rational study programs. Parents were often misled by adjudicators who mistook a creditable fifteen-minute performance by a child who had been practising the material for a year for real talent. Too often, this built up false hopes of parents and children about musical careers, with nothing but frustration and failure as the outcome.

The article was somewhat exaggerated and stirred up controversy and irate letters to the editor – probably just what Payzant wanted. MacMillan, who saw the value of competitive festivals, wrote a rebuttal, stating that, although festivals are 'subject to abuse,' they stimulate musical activity, particularly among the more general run of students, and encourage high standards of performance.[32] Twenty years earlier he had written that festivals give the student 'a sense of proportion, showing him where he stands in relation to others,' and give the festival audience 'a critical taste' for what it hears.[33] MacMillan based his conclusions on his own adjudicating experiences – in the 1930s and 1940s alone, he had adjudicated at twenty-nine festivals across Canada.[34] And how could he forget Winnie-Ha-Ha? He did agree with Payzant on one point, that *group* competitions, like choral festivals, were desirable. From all of this discussion came a CMCl-sponsored conference in Toronto in 1965 on the pros and cons of competitive music festivals, with Ernest as conference head. Well-organized and well-attended, it gave both festival advocates and opponents their say.[35]

The next year, his last as CMCl president, MacMillan led a CMCl conference in Ottawa with the omnibus title 'Music in Canada, Its Resources and Needs,' or, as he aptly called it in his introductory remarks, 'Music and Money.'[36] Arnold Walter, who would succeed him as president, planned the event, and invited a wide assortment of speakers, from MPs to American fund - raisers and sociologists. With the Canadian Music Centre thriving, the conference now recommended that the CMCl be sufficiently funded to serve as an information centre (collecting data, conducting studies, publishing reports), to advise musical groups in matters such as fund-raising, grant giving, and legislative proposals, and to establish and supervise a management agency to assist the Canadian performer. (It would take ten years to establish the information centre, which, at best, then performed only *some* of the recommended tasks.)

This wasn't all. The conference addressed the lack of good musical training for the gifted and urged that special music high schools be established in major cities. More controversially, it spoke against decentralizing post-secondary professional training, preferring that it be given by only a few of the largest schools in the country. Such forthrightness (Walter was behind this) did not sit well with directors of smaller music schools. Ernest remained silent. He knew from his travels that, with the country more affluent than it had ever been, new schools were inevitable and perhaps even desirable.

Ernest also prepared a CMCl brief in 1965 for the follow-up committee of the 1956 Fowler commission on broadcasting.[37] Serious live music was beginning to lose its priority on CBC radio in the mid-1960s: the CBC Symphony Orchestra had disbanded in 1964, Canadian-produced opera was no longer given on radio, and TV opera was prohibitively expensive. It was alarming that the CBC was putting more and more of its funds into popular television that aped programs produced in the United States or towards relaying American shows for viewing on the CBC. In competing with American television for viewers in this way, the CBC was not, of course, fulfilling its mandate to express Canadian life through its services.

The CMCl brief called for 'a rebirth of CBC Radio' and the creation of an FM network to provide 'alternative programming' for the serious listener. It proposed that both AM and FM networks be 'commercial-free' and that the CBC be given long-term financing to enable it to chart its policies for the future. (The CBC was funded annually.) And, since colour television was imminent, it urged that the money needed to implement it not be taken from funds presently allocated to music and quality broadcasting. Finally, the brief asked the commission to urge that private stations be required to employ professional musicians for a larger percentage of their broadcast time. This was not done. However, commercial-free CBC AM and FM networks eventually came to pass. But the golden age of studio-produced live music on the CBC was over forever.

If the Canadian Music Council was no longer the catalyst it had been in the 1950s, it could still boast of one success story, the Canadian Music Centre. Sadly, John Adaskin, its executive secretary, died suddenly in 1964, and, after a careful search, Keith MacMillan was, to his father's delight, chosen to succeed him. Keith seemed born for the job and under his leadership the centre grew steadily to reach new heights in Canada's centennial year, 1967. For those like Ernest who had worked so hard to create the centre, it was all quite incredible.

Thanks to a special grant from Canada's Centennial Commission, the CMC commissioned *forty-four* new works for performance in major centres from coast to coast.[38] As for its 'routine' work, in 1967 alone it acquired 208 new scores, 143 tapes of new works, and 45 new works on commercial discs. It funded the copying of 194 orchestra scores, 52 sets of orchestral parts, 122 chamber scores, and 67 choral and vocal scores – expensive enterprises to be sure. Further, it published a catalogue of Canadian chamber and vocal music and a definitive catalogue of Healey Willan's works, and started its new magazine *Musicanada*. And it gave out a great deal of information on Canadian music, shipped music to performers, dispatched seven articles written by Keith to encyclopedias and the like, and promoted the John Adaskin Project, which addressed the use of Canadian music in education. Ernest could not have asked for anything more.

Caught up in the centennial celebrations, he took the tune of 'The Maple Leaf Forever' and reworded some of the lyrics, in an amusing mix of French and English, to show his optimism about a future for one Canada:

> In days of yore from many a shore
> Countless human beings came:
> Cherchons-nous donc un beau drapeau
> Dont le Canada s'ra le thème.
> Here may it wave in modest pride
> And, if we're not in error,
> Quoiconque soit son d'ssin final
> Il peut nous satisfaire.
>
> Refrain:
> Célébrons donc notr' Centenaire
> With our new flag - and, damme
> Why not combine the fleur de lys
> Et feuille d'érable pour jamais?

19. A Theatre Is Named

The early 1960s were rewarding years for Ernest MacMillan. His health was relatively good, and his phone kept ringing with offers of engagements. Some were fun, if only because they were so challenging. Just after his father's death, and on short notice, he gamely agreed to conduct the Vancouver Symphony on a strenuous week's tour in the mountainous southeast corner of British Columbia, replacing VSO conductor Irwin Hoffman, who was filling a prestigious engagement elsewhere.[1] (Ernest had long been a hero in British Columbia, thanks to the MacMillan Fine Arts Clubs and more than two decades of guest conducting the VSO.)

To start the tour, the intrepid sixty-seven-year-old traveller left Vancouver at 5:00 p.m. and drove with the VSO's manager Ian Dobbin over the coast range and through the Allison Pass in a blinding snowstorm to Grand Forks in the heart of Doukhobor country. The next day he conducted noon and evening concerts there. It was just a prelude of things to come – for the rest of the week he bounced by bus and car over twisting mountainous roads from one small centre to another, conducting two concerts daily (one for schoolchildren). And, when the tour was over, undaunted, he boarded a small courier plane in Kimberley, made several plane changes, and arrived in Montreal just in time for a CBC Talent Festival rehearsal and evening performance. It was 'a killing schedule,' Dobbin said, 'for any lesser man.'[2]

Two years later he helped the VSO again. Beset with money problems since its founding in 1930, it was again embroiled in a financial crisis, which came to a head in November 1963 when

Ernest happened to be in Vancouver to conduct the CBC Talent Festival and the Vancouver Chamber Orchestra. Board and players had reached an impasse over salaries and other contentious matters and it looked as if the VSO would fold. Trying to help, Ernest spoke informally to both players and board members. Principal horn player Robert Creech remembered an all-night session that he and several other players had with Ernest at his hotel. The next day Creech heard that the board was ready to talk with them; Ernest had obviously done some work behind the scenes.[3] Music critic Francean Campbell summed it up publicly a few weeks later when she wrote that it was Sir Ernest MacMillan who had made both parties see reason.[4] Canada's national musician was immutable on one point – Vancouver *must* have a symphony.

In commemoration of United Nations Day on 24 October 1961, Ernest conducted the CBC Symphony Orchestra at the United Nations General Assembly Hall in New York. He began the concert with Godfrey Ridout's delightful *Fall Fair*, a work commissioned for the occasion. Honours continued, including a Canada Council medal in recognition of his six years of service and honorary presidencies of a number of musical organizations. He opened a new Heintzman piano factory in Hanover, Ontario, in 1962 (there were practically no Canadian piano manufacturers left in the country, and the few left needed encouragement) and a new music building at Brandon University in Manitoba in 1963, where he praised this small but effective school for preparing its students so well for careers as teachers. Brandon's music school was one of a number that were developing rapidly in response to Canada's burgeoning musical life. In his talk there, MacMillan referred admiringly to the pedagogical methods developed by Carl Orff in Germany and Austria to bring out children's natural affinity to rhythm and melody with devices such as speech patterns, rhythmic movement, pentatonic tunes, and improvisation. (He had become acquainted with Orff at a Toronto Orff conference the previous summer.) The 'Orff Schulwerk' was a new and promising variation on how Ernest, himself, thought ear training should be taught – procedures which he had espoused so well in his 1937 text, *On the Preparation of Ear Tests*.

Although Ernest had had nothing to do with the Royal Conservatory since his retirement in 1952, he could not help but notice the progress of its Faculty of Music under Arnold Walter's direction. Walter was a wise and persuasive leader and nothing like the image of the 'Prussian' dictator his detractors had flaunted during the fracas. Boyd Neel, an English physician and founder-conductor of the Boyd Neel Orchestra, had been appointed dean of the conservatory in 1953. Although he was little more than a figurehead and dissociated himself from academic matters, he was at least congenial, and he did accomplish one important thing: he got the approvals and funds from the university and the province for a much-needed new building. In fact, *two* buildings were the outcome, thanks to some adroit exchanges of money and properties by the provincial government, which took more from the conservatory than it gave. Ontario Hydro purchased the conservatory's choice location at the corner of College Street and University Avenue for the ridiculously low price of about $2,500,000. In return, the province, through the university, gave the Faculty of Music and the Opera School the Edward Johnson Building, a new building tucked well behind others on Queen's Park Crescent, and gave the School of Music a run-down eighty-two-year-old building on Bloor Street, about 120 metres away. The physical separation of the conservatory's two units would hasten their final separation in 1970.

On 26 January 1962, Claude Bissell, president of the University of Toronto, informed Ernest that, subject to his (Ernest's) approval, the splendidly appointed 815-seat opera theatre in the faculty's new building would be named the 'MacMillan Theatre.'[5] He went on, 'Inasmuch as the theatre will be a meeting place of the Conservatory and the city – to each of which you have made a major contribution – I can think of no more appropriate way of designating it.'

But how appropriate was it? Shouldn't the *entire* building have been named after MacMillan, if it was going to be named after anybody? But of course, it was too late. The building had already been named after Edward Johnson, whose services to the university added up to fourteen years on university boards – its board of governors and the conservatory board – and one year overseeing the conservatory's reorganization prior to Neel's appointment. In honouring Johnson, a distinguished Canadian whose international reputation lay in opera but whose service to Canadian music and to the university had been slight compared to MacMillan's, it would have been more appropriate to name the *opera theatre* after him. And, if the opera theatre was really supposed to be the meeting place of town and gown, as Bissell suggested with every good intention, it should have been twice as large (as proposed in original discussions about the building) and then Toronto would have had the opera house it still lacked thirty years later.

But Ernest had mellowed and took it all in becoming style. After the naming of the theatre was announced, he told the *Globe and Mail* that there was 'a definite place for a theatre of this type. Some of the finest opera houses in the world are about the same size.'[6] Of course he was mainly referring to eighteenth-century opera theatres, but he diplomatically skirted this point. He also agreed that the Kenneth Forbes portrait of him, which he had angrily removed from the conservatory at the conclusion of the 1952 fracas, could once more grace the university's walls, this time in the vestibule of the MacMillan Theatre.

CAPAC then rose to the occasion and announced its intention to underwrite an annual lecture series by leading personages in the musical world, to be called 'The MacMillan Lectures' and to be given in the MacMillan Theatre. Ernest was to give the first set of three lectures in July 1963, but was unable to because he was recovering from a serious eye operation. The previous January he had lost the sight of his right eye, after a fall at the Toronto airport, which, indirectly, could have been due to arteriosclerosis. A June operation had failed to restore it. It was a major set-back. He asked Glenn Gould, whom he had known since Gould's early teens, to be the first MacMillan lecturer, and Gould readily agreed. His first paper, 'Forgery and Imitation in the Creative Process,' was, as Ernest predicted in his introductory remarks, 'stimulating and illuminating,' and the capacity house thoroughly enjoyed his sparkling, if unnecessarily complex and wordy, presentation.

In March 1964, MacMillan obligingly presided over the official opening of the Edward Johnson Building (Johnson had died in 1959). There was a fanfare and speeches. Ernest spoke first, praising the building and the man whose name it bore. After mentioning some salient points in the development of music at the university, he noted wistfully that the University had not always been as generous in fostering musical studies as it now was, with this fine new building with its two halls – the other one was a 500–seat concert hall later named Walter Hall – and spacious library. Towards the end of his talk, he mentioned the 1952 reorganization and how it had come to pass, in case anyone had forgotten. To set the record straight, he said that he had given the plan his 'personal approval' and had been 'happy to retire, for I had become very much involved in other activities ... Under the new arrangement my own office ceased to exist, so I was spared the necessity of resigning.' He ended with a phrase from one of his last letters to President Smith during the fracas: 'On June 30, 1952, I ceased upon the midnight with no pain.'[7]

The opening ceremonies also included MacMillan conducting the university symphony and chorus for Parts One and Two of *England*, its first performance since the CBC's in 1941. The festivities lasted for an entire week. At one concert, MacMillan and Neel shared the podium to conduct the soon-to-be-dissolved CBC Symphony Orchestra, MacMillan doing Oskar Morawetz's *Carnival* Overture and the première of John Beckwith's Concertino for Horn and Orchestra, with Eugene Rittich as soloist. Morawetz, of Czech-Jewish ancestry, had come to Canada in 1939. When Ernest had first programmed his overture with the TSO in 1948 it had no name, like his own 1924 overture. Deciding that it deserved a better fate, and, no doubt thinking of Antonin Dvořák, he named it – with Morawetz's approval – *Carnival*. It has since been performed well over one hundred times.[8] The Opera School did Benjamin Britten's *Albert Herring* in the same week.

The MacMillan Theatre is ideal for chamber, baroque, and classical opera. Its acoustics are good for voices, especially with a full house, but, because of hard-surfaced material in the orchestra pit, even a Mozart-sized orchestra often overpowers the singers. Backstage facilities are excellent, including a large workshop to build scenery and props. There was, however, one embarrassment in 1964 – the small balcony could not be used because it hadn't been angled sharply enough. This flaw was later remedied, but only partially.

The next year Ernest took his turn as the MacMillan-CAPAC lecturer. Not one to take lightly a lecture series bearing his name in a theatre bearing his name, he spoke soberly and with substance. His first talk, 'In Quires and Places Where They Sing,' was an overview of choral music from plainsong to the present, with special emphasis on its religious role. Ernest drew on his lifelong knowledge of the subject and expressed his thoughts, as always, simply, clearly, and unassumingly. In the second talk, a week later, he addressed 'The Bard and His Music,' and, with the help of recorded examples, showed how Shakespeare's writings had inspired a wide variety of music over the centuries – including incidental music for the plays, music for the songs in the plays, and full-scale works such as operas. To conclude, he spoke at some length about Vaughan Williams's Falstaff opera, *Sir John in Love*, which he felt merited more attention in the operatic world than it was getting. (It took twenty years, but the Canadian première of *Sir John in Love* was given by the University of Toronto opera school at the MacMillan Theatre in 1984.)

In his final lecture, the 'Canadian Musical Public,' he first praised 'mechanical reproduction' for bringing to life so much unknown music of the past, for popularizing serious music generally, and for familiarizing listeners with the great classics. But, he was quick to add, mechanical reproduction does not replace a live performance: 'The fusion of performer and listener, like that of two chemical elements, produces a third indefinable something.' Concerning taste, Ernest feared that Canadians listened to music too casually and would do better to show 'greater elation at the first rate, and less tolerance of the mediocre.'

Moving on to the composer-audience relationship, he said: 'For us in Canada, it is a matter of public duty to cherish what we have and foster the development of what we need ... We must give every reasonable encouragement to our younger composers.' However, he cautioned, 'the composer can scarcely have it both ways. If he deliberately speaks a language comprehensible only to himself (and I sometimes wonder if it always *is*) he cannot reason-

ably complain if he finds his audience unresponsive ... Evidently
something has gone wrong ... The blame does not lie exclusively
with the audience. If a composer has an hospitable audience he
must not repay it with a standoffish, take-it-or-leave-it attitude.'
Ernest then added, 'No composer would be wilfully unintelligible
in his compositions.'

One positive way to help listeners to know and evaluate highly
individual and complex new works, he said, would be through
listening to recordings of them.

Anything that has to stand its chance with the public on the strength of
one or two performances labours under a serious disadvantage ... The
relationship must be a matter of give and take: all take and no give will
end in divorce, as it often does in marriage. *The audience* must realize
that music, like everything else, is bound to change its character in the
course of time and that its resources are well-nigh inexhaustible. *The
composer* must remember that while most of their great predecessors
were ahead of their time, they were not so far ahead as to render it
impossible for their audiences to catch up. If the audience does not
catch up, it *may* be because the composer has wandered up a blind
alley: there have been many blind alleys in musical history. Music lovers
think of music as nourishment for the soul. If they ask the composer for
bread, will he give them a stone?

The CBC thought enough of the lecture to broadcast it in full the
following year.

Ernest was entering a time of life which, inevitably, means the loss
of family, friends, and colleagues. Two of his three sisters had
died young – Dorothy had died just a year after Winifred, the
victim of chronic circulatory problems. In 1959, it was Amice
Calverley, with whom he had many happy times in London and
Salzburg, and, a year later, the kindly Elie Spivak, whom Ernest
described as 'a musician of the highest ideals.' It had been twelve
years since Ernest had forced Spivak to resign as TSO concert-
master and, following Spivak's death, he felt compelled to explain
why: 'I now know that the mounting nervousness in his playing
(he was always sensitive and highly strung) was an early symptom

of the long and lingering disease which was, in the end, to prove fatal. With his unselfish nature and dedicated spirit he would have been the last person to put consideration of his own good before that of the orchestra. His resignation was painful for both of us but we remained fast friends until the end.'[9]

It was equally hard for him to accept the deaths of close friend Fred MacKelcan and colleague John Adaskin, and, perhaps still harder, of two of his favourite young musicians: brilliant baritone James Milligan, who died in 1961 at thirty-three, and Rowland Pack, cellist, keyboard player, and choir director, who died in 1964 at thirty-seven. Pack had joined the TSO's cello section in 1947 when he was twenty and had become principal seven years later. In his tribute, Ernest caught the essence of this superb musician:

I first knew him as a Conservatory student when he frequently played cello in string quartets and I was particularly struck by his complete absorption in the music. He never seemed to look at the printed sheet but always watched his colleagues, listening intently to the sounds around him ... Rolly's utter sincerity and absence of display must have struck everyone who knew him ... He was never fulsome in bestowing praise and, on the few occasions when he shyly complimented me on something I had done, I felt a glow of satisfaction far stronger than I derived from the more effusive praises of many others.[10]

Still another loss was that of the gifted English-American pianist Alec Templeton, who died in 1963. Blind from birth, Templeton was a keyboard parodist and improviser after Ernest's own heart. He could convulse audiences – the more musically knowledgeable the better. He had a natural talent for comedy and loved to make fun of serious music, to rid it of pretence, affectation, and inflated values, to remove it from its pedestal and bring it down to earth with the help of a good laugh.

Templeton appeared five times with Ernest and the TSO in the 1950s. For his first visit, on 23 November 1951, he played the solo part in Franck's Symphonic Variations and then 'led the orchestra on anything but a dignified chase through his "Mozart Matriculates" and "Have a few on Dinicu"'[11] He also did take-offs on operatic arias, in the style of the composer, and made a travesty of an ultramodern Webern song cycle, in which he would cough to mark the end of each song, because the music for each is so sparse and the rests so frequent. On other visits, Templeton would, typically, play one serious piece – Gershwin's *Rhapsody in Blue* on one occasion, the first movement of the Schumann Piano Concerto on another – and then take the audience on a hilarious musical voyage – 'Bach Goes to Town,' 'Debussy in Dubuque,' 'Haydn Takes to Joyridin'' were three. At parties, MacMillan would often do Templeton-like burlesques at the keyboard, and, when Templeton stayed with the MacMillan's on his Toronto visits, the two would combine their talents at the piano with side-splitting results. More's the pity that Templeton never performed on a Christmas Box program. Ernest had 'treasured memories' of Alec and paid him special tribute on the CBC a few months after his death.

On a happier note, Ernest's growing family (in all he had six grandchildren) gave him more and more pleasure as he grew older, and he welcomed family gatherings at Christmas and other times during the year. At one party in particular the resourceful Elsie hired a magician to entertain the younger children – in those days a rare event to be sure.[12] One of Elsie's grandsons, Don MacMillan, has said, insightfully, that putting zest and delight into entertaining was Elsie's way of putting her 'sense of artistry into her life,' her way of doing something that was hers alone.[13] She had designed the house for entertaining, kept a lovely garden, and cooked with the best of them. Don remembered too his petite grandmother's entrances at parties. She would stand at the top of the steps leading to her sunken living-room so that all present would look up and see her, invariably chic and smiling. Actually, Elsie was the principal conversationalist at MacMillan parties, not Ernest. Only when he launched into one of his many stories, preferably with a Scottish accent, or sat down at the piano and did one of his comedy routines, did he become the centre of attention.

Besides providing fun and games, Ernest and Elsie, who took being Canadian seriously, made it a practice to give *Canadian* books to the younger members of the family. They rarely saw

Jocelyn after she moved back to England, but Andrea and Clare Mazzoleni visited Park Road frequently, even after Ernest's split with Mazzoleni in 1952. Andrea was close enough to Ernest to share with him the news, in 1961, that she had joined the Catholic church. She was greatly relieved at his encouraging response: 'I think its the best thing I have heard in ages.'[14] Ernest thought the Catholic liturgy the most sympathetic to music.[15]

While recovering from his eye operation in June 1963, Ernest grew a beard which he would retain for the rest of his life. It made him look older and, some thought, frailer, although the also-bearded R. Murray Schafer thought otherwise. Ernest sent Schafer a photograph that showed off his new beard, and the composer's reply must have given him a few chuckles. Schafer thanked him for the photo with characteristic irreverence and went on to say that Ernest's beard was superb and that he should have grown one years earlier. Promising to keep the photo on his desk, Schafer went on: 'You must know that you are held in high esteem by many people here [Schafer had recently been appointed artist-in-residence at Memorial University in St John's, Newfoundland] ... and I am counting on your picture ... to help ingratiate me with many people who might otherwise find the prospect of a bearded composer of serial music a little too bizarre to tolerate.'[16]

In August 1963, Canada's media, its musical world, and Ernest's colleagues and friends all helped him to celebrate his seventieth birthday. The July–August issue of the Canadian Music Centre's short-lived *Music across Canada* was entirely devoted to Ernest. On its cover was the photograph he had sent to Schafer, and the journal itself was full of formal and informal tributes (including one from Governor General George Vanier, with whom he had served on the Canada Council), articles by several of his musical colleagues, information about his life and his accomplishments, and reproductions of numerous photographs and awards.

To select just one tribute from the journal, the organist-choirmaster Alfred Whitehead related an incident which shows demonstrably how much Ernest loved to *sing* choral music.[17] One day in early 1947 he found Ernest waiting in the vestry of the Anglican Christ Church Cathedral in Montreal. 'I'm on my way

to Nova Scotia and have an hour or so to spare,' said Ernest, 'so
I can sing in your choir.' Whitehead continued:

Now Ernest's vocal powers are not the most distinguished part of his
musical equipment, but I quickly decided that this slight deficiency
would be more than balanced by the joy my choristers would feel at
having the great man with us. We found ample-sized robes for him,
placed him in line, and my wife in her pew and many in the congregation recognized Canada's leading musician singing his head off in the
processional hymn. I'm not sure how this Presbyterian – United Church-
man got on in the singing of the Psalms, but he was quite at home in
the Stanford *a cappella* motet.

One of the most heart-warming birthday wishes was a personal
one from Boris Berlin, the pianist who had come from Russia to
Toronto in 1925 and had worked with MacMillan on piano pedagogy and ear training at the conservatory in the 1930s, those
difficult years of the Great Depression when the conservatory was
debt-ridden and its teachers so moneyless that they literally held
a party when a new pupil enrolled.[18] Berlin wrote, 'How I wish to
shake your hand on this day and to tell you that you were always
an inspiration to me. More than that you were a beacon pointing
the direction for me and for many others like me to a better life
and harder work in music. For me you are more than a friend
and a guiding spirit but an older brother whom I respected and
loved and still respect and love.'[19]
    Not to be outdone, Keith's four children composed a four-
stanza poem – a take-off on *Hiawatha* – which began:

> From the land of lake and forest
> From the shining inland water
> (Rather small but clearish water)
> Come these HAPPY BIRTHDAY greetings
> To our very special Grampa

To which the delighted Grampa responded in *seven* stanzas, also
with apologies to Hiawatha, about how he spent his birthday with

doorbells and telephones ringing, with wires arriving, and with interviews from 'the Tribe of Television.' Finally there was dinner:

> Such a one as only Granny
> Could prepare for such occasion
> Featuring some luscious lobster

and a touch of sibling teasing:

> Which Aunt Jean refused to share in
> Although she sipped a small Campari
> Also Chablis and Drambuie.

20. A Life Draws to a Close

Ernest's health deteriorated noticeably in the mid-1960s. His swift and purposeful gait gradually changed to the slower and more careful pace of an aging man. In a letter to Marjorie Agnew in April 1965 he told her that he was cutting out some Talent Festival conducting because he didn't want to work anymore![1] Making light of it so as not to concern her, since she was in poor health herself, he related a joke about a sailor who went to the ship's doctor. When asked 'What's the matter?' he replied, 'Well sir, I don't rightly know. I eat hearty, I sleeps well, and I drinks a lot, but when I see a bit of work in front of me I'm all of a dither.'[2] But he was in worse shape than he made out. Less than three weeks later he wrote Marjorie again: 'I managed to get through the *St John Passion* without mishap, although I had to be helped on and off the platform.' He mentioned that 3,000 people had attended the performance and more had been turned away.[3] Obviously, the MacMillan name still had magic.

In May 1966, in Karlovy Vary (Karlsbad), Czechoslovakia, while taking a break from a CISAC conference in Prague, he had a bad fall. Thanks to Elsie and the Canadian ambassador, he received excellent treatment but remained infirm and, after two weeks, was taken by ambulance to the airport and flown home. (He and Elsie had to abandon a trip to Greece which was to follow the Prague conference – it would have been their first time there.)[4] Arteriosclerosis, which was gradually destroying his fundamentally strong constitution, contributed to the fall, as did his faulty eyesight. It was becoming clear that he would not be blessed with his beloved father's longevity.

As Ernest's Talent Festival conducting wound down, the CBC began providing him with a variety of non-conducting assignments – he still had knowledge, wisdom, and experience to share with others. The list of shows he was on is impressive: 'Records in Review,' 'Music from Two Worlds,' 'Music in Canada,' 'Theme and Variations,' 'Celebrity Series,' 'TBA,' 'Sir Ernest's Christmas Album,' 'Music Diary,' 'Encore,' and 'The Day It Is.' By the late 1960s his speaking voice had grown a shade darker, but he spoke as always with clarity, economy of language, and to the point. True, many of his texts were prepared in advance, but on interview shows he was as quick, responsive, and reasonable as ever.

There were more deaths. First it was Frederick Silvester in 1966 and then Healey Willan in early 1968. Willan, who was thirteen years older than Ernest, had retained his youthful demeanour until almost the end. On Christmas Day 1967, Ernest, knowing that Willan was failing, used the CBC program 'Sir Ernest's Christmas Album' to pay him tribute and reminisce about almost half a century of attending Willan's St Mary Magdalene Church on Christmas Eve to hear his High Anglican choir sing carols in its uniquely effective way. Back in the 1920s, he and Elsie had often stayed on with Willan until the 'wee hours' (perhaps toasting in the season with strong brew – Ernest said nothing of this on the air) and then would rush home to decorate their Christmas tree and fill the stockings 'of two lively boys who would be up at dawn.'[5]

The seventy-fifth birthday celebrations in 1968 were quieter than those for the seventieth, although the TSO and the Mendelssohn did honour him at Massey Hall in November by performing his music and presenting him with a plaque to thank him for conducting the choir for fifteen years. The concert was followed by a civic reception. The CBC broadcast the concert and filmed it for showing later on television under the title 'Sir Ernest Laudamus.' The program was the brainchild of Mendelssohn Choir conductor Elmer Iseler, who asserted that he 'wouldn't be swinging a baton today were it not for the encouragement of

Canada's first musical knight.'[6] Ernest conducted for the last time the following Good Friday at St Paul's Church and, because of his frailness, remained seated throughout. Kenneth Winters's review of the concert in the *Telegram* was from the heart: 'One went to St. Paul's Church on Good Friday night as much to pay one's respect to conductor Sir Ernest MacMillan as to hear Rossini's Solemn Mass.'[7]

It says much for Ernest MacMillan's generosity of spirit that, when Arnold Walter retired as director of the Faculty of Music in 1968, Ernest wrote him, 'Your period of office both before and after the re-constitution of the Royal Conservatory in 1952 has seen a notable expansion of its activities and its influence. No one knows better than I for what a large proportion of these changes and improvements you are personally responsible.'[8] He went on to note Walter's work in the Senior School, the Opera School, and the courses for music educators. 'I hope that everyone who admires the Edward Johnson Building and the Theatre that bears my name is fully aware of the time and effort which you devoted to its planning. Although others have played an important part in this achievement, no one has a greater right to exclaim, "Si monumentum requiris, circumspice."'

In August 1968, John Beckwith interviewed Ernest at some length and interspersed his own commentary.[9] Beckwith hypothesized that 'since no model of great musical eminence had appeared among MacMillan's teachers, the real model in his life was perhaps religious and ethical rather than musical,' and that 'the concept of a life of service to others had been responsible for his acceptance of many onerous administrative positions at early stages of the Canadian musical expansion, when free artistic impulse might well have dictated refusal.' Ernest agreed that both points were well taken and added that he did what he had to do because it was 'instilled into me and I come by it to a certain extent naturally ... I just had to buckle down and work.'

Yes, conducting was one of his great joys. 'I never had lessons in conducting; I should have had. It would have been much better if I had, but having been plunged into it I carried on as best I could.' He remembered his fine recording of the 'Haydn Serenade' in 1941 and modestly attributed it to the fine string players the TSO had at that time; and, in the same vein, he said that if the Amadeus Quartet's recent recording of his string quartet is successful 'it will be due largely to the playing rather than to the music itself.'

Beckwith moved the conversation on to other composers, asking Ernest which of the many Canadian works he had introduced were the best and the most enduring. Ernest, describing himself as a 'canny Scot,' refused to name any, saying instead that 'The public will decide in the long run, there's no question about it.' And then, towards the end of the interview, Ernest confessed that he could no longer play anything on the keyboard because his fingers were too stiff, and that now he only listened to Bach, Beethoven, Brahms, and, most especially, to Bach cantatas, of which he never tired. Beckwith suggested that such works defined for him 'what music is, in a way that some of the contemporary things don't,' and that they were more than 'old friends' and represented 'values which you very much like to cling to.' Ernest replied succinctly to this searching and provocative comment: 'Melodic lines and counterpoint and musical forms are of course necessary, and definite shapes are things that I think should belong to practically any kind of music.' When Beckwith closed by chiding him politely about his 'habitual modesty,' he retorted, 'As the Scot said, "Lord gi' us a guid conceit o' ourselves," (light laugh) and I think I've got my share, but I hope I don't obtrude it on everybody else.'

Unlike some gifted people who look back on their lives with misgivings that they should have done more and been recognized more, Ernest in his old age, was content, with his lot. He had not competed for a place on the world stage, preferring to use his God-given gifts in a smaller arena, Canada. He had simply competed with himself – he knew the meaning of excellence and had tried to achieve it in whatever he did throughout his life. It was excellence that drove him, not ambition. He was confident of his place in history.

Yet another old friend, Marius Barbeau, died the following year. In his tribute, Ernest looked back on a holiday he and Elsie had taken with Barbeau on the Île d'Orléans.[10] With considerable amusement they had watched Barbeau pursue *objets d'art* in his

relentless search for Canadiana. 'In the churches many of the
priests had discarded some of the fine old wooden carvings and
had substituted some rather ugly plaster figures and things of that
kind. Barbeau would discover carvings in the attic and then dick-
er with the priest whenever he could to buy them.' Success came
after getting the priest 'in a suitable state of intoxication so that
he wouldn't be too cautious and yet be cautious enough – just a
happy medium.' Evidently, they preferred selling these things to
Barbeau rather than to a museum.

Barbeau's infectious enthusiasm had stimulated both Ernest
and Healey Willan to set to music French-Canadian folk-songs,
and so the great folklorist had been disappointed that the next
generation of composers showed less interest. Ernest, too, had to
say, regretfully, that 'the use of folk song as such is now, I fear,
very much looked down upon by most of our young composers,
who are much more internationally minded. There's less of the
nationalistic flavour nowadays, not only in Canada but in other
countries as well.' He did, however, single out Harry Somers,
who, in his *Riel*, had made 'effective use of a Barbeau West Coast
Indian song, but set to Cree words and "transplanted" to Mon-
tana.' Barbeau had recorded the song in the summer of 1927,
and it was, Ernest pointed out without rancour, 'a lament for a
chief ... not a lullaby as in the opera.'[11]

He had more and more trouble walking, attending meetings,
going to concerts. He resigned as CAPAC president in February
1969 (he had retired as president of the Canadian Music Council
three years earlier) and on 11 June, CAPAC gave him a magnificent testimonial dinner at the Royal York. Two weeks later Governor General Roland Michener informed MacMillan that he had
been appointed a Companion of the Order of Canada, the country's highest honour. Since MacMillan was not well enough to
make the trip to Ottawa for the investiture, Michener went to
Park Road and personally presented him with the award, only to
find that MacMillan's surname was spelled MacMillian on the
certificate – shades of Harvard in 1914!

Now he was housebound, but countless visitors continued to
attend him there, and he kept up his letter-writing, thanks to
Maria Baumeister's weekly visits. To Marjorie Agnew he wrote that

he was leading a 'sedentary life' and using a cane 'inherited' from his father.[12] He was troubled that Elsie had to carry his meals up to the second floor where he stayed nearly all the time. She was finding all the fetching and carrying up and down stairs too much, and so, to alleviate the problem, the second floor was expanded into a self-contained flat. During the renovation, there was a bit of a wrangle over the new kitchen. A city by-law did not permit the installation of a kitchen sink, but a kindly inspector, who had been a Second World War prisoner of war and knew of Ernest's work for POWs, looked the other way as a 'bar sink' was put in. Once the renovation was completed, Keith MacMillan and his family moved into the rest of the house. Elsie was particularly appreciative of Keith's wife, Pat, for the help she gave Ernest: 'There was an affection, understanding, and trust between them that made many difficult things easy as well as being a lovely thing to see.'[13]

Clifford McAree, a prominent organist and a conservatory branch principal, was among the many friends, former students, and colleagues who wrote him encouraging notes to get well. Years later McAree related how, at Christmas 1969, he had sent greetings and words of gratitude to Ernest for the great influence Ernest had had on his life; and, then, having been away over the holiday, returned to find that Ernest had been ringing him all week to thank him for the note.[14] McAree also recalled another memorable incident. He had attended one of Ernest's lectures on Bach's *Well-tempered Clavier* in 1948, and at its conclusion Ernest had sought him out and exclaimed, 'Clifford, if I had known you were going to be here I would have asked you to play the *B Flat Minor* from the second book.' Seven years earlier, McAree had played that Prelude and Fugue for his licentiate piano recital! The phenomenal MacMillan memory was always at work.

Ernest went to Toronto General Hospital in May 1971 for a full check-up and removal of kidney stones. While there he suffered a severe stroke and was hospitalized for three months. (Eight years earlier, at the end of March 1963 and two months after his eye accident, he had a slight stroke while attending a JMC dinner in Montreal, but had been hospitalized for only a day.) Then he was moved to Riverdale Hospital to convalesce, a most unfortunate decision – the quarters were uncomfortable and crowded and there were no private rooms available. Furthermore, in the space of just one week, five patients in Ernest's room died. Depressed and losing his will to live, he insisted on going home, even though his doctors felt he needed hospital care. As it turned out, wrote Elsie to a friend, his judgment was sound, 'so rapid was his improvement in every way – general health, speech, and awareness ... We brought in our own complete hospital equipment and arranged for nursing and therapeutic services. I took over meals and medication and learned some simple nursing techniques and with the superb help of Keith and Pat found we could make a go of it.'[15]

There was one bright spot in Ernest's several unhappy weeks at Riverdale. The sculptor Frances Gage visited him to present him with a bas-relief of his head, the outcome of six one-hour sittings done before he was hospitalized. She had portrayed him in a 'heroic cast,' her only regret being that she had not had the chance to do his head in the round.[16] The relief had been commissioned by Spencer Clark of Toronto, who wanted lasting impressions of great Canadian artists. (Gage had already done reliefs of Willan, and painters Fred Varley and A.Y. Jackson.)

Frances Gage remembered Ernest as an exciting subject. At seventy-seven, he was 'a handsome man, his features were small but his bones were good, as was the shape of his skull. His hair stood up most attractively.' The sculptor recalled how he had feigned embarrassment at the attention she gave him during the sittings. He talked freely about his sons and how, like most busy fathers, he wished he had spent more time with them when they were young. Full of self-reproach, he also suggested that his dear Elsie, with the best of intentions, had often kept them away from him so that he could get on with his work. While Gage worked, she saw Elsie in action, constantly hovering about, guarding Ernest, protective as always.

In their conversations he revealed his continuing interest in things musical and spoke warmly of Karel Ančerl, the meticulous and demanding Czech conductor who had taken over the TSO in 1969. Ernest saw a kindred spirit in Ančerl, who was committed to building the orchestra at some expense to his personal popularity, much as he, Ernest, had done forty years earlier. This kind of commitment was becoming rarer, as jet travel enabled conductors to hold two or even three positions around the world. In fact, both MacMillan and Ančerl may well have been members of a dying breed of community-focused conductors content to serve one orchestra only.

Elsie wrote that Ernest's final year 'was a time of real happiness, with the grandchildren bringing in their friends for chamber music (everyone plays), chatter, and cokes, and "Tea at 4," a daily happening for family and friends, with Ernest in his wheel chair fully aware of and enjoying the lively talk going on around him – sometimes joining in.'[17] It gave him much satisfaction to know that there would be musical MacMillans for a long time.

Ernest MacMillan died on 6 May 1973. He had a brain haemorrhage ten days earlier and was, after that, unconscious until the end. As expected his passing was national news – the daily press, radio, and television all carried lengthy obituaries about the most important and prominent Canadian musician of the century, the man who was responsible for 'Canada's musical coming of age.'[18]

There was a small funeral service at Park Road, and then, on 15 May, a public memorial service at Convocation Hall where he had played the organ as a student and conducted the *St Matthew Passion* for so many years. There were several musical tributes. Elmer Iseler conducted members of the Mendelssohn Choir and the Festival Singers, and a small orchestra of TSO players, including some who had played with MacMillan in his very first year – Isidor Desser, Frank Fusco, Berul Sugarman, and Harold Sumberg – and others from the early 1930s – Albert Pratz and Robert Warburton. Lois Marshall, Ernest's favourite soprano, sang one of his little-known songs, 'I sing of a maiden,' and the recitative 'Although our eyes with tears' and the aria 'Jesus, Saviour, I am Thine' from the *St Matthew Passion.* (Wherever he was, did Ernest weep too?) University organist Charles Peaker played Ernest's *Cortège académique,* and the TSO players did his *Two Sketches for Strings.* Hymns opened and closed the service.

There were eulogies, too. Albert Trueman, Robertson Davies, Charles Peaker, and John Beckwith talked in turn about Ernest's

achievements and about what he had meant to each of them
personally. Trueman spoke mainly about Ernest at the Canada
Council, Davies about being one of Ernest's attentive listeners,
Peaker as a fellow organist, and Beckwith (then dean of the
Faculty of Music) as a former student. There were other tributes
at the Arts and Letters Club and at the Royal Canadian College
of Organists, where Muriel Gidley Stafford reminded her fellow
organists 'that to watch and listen to MacMillan at the organ was
sheer magic.' Even though he had been out of the public eye for
some years, the many hundreds of thousands who had grown up
musically with Dr and then Sir Ernest MacMillan felt a deep sense
of loss.

CAPAC's *The Canadian Composer* proudly devoted its entire July
1973 issue to MacMillan, with articles on his conducting, organ
playing, and composing, his work with Barbeau, his *St Matthew
Passion*, his work on the Canada Council and at CAPAC, and a list
of his works and recordings. *Not* included was his work as teacher,
academic administrator, examiner and adjudicator, writer, accompanist, and chamber music player. Quite a man!

To be sure, there had hardly been an area of Canadian music
that had not fallen under his influence. He had understood the
country and its musical needs better than anyone else. He had
been a leader, chairman, president, standard-bearer, and master
builder – wise, temperate, tolerant, and impartial. He had been
approachable, tactful, patient, and politic, and moved people
along through compromise and reason. Gains may have been
small or even non-existent from year to year, but, thanks to his
tenacity, in the end they added up to solid accomplishment.
There had been two motivating forces in his life: his Presbyterian
sense of social responsibility and community, and, emanating
from that, his resolve to convert musical Canada from a colony to
a nation. Since the end of the Great War, nationalism had been
at the root of most of Canada's actions. Music expressed this national feeling, but it was not until after the Second World War
that substantial advances in composition, performance, and education were made. The 1940s and 1950s were the decades when
Canadian music had finally found itself, and no one had contributed to the process more than Ernest MacMillan.

He had written in 1954 that 'there *is* an ultimate purpose in things,' and that 'one must strive to understand that purpose and then devote oneself to playing a part, however small, in fulfilling that purpose – this, whatever one's conception of the Deity may be, is to glorify God and to enjoy Him forever.'[19] But was it God or was it the very real and human world around him that had defined his purpose in life? One cannot but think it was the latter.

It took the writer Robertson Davies to put Ernest's death into focus and to say what he meant to Canada:

It is on the achievements of such men that a culture of a country rests. To say that they teach us is a poor description of what they do, for in reality they reveal to us things that we are eager to know but which we cannot understand unaided. Their work is not education, but revelation, and there is always about it something of prophetic splendour. Sometimes, before they die they become heroes of legend, and when they die we are aware, not of loss, but only a growing splendour in the legend.[20]

Elsie MacMillan died suddenly of a cardiac arrest on 2 August 1973, only three months after Ernest's death. She had congestive heart problems, aggravated by the stress and strain of caring for Ernest in his final two years. Elsie was also exhausted from replying by hand to the hundreds of letters of condolence she had received on the death of her beloved husband, a daunting task for a woman in her eighties. Her funeral was at St Andrew's Presbyterian Church, where she had been married. Her death may have been a blessing. Elsie and Ernest had waited six years to marry and then had spent fifty-three exciting and happy years together. Perhaps the thought of a life without him was too much for her to bear.

Notes

All unpublished papers in these notes are in the Sir Ernest MacMillan fonds, Music Division, National Library of Canada, unless otherwise noted.

Chapter 1

1 Alexander MacMillan, 'Looking Back: Reminiscences of the Rev. Alexander MacMillan, D.D., Mus.D., 1864–1961,' ed. Keith and Patricia MacMillan (unpublished, 1987–8), 7 (KMF). Much of the material dealing with Alexander's early years in Canada is based on this source.
2 Ibid., 9–10.
3 Ibid., 23. The Auburn church was demolished in the mid-1920s. The Smith's Hill church still stands.
4 Ibid., 25.
5 Alexander Ross, 'Reminiscences of the Reverend Alexander Ross, May 1830–December 19, 1919,' ed. Keith and Patricia MacMillan (unpublished, 1988), Book B, 36–7 (KMF).
6 Marion LeBel, interview with the author, 14 March 1992. LeBel is the granddaughter of Winnie's sister Christina Ross Gunn.
7 In turn, Keith MacMillan, Ernest's older son, referred to his father as his 'Most Unforgettable Character' in *Reader's Digest* itself (February 1978).
8 ECM, 'Memoirs' (unpublished, n.d.), ch. 14, 3–4 (KMF). 'Memoirs' was written mainly between 1957 and 1959.
9 Ibid., ch. 14, p. 8.
10 Ibid., ch. 14, p. 1.
11 William Westfall, *Two Worlds, The Protestant Culture of Nineteenth-Century Ontario* (Montreal and Kingston 1989), 6–8. This volume has been very helpful to the author.
12 Ibid., 7.
13 See Carl Morey, 'Orchestras and Orchestral Repertoire in Toronto before 1914' in *Musical Canada*, ed. John Beckwith and Frederick A. Hall (Toronto 1988), 100–14.

14 N. Keith Clifford, 'The Contribution of Alexander MacMillan to Canadian Hymnody' (unpublished, n.d.) (KMF). The revised hymnal was published in 1904 by Oxford University Press.

15 Alexander MacMillan, 'Looking Back,' 36.

16 Ibid.

17 St Enoch's is now the home of the Toronto Dance Theatre.

18 Alexander MacMillan, 'Looking Back,' 50.

19 Nora van Nostrand Wedd, interview with the author, 20 April 1992. Wedd was the 'young friend.'

20 ECM, 'Memoirs,' ch. 1, p. 2.

21 Alexander MacMillan, 'Looking Back,' 50.

22 ECM, 'History of My Life' (hand-written, n.d.), 1. This was a term paper written for a university English course, probably in 1911–12.

23 Nora van Nostrand Wedd interview. Wedd was in the second sled.

24 Jessie Greenaway, letter to Keith MacMillan, 11 February 1978 (KMF).

25 ECM, letter to his mother, 2 January 1903.

26 ECM, 'Memoirs,' ch. 1, p. 5.

27 Alexander MacMillan, 'Looking Back,' 51.

28 ECM, 'Memoirs,' ch. 1, p. 5.

29 Ibid., ch. 1, pp. 5–6.

30 Ibid., ch. 1, p. 6.

31 One of the members of the Blakeley trio was Arthur Beverley Baxter, who would go on to a brilliant career in England as a statesman and writer (for many years he wrote a London letter for *Maclean's*) and would, like Ernest, be knighted.

32 Alexander MacMillan, 'Looking Back,' 51–2.

33 ECM, 'Memoirs,' ch. 1, p. 2.

34 Ibid., ch. 1, pp. 2–3.

35 Alexander MacMillan, 'Looking Back,' 50–1.

36 ECM, 'Memoirs,' ch. 1, p. 14.

37 Ibid., ch. 1, p. 8.

38 Ibid., ch. 1, p. 12.

39 The hall was originally named Massey Music Hall but the public always referred to it as Massey Hall.

40 *Toronto Daily Star*, 5 April 1904.

41 ECM, 'The Organ Was My First Love,' *CMJ*, Spring 1958, p. 19. Five decades later ECM wrote that Lemare played the *Ride of the Valkyries*. However, press accounts of the concert do not mention this.

42 *Hollywood Citizen-News*, 17 June 1936. Blakeley was interviewed when ECM conducted the Hollywood Bowl orchestra.

43 ECM, 'The Organ Was My First Love,' 20.

44 Alexander MacMillan, 'Looking Back,' 53–4.

45 ECM, 'Memoirs,' ch. 2, p. 5.

46 Ibid., ch. 2, p. 6.

47 Ibid., ch. 2, p. 4.

48 Julius Morison, several letters to ECM, March–December 1907 (KMF).
49 ECM, 'Memoirs,' ch. 2, p. 3.
50 Alexander MacMillan, 'Looking Back,' 53.
51 ECM, letter to his father, 3 December 1906.
52 ECM, 'Memoirs,' ch. 2, p. 7.
53 Winnie MacMillan, letter to her sister Christina Ross Gunn, 26 December 1907 (Marion LeBel papers).

Chapter 2

1 ECM, 'Memoirs,' ch. 2, p. 9.
2 J. Wilson Gray, letter to ECM, 18 December 1909.
3 Unidentified press clipping. The manuscript has disappeared.
4 *Saturday Night*, 2 October 1909, p. 15.
5 ECM, 'Memoirs,' ch. 2, pp. 8–9.
6 Keith MacMillan, ECM biography (unpublished, n.d.), ch. 4A, p. 10 (KMF). This is an unfinished manuscript which Keith MacMillan was working on until his death in May 1991. Alexander MacMillan, in 'Looking Back,' 55, states that Ernest was by far the youngest candidate.
7 ECM, 'Memoirs,' ch. 2, p. 12.
8 Polly Lothian, letter to Alexander MacMillan, 16 August 1911 (KMF).
9 Lilian Hardie's name crops up in a letter from Polly Lothian to Alexander MacMillan dated 12 February 1922 in which she wrote that 'Ernest might be interested to hear that Lilian Hardie is going to be married,' and again in a letter from ECM to Elsie in February 1927 in which he mentions having seen Lilian Hardie, 'who now has two children' (KMF).
10 ECM, letter to his father, 20 December 1910.
11 ECM, letter to his father, 4 February 1911.
12 ECM, 'Memoirs,' ch. 2, p. 10.
13 Frederick George Killmaster, 'Reminiscences of a Canadian Musician' (unpublished, n.d.) (author's papers).
14 *The University Hymn Book*, ed. Alexander MacMillan and W.S. Milne (Toronto 1912).
15 The author is indebted to John Beckwith for his remarks on this hymn at Parry Sound, Ontario, 17 July 1993.
16 Isabel Gunn, letter to her mother, Christina Ross Gunn, 23 July 1912 (Marion LeBel papers).
17 Isabel Gunn, letter to Christina Ross Gunn, 28 July 1912.
18 Keith MacMillan, ECM biography, ch. 4A, p. 7.
19 ECM, 'Memoirs,' ch. 3, p. 5. One of the churchgoers was former U.S. President William Howard Taft, who, according to Ernest, occupied space for three ordinary people at Sunday services.
20 Keith MacMillan, ECM biography, ch. 4A, p. 19.
21 ECM, letter to Elsie, 25 June 1913.
22 ECM, letter to Elsie, 26 June 1913.

23 ECM, letter to Elsie, 2 July 1913.

24 ECM, letter to Elsie, 4 July 1913.

25 ECM, letter to Elsie, 29 June 1913.

26 ECM, letter to Elsie, 25 July 1913.

27 ECM, letter to Elsie, 11 July 1913. The Montreal pianist was probably Willie Eckstein.

28 ECM, letter to Elsie, 3 January 1914.

29 ECM, letter to Elsie, 4 January 1914.

30 ECM, letter to Elsie, 29 December 1913.

31 ECM, letter to Elsie, 7 January 1914.

32 ECM, 'Memoirs,' ch. 3, p. 4.

33 Ibid., ch. 3, pp. 4–5.

34 Ibid., ch. 3, p. 4.

35 ECM, letters to Elsie, 14, 16 March 1914.

36 ECM, letter to Elsie, 16 April 1914.

37 The Burgesses, mother and daughter, were firm fixtures in ECM's life by this time. In 1927 he dedicated his arrangement of a sixteenth-century Christmas carol, 'The Storke,' to Antoinette, and in 1940 he played the organ for Barbara's wedding.

38 ECM, letter to Elsie, 22 June 1914.

39 ECM, letter to Elsie, 27 June 1914.

40 ECM, letter to Elsie, 27 July 1914.

41 Muck returned to the Boston Symphony in 1914. Three and a half years later, American anti-German hysteria led to his arrest, and he was interned for the remainder of the war.

42 With apologies to the late Barbara Tuchman.

43 ECM, 'Memoirs,' ch. 3, pp. 7–8.

44 The old town of Nuremberg was almost totally obliterated by bombings in the Second World War but has since been rebuilt.

45 Polly Lothian, letter to Winnie MacMillan, 8 February 1915.

46 Antoinette Burgess, letter to Alexander MacMillan, 10 February 1915.

47 ECM, letter to his parents, 14 February 1915.

48 ECM, 'Memoirs,' ch. 3, pp. 8–10.

Chapter 3

1 J. Davidson Ketchum, *Ruhleben: A Prison Camp Society* (Toronto 1965). This book deals with the camp's social organization and includes statistics on its population and a bibliography of writings about Ruhleben.

2 Ketchum, *Ruhleben*, 117.

3 ECM, 'Memoirs,' ch. 4, pp. 5–6. Winzer was a Polish-born painter and book illustrator.

4 ECM, Ruhleben diary, September–October 1915. These were the only months that ECM kept a diary at Ruhleben.

5 ECM, 'Memoirs,' ch. 4, pp. 8–9.
6 Israel Cohen, *The Ruhleben Prison Camps* (London 1917), 162–3. Cohen was released from Ruhleben in June 1916 and wrote this book as soon as he returned to England.
7 ECM, letter to Elsie, 21 April 1915.
8 ECM, letter to 'My Dear Everybody,' 15 December 1916.
9 ECM, 'Memoirs,' ch. 4, p. 9.
10 Cohen, *Ruhleben Prison Camps*, 161.
11 ECM, 'Memoirs,' ch. 4, p. 11.
12 ECM, letter to Elsie, 12 August 1917.
13 ECM, letter to Elsie, 2 December 1917.
14 Keith MacMillan, ECM biography, ch. 5, p. 20. Alexander wrote to Winnie on 12 February 1917 about the voyage but left out the frightening details.
15 Alexander MacMillan, letter to his wife, Winnie, 20 April 1917.
16 ECM, letter to Elsie, 20 July 1918.
17 Ibid.
18 ECM, TMC program note, reprinted in the *Toronto Globe*, 13 April 1921.
19 [George Gardner], 'A New Choral Writer,' *The Musical Times*, 1 September 1920, p. 621.
20 *Sheffield Daily Telegraph*, 18 March 1921.
21 *Toronto Daily Star*, 13 April 1921.
22 *Toronto Mail and Empire*, 13 April 1921.
23 The first and third of the *Three Songs for High Baritone* are published in *Songs IV to English Texts*, ed. Frederick A. Hall, CMH, vol. 14 (Ottawa 1993), 122–7. There are also several other ECM songs in this collection. There is no evidence that *The Countess Cathleen* was ever performed at Ruhleben.
24 ECM, letter to Elsie, 15 July 1915.
25 Elsie Keith, letters to ECM, 20 October and 17 November 1916.
26 ECM, letter to Elsie, 30 November 1916.
27 ECM, letter to Elsie, 4 November 1917.
28 Elsie Keith, letter to ECM, 20 July 1918. Ernest's sister Dorothy wrote to him on 25 June 1918: 'Oh, the appalling dignity of it! I suppose you will be a "Sir" next! Only, don't call yourself "Sir Ernest" – it doesn't sound a bit nice – "Sir Campbell" is much preferable.'
29 Elsie Keith, letter to ECM, 17 June 1917.
30 ECM, letter to Elsie, 25 March 1918.

Chapter 4

1 ECM, letter to his father, 2 December 1918.
2 ECM, 'Memoirs,' ch. 5, p. 2.
3 ECM, letter to his father, 2 December 1918.
4 ECM, 'My Most Memorable Meal,' *Maclean's*, 17 August 1957, p. 42.

5 ECM, 'Memoirs,' ch. 5, pp. 4–5.

6 Ibid., ch. 5, p. 5.

7 Alfred Hollins, *A Blind Musician Looks Back* (London 1938), 382.

8 Peggy Maclean, letter to Alexander MacMillan, 18 January 1919 (KMF).

9 Peggy Maclean, letter to Alexander MacMillan, 31 May 1919 (KMF).

10 Alexander MacMillan, letter to his wife, Winnie, 28 January 1919.

11 Robertson Davies, CBC interview with Whitney Smith, 12 September 1982. This program was one of six devoted to ECM in August–September 1982. The series was titled 'The Music Builder.'

12 Ethelwyn Wickson, interview with the author, 12 March 1992.

13 Elsie Keith, letter to ECM, 23 April 1919. The letter she referred to was in the *Toronto Daily Star*, 22 April 1919.

14 ECM, letter to Elsie, 1 May 1919.

15 ECM, letter to Elsie, 26 April 1919.

16 Charles Peaker, address at the ECM memorial service, Convocation Hall, University of Toronto, 15 May 1973.

17 ECM, letters to Elsie, 16, 25 April, 1, 6 May 1919.

18 ECM, 'Memoirs,' ch. 5, pp. 7–8.

19 Elsie MacMillan, letter to ECM, 15 May 1922.

20 Evangeline Harris Olmsted, 'Dorothy MacMillan 1909–1940' (unpublished, n.d.) (Jocelyn Podhalicz papers). Olmsted, bright and astute, was Dorothy's close friend. She visited the MacMillan home frequently between 1912 and 1922.

21 Ibid.

22 *Saturday Night*, 2 April 1921, p. 6.

23 *Toronto Mail and Empire*, 24 March 1921.

24 *Saturday Night*, 26 March 1921, p. 1

25 ECM, 'Memoirs,' ch. 6, p. 2.

26 'Chicago Convention Soars to High Point,' *The Diapason*, 1 September 1922, p. 3.

27 *Toronto Globe*, 14 March 1925.

28 ECM,'Bach's Catechism,' lecture given at the Metropolitan United Church, 23 September 1947.

29 ECM, 'The Bach Bi-Centenary,' *CBC Times*, 12 April 1950.

30 The quotations are from unidentified New York and Washington newspapers, cited in the *Toronto Mail and Empire*, 1 December 1923 and 29 November 1924, respectively.

31 *New York Evening Post*, 26 November 1924.

32 *Saturday Night*, 27 March 1926, p. 11.

33 *Saturday Night*, 24 January 1925, p. 7.

34 Elsie MacMillan, quoted in the *Toronto Evening Telegram*, 19 April 1950.

35 *Toronto Daily Star*, 28 March 1923.

36 Elsie MacMillan, quoted in the *Toronto Evening Telegram*, 19 April 1950.

37 ECM, 'Memoirs,' ch. 6, p. 5.

38 Ibid., ch. 6, p. 7.
39 Ibid., ch. 6, p. 6.
40 ECM, CBC TSO intermission talk, 25 March 1953.
41 There were a few minor cuts. MacMillan was concerned that the complete work might be too long for the audience.
42 TMC program note, 25 March 1953.
43 Two years were missed: 1933, because of lack of funds, and 1955, when MacMillan did the *St John Passion* instead.
44 Reginald Godden, 'Ernest Alexander Campbell MacMillan,' *Arts and Letters Monthly Letter*, September 1973.

Chapter 5

1 ECM, letter to William Burden, 12 June 1925. Burden was chairman of the Eaton Memorial Music Committee.
2 N. Keith Clifford, 'The Contribution of Alexander MacMillan to Canadian Hymnody,' 7. The United Church of Canada was a union of all Canadian Methodist and Congregational churches, approximately two-thirds of Canadian Presbyterian churches, and the General Council of Local Union Churches of Saskatchewan.
3 A.S. Vogt, letter to ECM, 29 March 1923. Vogt praised ECM for the 1923 *Passion* performance but made no mention of leaving at intermission.
4 Muriel Gidley Stafford, 'Tributes: Sir Ernest MacMillan (1893–1973),' *Music*, August 1973, 19. *Music* was the publication of the American Guild of Organists and the Royal Canadian College of Organists.
5 A Successful Teacher of Music and a Former Pupil, 'Sir Ernest MacMillan – A Student's Eye View' (unpublished, n.d.).
6 Boris Berlin and ECM, *The Modern Piano Student* (Oakville, Ont., 1937).
7 ECM, 'The Responsibility of the Music Teacher,' lecture given to the Ontario Music Teachers' Association, 28 March 1940.
8 ECM, 'Making Music for Oneself and for Others,' talk on Radio Station ZQI, Kingston, Jamaica, 21 November 1940. A second version was printed in the *Vancouver Sun*, 6 November 1949.
9 ECM, 'Memoirs,' ch. 6, p. 11.
10 Ibid., ch. 6, p. 12.
11 ECM, 'Augustus Stephen Vogt – An Appreciation,' *University of Toronto Monthly*, October 1926, pp. 20–1.
12 This judgment is based on a review of the ECM fonds at the NLC.
13 Alexander MacMillan, letter to ECM, 6 October 1926.
14 ECM, travel diary, 15 December 1926–15 January 1927.
15 ECM, letter to Elsie, n.d. Probably 10 January 1927.
16 Healey Willan had been a choirboy and organ student at All Saints Church.
17 Louis Applebaum, interview with the author, 3 February 1992.

18 Willan, Mouré, and Fricker had all been awarded honorary doctorates by the University of Toronto following their appointments – Willan in 1920, Mouré in 1921, and Fricker in 1923 (UTA).

19 Leo Smith was a contributing editor to the *Conservatory Quarterly Review*, which ran from 1918 to 1935. His frequent editorials and articles have interest and charm.

20 ECM, 'Those Music Exams!' *Chatelaine*, November 1933, pp. 15, 48, 62.

21 ECM, lecture given to the Gregorian Association, 15 September 1964.

22 *Toronto Evening Telegram*, 1 March 1928.

23 *Toronto Globe*, 1 March 1928.

24 *Toronto Globe*, 30 January 1930.

25 Ettore Mazzoleni, CBC tribute to ECM, 11 May 1973. Mazzoleni had taped this anecdote in 1968, shortly before his death.

26 Louis Applebaum, CBC tribute to ECM, 11 May 1973.

27 *Toronto Daily Star*, 17 April 1928.

28 *Toronto Globe*, 17 April 1928.

29 *Toronto Mail and Empire*, 21 April 1928.

30 See Patricia Wardrop, 'CPR Festivals,' *EMC2*, 326–7; John Murray Gibbon, *A Canadian Mosaic* (Toronto 1938).

31 *Saturday Night*, 23 November 1929, pp. 7, 14.

32 *Toronto Daily Star*, 18 November 1929.

33 *Toronto Evening Telegram*, 16 November 1929.

34 'Hugh the Drover,' *Musical Courier*, 30 November 1929, pp. 26, 34.

35 *Vancouver Province*, 29 December 1929.

Chapter 6

1 ECM, review of Marius Barbeau and Edward Sapir, *Folk Songs of French Canada* (New Haven 1925), *Canadian Forum*, December 1925, pp. 79–81.

2 *Two Sketches for Strings* is dedicated to the Hart House String Quartet, whose scrapbooks are in the library of the University of Toronto's Faculty of Music.

3 ECM, 'Memoirs,' ch. 13, p. 5.

4 ECM, letter to Elsie, 4 August 1927.

5 Marius Barbeau, 'The Thunder Bird of the Mountains,' *University of Toronto Quarterly*, October 1932, p. 96.

6 Peter Haworth, 'MacMillan and Barbeau on the Nass River,' CBC radio documentary, 30 September 1974.

7 ECM, 'Memoirs,' ch. 13, pp. 7–8.

8 Marius Barbeau, 'The Thunder Bird of the Mountains,' 93–4.

9 Ibid., 105–6.

10 ECM, 'The Folk Songs of Canada,' address to the Zonta Club, Toronto, 20 October 1930.

11 Marius Barbeau and ECM, 'Saving the Sagas,' presented by B.E. Norrish (Ottawa 1927), N.F.A. 3796, 3797.

12 Marius Barbeau, *Three Songs of the West Coast*, English versions by Duncan

Campbell Scott, transcribed and arranged by Ernest MacMillan (London 1928). Jon Vickers recorded these songs in 1986, and they are included on CMC-CD 4993, 1993.

13 V. Garfield, P. Wingert, and M. Barbeau, *The Tsimshian, Their Arts and Music* (New York 1951).

14 ECM, *Six Bergerettes du bas Canada*, collected by Marius Barbeau (Toronto 1935).

15 Both the Toronto Mendelssohn Choir and the Festival Singers have re-corded this song on the CBC SM label. Elmer Iseler conducted both re-cordings. The TMC is on CMC-CD 4993, 1993.

16 *Twenty-one Folk Songs of French Canada*, ed. ECM, English translations and an introduction (in French only) by John Murray Gibbon (Oakville, Ont., 1928). ECM was one of five arrangers.

17 These songs are still unpublished but are available from the Canadian Music Centre.

18 ECM, 'Preface,' *Canadian Song Book* (Toronto 1928). There were several reprints. ECM earned between $100 and $150 in royalties annually for many years, a fair sum for such a publication. It was revised in 1949.

19 *London Observer*, fragment of a clipping, n.d.

20 Frederick A. Hall, 'Introduction,' *Songs IV to English Texts*, ed. Frederick A. Hall, CMH, vol. 14 (Ottawa 1993), ix.

21 ECM, letter to Marius Barbeau, 10 February 1957.

22 Kenneth Peacock, 'Canadian Folklore, the Source of So Much Music,' *The Canadian Composer*, July 1973, p. 18.

23 ECM, 'The Folk Songs of Canada.'

24 ECM, 'Memoirs,' ch. 13, pp. 2–3.

25 Keith MacMillan, quoted in the *Toronto Evening Telegram*, 10 August 1968.

26 Keith MacMillan, 'Parallel Tracks: Ernest Campbell MacMillan in the 1930s and 1940s,' *Canadian Music in the 1930s and 1940s*, ed. Beverley Cavanagh [Kingston, Ont., 1987], 13.

27 Ross MacMillan, interview with the author, 13 May 1992.

28 Juliette Bourassa-Trépanier, 'Rodolphe Mathieu,' *EMC2*, 818–19.

29 See Robin Elliott, 'The String Quartet in Canada,' PhD dissertation, University of Toronto, 1990, pp. 215–19.

30 ECM's String Quartet in C Minor was recorded by the Amadeus Quartet in 1968 and is now on CMC-CD 4993, 1993. ECM's description of the work on the record jacket notes that it was first performed by the Hart House Quartet in 1924, but on that occasion only three of the movements were played.

31 There is another version of how Ernest got this work performed: he showed the completed score to von Kunits, who agreed to perform it and asked Ernest to conduct it.

32 ECM's Overture has been recorded by the TSO with conductor Andrew Davis on CBC SM 5068.

33 ECM, letter to Allard de Ridder, 29 June 1936.

Chapter 7

1 Alexander MacMillan, letter to ECM, 7 July 1931.
2 ECM, quoted in the *Toronto Daily Star*, 3 October 1931.
3 ECM, 'Memoirs,' ch. 8, p. 2.
4 *Toronto Globe*, 11 June 1932.
5 Henry Saunders, letter to Mrs von Kunits and family, 22 October 1931 (TSO archives).
6 ECM, 'Memoirs,' ch. 8, p. 3.
7 Marcus Adeney, interview with Keith MacMillan, 25 September 1984.
8 ECM, letter to TSO members, 24 October 1931.
9 TSO program note, 27 October 1931.
10 Hamilton-born Ernest Seitz was a frequent soloist with the TSO. He is most famous for his song 'The World is Waiting for the Sunrise.'
11 ECM, 'Memoirs,' ch. 8, p. 2.
12 *Saturday Night*, 19 December 1931, p. 179.
13 *Toronto Mail and Empire*, 21 April 1932.
14 *Toronto Daily Star*, 24 February 1932.
15 *Toronto Globe*, 24 February 1932.
16 ECM, letter to TSO members, 26 January 1932.
17 *Saturday Night*, 30 April 1932, p. 6.
18 TSO program note, 20 April 1932.
19 Vincent Massey would become Canada's High Commissioner to London and, later, its first native-born Governor General.
20 William Kilbourn, *Intimate Grandeur: One Hundred Years at Massey Hall* (Toronto 1993), 82–6. The hall was officially renamed Massey Hall at this time.
21 Vincent Massey, letter to J.P. Girven, 7 November 1932; J.P. Girven, letter to Vincent Massey, 9 November 1932 (UTA).
22 *Toronto Globe*, 5 October 1932.
23 See Carl Morey, 'Orchestras and Orchestral Repertoire in Toronto before 1914,' *Musical Canada*, ed. John Beckwith and Frederick A. Hall (Toronto 1988), 112. Frank Fusco, a first violinist in the TSO, told the author that this was still the custom in the 1930s.
24 *Toronto Globe*, 5 October 1932.
25 John Adaskin, 'MacMillan as Conductor,' *Music across Canada*, July–August 1963, pp. 25–8.
26 *Toronto Evening Telegram*, 22 March 1933.

Chapter 8

1 An anecdote which underlines Ernest's national fame for his ability to do any and all things musical is about a TSO cellist (Philip Spivak) returning to Canada after having had his instrument repaired by a prominent luthier in New York. After explaining the purpose of his visit to a Canada

Customs official, the latter queried, 'Why didn't you ask Sir Ernest Mac-Millan to do it?'

2 Irene Rowe, 'The History and Development of School Concerts by the Toronto Symphony Orchestra from 1925 to 1957,' MM dissertation, University of Western Ontario, 1989, p. 33.

3 Ibid., 34.

4 Ibid., 36.

5 ECM, 'Memoirs,' ch. 15, p. 1.

6 *Toronto Globe*, 18 December 1935.

7 ECM, 'Memoirs,' ch. 15, pp. 1–3.

8 *Toronto Daily Star*, 16 December 1936.

9 *Toronto Evening Telegram*, 16 December 1936.

10 ECM, 'Memoirs,' ch. 15, p. 2.

11 ECM, tape and transcript of the TSO's 1950 Christmas Box performance (KMF).

12 Anna Russell, interview with Keith MacMillan, 19 June 1985 (KMF), and conversation with the author, 10 December 1993.

13 *Toronto Mail and Empire*, 3 July 1934.

14 C.V. Pilcher did the text.

15 *Toronto Daily Star*, 3 July 1934; *Toronto Mail and Empire*, 3 July 1934.

16 ECM, 'Memoirs,' ch. 8, p. 10.

17 ECM, 'Three Notable British Composers,' *TCM Quarterly*, August 1934, pp. 5–7. Reprinted in the TSO program, 6 February 1935.

18 Mary Barrow, conversation with the author, 5 November 1992.

19 ECM, letter to Arthur Judson, 11 November 1937.

20 *Toronto Daily Star*, 10 November 1937.

21 *Saturday Night*, 20 November 1937, p. 8.

22 *Toronto Evening Telegram*, 10 November 1937.

23 Heinz Unger, letter to ECM, 17 November 1937.

24 *Toronto Globe and Mail*, 30 November 1938.

25 *Toronto Evening Telegram*, 30 November 1938.

26 ECM, *On the Preparation of Ear Tests* (Oakville, Ont., 1938).

27 Floyd Chalmers, *Both Sides of the Street: One Man's Life in Business and the Arts* (Toronto 1983), 123–4.

28 Ibid., 122.

29 Godfrey Ridout, interview with Keith MacMillan, 15 February 1983 (KMF).

30 Ibid.

31 Keith MacMillan, 'Parallel Tracks,' 9.

32 Glen Morley, letter to Keith MacMillan, 10 January 1986 (KMF).

33 Ernest Hutcheson, 'Report on a Short Survey of the Toronto Conservatory of Music' (unpublished, n.d.) (UTA). The Carnegie Corporation, which contributed substantial funds to the arts in Canada between the wars, paid for the survey.

34 *Toronto Globe*, 31 May 1934. The quote is from a Columbia University *Bulletin of Information*.

35 *Toronto Daily Star*, 8, 9 May 1934.
36 ECM, quoted in the *Toronto Daily Star*, 9 May 1934.
37 ECM, quoted in the *Toronto Mail and Empire*, 31 May 1934.
38 *Toronto Evening Telegram*, 31 October 1934.
39 Faculty of Music, *Calendar*, 1935–6.
40 ECM, 'The Place of Music in a University Curriculum,' *Proceedings*, Eleventh National Conference of Canadian Universities, University of Western Ontario, 31 May–2 June 1927, pp. 66–75.
41 ECM, letter to H.J. Cody, president of the University of Toronto, March 1937 (UTA).

Chapter 9

1 R.B. Bennett, letter to ECM, 18 May 1935.
2 ECM, wire to Frederick Harris, 13 March 1935.
3 Elsie MacMillan, letter to ECM, 20 May 1935.
4 Fred MacKelcan, wire to ECM, 21 May 1935.
5 ECM, letter to R.B. Bennett, 25 May 1935.
6 *Toronto Mail and Empire*, 3 June 1935.
7 *Toronto Daily Star*, 3 June 1935.
8 *Toronto Globe*, 4 June 1935; *Toronto Evening Telegram*, 4 June 1935.
9 *Toronto Mail and Empire*, 4 April 1932.
10 Keith MacMillan, 'Broadcasting,' *EMC2*, 162–7.
11 ECM, letter to Gladstone Murray, 6 March 1937.
12 ECM, letter to John P.L. Roberts, 20 May 1966.
13 ECM, 'Canadian Musical Life,' *Canadian Geographic Journal*, December 1939, pp. 330–6.
14 ECM, letter to Gladstone Murray, 15 January 1940; Murray, letter to ECM, 15 February 1940.
15 *The Times*, 20 July 1933; *The Daily Telegraph*, 20 July 1933.
16 *Toronto Globe*, 21 July 1933.
17 ECM, letter to Elsie, 16 July 1933.
18 ECM, letter to Elsie, 28 July 1933.
19 ECM, letter to Elsie, 6 August 1933.
20 ECM, 'Memoirs,' ch. 11, p. 14.
21 Ibid., ch. 11, p. 17.
22 ECM, letters to Elsie, 13, 21, 28 July 1935.
23 Muriel Gidley Stafford, interview with the author, 28 July 1992; Stafford, letter to the author, 3 November 1993.
24 'The London Conference of Organists,' *The Musical Times*, September 1935, p. 828.
25 Edith Milligan Binnie, interview with the author, 10 June 1992.
26 ECM, 'Emmy Heim,' *Royal Conservatory Bulletin*, November 1954.
27 Emmy Heim, 'A Self Portrait,' jacket note on Hallmark record SS2.
28 ECM, 'Memoirs,' ch. 8, p. 6.

29 ECM, letter to Elsie, 17 August 1935.
30 ECM, 'Memoirs,' ch. 11, p. 18.
31 *Los Angeles Times*, 5 August 1936.
32 *Los Angeles Evening Herald*, 5 August 1936.
33 ECM, 'Memoirs,' ch. 9, pp. 7–10.
34 Ibid., ch. 9, p. 9.
35 Ibid., ch. 9, p. 10.
36 ECM, 'The Value of Music in Education,' graduation address, University of British Columbia, 7 May 1936; repr. *University of Toronto Monthly*, June 1936, 285–7.
37 Sir Ernest MacMillan Fine Arts Clubs files (NLC).
38 William Littler, interview with Keith MacMillan, 16 July 1984.
39 Wilfrid Pelletier, letter to ECM, 29 October 1936.
40 *Montreal Gazette*, 12 December 1936; *Montreal Star*, 12 December 1936.
41 *Chicago Journal of Commerce*, 3 July 1937.
42 *Chicago Herald-Examiner*, 3, 4 July 1937.
43 *Chicago Tribune*, 7 July 1937.
44 *Washington Post*, 24 January 1938.
45 ECM, 'Memoirs,' ch. 11, p. 11.

Chapter 10

1 ECM, 'Memoirs,' ch. 8, pp. 3–4.
2 ECM, notes prepared for Lazare Saminsky, undated but probably 1956. Saminsky's *Essentials of Conducting* was published in New York in 1958.
3 Victor Feldbrill, interview with author, 21 November 1991.
4 Victor Feldbrill, interview with Keith MacMillan, 10 December 1987 (KMF).
5 ECM, letter to Arthur Judson, 6 September 1938.
6 Arthur Judson, letter to ECM, 8 September 1938.
7 ECM, letter to J.E. Hahn, 4 January 1939. Hahn was TSO president.
8 Trevor Owen was a prominent diagnostician interested in the interaction of physical and mental illness.
9 ECM, letters to A.L. Bishop, 11 April 1939.
10 Elsie MacMillan, letter to ECM, undated but probably 18 April 1939.
11 ECM, letter to Elsie, 29 April 1939.
12 ECM wrote 'The Song of Winnie-Ha-Ha' on 29 April 1939 on Edmonton's MacDonald Hotel stationery.
13 ECM, letter to Elsie, 3 June 1939.
14 ECM, 'Memoirs,' ch. 11, pp. 9–10.
15 *Philadelphia Record*, 3 August 1939.
16 *Philadelphia Evening Bulletin*, 3 August 1939.
17 ECM, 'Memoirs,' ch. 11, pp. 13–14.
18 ECM, letter to Walter F. Evans, 12 September 1939. Evans was manager of the VSO.

19 ECM, 'Hitler and Wagnerism,' lecture given to the Vancouver Institute, 7 October 1939. A more polished version appeared in the *Queen's Quarterly*, Summer 1941, pp. 97–105.

20 William Lyon Mackenzie King, letter to ECM, 13 September 1943.

21 William Lyon Mackenzie King, quoted in Irving Abella and Harold Troper, *None Is Too Many* (Toronto 1983), 36–7.

22 Ibid.

23 ECM, 'Memorandum Regarding Music in Canada's War Effort,' 8 September 1942. The date is pencilled in. It is possible that ECM refined and renamed the paper before sending it to King.

24 William Lyon Mackenzie King, letter to ECM.

25 ECM, 'The Future of Music in America,' *Proceedings of the Music Teachers National Association Conference*, Cleveland, 30 December 1940, pp. 28–40.

Chapter 11

1 ECM, letter to J.E. Hahn, 11 September 1939.

2 ECM, letter to Elsie, 18 June 1940.

3 Jocelyn Podhalicz, interview with the author, 17 March 1992.

4 There are various letters from ECM to prospective employers in the ECM fonds at the NLC.

5 Jocelyn Podhalicz, interview with the author.

6 ECM, 'The Arts in Wartime,' speech to the Toronto Board of Trade, 9 December 1940. An incendiary bomb destroyed Queen's Hall the following spring.

7 Other student presidents who went on to become prominent in the Canadian music scene include pianist Margaret-Ann Ireland, conductor George Crum, musicologist George Proctor, and writer Patricia Wardrop.

8 ECM, 'Memoirs,' ch. 12, p. 6.

9 ECM, 'Memorandum regarding Music in Canada's War Effort,' n.d.

10 See the ECM fonds at the NLC on the YMCA's aid to war prisoners.

11 ECM, 'Memoirs,' ch. 12, pp. 8–9.

12 See Eric Koch, *Deemed Suspect: A Wartime Blunder* (Toronto 1980).

13 ECM, letter to F.C. Blair, 6 March 1942. See also Abella and Troper, *None Is Too Many*.

14 Thomas Holland, letter to ECM, 4 March 1941. Holland was principal of Edinburgh University. Tovey had died in July 1940.

15 Adrian Boult, letter to ECM, 24 February 1941.

16 ECM, letter to Thomas Holland, 10 April 1941.

17 ECM, 'A Moment of Decision,' memorandum to C.A. Wainwright, October 1965.

18 *Toronto Globe and Mail*, 19 April 1941; *Toronto Daily Star*, 19 April 1941; *Toronto Evening Telegram*, 26 April 1941.

19 *Toronto Globe and Mail*, 27 June 1941; *Toronto Daily Star*, 5 July 1941.

20 *Toronto Globe and Mail,* 7 August 1941.

21 Charles Peaker, draft biography of ECM, 1958 (KMF).

22 ECM, letter to Elsie, 23 December 1941.

23 Samuel Richard Gaines, letter to ECM, 31 December 1941.

24 ECM, letter to Samuel Chotzinoff, 5 January 1942.

25 Hyman Goodman, letter to Keith MacMillan, 24 January 1988 (KMF).

26 ECM, 'Musical Composition in Canada,' *Culture,* vol. 3, 1942, p. 153.

27 Gladstone Murray, 'Broadcasting – Everybody's Business,' address to the Canadian Club, Ottawa, 14 January 1942.

28 ECM, letter to F.H. Deacon, 27 April 1942. The Mendelssohn Choir appointment was first announced on 1 October 1941 and subsequently approved by the TCM.

29 Chalmers, *Both Sides of the Street,* 122. Chalmers said the conservatory was 'virtually insolvent,' a bit of an exaggeration.

30 See Floyd Chalmers, 'Toccata,' *Saturday Night,* 12 February 1938, p. 11. 'Toccata' is a photo study of Reginald Stewart.

31 ECM, letter to Elsie, 5 May 1942.

32 ECM, quoted in the *Varsity,* 15 December 1943. The *Varsity* is a University of Toronto student newspaper. The portrait is now at the Edward Johnson Building, University of Toronto.

33 Harvey Perrin, interview with the author, 20 November 1991.

34 ECM, notes prepared for Lazare Saminsky.

35 Ralph Vaughan Williams, 'Conducting,' *Grove's Dictionary of Music and Musicians,* 5th ed., ed. Eric Blom (London 1954).

36 Maud McLean, 'Sir Ernest: A Tower of Strength in Choral Music,' *The Canadian Composer,* July 1973, p. 30.

37 Maud McLean, interview with the author, 22 December 1992.

38 William Rogers, interview with the author, 2 February 1993.

39 Unidentified quotation.

40 *Toronto Globe and Mail,* 30 December 1942.

41 ECM, quoted in the *Toronto Globe and Mail,* 21 December 1946.

42 ECM, review of Handel's *Messiah,* ed. Watkins Shaw (London 1958), *CMJ,* Winter 1960, pp. 57–60.

43 These RCA Victor recordings include Elgar's *Pomp and Circumstance Marches, Op. 39, Nos. 1–4,* Gustav Holst's *The Planets,* Gordon Jacobs's *A William Byrd Suite,* and the 'Haydn Serenade.'

44 Jack Elton, quoted in the *Toronto Daily Star,* 17 October 1944.

45 *Toronto Globe and Mail,* 19 August 1943.

46 ECM, 'Memoirs,' ch. 12, p. 8.

47 Ibid., ch. 12, p. 8.

48 Dmitri Shostakovich, letter to ECM, 23 June 1943. Shostakovich also asked ECM to convey his greetings to Boris Fedorovich Berlin, 'about whose pedagogical work, we Soviet musicians are well informed.'

49 ECM, speech given at the Royal York Hotel, Toronto, 22 June 1943.

50 David Josephson, 'Grainger, (George) Percy (Aldridge),' *The New Grove Dictionary of American Music*, ed. H. Wiley Hitchcock and Stanley Sadie (London 1986).
51 Percy Grainger, letter to ECM, 21 November 1945.

Chapter 12

1 ECM, letter to Bernard Heinze, 14 May 1937.
2 Arthur Judson, letter to ECM, 4 September 1937.
3 Davidson Dunton, letter to ECM, 25 October 1944. Dunton was general manager of Canada's Wartime Information Board.
4 Eugene Ormandy, letter to ECM, 8 November 1944.
5 ECM, letter to Davidson Dunton, 27 October 1944.
6 ECM, 'A Canadian Musician in Australia,' CBC broadcast, 31 August 1945.
7 *Sydney Morning Herald*, 14 April 1945.
8 *Sydney Morning Herald*, 23 April 1945.
9 Neville Cardus, letter to ECM, 3 May 1945.
10 ECM, letter to Neville Cardus, 7 May 1945.
11 ECM, 'Music Critics, by One of Their Targets,' *TSO News*, September 1963.
12 *Australian Women's Weekly*, 5 May 1945.
13 Unidentified press clipping.
14 *Melbourne Sun*, n.d.
15 ECM, 'Memoirs,' ch. 10, p. 8.
16 Ibid., Ch 10, p. 1.
17 *Toronto Globe and Mail*, 10 August 1945.
18 N.K. Ryan, letter to ECM, 11 May 1944.
19 ECM, letter to N.K. Ryan, 5 June 1944.
20 Claude Champagne, letter to ECM, 15 August 1945.
21 Claude Champagne, letter to ECM, 5 September 1945.
22 ECM, letter to Claude Champagne, 14 November 1945.
23 José Siqueira, letter to ECM, 6 December 1945.
24 T.W.L. MacDermot, letter to ECM, 30 January 1946.
25 Jean Desy, wire to ECM, 4 March 1946.
26 Claude Champagne, letter to ECM, 17 April 1946.
27 Bruno Zirato, letter to ECM, 18 April 1946.
28 Walter Brown, letter to José Siqueira, 25 May 1946.
29 Elsie MacMillan, 'Rio in Retrospect' (unpublished diary).
30 Ibid. The author visited Rio twenty-five years later and found conditions much the same.
31 ECM, 'Rolling Round in Rio,' *TSO News*, December 1946.
32 ECM, diary of the Rio trip, book 2, p. 42.
33 José Siqueira, quoted in the *Toronto Globe and Mail*, 4 September 1946.
34 ECM, quoted in the *Toronto Evening Telegram*, 2 October 1946.
35 ECM, 'Rolling Round in Rio.'

36 ECM, address at Toronto's civic reception, 10 October 1946.
37 Keith MacMillan, interview with Whitney Smith, 7 June 1981 (KMF).
38 *The Toronto Symphony under the Direction of Sir Ernest MacMillan*, National Film Board film, 01–45–119, 01–45–120.
39 ECM, quoted in *Le Soleil* (Quebec City), 20 March 1947.
40 *Washington Post*, 14 February 1946.
41 *Indianapolis Star*, 4 February 1946.
42 *Buffalo Courier-Express*, 6 March 1950.
43 Arnold Edinborough, *A Personal History of the Toronto Symphony* (Toronto 1972).
44 Ibid. Edinborough points out that, for many years, the women's committee raised more money than did the directors. In 1947–8, for example, the women raised $30,000 and the directors $22,000.
45 Elie Spivak, letter to ECM, 3 April 1948.
46 Elie Spivak, letter to ECM, 10 May 1948.
47 ECM, letter to Elie Spivak, n.d.
48 Jack Elton, quoted in the *Toronto Daily Star*, 14 May 1948.
49 Paul Scherman, interview with Keith MacMillan, 12 December 1984 (KMF). ECM conducted the Bartók on 31 January 1950.
50 Heinz Unger, letter to ECM, 6 October 1944.
51 Victor Feldbrill, interview with the author, 21 November 1991.
52 Heinz Unger, letter to ECM, 6 October 1949.
53 *Toronto Evening Telegram*, 15 January 1947.
54 *Toronto Globe and Mail*, 15 January 1947.
55 Patricia Parr now teaches at the University of Toronto and is a leading sonata and chamber music player.

Chapter 13

1 Wayne Gilpin, *Sunset on the St. Lawrence* (Oakville, Ont., 1984), 68–74.
2 Floyd Chalmers, letter to Leslie Frost, 22 December 1944. Frost was the provincial treasurer (UTA). See also Chalmers, *Both Sides of the Street*, 188.
3 Tom Canning, also an Eastman graduate, was appointed to teach musical theory, but he left after a year.
4 Robert Rosevear, tape prepared for the author, 6 November 1992.
5 ECM, memorandum to Sidney Smith, 29 October 1948 (UTA).
6 Harvey Perrin, interview with the author, 20 November 1991.
7 ECM, quoted in the *Toronto Globe and Mail*, 2 October 1946.
8 ECM, letter to Vincent Massey, 29 February 1944.
9 Elizabeth Wynn Wood, letter to ECM, 19 April 1944. Her article was published in the March–April 1944 issue of *Canadian Art*, pp. 93–5, 127–8.
10 ECM, letter to Elizabeth Wynn Wood, 28 April 1944.
11 House of Commons. Special Committee on Reconstruction and Re-establishment. *Minutes of Proceedings and Evidence*, no. 10, 21 June 1944. See Appendix J, pp. 373–4, for the music brief.

12 *Toronto Globe and Mail,* 22 June 1944.
13 'Report of the first National Meeting of the Council,' 2 July 1946 (Robert Creech papers).
14 CMCI, 'Brief to the Royal Commission on National Development in the Arts, Letters and Sciences' (Robert Creech papers). It was one of about thirty-five from music groups nationwide.
15 ECM, 'Music,' *Royal Commission Studies* (Ottawa 1951), 353–67. Ernest's essay was one of twenty-eight solicited by the commission.
16 Royal Commission on National Development in the Arts, Letters and Sciences, 1949–1951. *Report* (Ottawa 1951).
17 Paul Litt, 'The Care and Feeding of Canadian Culture,' *Toronto Globe and Mail,* 31 May 1991. See also Paul Litt, *The Muses, the Masses, and the Massey Commission* (Toronto 1992).
18 CAPAC became the successor to the Canadian performing Rights Society in 1945 and was in turn succeeded by the Society of Composers, Authors and Music Publishers of Canada (SOCAN) in 1990.
19 ECM, quoted in a TSO news release, 8 January 1948.
20 *Toronto Globe and Mail,* 11 March 1950.
21 Helmut Kallmann, 'The Canadian League of Composers/La Ligue canadienne de compositeurs,' *EMC2,* 201.
22 John Weinzweig, interview with the author, 2 December 1992.
23 Sandy Stewart, conversation with the author, 22 January 1993. Stewart, a CBC radio and television producer, was at the concert with Keith MacMillan and sat immediately behind ECM and Elsie.
24 *Financial Post,* 3 April 1948.
25 Cantata No. 53 is now thought to be by Melchior Hoffmann, not Bach.
26 Keith MacMillan, 'Parallel Tracks,' 11.
27 D.W. Insley, letter to ECM, 27 July 1951.

Chapter 14

1 Sidney Smith, letter to Edward Johnson, 18 February 1948 (UTA).
2 Edward Johnson, letter to Sidney Smith, 21 June 1951 (UTA).
3 ECM, letter to Sidney Smith, 6 March 1952 (UTA).
4 Sidney Smith, letter to ECM, 7 March 1952 (UTA).
5 ECM, letter to Sidney Smith, 18 March 1952 (UTA).
6 Ettore Mazzoleni, letter to Sidney Smith, 18 March 1952 (UTA).
7 Sidney Smith, letter to Edward Johnson, 20 March 1952 (UTA).
8 ECM, letter to Sidney Smith, 22 March 1952 (UTA).
9 ECM, 'Summary and Commentary on My Correspondence with the President of the University of Toronto,' n.d.
10 Andrea Mazzoleni, interview with author, 12 December 1991.
11 ECM, letter to Sidney Smith, 10 April 1952 (UTA).
12 Sidney Smith, letter to ECM, 14 April 1952 (UTA).
13 Keith MacMillan, letter to Whitney Smith, 6 July 1982 (KMF).

14 ECM, letter to members of the Faculty of Music, 21 April 1952 (Robert Rosevear papers).
15 Ettore Mazzoleni, letter to Edward Johnson, 22 April 1952 (UTA).
16 Ettore Mazzoleni, letter to faculty members of the Conservatory, 23 April 1952 (UTA).
17 *Toronto Globe and Mail*, 28 April 1952.
18 R.H. Loken, letter to Sidney Smith, 29 April 1952 (UTA).
19 Eric Phillips, quoted in the *Toronto Daily Star*, 28 April 1952.
20 *Toronto Globe and Mail*, 2 May 1952.
21 John Weinzweig, interview with the author, 2 December 1992.
22 R.H. Loken, wire to Ettore Mazzoleni; Mazzoleni, wire to R.H. Loken, 3 May 1952 (UTA).
23 *Toronto Globe and Mail*, 7 May 1952.
24 Elsie MacMillan, letter to Dalton Wells, n.d. Wells was later chief justice of the High Court of Ontario.
25 ECM, quoted in the *Toronto Globe and Mail*, 28 April 1952.
26 ECM, letter to Kate Buckerfield, 25 April 1952.

Chapter 15

1 'Summary of Reports on Twenty-Nine Symphony Orchestras,' Conference of Managers, Denver, Colorado, 3–5 June 1952.
2 Minneapolis's recording reputation had initially been made by Dorati's predecessor, Dimitri Mitropoulos.
3 ECM, 'The Sinews of Symphonies,' *TSO News*, October 1951.
4 Lois Marshall, interview with the author, 25 January 1993.
5 TSO, board minutes, 21 April 1952.
6 ECM, interview with a *Hamilton Spectator* reporter on the CHCH television program 'Portrait,' 1962 (KMF).
7 TMA, executive minutes, 16 May 1952.
8 *Toronto Globe and Mail*, 21 May 1952.
9 Walter Murdoch, quoted in the *Toronto Evening Telegram*, 21 May 1951.
10 *Toronto Daily Star*, 22 May 1952.
11 *Toronto Globe and Mail*, 22 May 1952.
12 TSO, board minutes, 26 May 1952.
13 *Toronto Globe and Mail*, 30 May 1952; *Toronto Daily Star*, 30 May 1952.
14 Morry Kernerman, interview with the author, 12 November 1991.
15 *Toronto Globe and Mail*, 30 May 1952.
16 *Toronto Globe and Mail*, 5 June 1992.
17 See Len Scher, *The Un-Canadians: True Stories of the Blacklist Era* (Toronto 1992) for oral accounts by Symphony Six members Ruth Budd and Steven Staryk, and by Harry Freedman, who was in the TSO and on the TMA executive at the time.
18 ECM, letter to Frank Park, 10 February 1947. Park was president of the Council for Canadian-Soviet Friendship.

19 ECM, letter to the editor, *Toronto Globe and Mail,* 5 July 1950.

20 Eleanor Roosevelt, quoted in *The New York Times,* 11 December 1950.

21 Trygve Lie, letter to ECM, 10 December 1950; ECM, letter to Lie, 12 December 1950.

22 ECM, letter to A.C. Nielsen, 1 November 1950. Nielsen was the American consul-general.

23 Immigration procedures for entry to the United States are carried out at major Canadian airports.

24 ECM, letter to the American Consulate, 10 January 1952.

25 Dan Cameron, letter to ECM, 22 October 1952; ECM letter to Cameron, 26 November 1952.

26 *Toronto Globe and Mail,* 15 August 1952.

27 John Moscow, quoted in the *Toronto Daily Star,* 15 August 1952.

28 *Toronto Daily Star,* 26 August 1952.

29 TSO, board minutes, 8 September 1952.

30 TSO, association minutes, 22 September 1952; *Toronto Daily Star,* 23 September 1952.

31 TSO, board minutes, 29 September 1952.

32 Lester Pearson, quoted in the *Toronto Globe and Mail,* 1 October 1952.

33 *Toronto Daily Star,* 2 September 1952.

34 ECM, letter to the American Consulate, 20 April 1953.

35 Gwenlyn Setterfield, interview with the author, 10 February 1993. Setterfield is the author of an unpublished biography of Staryk.

36 For a critical appraisal of the Symphony Six episode forty years after the fact, see Gerald Hannon, 'The Big Chill,' *Toronto Globe and Mail,* 29 February 1992, and responses to it from Ross MacMillan, 14 March 1992, and Robertson Davies, 21 March 1992.

37 TSO, board minutes, 12 January 1953.

38 Leslie Hannon, 'The Elegant Enigma of Sir Ernest,' *Mayfair,* February 1953, p. 59.

39 *Toronto Globe and Mail,* 23 June 1953; TSO, board minutes, 22 June 1953.

40 ECM, 'European Odyssey (... Potted Version),' *The Mendelssohn Chorister,* November 1952.

41 Ibid.

42 ECM, *Saturday Night,* 4 October 1952, pp. 10, 18. ECM, *TSO News,* April 1953.

43 ECM, *Saturday Night,* 18 October 1952, pp. 23–4.

44 Gwenlyn Setterfield, interview with the author.

45 ECM, *Saturday Night,* 25 October 1952, pp. 13, 18.

46 Ibid.

47 ECM, 'European Odyssey.'

48 *Salt Lake Tribune,* cited in *The Mendelssohn Chorister,* December 1953.

49 Leslie F. Hannon, 'The Elegant Enigma of Sir Ernest,' *Mayfair,* February 1953, pp. 29–31, 56–59, 64.

50 F.C.A. Jeanneret, letter to ECM, 25 March 1953.

51 ECM, letter to F.C.A. Jeanneret, 8 April 1953.

52 Ibid., 23 April 1953.

Chapter 16

1 The three recordings are: Handel's *Messiah*, Beaver LPS-001; Bach's *St Matthew Passion*, Beaver LPS-002; Handel's *Messiah* Highlights, Beaver LP-1003. They were issued in the United States by RCA Victor.

2 Beaver LPS-1002.

3 Fred MacKelcan, letter to ECM, 25 May 1953.

4 Alfred Frankenstein, *High Fidelity Magazine*, September 1954, p. 53.

5 C.G. Burke, *High Fidelity Magazine*, January 1955, p. 52.

6 Henry T. Finck, cited by Ocean G. Smith, in 'After Thirty Years,' *The Mendelssohn Chorister*, March 1954.

7 *The New York Times*, 28 April 1954.

8 *The New York World Telegram and Sun*, 28 April 1954.

9 *The New York Times*, 30 April 1954.

10 *The New York World Telegram and Sun*, 30 April 1954.

11 *New York Journal-American*, 30 April 1954.

12 *New York Herald Tribune*, 30 April 1954.

13 *Peterborough Examiner*, 27 March 1953.

14 *Toronto Globe and Mail*, 27 October 1954.

15 ECM, letter to Trevor Moore, 12 January 1955; repr. *TSO News*, March 1955.

16 TSO, board minutes, 13, 26 January 1955.

17 TSO, board minutes, 7 April 1955.

18 *Toronto Globe and Mail*, 13 April 1955.

19 *Toronto Globe and Mail*, 21 December 1955.

20 *Toronto Evening Telegram*, 9 April 1956.

21 ECM, quoted in the *Toronto Daily Star*, 10 April 1956.

22 John Beckwith, 'Music,' *The Culture of Contemporary Canada*, ed. Julian Park (Ithaca, NY, 1957), 149.

23 *Toronto Globe and Mail*, 18 January 1955.

24 *Toronto Globe and Mail*, 9 April 1956.

25 Nathan Phillips, on CKEY radio, 15 April 1956.

26 University of Rochester, citation for ECM, quoted in the *Toronto Globe and Mail*, 11 June 1956.

27 Walter Herbert, quoted in the *Toronto Globe and Mail*, 9 August 1956.

28 L.M. Allison, 'Mount Allison Summer Institute,' *CMJ*, Autumn 1956, p. 53.

29 *San Antonio News*, 28 February 1954.

30 *San Antonio Light*, 28 February 1954.

31 Letters and other information about ECM in England and Europe at that time are in the Sir Ernest MacMillan file at the BBC Written Archives Centre, RCONT1 – Sir Ernest MacMillan.

Chapter 17

1 Lester B. Pearson, letters to ECM, 13 February, 6 March 1953.
2 CMCl, brief to the Royal Commission on Patents, Copyrights, Trademarks and Industrial Designs, 14 October 1954 (Robert Creech papers).
3 John Mills, 'A Role in the Fight for the Protection of All Composers,' *The Canadian Composer,* July 1973, p. 36.
4 *Music in Canada,* ed. Ernest MacMillan (Toronto 1955).
5 *Toronto Globe and Mail,* 9 April 1955.
6 William Krehm, 'CBC Views the Shows,' 22 May 1955, transcript.
7 Geoffrey Payzant, interviews with the author, 26 February 1992, 16 February 1993. Payzant, interview with Keith MacMillan, 26 June 1986 (KMF).
8 CMCl, minutes, 5 November 1956 (Robert Creech papers).
9 ECM, quoted in the *Toronto Globe and Mail,* 26 June 1956.
10 Bernard Ostry, *The Cultural Connection* (Toronto 1978), 67–9. See also J.L. Granatstein, *Canada 1957–1967* (Toronto 1986).
11 Ostry, *Cultural Connection,* 67.
12 The Canada Council, *First Annual Report,* to 31 March 1958. All data about the council are from this report and annual reports which followed, unless noted otherwise.
13 CMCl, minutes, 24 November 1956 (Robert Creech papers).
14 Canada Council, *Third Annual Report,* 1959–60, p. 71.
15 Heinz Unger, letter to Albert Trueman, 28 July 1958.
16 ECM, letter to Albert Trueman, 6 August 1958.
17 Albert Trueman, 'An Obvious Choice to Help Begin the Canada Council,' *The Canadian Composer,* July 1973, p. 32.
18 ECM, 'Brief to the Canada Council Presented by the Canada [sic] Music Council,' undated but probably spring 1957 (Robert Creech papers).
19 'Memorandum of Agreement in the Application to the Secretary of State to Incorporate the Canadian Composers' Centre,' February 1958 (Robert Creech papers).
20 Jean Papineau-Couture, letter to ECM, 4 June 1958.
21 ECM, letter to Jean Papineau-Couture, 10 June 1958.

Chapter 18

1 *Toronto Globe and Mail,* 2 January 1957.
2 ECM, 'A Favourite Vacation Spot,' (unpublished, n.d.).
3 ECM, 'Memoirs,' introduction, p. 2.
4 ECM, 'Music and the Sea,' *Imperial Oil Fleet News,* Spring, 1956, pp. 3–5.
5 Adrian Boult, letter to ECM, 13 April 1957.
6 ECM, letter to Adrian Boult, 23 May 1957.
7 Charles Peaker, draft biography of Sir Ernest MacMillan (KMF).
8 Alexander Brott, letter to ECM, 11 May 1956.
9 ECM, letter to Alexander Brott, 25 May 1956.

10 Alexander Brott, letter to ECM, 25 July 1957; ECM, letters to Brott, 24 August 1957, 23 October 1957.

11 Alexander Brott, letter to ECM, 15 February 1959; ECM, letter to Brott, 20 February 1959.

12 Ian MacDonald, letter to Keith MacMillan, 5 July 1984 (KMF).

13 Keith MacMillan, letter to Ian MacDonald, 5 June 1984 (KMF).

14 Elsie MacMillan, letter to Keith and Patricia MacMillan, 16 October 1958 (KMF).

15 Ibid.

16 Maria (Baumeister) Kiors, interview with the author, 12 February 1992.

17 Ian MacDonald, letter to Keith MacMillan, 5 July 1984 (KMF).

18 Eddy Bayens, conversation with the author, 9 August 1993.

19 ECM, letter to Jack Elton, 24 April 1959.

20 Carl Little, letter to the author, 25 March 1993.

21 Ibid.

22 ECM, quoted in the *Toronto Globe and Mail*, 16 March 1963.

23 ECM, presentation to the Board of Broadcast Governors, 16 March 1960.

24 Elsie MacMillan, Christmas letter to friends, December 1960.

25 Gilles Lefebvre, letter to the author, April 1993.

26 Graham George, 'International Folk Music Council,' *CMJ*, Autumn 1961, pp. 36–8.

27 *Three French Canadian Sea Songs* (1930).

28 TSO, board minutes, 8 January 1962.

29 CMCl, minutes, 5 May 1952.

30 ECM, 'Announcement to Our Readers,' *CMJ*, Summer 1962, p. 3.

31 Geoffrey Payzant, 'The Competitive Music Festivals,' *CMJ*, Spring 1960, pp. 35–46.

32 ECM, 'The Music Festival Controversy,' *CMJ*, Autumn 1960, pp. 30–2.

33 ECM, 'Problems of Music in Canada,' *Yearbook of the Arts in Canada 1936*, ed. Bertram Brooker (Toronto 1936), 199. Also cited in Maria Tippett, *Making Culture* (Toronto 1990), 56.

34 Keith MacMillan, 'Parallel Tracks,' 9.

35 CMCl Conference Report, 'The Pros and Cons of the Festival Movement in Canada,' Toronto, 9, 10 April 1965 (Robert Creech papers).

36 *Proceedings*, CMCl Annual Meeting and Conference, 'Music in Canada, Its Resources and Needs,' Ottawa, 31 March, 1, 2 April 1966 (author's papers).

37 ECM, 'Brief of the Canadian Music Council to the Fowler Committee on Broadcasting,' 26 February 1965 (Robert Creech papers).

38 Keith MacMillan, CMC, 'Summary Report of Activities for 1967,' 6 April 1968 (Robert Creech papers).

Chapter 19

1 Ian Dobbin, *Music across Canada*, July–August 1963, p. 43.

2 Ibid.

3 Robert Creech, interview with the author, 8 September 1991.

4 *Vancouver Province*, 7 December 1963.

5 Claude Bissell, letter to ECM, 26 January 1962 (UTA).

6 ECM, quoted in the *Toronto Globe and Mail*, 3 March 1962.

7 ECM, paper given at the opening of the Edward Johnson Building, 2 March 1964.

8 Oskar Morawetz, interview with the author, 30 October 1992.

9 ECM, 'Elie Spivak As I Knew Him,' *TSO News*, October 1960.

10 ECM, 'Rowland Pack,' *TSO News*, January 1964.

11 *Toronto Daily Star*, 24 November 1951. Dinicu composed the charming miniature 'Hora Staccato,' and Jascha Heifetz popularized it.

12 Clare (Mazzoleni) Piller, interview with the author, 14 February 1992.

13 Donald MacMillan, interview with Whitney Smith, 23 June 1982 (KMF). Donald MacMillan, interviews with the author, 17 February 1992, 1 April 1993.

14 Andrea Mazzoleni, interview with the author, 12 December 1991.

15 Keith MacMillan, interview with Whitney Smith (KMF).

16 R. Murray Schafer, letter to ECM, 18 September 1963.

17 Alfred Whitehead, 'What a Man! What a Wife!' *Music across Canada*, July–August 1963, p. 44.

18 Gordon Hallett, interview with the author, 6 January 1992.

19 Boris Berlin, letter to ECM, 18 August 1963.

Chapter 20

1 The University of British Columbia had awarded Marjorie an honorary doctorate the year before; Ernest had written a letter of support to the university's president John B. MacDonald on 30 March 1961, when she was first being considered for the degree.

2 ECM, letter to Marjorie Agnew, 2 April 1965.

3 ECM, letter to Marjorie Agnew, 20 April 1965.

4 Elsie MacMillan, letter to Keith MacMillan and family, 16 June 1966.

5 ECM, 'Sir Ernest's Christmas Album,' CBC radio, 25 December 1967.

6 William Littler, 'Sir Ernest Laudamus,' *Toronto Star TV Weekly*, 14 December 1968.

7 *Toronto Evening Telegram*, 15 April 1968.

8 ECM, letter to Arnold Walter, 28 March 1968.

9 ECM, CBC interview with John Beckwith, 'Words about Music,' 28 November 1968.

10 ECM, 'Some Reminiscences of Marius Barbeau,' *Musicanada*, April 1969, pp. 10–11, 15.

11 Ibid.

12 ECM, letter to Marjorie Agnew, 24 September 1969.

13 Elsie MacMillan, letter to Kay Irwin Wells, n.d., but following Ernest's death.
14 Clifford McAree, letter to Keith MacMillan, 2 May 1985 (KMF).
15 Elsie MacMillan, letter to Kay Irwin Wells.
16 Frances Gage, interview with the author, 13 February 1992.
17 Elsie MacMillan, letter to Kay Irwin Wells.
18 William Littler, conversation with the author, 10 July 1993.
19 ECM, 'This I Believe,' on Edward R. Murrow's CBS show, 31 December 1954.
20 Robertson Davies, 'A Leader of Us Who Faced the Music,' *The Canadian Composer*, July 1973, p. 16.

Interviews

With Keith MacMillan:

Frances James Adaskin, Marcus Adeney, Louis Applebaum, Paul Baby, John Beckwith, Hunter Bishop, Ian Cameron, Victor Feldbrill, Reginald Godden (and Harry Somers), Flora Goulden, Richard Johnston, Greta Kraus, Trudi Le Caine, Brock McElheran, Zara Nelsova, Geoffrey Payzant, Anna Russell, Paul Scherman, Molly Sclater, Harold Sumberg, Muriel Dagger Temple, and Kay Irwin Wells.

With Ezra Schabas:

Louis Applebaum, John Beckwith, Helen Bickell, Edith Binnie, John Cozens, Victor Feldbrill, Frances Gage, Gordon Hallett, Maria Baumeister Kiors, John Lawson, Marion LeBel, Roy Loken, Donald MacMillan, Patricia MacMillan, Ross MacMillan, Lois Marshall, Mary Mason, Andrea Mazzoleni, Oskar Morawetz, Geoffrey Payzant, Harvey Perrin, Clare (Mazzoleni) Piller, Jocelyn Podhalicz, Laure Rièse, Paul Scherman, Muriel Gidley Stafford, Jean Tory, Nora van Nostrand Wedd, John Weinzweig, and Ethelwyn Wickson.

Archival Material

The Sir Ernest MacMillan fonds is housed in the Music Division of the National Library of Canada in Ottawa. These archives consist of some 17.5 metres of documents, 284 sound recordings, and over 800 photographs. The fonds is divided into 14 series: Career and Other Activities/Subject Files; Correspondence; Compositions; Writings; Programmes; Sound Recordings; Writings about MacMillan by Others; Sir Ernest MacMillan Fine Arts Clubs of Canada; Photographs and Drawings; Personal Documents; Awards, Honours, Titles; Financial Documents; MacMillan's Library; Memorabilia. Certain documents are under restriction.

The Keith MacMillan fonds includes correspondence, audiotapes and discs, photographs, programs, music, and other material. Keith MacMillan also prepared a daily diary of Sir Ernest's life, a selection of excerpts from Sir Ernest's and Lady MacMillan's letters, and numerous listings including Sir Ernest's TSO programs, his writings and speeches, articles about him, concert reviews, photographs, and audiotapes. The Keith MacMillan fonds has been deposited in the National Library.

The CBC archives in Toronto and Ottawa have many audiotapes and some kinescopes of interest to ECM researchers. Sir Ernest conducted the Toronto Symphony Orchestra on CBC broadcasts from the late 1930s until 1956. The CBC did several revealing radio interviews with him: 'Experience of Life,' interview by Ron Hambleton, 26 February 1955; 'Assignment,' interviews by Tony Thomas, five shows 17–21 June 1957; interview by Clyde Gilmour, 29 August 1966; and interview by John Beckwith, 28 November 1968. Warren Davies interviewed him on CBC television on 'The Day It Is,' 20 November 1968.

Sir Ernest also appeared on many CBC radio and television music and talk shows in the 1960s. On 11 May 1973, shortly after his death, CBC radio broadcast a two-hour program titled 'Tribute to Sir Ernest MacMillan,' which included some of his music and featured commentaries by leading musicians who knew him well. On 30 September 1974, the CBC did a radio documentary, 'MacMillan and Barbeau on the Nass River,' which included recordings of the work the two men did together in 1927. In August and September 1982, Whitney Smith presided over 'Sir Ernest MacMillan, the Music Builder,' six one-hour radio documentaries dealing with MacMillan's life. Louis Applebaum, Floyd Chalmers, Robertson Davies, Keith MacMillan, and Godfrey Ridout were among the participants. Smith also did two one-hour shows on Sir Ernest and Arnold Walter in 1983. The CBC radio archives (Toronto) has prepared a partial list of its holdings of tapes that MacMillan did for the CBC.

The Toronto Symphony Orchestra archives contain board and players' committee minutes, programs, TSO publications, audiotapes of interviews with players, photographs, scrapbooks, and memorabilia. The University of Toronto archives have Royal Conservatory and Faculty of Music correspondence, board minutes, journals, and miscellaneous material. The archives of the Toronto Mendelssohn Choir, the BBC Written Archives Centre, the Toronto Arts and Letters Club, the Metropolitan Toronto Reference Library (Music Section), and the Toronto Musicians' Association include relevant correspondence, articles, minutes, and other material. The Canadian Music Centre (Toronto) has a considerable collection of MacMillan scores and audiotapes.

Bibliography

Selected Books and Parts of Books

Abella, Irving, and Harold Troper. *None Is Too Many.* Toronto: Lester Publishing Limited, 1983.

Beckwith, John. 'MacMillan, Sir Ernest.' In *Encyclopedia of Music in Canada*, 2d ed, edited by Helmut Kallmann and Gilles Potvin, 788–91. Toronto: University of Toronto Press, 1992.

– 'Music.' In *The Culture of Contemporary Canada*, edited by Julian Park, 143–63. Ithaca, NY: Cornell University Press, 1957.

Bothwell, Robert, et al. *Canada 1900–1945.* Toronto: University of Toronto Press, 1987.

Canada Council. *Annual Reports.* 1958–63.

The Canadian Musical Heritage Series. Ottawa: Canadian Musical Heritage Society, 1984–93. Vol. 5: John Beckwith, ed. *Hymn Tunes* (includes scores of four MacMillan hymns); Vol. 8: Helmut Kallmann, ed. *Music for Orchestra* (includes MacMillan's Overture); Vol. 13: Robin Elliott, ed. *Chamber Music II: String Quartets* (includes MacMillan's String Quartet and *Two Sketches*); Vol. 14: Frederick A. Hall, ed. *Songs IV to English Texts* (includes scores of seven of MacMillan's songs).

Careless, J.M.S. *Canada: A Story of Challenge.* Toronto: Stoddart, 1970.

Chalmers, Floyd S. *Both Sides of the Street: One Man's Life in Business and the Arts in Canada.* Toronto: Macmillan, 1983.

Cohen, Israel. *The Ruhleben Prison Camps.* London: Methuen, 1917.

Edinborough, Arnold. *A Personal History of the Toronto Symphony.* Toronto: Rothmans, 1972.

Filion, John, ed. *The Canadian World Almanac 1988.* Toronto: Global Press, 1987.

Granatstein, J.L. *Canada 1957–1967: The Years of Uncertainty and Innovation.* Toronto: McClelland and Stewart, 1986.

Green, J. Paul, and Nancy F. Vogan. *Music Education in Canada: A Historical Account.* Toronto: University of Toronto Press, 1991.

Hitchcock, H. Wiley, and Stanley Sadie, eds. *The New Grove Dictionary of American Music.* London: Macmillan, 1986.

Hollins, Alfred. *A Blind Musician Looks Back.* London: W. Blackwood, 1938.

House of Commons. Special Committee on Reconstruction and Establishment, *Minutes of Proceedings and Evidence,* no. 10, 21 June 1944. See Appendix J, pp. 373–4, for the music brief.

Jones, Gaynor. 'The Fisher Years: The Toronto Conservatory of Music 1881–1913.' *Three Studies,* CanMus Documents 4. Toronto: Institute for Canadian Music, 1989.

Kallmann, Helmut. *A History of Music in Canada 1534–1914.* Toronto: University of Toronto Press, 1960. Reprint, 1987.

Kallmann, Helmut, and Gilles Potvin, eds. *Encyclopedia of Music in Canada,* 2d ed. Toronto: University of Toronto Press, 1992.

Ketchum, J. Davidson. *Ruhleben: A Prison Camp Society.* Toronto: University of Toronto Press, 1965.

Kilbourn, William. *Intimate Grandeur: One Hundred Years at Massey Hall.* Toronto: Stoddart, 1993.

Lazarevich, Gordana. *The Musical World of Frances James and Murray Adaskin.* Toronto: University of Toronto Press, 1988.

Litt, Paul. *The Muses, the Masses, and the Massey Commission.* Toronto: University of Toronto Press, 1992.

MacMillan, Alexander, and W.S. Milner, eds. *The University Hymn Book.* Oxford: Oxford University Press, 1912.

MacMillan, Keith. 'Ernest MacMillan: The Ruhleben Years.' In *Musical Canada: Words and Music Honouring Helmut Kallmann,* edited by John Beckwith and Frederick A. Hall, 164–82. Toronto: University of Toronto Press, 1988.

– 'Parallel Tracks: Ernest MacMillan in the 1930s and 1940s.' In *Canadian Music in the 1930s and 1940s,* edited by Beverley Cavanagh, 2–14. [Kingston, Ont.: Queen's University School of Music, 1987].

MacMillan, Keith, and John Beckwith, eds. *Contemporary Canadian Composers.* Toronto: Oxford University Press, 1975.

Marsh, James H., ed. *The Canadian Encyclopedia.* Edmonton: Hurtig Publishers, 1985.

[McLean, Maud]. *A Responsive Chord: The Story of the Toronto Mendelssohn Choir 1894–1969.* Toronto: Toronto Mendelssohn Choir, 1969.

Ostry, Bernard. *The Cultural Connection.* Toronto: McClelland and Stewart, 1978.

Proctor, George A. *Canadian Music of the Twentieth Century.* Toronto: University of Toronto Press, 1980.

Royal Commission on National Development in the Arts, Letters and Sciences, 1949–51. *Report.* Ottawa: Edmond Cloutier, 1951.

Scher, Len. *The Un-Canadians, True Stories of the Blacklist Era.* Toronto: Lester Publishing Limited, 1992.

Thompson, John Herd, with Allen Seager. *Canada 1922–1939: Decades of Discord.* Toronto: McClelland and Stewart, 1985.

Tippett, Maria. *Making Culture: English-Canadian Institutions and the Arts before the Massey Commission.* Toronto: University of Toronto Press, 1990.

Walter, Arnold, ed. *Aspects of Music in Canada.* Toronto: University of Toronto Press, 1969.

Westfall, William. *Two Worlds: The Protestant Culture of Nineteenth-Century Ontario.* Montreal and Kingston: McGill-Queen's University Press, 1989.

Selected Articles

Barbeau, Marius. 'Canadian Folk Songs As a National Asset.' *Conservatory Quarterly Review* (Summer 1928), 154–7.

– 'The Thunder Bird of the Mountains.' *University of Toronto Quarterly* (October 1932), 92–110.

Beckwith, John. 'Tributes: Sir Ernest MacMillan (1893–1973).' *Music* (August 1973), 19. (*Music* is a publication of the American Guild of Organists and the Royal Canadian College of Organists.)

Charlesworth, Hector. 'Hugh the Drover.' *Saturday Night* (23 November 1929), 7, 14.

'Chicago Convention Soars to High Point.' *The Diapason* (1 September 1922), 3.

[Gardner, George]. 'A New Choral Writer.' *Musical Times* (1 September 1920), 620–1.

Godden, Reginald. 'Ernest Alexander Campbell MacMillan.' *Arts and Letters Monthly Letter* (September 1973).

Hannon, Leslie F. 'The Elegant Enigma of Sir Ernest.' *Mayfair* (February 1953), 29–31, 56–9, 64.

'Hugh the Drover.' *Musical Courier* (30 November 1929), 26, 34.

Kraglund, John. 'Sir Ernest's 75th: Special Musical Celebration.' *The Canadian Composer* (December 1968), 12–13.

Littler, William. 'Sir Ernest Laudamus.' *Toronto Star TV Weekly* (14 December 1968).

'Lord's Day Alliance.' *Saturday Night* (26 March 1921), 102.

MacKelcan, F.R. 'Sir Ernest MacMillan.' *Queen's Quarterly* (Winter 1936–7), 408–14.

MacMillan, Elsie. 'Life with Ernest.' *TSO News* (October 1949).

MacMillan, Keith. 'Unforgettable Sir Ernest MacMillan.' *Reader's Digest* (February 1978), 56–60.

Mason, Lawrence. 'Of Orchestra Concerts.' *Toronto Globe* (22, 29 December 1934; 12, 19, 26 January 1935).

McStay, Angus. 'Prodigy's Progress.' *Maclean's* (October 1940), 16, 36–9.

'Sir Ernest MacMillan, 1893–1973.' *The Canadian Composer* (July 1973). (This issue, which appeared two months after Sir Ernest's death, is devoted entirely to him. It includes contributions from leading Canadian musicians and writers.)

Smith, Ocean G. 'After Thirty Years.' *The Mendelssohn Chorister* (March 1954).

Smith, Whitney. 'Reassessing Sir Ernest MacMillan.' *The Canadian Composer* (May 1983), 28, 30

Stafford, Muriel Gidley. 'Tributes: Sir Ernest MacMillan,(1893–1973).' *Music* (August 1973), 19. (*Music* is a publication of the American Guild of Organists and the Royal Canadian College of Organists.)

A Tribute to Sir Ernest MacMillan.' *Music across Canada* (July–August 1963). (This issue is devoted entirely to ECM to mark his seventieth birthday. It includes contributions from leading Canadian musicians and writers.)

Winters, Kenneth. 'Sir Ernest at Seventy-five.' *Toronto Evening Telegram* (10 August 1968).

Unpublished Papers

Canadian Music Council, 1949–68. Minutes, including those for the Music Committee, 1944–9 (Robert Creech papers).

– 'Brief to the Royal Commission on Patents, Copyrights, Trademarks and Industrial Designs,' 14 October 1954 (Creech papers).

– ECM, 'Brief to the Canada Council Presented by the Canada [sic] Music Council,' undated but probably Spring 1957 (Creech papers).

– 'Memorandum of Agreement in the Application to the Secretary of State to Incorporate the Canadian Composers' Centre,' February 1958 (Creech papers).

– ECM, 'Brief of the Canadian Music Council to the Fowler Committee on Broadcasting,' 26 February 1965 (Creech papers).

– Conference Report, 'The Pros and Cons of the Festival Movement in Canada,' Toronto, 9, 10 April 1965 (Creech papers).

– *Proceedings*, Annual Meeting and Conference, 'Music in Canada, Its Resources and Needs,' Ottawa, 31 March, 1, 2 April 1966 (Author's papers).

Clifford, N. Keith. 'The Contribution of Alexander MacMillan to Canadian Hymnody,' (n.d.) (KMF).

Elliott, Robert W.A. (Robin). 'The String Quartet in Canada,' Ph.D. dissertation, University of Toronto, 1990.

Hutcheson, Ernest. 'Report on a Short Survey of the Toronto Conservatory of Music,' (n.d.) (UTA).

Killmaster, Frederick George. 'Reminiscences of a Canadian Musician,' (n.d.) (Author's papers).

MacMillan, Alexander. 'Looking Back: Reminiscences of the Rev. Alexander MacMillan, D.D., Mus.D., 1864–1961.' Edited by Keith and Patricia MacMillan (1987–8) (KMF).

MacMillan, Keith. Alphabetical and chronological lists of Sir Ernest's periodical articles and speeches (KMF).

– CMC, 'Summary Report of Activities for 1967.' 6 April 1968 (Robert Creech papers).

– 'Diary of Sir Ernest MacMillan.' (KMF). (This is a chronological diary with over 3,000 entries in the life of Sir Ernest MacMillan.)

– Draft biography (five chapters) of Sir Ernest MacMillan (KMF).
– 'Toronto Symphony Orchestra Programmes, 1931–1956.' (KMF). (These are computerized lists of program information by date, composer and work, conductor, soloist, type of concert, and Canadian music.)

Olmsted, Evangeline Harris. 'Dorothy MacMillan 1909–1940.' (Jocelyn Podhalicz papers).

Peaker, Charles. 'Draft biography and notes of Sir Ernest MacMillan.' 1958 (KMF).

Ross, Alexander. 'Reminiscences of the Reverend Alexander Ross, May 1830–December 1919.' Edited by Keith and Patricia MacMillan (1988) (KMF).

Rowe, Irene. 'The History and Development of School Concerts by the Toronto Symphony Orchestra from 1925 to 1957,' M.M. dissertation, University of Western Ontario, 1989.

Smith, Whitney. 'Sir Ernest MacMillan and Dr. Arnold Walter: A Counterpoint of Musical Heritage.' (1983) (Author's papers).

Selected Writings by Sir Ernest MacMillan

These writings are principally in the Sir Ernest MacMillan fonds, Music Division, National Library of Canada. They are listed here in chronological order.

Books and Parts of Books

'Problems of Music in Canada.' *Yearbook of the Arts in Canada*, vol. 2, edited by Bertram Brooker, 185–200. Toronto: Macmillan, 1936.

– and Boris Berlin. *The Modern Piano Student.* Oakville, Ont.: Frederick Harris, 1937.

On the Preparation of Ear Tests. Oakville, Ont.: Frederick Harris, 1938.

– and Boris Berlin. *Twenty-One Lessons in Ear-Training.* Oakville, Ont.: Frederick Harris, 1939.

– and Healey Willan. *Graded Sight-Reading Exercises for Piano.* Oakville, Ont.: Frederick Harris, 1939.

'Music in Canada.' *Royal Commission Studies*, 353–67. Ottawa: King's Printer, 1951.

'Introduction' and 'Choral Music.' *Music in Canada*, edited by Ernest MacMillan. Toronto: University of Toronto Press, 1955.

'Music – Concert Performance.' *Encyclopedia Canadiana*, edited by John Robbins, 222–8. Toronto: Grolier, 1958; rev. eds. 1966, 1975.

'Canada.' *La Musica, Parte Prima: Enciclopedia Storica*, 43–6. Turin: Unione Tipografico Editrice Torinese, 1966.

Articles

'Potted Music.' *Canadian Forum* (January 1922), 496–7.

'Tendencies in Modern British Music.' Parts 1 and 2. *Canadian Forum* (July 1923), 308–10; (September 1923), 371–2.

'Our Musical Public.' *Canadian Forum* (July 1924), 306–8.

'A Few Aphorisms.' *Conservatory Quarterly Review* (February 1925), 10.

'The University and Music.' *University of Toronto Quarterly* (March 1926), 263–4.

'Music at the Educational Conference.' *Conservatory Quarterly Review* (Spring 1926), 85–7.

'The Place of Music in a University Curriculum.' *Canadian Universities Conference Report* (31 May–2 June 1927), 66–75.

'The Folk Song Festival at Quebec.' *Conservatory Quarterly Review* (Summer 1927), 130.

'The Musical Amateur.' *Toronto Globe* (15 September 1927). (This was a special music edition.)

'Some Notes on Schubert.' *The School* (October 1927), 120–5.

'The Musical Season in Toronto.' *Canadian Forum* (May 1928), 642–3.

'Suggestions for a Course of Music Study for High Schools.' *Ontario Educational Association Report* (1928), 188–91.

'Hymns and Hymn Singing.' *The Diapason* (1 October 1929), 32–3.

'Choral and Church Music.' *Conservatory Quarterly Review* (Winter 1929), 57, 59.

'Organ Accompaniments in Church Services.' Parts 1 and 2. *Conservatory Quarterly Review* (Winter 1931), 46–8; (Spring 1931), 109–12.

'Impressions of the Lausanne Conference.' *Conservatory Quarterly Review* (Autumn 1931), 6–7.

'Musical Relations Between Canada and the U.S.A.' *Proceedings of the Music Teachers' National Association* (1931), 36–44.

'Music Education in Canada.' *Music Supervisors National Conference Yearbook* (1932), 80–5.

'Those Music Exams.' *Chatelaine* (November 1933), 15, 48, 62.

'Three Notable English Composers.' *Conservatory Quarterly Review* (August 1934), 5–9.

'School Life and Music.' *Annual of the Ontario Educational Association* (1934), 89–93.

'The Value of Music in Education.' *University of Toronto Monthly* (June 1936), 285–7.

'Music and Adult Education.' *Saint John Telegraph-Journal* (12 February 1938).

'Canadian Musical Life.' *Canadian Geographical Journal* (December 1939), 330–6.

'Hitler and Wagnerism.' *Queen's Quarterly* (Summer 1941), 97–105.

'The Future of Music in America.' *Proceedings of the Music Teachers' National Association* (1940), 28–40.

'Musical Composition in Canada.' *Culture* (Quebec) (vol. 3, 1942), 149–54.

'Music in Wartime.' *Music Bulletin No. 10* of the Oxford University Press (15 October 1942).

'We Need Music.' *Chatelaine* (December 1942).

'Orchestral and Choral Music in Canada.' *Proceedings of the Music Teachers' National Association* (1946), 87–93.

'Some Notes on Messiah.' *Toronto Globe and Mail* (21 December 1946).

'Musical Composition in Canada.' *TSO News* (April 1947).

'The Outlook for Canadian Music.' *International Musician* (October 1948).

'Making Music for Oneself and for Others.' *Vancouver Sun* (26 November 1949).

'Program Building, A Jigsaw Puzzle.' *TSO News* (13 September 1950).

'Why Not Canadian Festivals.' *Saturday Night* (4 October 1952), 10, 18.

'Edinburgh's Varied Offerings.' *Saturday Night* (18 October 1952), 23–5.

'After Edinburgh – Home Thoughts from Abroad.' *Saturday Night* (25 October 1952), 28.

'Pageantry and Festivals.' *TSO News* (March 1953).

'I Got a Great Kick Outa That.' *TSO News* (March 1954).

'Mount Allison Summer Institute.' *Toronto Globe and Mail* (13, 14, 17, 20 August 1956).

'The Canadian Music Council.' *Canadian Music Journal* (Autumn 1956), 3–6.

'Is Canada Progressing Musically?' *Mount Allison Record* (Autumn 1956), 97–108.

'Some Problems of the Canadian Composer.' *Dalhousie Review* (Autumn 1956), 130–43.

'Music in Canadian Universities.' *Canadian Music Journal* (Spring 1958), 3–11.

'The Organ Was My First Love.' *Canadian Music Journal* (Spring 1959), 15–25.

'The Music Is Alive.' *Saturday Review* (24 October 1959), 23, 50.

'Healey Willan As I Have Known Him.' *American Organist* (August 1960), 10–11.

'Messiah: One of the Greatest Works of All Time.' *Toronto Globe and Mail* (17 December 1960).

'What Is Good Music.' *New York Herald Tribune* (21 May 1961).

'A Case For O Canada.' *Toronto Globe and Mail* (16 March 1963).

'Music Critics by One of Their Targets.' *TSO News* (September 1963).

'Some Reminiscences of Marius Barbeau.' *Musicanada* (April 1969), 10, 11, 15.

Book Reviews

Barbeau, Marius, and Edward Sapir. *Folk Songs of French Canada. Canadian Forum* (December 1925), 79–82.

Hutchings, Arthur. *Delius: A Critical Biography. University of Toronto Quarterly* (January 1949), 210–12.

Myers, Robert Manson. *Handel's Messiah: A Touchstone of Taste. University of Toronto Quarterly* (January 1949), 210–12.

D'Harcourt, Marguerite, and Raoul d'Harcourt. *Chansons Folkloriques françaises au Canada. Canadian Music Journal* (Winter 1957), 77, 79.

Shaw, Watkins, ed. *G.F. Handel: Messiah. Canadian Music Journal* (Autumn 1959), 57–60.

Sharp, Cecil, ed. *English Folk Songs. Canadian Music Journal* (Autumn 1960), 73–7.

Vaughan Williams, Ralph, and A.L. Lloyd, eds. *The Penguin Book of English Folk Songs. Canadian Music Journal* (Autumn 1960), 73–7.

Barbeau, Marius. *Le Rossignol y Chante. Canadian Author and Bookman* (Winter 1962), 11, 13.

Unpublished Papers and Talks

'Ruhleben Diary,' September 1915.
Ruhleben talks: 'The Viennese Classicists,' 'A Sketch of Russian Music,' 'Debussy,' 'Beethoven's Symphonies,' 'English Music,' 1915–18.
'Music at Ruhleben, Part I,' 13 February 1919 (talk).
'Diary, December 1926–January 1927.'
'The Second Book of Bach's Forty-eight,' 11 March 1930 (talk to Duet Club, Hamilton).
'The Folk Songs of Canada,' 22 October 1930 (talk to Toronto Zonta Club).
'Music Credits in High School,' ca. 1935.
'Music and the Nation,' 1 September 1938 (talk to director's luncheon, Canadian National Exhibition, Toronto).
Broadcast for children, 24 November 1938 (introductory talk for TSO Childrens' Concerts CBC broadcast).
'Responsibility of the Music Teacher,' 28 March 1940 (talk to Ontario Music Teachers' Association, Toronto).
'The Arts in Wartime,' 9 December 1940 (talk to Toronto Board of Trade).
'Canadian Music and Its Place in the Music of the New World,' 10 October 1942 (talk to Institute of Inter-American Affairs, Columbia University, New York City).
'Salute to Our Russian Ally,' 22 June 1943 (talk to Writers, Broadcasters and Artists War Council, Royal York Hotel, Toronto).
'Diary of a Trip to Brazil,' August 1946.
'What Radio Has Meant to the Life of Radio Artists and Musicians,' 18 April 1947 (talk to radio artists dinner, Toronto).
'Bach's Catechism,' 23 September 1947 (talk to Canadian College of Organists at Metropolitan United Church, Toronto).
'The Enjoyment of Music,' 20 December 1951 (talk to Empire Club, Toronto).
'Diary, Continental trip,' Autumn 1952.
'This I Believe,' 31 December 1954 (prepared statement for Columbia Broadcasting System's Edward R. Murrow show).
'Memoirs,' undated but mainly written 1957–9 (KMF).
'Patronage and the Arts,' 21 May 1957 (talk to Brantford Music Club).
MacMillan Lectures (CAPAC): 'In Quires and Places Where They Sing,' 7 July 1964, 'The Bard and Music,' 14 July 1964, 'The Audience and the Composer,' 21 July 1964 (lectures at the University of Toronto).
Address to Gregorian Association, Toronto, 15 September 1964 (excerpts from Sir Ernest's 'curiosities' files).
Alumni Address: Reminiscences 1912–18, 5 June 1965 (given at University College, University of Toronto).

Selected Musical Works by Sir Ernest MacMillan

This list includes most of Sir Ernest MacMillan's compositions, arrangements, and transcriptions. Nearly all of his student works prior to 1914 have been omitted. Manuscripts in the Sir Ernest MacMillan fonds at the National Library are indicated by NLC. For works in the *Canadian Musical Heritage Series* see CMH. Entries marked CMC are at the Canadian Music Centre in Toronto. Information on recordings of MacMillan's works is included.

Stage

The Mikado (W.S. Gilbert and A.S. Sullivan). Scored by A.G. Claypole, B.J. Dale, W. Paner, E.C. MacMillan, Charles Webber. Ruhleben 1916. Solo voices, chorus, orchestra. NLC.

The Peasant Cantata (J.S. Bach). Transcription and stage version by ECM. n.d. Solo voices (SATB), string quintet, cembalo. NLC.

Prince Charming, ballad opera (text by J.E. Middleton; music arr. from Scottish and French tunes by ECM). Banff 1931. Seven soloists, small orchestra, chorus. NLC.

Orchestra, Orchestra and Choir, Band

Overture 'Don't Laugh.' 1915. Orchestra. NLC.

Overture 'Cinderella.' 1915. Medium orchestra. NLC.

Scherzo, Third Piano Suite (York Bowen). Arr. (unfinished) 1916. Orchestra. NLC.

England: An Ode (Swinburne). 1918. Solo voices, chorus, orchestra. Novello, 1921. NLC. CMC.

Overture. 1924. Orchestra. CMH, vol. 8. NLC. CMC. CBC SM-5068 (Toronto Symphony, Andrew Davis conductor).

Sonata, Op. 27, No. 2 'Moonlight' (Beethoven). Transcribed for orchestra by ECM. 1928. NLC.

'O Canada' (A. Routhier; English version by Stanley Weir and J.W. Garvin). Arr. 1930, rev. 1966–7. SATB (or SATB with orchestra, or solo voice and piano). Whaley Royce, 1930. NLC. CMC.

Two Chorale Preludes from the 'Little Organ Book' (J.S. Bach). Arr. 1932. Orchestra. NLC.

Scotch Broth, or What's Intil't? (As One Scot to Another). 1933. Orchestra. NLC.

'Hail to Toronto' (C.V. Pilcher). 1934. SATB, band (piano reduction). Gordon V. Thompson, 1934 (SATB only). NLC.

'God Save the King.' Arr. 1934. Full orchestra (SATB, orchestra or piano). Frederick Harris, 1957. NLC. Les Smith LSP–6302 (Ontario Department of Education Music Summer School Choir) (SATB, orchestra) 1976. Audat WRC–204 (Ontario Ministry of Education Summer School Choir and Orchestra). CMC.

Te Deum Laudamus. 1936. SATB, orchestra. NLC. CMC.

'It's a Grand Life, If We Don't Weaken: A Marching Song' (Dorothy Hill). Frederick Harris, 1940 (SATB, orchestra; also voices, piano). NLC.

A Song of Deliverance (based on Genevan Psalm Tune, Old 124th; words from Scottish Psalter 1650). Arr. 1944. SATB, orchestra (organ). Oxford University Press, 1945. NLC. CMC.

Christmas Carols. Arr. 1945. Orchestra. NLC. CMC.

Nocturne in E-flat, Op. 9, No. 2 (Chopin). Arr. 1945. Orchestra. NLC. CMC.

Fantasy on Scottish Melodies (original title *A St Andrew's Day Medley*). 1946. Orchestra. NLC. CMC.

Fanfare for a Festival. 1959. Brass, percussion. NLC. CMC.

Fanfare for a Centennial. 1967. Brass, percussion. NLC. CMC.

Adagio, First Organ Sonata (Mendelssohn). Arr. n.d. Medium orchestra. NLC.

'And They Entered in,' (Luke 15: 3). n.d. Soprano, small orchestra. NLC.

Extract from Cyril Scott's Pianoforte Sonata. Arr. (unfinished) n.d. Orchestra NLC.

'Good King Wenceslas.' Arr. n.d. Orchestra. NLC.

Minuet from Berenice (Handel). Arr. n.d. Small orchestra. NLC.

Organ Fugue in G Minor (Bach). Arr. (unfinished) n.d. Orchestra. NLC.

Prelude and Fugue in G Minor (Bach). Arr. n.d. Orchestra. NLC.

Sonata in D Minor, Op. 31, No. 2 (Beethoven). Arr. (unfinished) n.d. Orchestra. NLC.

Spirit Song from the Nass River. Arr. by ECM for orchestra. n.d. NLC.

'Twanky-dillo' (Old Sussex Song). Arr. n.d. Orchestra. NLC.

Twilight Fancies (Delius). Arr. n.d. Small orchestra. NLC.

Valse. n.d. Medium orchestra. NLC.

Chamber Music

Fugue in G. 1917. String Quartet. NLC.
Fugue in A Minor. 1917. String Quartet. NLC.
Fugue on a Theme of Benjamin Dale. 1917. String Quartet. NLC.

String Quartet in C Minor. 1914–21. CMH, vol. 13. NLC. CMC. CMC–CD 4993 (Amadeus Quartet).

Two Sketches for String Quartet Based on French-Canadian Airs. 1927. Also arr. for string orchestra. Oxford University Press, 1928, and CMH, vol. 13 (string quartet version). NLC. CMC. CMC–CD 4993 (Amadeus Quartet). Centre-discs CMC–2887 (VSO, Mario Bernardi conductor). For other versions see *EMC2*, 790.

À la claire fontaine. Arr. 1928. Violin, piano. NLC.

Six Bergerettes du bas Canada (traditional, translated by Mrs H. Ross). Arr. 1928. SAT, harp, viola, cello, oboe. 1928. Oxford University Press, 1935. NLC. CMC. CBC SM–204 (Vancouver chamber group, Simon Streatfeild conductor).

Three French Canadian Sea Songs (traditional). 'Le Long de la mer jolie,' 'Sept ans sur mer,' 'À Saint-Malo.' Arr. 1930. Medium voice and string quartet (orchestra). NLC. CMC.

There Was an Old Woman (traditional nursery rhyme). 1946. Mezzo-soprano, strings. NLC. CMC.

Écossaises (Beethoven). Arr. n.d. String quintet and 3 winds. NLC.

Let Us Now Praise Famous Men (R. Vaughan Williams). Arr. n.d. Winds. NLC.

'Sumer Is Icumen In': A Passacaglia on the 'Pes.' N.d. Recorder, viola da gamba, harpsichord. NLC.

'Sweet Chance That Led My Steps Abroad' (Michael Head). Arr. n.d. String quintet. NLC.

Trio in B-flat (unfinished). n.d. NLC.

Keyboard

Chorale Prelude for Organ and *Chorale Prelude for Organ on a Melody by Max Reger.* 1917. NLC.

Notturne, Quartet in D Major (Borodin). Arr. n.d. Organ. NLC.

Gavotte. N.d. Piano. NLC.

Cortège académique. 1953. Organ. Novello, 1957. NLC. CMC. CMC–CD 4993 (Andrew Davis organ).

D'où viens-tu bergère? (folk tune). Arr. n.d. Piano 4 hands. In *Meet Canadian Composers at the Piano*, Gordon V. Thompson, 1958. CMC.

Suite in G (Purcell). Arr. from harpsichord works n.d. Organ. NLC.

Voice, Choir

Magnificat in B-flat. 1908. SATB, organ. NLC.

Sleepy Time Songs (Katharine M. Jackson). 1 'Slumber Song'; 2 'The Dream Swing'; 3 'The Magic Gate.' 1910. Voice, piano. NLC.

'Love's Retreat' (Katharine M. Jackson). 1911. Voice, piano. NLC.

Four Hymns: 1 'Deus Refugium Nostrum' (F.R. Tailour); 2 'Laus Deo' (William C. Gannett); 3 'Benedicte omnia opera' (Milton); 4 'Arthur' (Arthur

P. Stanley). 1911–12. SATB. *The University Hymn Book*, Oxford University Press, 1912. CMH, vol. 5.

'Love's Parting.' 1913. Voice, piano. NLC.

'Du bist wie eine Blume' (Heine). 1913. Voice, piano. NLC.

'O Mistress Mine, Where Are You Roaming?' (Shakespeare). 1917. Voice, piano. NLC.

Three Songs for High Baritone from 'The Countess Cathleen' (Yeats). 1 'Were I but Crazy for Love's Sake'; 2 'Impetuous Heart Be Still'; 3 'Lift up the White Knee.' 1917. Voice, piano. 1 and 3 in CMH, vol. 14. NLC.

Magnificat (Palestrina). Arr. 1917. SATB.

Songs from 'Sappho' (Bliss Carman). 1920. Voice, piano. CMH, vol. 14. NLC.

'That Holy Thing' (George MacDonald). Arr. 1925. Voice, piano. NLC.

Two Christmas Carols 'I Sing of a Maiden' (carol); 'The Storke' (A Christmas Legend). 1925. Voice, string trio (piano). Frederick Harris, 1927. CMH, vol. 14. NLC. CMC.

'Sonnet' (E.B. Browning). 1928. Voice, piano. Frederick Harris, 1928. CMH, vol. 14. CMC.

Three Songs of the West Coast 1 'A Spirit Song'; 2 'Na Du – Na Du'; 3 'Stop All This Idle Chatter.' Edited by Marius Barbeau, transcribed by ECM, English version by Duncan Campbell Scott. 1928. Voice, piano. Frederick Harris, 1928. NLC. CMC. CMC–CD 4993 (Jon Vickers).

Four French-Canadian Folk Songs (translated by J.M. Gibbon). 1 'Au cabaret/At the Inn'; 2 'Blanche comme la neige/White as Cometh the Snowflake'; 3 'C'est la belle Françoise/The Fair Françoise'; 4 'Dans tous les cantons/In All the Country Round.' Male voices. Arr. 1928. Boston Music, 1928. 'Blanche comme la neige' rev. 1958 for SATB, Gordon V. Thompson, 1968. NLC. CMC. CMC–CD 4993 (Toronto Mendelssohn Choir, Elmer Iseler conductor).

Twenty-one Folk Songs of French Canada. Edited by ECM. English translations and an introduction (in French only) by J.M. Gibbon. Frederick Harris, 1928. ECM was one of nine arrangers. Several songs listed above are included in this volume.

A Canadian Song Book. Dent, 1929. Rev. ed. 1948. (First ed. also published in Britain as *A Book of Songs.*)

'The Bluebells of Scotland.' Arr. 1929. SATB. Dent, 1929.

'Recessional' (Kipling). 1929. SATB, piano. NLC.

'Last Prayer' (Christina Georgina Rossetti). 1929. Voice, piano (string quintet). Boston Music, 1929. NLC.

'Spirit of Ahmek' (A. Eustace Haydon). Taylor Statten, 1930. Voice, piano.

'The King Shall Rejoice in Thy Strength' (Bible, Yattendon Hymnal). Ca. 1935. SATB, organ. Frederick Harris, 1935. NLC. CMC.

Northland Songs, No. 2 (J.M. Gibbon). Arr. 1938. Voice, piano. Gordon V. Thompson, 1938. CMC.

'Canadian Boat Song' (Thomas Moore). Arr. Voice, piano. Gordon V. Thompson, 1941.

'Debout, canadiens!/Canada Calls' (Adrien Plouffe). Voice, piano. Gordon V. Thompson, 1942.

'Land of the Maple Leaf' (C.V. Pilcher). 1943. SATB, piano (string quintet). Gordon V. Thompson, 1943. NLC. CMC.

'Raise the Flag' (Arthur Thomson). 1946. Voice, piano. NLC.

Ballads of B.C. (J.M. Gibbon). Arr. 1947. Voice, piano. Gordon V. Thompson, 1947. CMC.

'Vitai Lampada Tradens' (C.V. Pilcher). 1953. (School song for Havergal College.) Voices, piano. NLC.

'Alma Mater Song' (Winthrop Bell). 1956. (To Mount Allison University.) NLC.

'A toi, belle Hirondelle.' 1958. Soprano soloists, SSA. CMC.

Jongleur Songs of Old Quebec. Collected by Marius Barbeau, arr. by ECM. Rutgers University Press, 1962.

'L'amour de moi' (for Emmy Heim). Arr. n.d. NLC.

'Annie Laurie.' n.d. SATB. NLC.

'Christ ist Erstanden.' Arr. n.d. Voice, piano. NLC.

Communion Service in G. n.d. SATB. NLC.

'Good Friday' (John Masefield). n.d. Soprano. NLC.

'I Heard a Voice from Heaven.' n.d. SSAA. NLC. CMC.

'King of Glory, King of Peace.' n.d. SATB. NLC.

'Light of Light.' n.d. SATB. CMH, vol. 5.

'The Lord Is My Shepherd.' Arr. n.d. SATB. NLC.

'Ode to Brock' (J.D. Logan). n.d. SATB. NLC.

'One Bright May Morn' (Canadian folk-song). Unfinished, n.d. Voice, piano. NLC.

'Padded Footsteps' (A.J. Bourinot). n.d. Voice, piano. CMH, vol. 14. NLC.

'A Rabbit.' n.d. Voice, piano. NLC.

'The Songs of June.' n.d. Voice, piano (small orchestra, organ). NLC.

Three Folk-Songs from French Canada. 1 'Je sais bien quelque chose'; 2 'Mon doux berger'; 3 'Les Jeunes filles à marier.' Arr. n.d. Voice, piano. NLC.

Three French Canadian Airs. 1 'Plus matin que la lune'; 2 'La Prisonnière de la tour'; 3 'Lisette.' Arr. n.d. Voice, piano. NLC.

'Through the Day My Love Has Spared Us.' n.d. Voices. NLC.

'Les Trois dames de Paris.' Arr. n.d. Voice, piano. NLC.

'Under My Veil.' n.d. Voice, instrumental sextet. NLC.

'Vesper Hymn' (Longfellow). n.d. SSAATTBB.

'Weep You No More, Sad Fountains' (anon). n.d. Soprano, piano (mezzo-soprano, medium orchestra). NLC.

'Ye Banks and Braes' (Burns). n.d. Four male voices. NLC.

Discography

(Recordings of MacMillan's works are noted in *Selected Musical Works by Sir Ernest MacMillan*).

Recordings Conducted by MacMillan

Adaskin *Serenade Concertante*; Morel *Esquisse*; Fleming *Shadow on the Prairie*. TSO. 1956. Radio Canada International (RCI) 129/(Adaskin) 5–Anthology of Canadian Music (ACM) 23

Bach *Cantata No. 51*; Mozart *Exsultate, jubilate*. TSO. Marshall, soprano. 1953–4. Hallmark CS-2

Bach *St Matthew Passion*. Full orchestra, Toronto Mendelssohn Choir, Milligan (Jesus), Johnson (Evangelist), Marshall, Morrison, Newton, sopranos; Stilwell, alto; Lamond, tenor; Brown, Tredwell, baritones; Silvester, organ; Kraus, harpsichord. 1953–4. 3-Beaver LPS-002/3-RCA Victor LBC-6101

Coulthard *Ballade (A Winter's Tale)*; MacMillan *Two Sketches*; Weinzweig *Interlude in an Artist's Life*. TSO. 1946. CBC International Service Canadian Album No. 2/(Weinzweig) 5–Anthology of Canadian Music ACM 1/(Coulthard) 6–ACM 10

Elgar *Pomp and Circumstance Marches, Op. 39, No. 1–4*. TSO. 1942. 2-RCA Victor 8226, 8227

Elwell *Pastorale*. TSO. Marshall, soprano. 1953. Hallmark CS-1

Handel *Messiah*. Full orchestra, Toronto Mendelssohn Choir, Marshall, soprano; Palmateer, alto; Vickers, tenor; Milligan, bass; Silvester, organ; Kraus, harpsichord. 1952. 3-Beaver LPS-001/3-RCA Victor 6100/3-RCA Victor LM-6134. Excerpts: Beaver LPS-1003/RCA Victor LBC-1053/RCA Victor LM-2088

Holst *The Planets*: 4 movements. TSO. 1943. 4-RCA Victor 11-8412-8415/ Camden 204

Jacob *A William Byrd Suite*; Haydn (Hoffstetter) *Serenade*. TSO. 1942. 2-RCA Victor 8725–8726

McMullin *Rocky Mountain Suite* (Sketch No. 2); Rathburn *Images of Childhood*;
Freedman *Symphonic Suite*. TSO. 1950. Radio Canada International RCI 19

Milhaud *Suite Française*; Britten *Kermesse Canadien*; Benjamin *Red River Jig*.
TSO. 1950. RCI 18

Rachmaninoff *Concerto No. 3*. William Kapell, piano. TSO. 1948. International
Piano Archives IPA-507

Ridout – Morawetz – Somers – Rathburn – Weinzweig – Vallerand. TSO.
1951. RCI 41/(Vallerand) 3-ACM 19

Ronald 'O Lovely Night.' Kirsten Flagstad, soprano. 1938. 3–Legendary LR-
120/2-Legendary LRCD-1015-2

Tchaikovsky *Symphony No. 5*. TSO. 1953. Beaver LP-1001/Victor Bluebird LBC-
1093/RCA LBC-1068/Camden 374

Tribute to Her Majesty Elizabeth II: Handel anthems. CBC Orchestra, Vickers,
tenor. 1953. Beaver LPS-1002

Verdi 'Pace, Pace' from *La Forza del Destino*; Mozart *Exsultate, jubilate*. TSO.
Marshall, soprano. 1953. Hallmark SS-1

Recording with MacMillan as Pianist

Emmy Heim – A Self-Portrait. Emmy Heim, soprano. 1949–54. Hallmark SS-2

Index